Make This Town Big

Make This Town Big

THE STORY OF ROY TURNER
AND THE WICHITA WINGS

———

Tim O'Bryhim & Michael Romalis

ISBN: 1530856272
ISBN 13: 9781530856275

This book is dedicated to the memory of
"The Voice of the Wings"...
Public address announcer and loyal fan

J.B. Johnson

1939-2015

"And now Wichita...are...you...ready?!?"

(Photo Courtesy: Elaine Himes) J.B. Johnson in the
PA booth next to Alan Shepherd.

This book was made possible by major
contributions from the following sponsors:

Michael and Kathy O'Bryhim　　　　**Gene Rump**
Miriam and Brian Romalis　　　　　**Johnny Freedom**

Sporting Casey's

Additional funding was provided by the following sponsors:

Jackie Knapp Talley	Dick and Dena Elliott	Barbara Ray
Tim Nichols	Jared Cerullo	Bill Kentling
Rebecca Romalis	Jason Stuckless	Mark Weddle
Florence Asel		

Table of Contents

The MISL's Wichita Wings 1979-92

Authors' Notes & Acknowledgements

─────

I TURNED SIX-YEARS-OLD IN OCTOBER of 1982. My interests were fire trucks, ambulances and the TV show "CHiPs." I had, thanks to my teacher Miss Pam Dill, become a competent kindergartner at L'Ouverture Elementary School. I was learning new words, bigger numbers and brighter colors. Sometime after November 21, 1982 my favorite word became "Wings," my favorite number "21," and my favorite color "orange." That chilly Sunday night my family and I trekked up to the Kansas Coliseum in northern Sedgwick County to attend our first Wichita Wings indoor soccer game.

I remember the Kansas Coliseum was loud. LOUD. That night's event, against our hated rival to the east, the St. Louis Steamers, was unlike anything I'd ever seen. The crowd was a crazed mass of humanity dressed in orange and blue polyester-and-satin jackets, round orange hats, armed with horns attached to bottles of compressed air, and waving more orange-and-blue flags and banners than at a Sunkist union rally. I do specifically remember asking my mother, unironically, "What team do we want to win?"

My mother remembers that we went because the Wings were in the news so much. Friends talked it up. It was the place to be. My only exposure to the Wings to that point was at a soccer "clinic" in approximately 1980 at the Towne East Square shopping mall, held underneath the stage (now occupied by the food court.) My sister and I even won t-shirts. Going to the games just seemed like something we could do as a family. My father had had some health issues the previous spring, so we hoped it could quell what had been a stressful year.

The Wings became the defining element of my 1980s childhood. I received my first official MISL rocket-red and black soccer ball on Christmas Eve

1982. The sandy L'Ouverture playground fields were instantly transformed, in our minds, into pristine, green Astroturf fields as we played "games" during morning and afternoon recess. (I'm sure we spent more time debating who got to "be" Erik Rasmussen or Andy Chapman or Chico Borja than we actually played a game!) I also played many chilly, rainy, and muddy Saturday morning games on the Wichita United Soccer Association fields on East 13th Street. (Ask my mother how many newspapers she used to lay out on the back seat to protect our precious Buick interior from my muddy cleats!). And when Terry Nicholl, Tommy O'Neill, or Norman Piper came our school to put on a clinic, who do you think proudly wore his Wings jersey hoping he would be picked to "help" with the clinic? (Hint: it worked most of the time, but it was more fun to see our teachers get picked!)

I ate and breathed the Wings. I lived and died with those guys. Whether witnessing the events within the confines of the humid Kansas Coliseum with J.B. Johnson's voice reverberating throughout its concrete walls; or listening to the radio voices of Bruce Haertl, Jim Hawley, or Dave Phillips on my bedside radio; or the TV voices of Dave Armstrong, Steve Shaad, or Mark Allan on our '70s era Zenith TV on cold nights; my young heart always took a beating waiting for the end result. My vocabulary was enhanced thanks to the colorful language of our seatmates. Our cupboard at home was regularly stocked with white plastic cups (the Wichita Wings logo on one side, hockey's Wichita Wind on the other) that I would collect after the games. And given the extremes of Kansas weather, particularly in the winter, we would sometimes literally take our lives into our hands to drive to northern Sedgwick County en route to the Coliseum, or as we knew it, the brown barn on the hill. (And incidentally, my hero was no longer a fictional cop named "Ponch." It became a real lad from Linton, Derbyshire, UK named Jeff Bourne. He wore number 21.)

I stayed loyal to my childhood team, going to many if not most of the games through 1991-92, the franchise's last season in the MISL/MSL and my freshman year in high school. As I became older, my attendance waned: the franchise had switched to a different league with new rules and even newer players. My underlying hockey hunger (brought on by my Canadian roots) was satisfied in 1992-93 by the Wichita Thunder, a team in the newly reformed Central Hockey League. And my new responsibilities and stresses as a young adult began to take shape.

My interest in MISL and Wichita Wings history never left me, though. It was something I had retained since my earliest years as a kid and fan. One random night in about 2007, something occurred to me: despite all the excitement the Wichita Wings generated all those years ago, very little evidence of that excitement existed now. Though those golden (orange?) days may have remained in many hearts and minds throughout the Wichita area, there was nary a sign that the Wings ever existed...aside from a rusty "Catch Wings Fever" license plate on a car or someone wearing an old cap. The story of the Wichita Wings existed in the hearts and minds of former players, office staff, coaches, and fans. It lay within the pages of old *Missile Magazines*. And it rested in the old microfilm reels of Wichita newspaper archives. This was a story, a puzzle in fact, that was waiting to be told.

Eight years after that 2007 occurrence, my friend of over twenty years, Tim O'Bryhim, helped get the rocket-red ball rolling and we began to put this puzzle together. We may not have been able to interview everyone. And we may not have been able to include every detail. But we are proud to have been part of a project that we hope will ultimately be an accurate and well-researched history of the Wichita Wings

If you had told me when I was nine or 10 years old that 30-plus years later I would be sitting in Roy Turner's living room recounting the glorious days of the Wichita Wings with Turner, Kevin Kewley, and Kim Roentved, I would have not believed it. This book is a dream come true.

Michael Romalis
March, 2016

———

My Wings fandom did not reach the heights of a Mike Romalis in the 1980s. My strongest childhood memory from a Wings game was covering my ears because the air horns were so loud. But I played soccer on AYSO fields thanks to Wichita Wings players coming to Beech Elementary. And I wore an Andy Chapman jersey because I could watch him play on TV. Somewhere around 2010, Mike would insist on showing me old Wings games he had transferred from VHS tape to DVD. We would sit around and speculate about if it was possible for the Wings to return some day. Our discussion was prescient, because in 2011 I would write an article for *Splurge! Magazine* on that very idea coming to fruition. I bought season tickets for the new team and went to every single game, plus a few on the road. My indoor soccer obsession was now in full-swing.

In January of 2015, Johnny Freedom, Josh Kippenberger, and Anthony Villegas told me I should write a book about the Wichita Wings. If I had known at the time that it would become "the book that ate my life," I might not have done it! Josh set up the meeting with Roy Turner and Kim Roentved that set the wheels in motion, and I appreciate it greatly. I knew right away that I couldn't write this book without Mike Romalis, "unofficial historian of everything Wichita Wings." His previous research and relationships with former players and staff members were absolutely critical to being able to write a book about the Wings. Thanks to Mike patiently educating me on Wichita Wings history, I can now say I have a Bachelor's degree in Wings Studies...which is paltry compared to Mike's Ph.D. I couldn't have done any of this without him.

My mom (Kathy), dad (Mike), brother (Brendan), and sister-in-law (Iris), were there for me throughout this process; listening to me endlessly prattle on about an indoor soccer team from 30 years ago. They encouraged me without fail. To the "gentleman bastards" of my fantasy football league, and my brothers in the "Grey Company," I thank you for keeping me from spending every single minute of my day on this book. Your company was a welcome distraction. To Mrs. Freedom, Stephanie Lewis, and all the many other indoor soccer fans here in Wichita, thank you for all the camaraderie over the past few years.

Tim O'Bryhim
March, 2016

————

We owe a debt of gratitude to the many local journalists that did such a fabulous job of covering the Wings. *The Wichita Eagle-Beacon's* Mal Elliott, Lonnie Crider, Mike Limon, Gary Dymski, Steve Love, Tom Shine, Fred Mann, and

Randy Brown wrote essential articles that were vital in increasing our understanding of what the Wings were all about. You will find their names scattered throughout the text and endnotes of this book. Sadly, Elliott and Brown, who spent so many years covering the Wings, have passed away. Tom Shine was gracious enough to let us interview him for the book and provided a reporter's perspective on the Wings. Bruce Haertl, a sports broadcasting legend here in Kansas, talked to us about his time as the Wings radio announcer and what it was like to cover the team as a television reporter. We can't thank him enough.

This book couldn't have been published without the many financial contributions from family, friends, and Wings fans across the country. We thank you all. We want to give a shout-out to the several fans who contributed their memories to this book: Eric Scriven, Steve Rademacher, Louis McCluer, Nathan Moore, Anthony Villegas, Mark Weddle, David Weber, John Morrison, and Christy Roberts…all your contributions were fantastic. Thanks to Leroy Parks for looking at the first few chapters and giving us his thoughts.

We are grateful to Roy Turner's Dallas Tornado friends: Kenny Cooper, Al Miller, Norm Hitzges, and Steve Pecher. They spent their precious time on the phone with us, telling us about Roy Turner as a soccer player. In particular, it was kind of Mr. Pecher of the Steamers to humor a couple of hated Wings fans. They all gave us great material. Thanks to Doug Verb from the old MISL for giving us the league perspective; it was invaluable. MISL referee and former Wheathawk Alan Shepherd gave us a wonderful interview, and then, tragically, passed away just weeks later. The Wichita soccer community misses him every day. Many thanks to Chris Johnson for sharing stories about his dad J.B., the long-time Wings' public address announcer.

We are so thankful to the photographers who agreed to let us use their wonderful photos for our book: Don Marler, Greg Fox, Howard Eastwood, Elaine Himes, and Dan Moore, your photos help us tell the story. Former Wings staff members Virginia Creamer, Kevin Himes, and Charlie Minshull Ford gave us lots of jewels about life behind the scenes. We thank them for it. Dr. Jay Price, a history professor at Wichita State University, gave us insight into the broader issues that were going on in Wichita during the 1980s. His expertise was invaluable. Former Wings owners Bob Becker and Bill Oliver helped us understand the perspective of the men who funded the Wings over the years. They deserve much of the ultimate credit for having something to write about. Thanks to Ruth Ann Messner for allowing us to use some great photos originally published in *The Wichitan* magazine. Dan Cramer, thanks for all your wise advice during the process of putting this book together.

Many thanks to original Wings GM Tom Marshall for reliving so many of his experiences from the founding of the Wings. We know it wasn't easy dredging up some of those memories. Big thanks to another Wings GM, Steve Shaad, who provided us with great material from his time with the team, for which he wore several different hats. Thanks to Ray Denton: a great guy who did important organizational work for the Wings in year one. His insight into that season was vital to making this book an accurate record of what happened. Thank you to Tamara Pryor for sharing stories about her life as the wife of the coach of the Wichita Wings.

Chico Borja, Terry Nicholl, Dale Ervine, and Norman Piper all graciously agreed to do long telephone interviews with us. Each of them gave us frank accounts of their time with the team. We appreciate so much their candor about the difficult times and for sharing the fun times as well. This book wouldn't have been half as good without their contributions. Mike Dowler took the time to correspond with us all the way from Wales. His humor and sharp memory contributed a lot to this book. Andy Chapman poured his heart out to us over the course of several hours. We learned so much about his childhood and his motivation as a player. Thanks so much, Andy! Big thanks to our fellow Golden Buffalo and class of '93 graduate, Larry Inlow, who gave us a couple hours of his time to talk about his journey from a boy who watched the Wings, to an actual Wing.

We'd like to give very special thanks to Jackie Knapp. Her memories of the Wings were sharper than just about anyone else. It was almost as if she had written everything down and just read it back to us. The amount of details she recalled was astounding. We owe her a great debt of gratitude, and thank her for her insight and her friendship. Throughout this process, Bill Kentling has provided us with his insight and great wisdom. He was a fabulous interview subject and did anything and everything to help make this book possible. His sense of humor gives our book a little extra pep in its step. For that, and for his friendship, we thank him wholeheartedly.

Over the course of a couple months, we were able to sit down with Roy Turner, Kim Roentved, and Kevin Kewley several times; both together and separately. This was a wonderful experience. To any kid growing up in Wichita in the 1980s, these men were rock stars. But they sure don't act like it. We appreciate their graciousness and humility. It's natural to hold back a bit when talking to a couple guys writing a book. But when we talked to Kim Roentved and Kevin Kewley, we could tell that they weren't the kind of guys to hold back on the truth, even if it was a little awkward.

It's not easy to open up about your life to a stranger, but Roy Turner did so without reservation. He welcomed us into his home and helped put us in touch with many of the important figures from Wichita Wings history. Without his cooperation, we wouldn't have been able to do this subject justice. We are thankful for the trust he put in us to tell his story and the story of his beloved Wings.

Gameday

———

FOR ANY EIGHT-YEAR-OLD SOCCER FANATIC, the day of a Wichita Wings game was an exciting time. It was no different for this particular eight-year-old. Just like the players on the pitch, he too had a pre-game routine. It was vital to get suited up with the appropriate amount of Wings gear. Wearing the 1981-82 white home jersey was a must. Over that was the orange Wings jacket his parents had bought for him last Christmas. The choice of headgear was important. He had to have his orange flat cap, emblazoned with the Wings logo and fitted with various soccer pins and buttons (including one with Andy Chapman's face on it!) If there was a hat trick by Jeff Bourne, Chapman, Erik Rasmussen, or another of the usual suspects, the boy would toss it onto the field alongside dozens of others. He needn't worry though... he had written his name on the inside of the cap so he could retrieve it at the Wings office the next business day. For occasions like a hat-trick, it was good to have a back-up hat. His baseball cap with the flashing Wings "W" would do just fine. Of course, he'd need to remember to keep it charged up with a fresh 9-volt battery!

With the uniform and jacket on, and the cap on his head, the boy dug out the orange duffel bag from underneath his bed. It contained his back-up hat, a pair of binoculars (his interest in the Angels' dance routine was purely academic, of course), and various other accoutrements. If the Wings were playing Minnesota he'd stash one other item in there. You see, the Strikers' goalkeeper Tino Lettieri kept a stuffed parrot named Ozzie in the goal with him. Lettieri's antics throughout the game made the Orange Army froth at the mouth. It was important to taunt Lettieri with your very own similarly-named stuffed parrot.

It was time to head out. The boy would climb into mom's 1982 Buick Skylark, his heart already racing in anticipation of the game to come. But first, they were off to McDonald's to get as many McPizzas as he could stuff into his mouth. He'd need the calories for all the energy he'd expend over the course of the game. After eating, they'd avoid game traffic on I-135 by taking "the back way." If they went north on Oliver, west on 61st, and straight up Hydraulic to the Kansas Coliseum, they'd get there faster than a Kim Roentved rocket into the net.

Parking was never a problem, but the weather could be. If it had rained earlier in the day, the walk up the hill could be a muddy one. Also, the occasional livestock show at the Coliseum could make for an unpleasant walking experience. The boy would need to watch where he stepped. But normally, the biggest obstacle was the cold. Trudging up the hill with the freezing wind in your face was no fun. However, like a beacon of light, the Coliseum lay above, its warm confines beckoning the freezing fans. The boy remembered President Reagan talking about "a shining city on a hill." This must be it!

Tickets in hand, the boy and his mother walked through the doors into the instant warmth of the Coliseum. The boy wished he could bottle the smell...a perfect combination of cotton candy, hot dogs, beer, and cigarette smoke. Oh, the cigarette smoke. They'd get settled in section 117, row J, before heading to the concourse. There, you could get a *Missile Magazine* for just a dollar. The teams would be out on the pitch, warming up to the sounds of "I Know There's Something Going On" by Swedish pop sensation Frida. As the teams finished their warm-ups, the lights would begin to dim. Captain Kick would come out to bang his drum and the Angels dance team might follow that up with a routine to the Wings own song, "Go For It!"

The show was about to begin. J.B. Johnson would introduce the opposing team while Huey Lewis' "Power of Love" played in the background: "Ladies and Gentlemen, welcome to the beautiful Kansas Coliseum where your Wichita Wings will take on the..." Wings fans were always sportsmanlike... well, ALMOST always. They would applaud politely for the opposing team. But they'd still boo the players who deserved it. A former Wing would get a big cheer.

Then the clap began. That slow '80s clap, growing faster and faster as the lights turned off. Spotlights flashed all around the arena and the fans screamed their heads off. J.B. Johnson would then ask his famous question: "And now Wichita, are...you...ready?!?" The boy was definitely ready. Johnson would introduce all his heroes to the boy's favorite song: Maynard Ferguson's version of Bill Conti's "Gonna Fly Now"; better known as the theme song from *Rocky*. After the cheers died down, former Wings Angel Nancy Bogard would come out to sing the national anthem.

The game began and the boy glanced around him to look at the banners and signs displayed by his fellow fanatics. Air horns blared, cowbells chimed, and vuvuzelas blew, as the boy took it all in. At the half, he would run up to the concourse to buy a miniball. He and the other kids would inevitably start an impromptu soccer game in the hallway, only to be thwarted by the ever-vigilant ushers, who shooed them all away. As the game progressed, the boy hoped and prayed there would be no overtime. Overtime would cause him to be so overcome by nerves that he could hardly stand it. The worst thing in the world was a Sunday afternoon overtime loss...and returning home with homework for Monday yet to be completed.

The boy would come home that night and eagerly watch the local TV news highlights of the now completed game. Tomorrow, he'd read every Wings article the *Wichita Eagle-Beacon* printed. After he went to bed that night, his dreams would be filled with orange soccer balls and a screaming crowd... Angels dancing around him...Kevin Kewley slapping him on the back...He was just another one of Roy's lads. The Wings had made Wichita into something much bigger than it had been before...and this boy, and all the other kids, would remember that forever.

A Note on Format

——

CHAPTER 1 OF THIS BOOK is written in a traditional non-fiction format. Chapters 2 through 23, along with the epilogue, are in the "Oral History" format. In those chapters, the name of our interviewees will be followed by their direct quotations. Our commentary as authors will be *italicized* and interspersed between these many quotations. We feel that the Oral History format is the best way to tell the story of Roy Turner and the Wichita Wings.

CHAPTER 1

Humble Beginnings

———

"Everyone was struggling, so you just dealt with it."

- ROY TURNER

THE UNOFFICIAL BIRTH OF THE Wichita Wings indoor soccer team can be dated to March 30th, 1943. On that day, Harry and Olive Turner of Liverpool, England welcomed into the world their new son, Roy Turner. The utterance of the words "Wichita Wings" would not occur, at least in the context of soccer, until the late 1970s. However, the story of the Wings cannot be told without telling the story of the man who most embodied that team over the course of almost two decades. Without Roy Turner, it is doubtful the history of the Wichita Wings would be a story worth telling.

According to Turner, his story would never have begun had it not been for a weekend pass for Sergeant Harry Turner in 1942. While World War II raged in Europe and beyond, Sgt. Turner did his part by training recruits for the British Army. The addition of a "war baby" to the family meant a fourth table setting, with Olive having given birth to Roy's sister, Maureen, near the beginning of the war. Harry would be lucky enough to avoid the fate of his father Howard, who was killed on horseback at age 27 during World War I.

Life in Liverpool during the war was not a pleasant ordeal. This was particularly true in 1940 and 1941. "Liverpool was a port, so we were bombed unmercifully...My family had to go down to the bomb shelters every night," said Turner. Future Wichita Wing and fellow Liverpudlian, Kevin Kewley, was fortunate to have been born well after the war ended. According to Kewley, the war years were a topic his family didn't like to talk about. The devastation of the bombings had been bad enough that Kewley's parents sent his older brothers to northern Wales during the worst of the Blitz.

Simon Jones, Deputy Head of the Museum of Liverpool Life, described the effect of the bombings in Liverpool:

> Between May 1st and 8th, 1941, over seven consecutive nights, German planes dropped 870 tonnes of high explosive bombs and over 112,000 incendiary bombs, starting fires throughout Merseyside [greater Liverpool]....What happened in May was the culmination of a bombing campaign which left a total of 4,000 dead, probably the heaviest loss per head of population of any British city.[1]

Though his mother's family was originally from Derbyshire, Turner's father's family had been Liverpudlians for generations. The devastation wrought by the bombings must have been hard to stomach for long-standing residents like the Turners. The war would end in 1945, and with it, the worry of a Nazi occupation of the British Isles. However, Roy Turner's generation would grow up with a unique set of challenges in an England very different from that of the 1920s and 1930s.

———

To grow up in post-war England was to grow up "without." Shortages of basic necessities became commonplace for the population of Great Britain. According to Turner:

> Struggling was the norm for me. Ration books...trying to make sure you got enough to eat. Having a pair of soccer shoes was almost unheard of. I was 10 years old when I got my first pair. Everyone was struggling, so you just dealt with it. Looking back, I was very proud of my parents for just being able to get through it.

Like most English parents, Harry and Olive worked hard to make a better life for their children. Harry was a "breadman," delivering bread throughout Liverpool. Olive was a clerk at a sports gambling shop where she "marked the pools." People would guess which English soccer games would end in a "draw" or "tie" in a given period of time. If a lucky gambler picked a sufficient number of correctly chosen tied matches, he would win a cash prize.

Despite working hard, people like the Turners faced an underlying problem: the daily requirements of life weren't often available for purchase. This is best illustrated by one British housewife's 1946 quest for the ingredients of a Shepherd's Pie:

> On her first trip to the local shop they had no meat but "there should be some rabbits" soon. Went back a second time and was informed there were indeed rabbits, but they "weren't ready just yet." On her third trip there was already a line, with "only about three rabbits visible. However, I waited and more came up. I was lucky." [2]

"Meat, butter, lard, margarine, sugar, tea, cheese, jam, eggs, sweets, soap, and clothes were all rationed." [3] The long-awaited appearance of bananas in the supermarket caused great excitement for one English mother of two. "*Bananas. Yes, bananas!! The first for 6 years. They are Robin's [her son's] really, as they are only allowed for under 18's...*" [4]

The week's rations in 1947 for housewife Rose Uttin illustrate the limitations on the diet of the average English family: "Our rations now are 1 oz bacon per week - 3 lbs potatoes - 2 ozs butter - 3 ozs margarine - 1 oz cooking fat - 2 ozs cheese & 1 lb meat [all per week]...½ lb of bread per day." [5] In the context of 21st century America, where waste of food is commonplace, it can be difficult to imagine such shortages. To make matters worse, in the winter of 1946-47, coal and electricity was in short supply:

> "It was the start of Britain's most severe and protracted spell of bad weather during the twentieth century." On Jan. 29th...it was "the coldest day for more than 50 years, the lights went out not only in London but all over the country...gas in most big cities was at about a quarter of normal pressure..." [6]

English novelist Christopher Isherwood, disappointed by the false hope of the end of World War II, neatly summed up the frustrations of post-war life:

> We endured with misery and loathing the continual fuel cuts, the rooms private and public in which we shivered in our exhausted overcoats, while the snow blizzards swept through the country again and yet again. Were there to be no fruits of victory? The rationing cards and coupons that still had to be presented for almost every-thing from eggs to minute pieces of scraggy Argentine meat, from petrol to bed-linen and "economy" suits, seemed far more squalid and unjust than during the war...[7]

It was in this world that Roy Turner lived his formative years. Life in England would improve and eventually return to the economic dynamism of earlier years. However, during those difficult times after the war, it was no wonder that a 1948 Gallup poll of Britons indicated that 42% of them wished to leave the country for good and settle overseas.[8] Years later, Roy Turner would himself feel that desire to leave England, but for reasons relating to furthering a career in professional soccer.

———

In the northern suburbs of Liverpool, at Maghull Secondary School, Roy Turner discovered that he had a special talent for soccer. In the 1950s, there was little organization related to the development of young players. "Everybody played soccer...didn't matter who you were. No coaching, you just made games up and tried to be Chico Borja or something," said Turner. When he tried out for his school team, he met with immediate success. "I re-member walking in and seeing my name on the board of starters for the first time. I was a midget compared to these guys. I was starting as a freshman. They were so much bigger than me."

Like many talented players, Turner started out as a forward. "I liked scor-ing goals. Most great players start out at center-forward as a youth, but then they realize they'll have to play somewhere else," said Turner. Eventually, he would play in the middle of the field. But as a schoolboy, his talent put him up front. According to Turner, though the team was headed by the school's PE teacher, there was "very little coaching."

"I was on varsity in my first year of high school, but [had] no aspirations to be a professional. The more I played it became more apparent that I could continue on," stated Turner. Despite his laissez-faire attitude toward a future career in soccer, his talent had not gone unnoticed. Mickey Lill, of the English First Division team Everton, asked Turner if he had considered taking his game to the next level. "I said 'No,' and then he said, 'I think you should,'" Turner recalled. It was a good thing for Wichita that Turner took Lill's advice and turned pro at age 17.[9] Thus began a journey that would one day lead to Kansas.

Everton was only a dozen miles from Turner's home. However, getting to the games presented a problem: he had no transportation. Luckily, he could count on the support of his dad, Harry. According to Turner, "When I played my first game for Everton, I had no car or money to get to the game. My dad drove up in his bread [delivery] van and picked me up to play the game. He would have done anything to create a chance for me to make it to the games or do anything I needed to do." Olive, however, was a harder sell on the idea of Turner becoming a professional soccer player. Like many mothers, she wanted her son to have a practical career. As Turner remembers:

Mom was a fantastic mother. Loved me TOO much. She wanted me to get a real job and not take a chance on soccer. She was a bit more cautious than dad. She didn't want me to rush into it. Her love may have smothered me in some ways. They came from poverty, so money was very important. She worried I couldn't make it.

Despite being signed by Everton, it wasn't as simple as going from being a schoolboy to playing in the First Division of English soccer. Everton, like the other top teams, had a tiered system for its players. "They had teams that went from First, Second, A-team, B-team, and C-team. I never played for the first team, so I started realizing I had to get away from there in order to make it. I went what they call 'non-League.'" Turner made it as high as the A-Team before deciding to move on. He ended up playing for several lower division teams in both England and North America for the next few seasons.

Turner's first big-time opportunity came during the spring of 1967. He signed with the Toronto Falcons of the National Professional Soccer League (NPSL). Seeing their son make the decision to pursue a career in North America wasn't easy for Harry and Olive. "They cried when I said I wanted to go to America, but accepted it and then became so proud of everything I did," said Turner. He would also have to leave behind his sister Maureen, who had been crowned Miss Liverpool, and then had married and started a family. These were the sort of sacrifices required to pursue the career of a professional soccer player.

Turner made his way to Toronto and discovered he had something in common with virtually everyone on the team: he wasn't Canadian. The Falcons claimed only one actual Canadian on their roster. The rest of the team was a mix of South Americans and Europeans, with Britons making up a plurality.[10] The NPSL, in general, struggled to sign North American players. The other nine teams in the league were in the United States, and boasted a grand total of only four American-born players.[11] In his nine games with Toronto, Turner, wearing #4, scored one goal and made two assists. The barely mediocre Toronto team finished the season 10-17-5 (wins, losses, and ties).[12]

Turner, however, did not finish the season with Toronto. He asked for, and was granted, a trade to the Philadelphia Spartans prior to the midway point in the season. Switching to #15, Turner played 14 more games that season with the Spartans.[13] Owned by the Rooney family, who ran the Pittsburgh Steelers, the Spartans both outdrew and outplayed Toronto. They finished second in the Eastern Division, just behind the Baltimore Bays.[14] Turner neither scored nor assisted on any goals with the Spartans.[15] However, he proved he belonged as a midfielder in the new North American league. Furthermore, Turner discovered two fellow Liverpudlians on the roster: John Best and Peter "Petey" Short. These three men would find their soccer destinies bound together for some time.

Controversy was no stranger to the NPSL that season. A rival league, the United Soccer Association (USA), sprung up at the same time. Both leagues decided to move forward simultaneously. However, only one, the USA, had official backing from FIFA. Players for the NPSL could theoretically face sanctions for playing in a non-FIFA-approved league. Luckily for the NPSL, THEY were the league with a television contract. CBS promoted the league with their "Just For Kicks!" ad campaign. [16] According to soccer aficionado Steve Holroyd, the league struggled for legitimacy:

> ...the NPSL also lost substantial credibility as a result of, ironically, its television contract: on May 15, barely one month into the season, referee Peter Rhodes admitted that eleven of the 21 fouls he called in the televised Toronto-Pittsburgh match were to allow CBS to work in commercials - the first "official" timeouts in the sport's long history. On one occasion, Rhodes had to push one player down who was trying to get up and resume the game because the commercial hadn't finished. [17]

By the end of 1967, both leagues merged to form the North American Soccer League (NASL). After spending the off-season back in England, Turner, along with Petey Short and John Best, signed with the Cleveland Stokers of the new NASL. Notably, this team also featured Dutchman and future Wichita Wing, Hank Liotart. Turner would now wear #6, and continued to do so for the rest of his playing career. The Stokers were owned by a consortium led by future US Senator Howard Metzenbaum and future Cleveland Indians President Ted Bonda. Much of their lineup consisted of former Philadelphia Spartans. [18] They had a good season that year, winning the Lakes Division with a .609 winning percentage. [19] Cleveland made the playoffs but lost in the semifinals to the eventual champions, the Atlanta Chiefs. [20]

Turner's tenure in Cleveland did provide a bit of comic relief between him and his mother, Olive. His roommate that year was the Spanish defender Jesus Tartilan. According to a 1974 interview with *The Dallas Morning News*, Turner said, "I wrote my mother and said I was living with Jesus. She wrote back, 'Hallelujah!' She thought I was living with the One and Only." [21]

For both the league and for Turner, 1968 was a banner year. The superb Santos team from Brazil came to the US to play two exhibitions with NASL teams. What made this particularly important for the league was that Santos was led by Pele, the greatest soccer player of all-time. This was significant for Turner because one of Pele's exhibition games was against his very own Cleveland Stokers. Turner was tasked with "marking," or guarding, Pele. Not for the last time, Turner's team would defeat Pele's side in the course of their one-on-one matchup. According to Turner:

> When Pele played for Santos it was a big deal...he was huge. I had to mark him...I was nervous, but did quite well. But they are only human. It's amazing what you can do in order to beat them. You always appreciate why they are called the best players in the world but then realize they are real people who you can match up with. I can say this: I saw Pele from the back a lot more than from the front.

It was a testament to the quality of the NASL that Santos and Pele lost both those games. Throw in the fact that the Atlanta Chiefs defeated Manchester City, the reigning First Division English League champions, and it became clear that the NASL had legitimate talent.[22] In 1968, Turner had proven himself against the very best. He would head back to England in the fall to play non-League soccer. But Turner was soon to face what would be the greatest challenge of his young career, followed by an unexpected change in scenery.

CHAPTER 2

An Oral History

Digger the Destroyer

———

"I have a framed picture on my wall of Pele and I playing during
a game. I'm sure Pele has the same picture on his wall."

- ROY TURNER

*NOW A 25-YEAR-OLD VETERAN OF both American and English professional
leagues, Roy Turner returned to England in the fall of 1968 prepared to play for
Northwich Victoria, a non-League team about 35 miles southeast of Liverpool.
His role there didn't just include working hard on the pitch. He served as a
player-coach, allowing him to bridge the gap between the coach's world and the
player's world. Later, throughout his head coaching tenure with the Wichita
Wings, Turner would effectively utilize that unique position with George Ley,
Norman Piper, and Kim Roentved. Unfortunately, playing for Northwich that
year almost ended his soccer career.*

ROY TURNER, MIDFIELDER, NORTHWICH VICTORIA: I had a ter-
rible injury to my foot. There was a terrible infection and I was in the hospital
for two months. They thought I might never walk again. I thought it was not
only the end of my career but the end of a lot of things.

Despite this ordeal, Turner was presented with a new opportunity for the upcoming 1969 NASL season. The trio of Turner, Petey Short, and John Best were moving again...this time to Dallas, Texas. In 1968, the Dallas Tornado, along with the remnants of the USA, had merged into the newly created NASL. During that league's inaugural season, the Tornado set new records for soccer futility, finishing 2-26-4 (wins, losses, and ties).[1] The arrival of new coach Ron Newman and a bevy of new players, including Turner, would soon turn things around for the Tornado. In the meantime, Turner was still recovering. Dallas, led by owner Lamar Hunt, wasn't concerned about any long-term effects from the injury.

ROY TURNER: Ron Newman brought me to Dallas. They brought me only on reputation, despite the injury, but thank God he had confidence in me. I worked my butt off for six months and got to being myself again.

That 1969 season in Dallas would be an injury-plagued time for Turner. After playing in 13 of Dallas' games, Turner injured his knee on August 3rd. Later that week he would undergo surgery, ending his season.[2] It was a bad year for Turner's legs, but it was a much better year for the Tornado. They finished 8-6-2, and showed promise for the future.[3] Both the team and Turner would soon fulfill that potential.

Digger. The Destroyer.[4] "Like a bulldog gone mad," according to Dallas Coach Al Miller.[5] Turner earned all these monikers during his career in Dallas. Standing 5'10 and weighing around 170 pounds, Turner was not necessarily physically imposing. Yet, he still imposed his will on the men he played against. He made his reputation at the center midfield position, though he would play elsewhere if needed.

ROY TURNER: My nickname was "The Digger." I was good at tackling. A lot of the better players couldn't play without legs [laughs]. I was the man marker...the Pele marker. I enjoyed that role. I had a very high work rate. I'd win the ball.

AL MILLER, HEAD COACH, DALLAS TORNADO, 1976-80: [Roy] played in the middle of the midfield. He was what I would call a defensive midfield player and was a terrier on the field and a nice guy. Tough guy on, nice guy off.

Turner's teammate Steve Pecher, or as Wings fans would say, "Hated rival, Steve Pecher," agreed with Miller's assessment...

STEVE PECHER, DEFENDER, DALLAS TORNADO: A very hard player. Nowadays you'd consider him a defensive center midfielder. He was a guy you knew was going to win a majority of his tackles and distribute the ball out of that position. Very reliable and crafty in the ways of knowing how to read players and knowing where they are going with the ball, [so he could] cut things off before they get started.

NORM HITZGES, RADIO ANNOUNCER, DALLAS TORNADO: Roy was almost constantly moving, and a pest. If I were the other team I'd find it hard to play against him. He was always pressing. Sometimes there was a gentleman's agreement among soccer players that you would give them some room to move some of the time. That wasn't Roy's game. He was an in-your-face midfielder. He made building an attack difficult by the fact that he was always pressing at midfield.

KENNY COOPER, GOALKEEPER, DALLAS TORNADO: If you can imagine going in the ocean and all of a sudden you are out there swimming and an octopus wraps itself around you. That was how Roy Turner played. He was an incredible "effort player." He was all arms and legs. He would smother you like a blanket. He was a man-for-man marker. He would usually pick up the playmaker on the opposition. He would pound that guy into submission.... in 90 minutes he would outwork the guy and not give him a chance to breathe. That's a skill, and a hard job. He was NOT an enforcer...didn't get involved in fights. But he would impose his will on your game. Whether it was Pele or anybody, his goal was to take them out of their game, to the point where they couldn't perform as they were used to. Even in practice, he'd have his elbow in your ribs and you'd turn around and he'd be right there. He was a very good player with great energy and terrific endurance. He would sometimes surprise you by getting forward. Those players aren't around much these days because the tactics and systems of play are different now.

It is no coincidence that Cooper, Miller, and Hitzges use similar language when talking about Roy Turner's game. A television detective, when confronted by such similar descriptions, would inevitably accuse the subjects of rehearsing their stories. But, in this real-life example, it just proves how clear it was to everyone that Turner was one tough customer on the field. How tough?

KENNY COOPER: Roy would cover so much distance in hot weather. One game it was 120 degrees on the field and Roy lost seven pounds in a half. He would cover so much ground.

———

Despite the departure of Petey Short to Rochester, the 1970 season in Dallas began with good tidings. According to Coach Ron Newman, Turner had a solid pre-season training session.[6] This fine performance carried forward through the season, with Turner playing in 21 of the 24 games that year. For the Tornado, however, it was a disappointing year. They finished dead last in the Southern Division at 8-12-4.[7] However, Turner's individual performance gained him notice with the media. The Sporting News' NASL All-Star roster included Turner on their Second Team.[8]

It wasn't only on the field that Roy Turner made a good impression. Outside the lines, the qualities that would one day make him so beloved in Wichita were being displayed in Dallas.

NORM HITZGES: As the good solid player he was, he was even better off the field. He was a great ambassador for soccer here. He was happy, outgoing, friendly…really good in the locker room. Players and other people tended to gravitate to him. I could see how he could become a legend in Wichita, or anywhere for that matter. He is the kind of guy that makes lots of friends easily and becomes the kind of guy a community looks at as a leader.

It was that 1970 season that the Tornado signed a young English goalkeeper named Kenny Cooper. He and Turner began a lasting friendship that would eventually transform into a coaching rivalry once Cooper took over the Houston Summit and Baltimore Blast in the Major Indoor Soccer League (MISL) during the 1980s.

KENNY COOPER: I first met Roy in March of 1970...Once seen, never forgot! Just a really engaging guy. The fact that he was from Liverpool and I was from north of there in Blackpool, helped. After I moved here it was a bit overwhelming at first. But people like Roy made it easier to adjust. We ended up becoming lifelong friends. He's a wee bit older, so I listened to his advice...In those days were getting about $100 a game so you had to have a second job. You could stay in a hotel for a week or 10 days and then you were on your own. Roy made that easier. He was very involved in the community. There were a group of British guys that all lived in the same apartment, which helped. America is the greatest country in the world but can be a bit overwhelming at first. We traveled together to practice. Roy worked for a company called Overseas Motors, which was selling Jaguars and MGs. He was one of the top salespeople there. It made it easy because he'd drive us home in a Jaguar! The first year neither Phil [Tinney] nor I had a car so we depended on Roy.

We felt fortunate to be in Dallas. Ron Newman was the coach and Ron Best helped bring me over. We put our heart and soul into everything we did. That included promoting Dallas and the NASL. We played together and spent lots of time together off the field. Roy and I are very similar in how we approached living in America and trying to build soccer in Dallas. We had an attitude that we would become the heart and soul of the franchise.

Both Turner and Cooper had a love for traditional British pub songs and the wildly popular rock n' roll music that had recently emerged from their home country.

KENNY COOPER: We were bachelors...I didn't get married till I was 34. We worked hard and played hard. We loved a good time. All our parties were tied around music...Beatles and Rolling Stones. On the weekends we'd hold a party and there was a great family atmosphere. It was always centered around music.

Invariably, it was Roy Turner, Dick Hall, Mike Renshaw and myself who made sure everyone had a good time. You were expected to be part of the singing and dancing.

Over the years, Turner's love of singing became quite well-known in Dallas. As The Dallas Morning News *writer Temple Pouncey wrote, "It was in the wee hours of a summer night in 1971 that Roy Turner and his teammates walked down the ramp of an airplane at Love Field, the last strains of yet another English song wafting from his mouth." [9] Cooper and Turner did indeed love to sing and have a good time. Several years later, when Cooper left bachelorhood behind, Roy Turner wasn't going to let anything stop him from being the life of the party...not even Cooper's honeymoon.*

KENNY COOPER: I got married, and Roy was the best man. The players and Al Miller were there. We had a great time and the night was winding down and my new wife and I were getting ready to leave in the limo to go to the Hyatt downtown for our honeymoon, and the phone rings. It was Roy.

> He said, "Where are you?"
> [Cooper] "Roy, I'm going on my honeymoon."
> Roy says, "I want to join you."
> [Cooper] "I don't think that's a good idea."
> [Roy] "No? Where are you going to be?"

He shows up downtown with his girlfriend at the restaurant. My wife said to me, "What's going on? It's our honeymoon, what's Roy doing here?" But that was Roy. Always the life and soul of the party.

STEVE PECHER: When we were in Dallas, Roy threw some good parties.

It was all in good, clean, fun. And there was plenty of it. But they weren't about to let good times interfere with their performance on the field.

KENNY COOPER: ...We were hard-working players...first there, last to leave. We tried to set an example for the young players.

In 1971, Turner and his teammates' hard work paid off. The Tornado won the NASL Soccer Bowl against the Atlanta Chiefs. Though the Tornado didn't win the Southern Division regular season championship, they made the semi-final round of the playoffs by finishing second. Their first playoff opponent was the Rochester Lancers, with whom they would play a three-game series. The first game of that series, played on September 1st, 1971, became famous as the NASL's longest game. [10]

ROY TURNER: We ended up with only eight or nine guys by the end of the game...The struggle was just to finish...

A total of six 15-minute overtime periods were played. Unfortunately for the Tornado, they were scored on by Rochester in that final period. In Michael Lewis' definitive article on the game, he writes that the Lancers' star Carlos Metidieri was approached by a Tornado player after scoring the final goal. "Thank you Carlos for scoring a goal because we couldn't do it anymore," he reportedly quipped. Metidieri claimed that his teammates doused themselves with water, filled their mouths with ice, ate oranges, and even drank coffee in order to keep going. [11]

The Tornado overcame their defeat to win the two next games against Rochester, advancing them to the championship series against Atlanta. They would win that series in three games as well, becoming league champions. [12] Turner would play in all six of the playoff games. During that 1971 season, he scored twice and made one assist. These were Turner's first contributions to the points sheet as a Tornado. [13] Many Tornado players, coaches, and staff contributed to what would be their best year as a franchise. But there was one figure that deserved the underlying credit: owner Lamar Hunt.

Hunt helped found the American Football League, owned the Kansas City Chiefs, and would eventually help found Major League Soccer. But in the 1970s he spent much of his time building the Dallas Tornado.

ROY TURNER: [He was an] incredible man...here he was running World Champion Tennis, the Chiefs, and he still found time to go to every game we played. Always there. And I worked for him for 10 years.

KENNY COOPER: Fantastic ambassador and pioneer of the game. He invested millions in the game.

AL MILLER: Lamar cared about the league and the players, and when we were successful, he was just beaming.

The sweet success of the 1971 championship would never have happened without the support of a man who has become one of the great figures in American sports in the 20th century.

In 1972, Dallas failed to repeat as league champion, losing 1-0 to the New York Cosmos in the lone semi-final game. [14] *Turner played in every game again in 1972 and 1973, scoring one goal over the course of those two years.* [15] *He succeeded in gaining some personal glory by making the All-Star Honorable Mention list in 1973. Dallas upped their game that year, winning the Southern Division and achieving an 11-4-4 record with the help of rookie sensation Kyle Rote, Jr.* [16] *Rote would become known to many Wings fans as one of the USA Network's color commentators for televised games in the early 1980s.*

Turner achieved another important career milestone in 1973...

ROY TURNER: They called me up and said, 'Would you play for America?' I said, 'I'm not a citizen.' 'Would you play if you were?'"

For Turner, the answer was a definitive "yes." Within a month he began the process of becoming an American citizen. Turner joined another future Wichita Wing, Mike Ivanow, on the US National Team.

ROY TURNER: It was wonderful to play for Team USA in 1973, but there weren't that many guys on our team that spoke English. We lost to Poland 0-1. Only about 25% of our guys were born in America. We played in Chicago against Poland. It was like playing IN Poland. There was a 17-game swing through Europe that I decided not to play in because of my knees. We played Mexico in Mexico. They had no respect at all for American soccer.

Turner started the game against Poland, playing the entirety of the first half. Against Mexico, he came in as a substitute in the 24th minute. [17] *Though the American team had little success that year, Turner enjoyed the time he played for his newly adopted land. In the process, he earned two "caps" and the honor of representing his country. Three years later, on April 12th, 1976, the year of the bicentennial, Federal Judge Joe B. Estes made it official when he administered the oath of citizenship to Turner. On that day, Turner remarked, "I want people to accept me as just as much an American as any player...and for them to know I'm behind Americanization of soccer."* [18]

The 1974 season brought rule changes to the NASL. A shootout system was designed to eliminate ties. Each team would provide five players for the shoot-out. If neither team had an advantage at the end of that shoot-out, it became a sudden-death shootout, with additional players shooting those shots. For part of the year, Turner was included on the "first-five" shootout list. But a miss against the Boston Minutemen resulted in him losing his spot. He scored his lone goal that year in a shootout against the Los Angeles Aztecs. Turner had the pleasure of hosting his parents, Harry and Olive, for a couple weeks during the season, as they visited America to watch their son play. [19]

For part of the 1975 season, Coach Ron Newman moved Turner to defense at the center-back position. Turner felt he was more effective in the midfield, but was willing to play wherever the team needed him. Newman continued to use him to stop goal-scorers across the league, marking players like former league MVP Randy Horton from the Washington Diplomats. [20] *No matter his position, Turner was able to contribute. He added a goal and an assist to the score sheet in 1975.* [21]

A Brazilian phenomenon burst upon the American soccer scene in 1975 when Pele joined the New York Cosmos. Turner had played against him once before in an exhibition against Santos FC back in 1968. He would have several opportunities to defend against Pele over the course of his three-year stint with the New York Cosmos.

ROY TURNER: I have a framed picture on my wall of Pele and I playing during a game. I'm sure Pele has the same picture on his wall. [laughs]

CHAPTER 3

An Oral History

Texas Twister

_____

"I didn't want to go back to England anymore...I wanted to stay."

- ROY TURNER

1976 BROUGHT NEW FACES TO the Dallas Tornado. A young midfielder from Liverpool, England came to town. Sound familiar? This time it was Kevin Kewley, who would go on to become one of the greatest players the Wichita Wings ever put on the pitch. The biographies of Turner and Kewley were similar in many ways. Like Turner's father, who served in the British Army, Kewley's father also served in World War II. His service, however, was with the Royal Navy. He traveled back and forth across the U-Boat infested waters of the Atlantic Ocean on missions to Argentina. Also like Turner, Kewley had experienced the rough-and-tumble life of a working-class kid in Liverpool, albeit a few years later.

KEVIN KEWLEY, MIDFIELDER, DALLAS TORNADO: Life in Liverpool was tough but you didn't realize it was tough until you got out. You never had money for soccer shoes or that sort of thing. All of a sudden you go to London and see how other people live and realize that this was totally different from the way we grew up. I came from a family of eight kids and every one of us lived at home. We moved to Kirkby, a few miles from Liverpool, when I was two. The houses we had been in were condemned. It was like a new town, but it was the same people. They moved the whole block.

Like Turner, Kewley didn't have much coaching as a young player. But his level of talent became clear very quickly. Kewley began his career with Liverpool FC in the English First Division, a professional journey that started at a very young age.

KEVIN KEWLEY: The only time you got coaches was when one of the teachers would be in charge. Most of the time we'd go out and play in the field and be on our own. I played with everybody and seemed to be better than everybody. The scouts came and watched our schoolboy games. At 15 I started playing for Liverpool FC. In the afternoon I'd go to school, which Liverpool FC paid for. At 17, they'd decide if you were good enough to play professionally. They signed like 13 apprentices every year, and cut 11 or 12 of them. The chances were slim and everyone knew that, but still, it was worth it. At least you'd get an education that was paid for. It was the equivalent of a community college. You all practice together and they pick 14 to go for the first-team each different game.

I was playing in Liverpool, and Al Miller came over and recruited me to come to Dallas in 1976. I had an open mind about coming over in the off-season. It was a great opportunity to see America, stay fit, and get some experience. I got frustrated with not enough opportunities at Liverpool. Once I came to America, I knew I would be staying here. It was such a great experience. Where Roy [Turner] and I are from was a tough area. The atmosphere in Dallas was great....such great team spirit. We'd all get together after games and the camaraderie was fantastic. Dallas is a beautiful place...traffic was a lot better then!

There were teams interested in me in Europe, but I thought I could always come back if it didn't work out. I'd only be 24 in two years. I wanted quality of life and I knew guys in similar situations that they were struggling in lower leagues. My friend went to Hereford [England] and he hated it. I made more money in America than I did in England. I loved the life here in America so much. The weather can be horrendous in England. There's so much more to do here in America. A lot of the soccer players would go to the betting shop or watch the horse races. But I was an outside type of guy so it suited me better in America.

After two very successful years with Dallas in 1976 and 1977, scoring a total of 13 goals and assisting in eight more, Kewley decided he was going to give up playing back in England during the off-season.[1] Ironically, it was only after he made that decision that he met with his greatest success in English soccer. In Dallas, he had the confidence of the new head coach, Al Miller, and even earned a nickname: "Tiger." Joining him in Dallas was future St. Louis Steamer, and the bane of Wings fans, Steve Pecher.

KEVIN KEWLEY: It was weird for me because I had played over in Dallas and had made my mind up that I wouldn't likely make it on the First Team [for Liverpool]. I had an offer from Al Miller in 1977 to stay permanently. Dallas had me wait to announce it because there was no sense leaving before the season in America started. In my mind, I had already left for America. But Liverpool wasn't doing very well and I got called up. I was not ready for it whatsoever. I didn't play very well. It was the last thing on my mind...I thought, "Why would they play me, I belong to [Dallas]?" I played like 86 minutes against Middlesborough because after four minutes a midfielder, Terry McDermott, got injured.

AL MILLER, HEAD COACH, DALLAS TORNADO: Kevin Kewley was a really good young talent. A lot of fighting power, a lot of running in him...very skillful. Definitely an above-average midfielder in the league. He wasn't a star but was a terrific guy to have on your team. You could count on him. He did very well for me in Dallas. I had a pipeline in Liverpool and that's how I got Kewley. Liverpool at that time was one of the big clubs in the world. To get someone from them at that time was a big deal. Early in the NASL years, most of the guys were European non-League players or broken-down older players past their prime. But once New York brought Pele in, everything changed. All of a sudden you had first-team players and international players coming in. The teams started spending money like hell and it couldn't last.

KEVIN KEWLEY: Temple Pouncey was the writer for the Dallas paper that coined my nickname. "Kewley was a Tiger for the Tornado," went the headline. That's how the name started.

STEVE PECHER, FORWARD, DALLAS TORNADO: I got down [to Dallas] in February of 1976. Roy was one of the veterans on the team. It was the last few years of his [career] as a player. He and Kenny Cooper took me under their WINGS, no pun intended, and helped me through my first year. They showed me a lot of veteran leadership on and off the field...how to train, what's expected of you, and that kind of stuff.

After achieving undeniable success in his years with the Tornado, Head Coach Ron Newman departed after a rare losing season in 1975. Lamar Hunt hired Al Miller to replace him. In 1973, Miller had won the NASL Soccer Bowl with the Philadelphia Atoms by defeating the Dallas Tornado.[2] If you can't beat 'em, hire 'em.

AL MILLER: I was coaching in Philadelphia and the owner called me into his office and told me he was selling the team...It was a difficult time for him. While we were talking in the office, he called Lamar Hunt in Dallas. [Lamar] said he was looking for a coach because they were getting rid of Ron Newman. It was a formidable challenge, but Lamar was so humble and gracious that I knew we'd have a good relationship.

I took over a team that was disorganized in its operation. It wasn't what I would consider a professionally-run operation. I cleaned house and knew there was some troublesome players there because I had coached against them. The reputation of players gets around...Before I got there, they were a bit undisciplined...Some of the players threw [famous TV broadcaster] Verne Lundquist into the pool during one of Lamar's parties.

Roy was really one of the good guys of that club...the heart and soul of the team. I liked [Roy] instantly when I got to meet him. Roy has a personality you couldn't help but love. He's a man's man. I'll always have nothing but respect and admiration for him. I refused to hire coaches and players who didn't have character. And Roy and Kevin were at the top of the chain when it came to integrity and character.

Lamar was financially tight to the core. He knew the sport couldn't survive if we spent a lot of money on players. He was very much against buying players to win a championship. When he hired me, he sat down in my office, closed the door and said, "I want you to know that I have enough money to buy us a championship every year. But, if I do it, then the other owners will compete with me. And none of us can afford to break the league over buying a championship. So here's what I want you to do: make us competitive and disciplined like the team was in Philly. I want you to do the best job you can do in the community and I don't want you to embarrass me with the team." I looked at him and said, "Basically, you are asking me not to win?" He laughed and said, "No, I want you to win, but I don't want to buy a championship."

He was tough with the dollars. We survived on young players, and knew the college scene better than the foreign coaches, which helped. And we threw in some foreign players that really made a difference. He was genuinely interested in what was going on with the team. He never meddled. Ever. Never gave a lecture to the team. Never came in the locker room. Never complained when we lost. Never got too excited when we won. He would sit at the game and had a little notepad and would always take notes on the game operations; i.e. the national anthem was 45 seconds late, etc. He knew everything about game operations.

He brought in a guy from the San Francisco 49ers who ran their game operations, as our new general manager: Dick Berg. He had a million ideas. One of his ideas was to take the SMU practice football field and build it like a little soccer stadium. He had sponsor boxes and colorful hoopla that goes with game operations. He had fireworks whenever we scored a goal. SMU's campus in right in the heart of rich, old money Dallas mansions. We started scoring some goals and the fireworks were going off and the people started calling the city and complaining about it being noisy and dangerous. The fire chief came out and met with Lamar and Berg and said we'd probably need to put an end to it, especially since the grass could catch on fire. So, Lamar said, "I want to show you how this is done. It's simple and once you see how we do this, you'll change your mind." He walked him out behind the stadium, and we had a couple college kids we hired who were in charge of setting off the fireworks after each goal. In these practice fields, they had the cinder blocks and the rockets would go off into the air and let out a big boom. They were showing him how it worked. The fire chief starts going back to Lamar's box to watch the game, and wouldn't you know it, we scored a goal. These kids had a walkie-talkie so they'd know when to light the fireworks. One kid got nervous because Lamar and the fire chief were there and accidentally tilted the thing. It went off and ran across the ground, lighting the grass on fire, went past the fire chief and hit the ivy covered wall of the stadium. That was the end of the fireworks at the stadium.

As Miller's coaching stint continued, Roy Turner's role off the field became just as important as his performance inside the lines. Growing the game of soccer had always been important to Turner throughout his career in Dallas. But Turner began to take an even greater role in going into the community and demonstrating the sport. He and other future Wings, like George Ley, Jeff Bourne, and Glenn Myernick, were going out and trying to get young people interested in both soccer in general, and the Dallas Tornado in particular. They played scrimmages against high school kids in front of school assemblies. They showed up to scores of birthday parties, handing out souvenirs. They even had booths at local malls. Turner coordinated the player appearances throughout the Greater Dallas area.[3] He was a soccer evangelist and he was coming to a town near you.

ROY TURNER, MIDFIELDER AND COMMUNITY RELATIONS COORDINATOR, DALLAS TORNADO: There were 824 kids playing soccer when I arrived. There were 70,000 playing there by 1979. We became salesman of the game of soccer. We were basically paid to sell the game. We would participate in school programs, could be seen juggling balls at shopping malls. We went to fields to watch the kids play.

We initiated it politically in the high schools. There were virtually no high school programs when we got there. It's one of the biggest soccer programs in America now, with millions of kids playing. All the high school football AD's [Athletic Directors] made it difficult. It was a battle to get past American Football. Very hard for the coaches to accept it. Then we started traveling throughout Texas doing clinics...Kenny Cooper, Bobby Moffat, Mike Renshaw, and Dick Hall...We were the nucleus of people that lived there year round. I didn't want to go back home anymore, I wanted to stay.

NORM HITZGES, RADIO ANNOUNCER, DALLAS TORNADO: The Tornado was outrageously good at planting the seeds of soccer. They had camps and events for fans everywhere. Roy was in the middle of all that stuff.

AL MILLER: Roy became one of my go-to guys in the office. We hired him and he was doing a lot of community work. Dallas in those days was really known because the English players like Roy and Kenny Cooper and Bobby Moffat had done a classy job in getting Dallas youth soccer started. I'm an ex-teacher at heart, so I'm into clinics and teaching. Lamar felt a need for that. We developed an unbelievable youth workshop. Roy and I would go out. I talked and he demonstrated. We drew big crowds, not only in Dallas, but around the region. We took it to Tulsa and Oklahoma City. We kind of toured and did these things. It was a smashing success.

Many of the things we did are still being used in youth soccer because I created a bunch of elementary play games that involved soccer skills so that all the moms and dads that were coaching, and didn't know anything about the sport, would be able to use our script. They could plug these games in and teach skills without the kids realizing it. We would play tag but you had to dribble a soccer ball. They have to do all the things that dribbling entails. We brought the parent-coaches out on the floor after demo-ing these things and had them play the games. We sold them that this was the way to go.

We were in the Dallas Cowboys building and Roy and I were working and had a late start and left to do a three hour workshop. We were racing to this thing. Roy said, "Boss,"...he always called me "Boss,"..."I'm starving. Let's make a quick pit stop at McDonalds." We order our food, pay for it, and take off. Just before we got to the clinic, Roy said, "We forgot to bring the food." We went 30 miles without realizing it.

The youth soccer promotions were one of the things that Lamar Hunt realized would grow the game. That's probably why he brought me on, because I was doing videos about the skills of the game. The league was using me to write youth coaching articles in the game programs, etc. Back in those days I was the only American and everybody else was a foreign coach. I kept saying, "I'm not a dummy, I know how to recruit and convince players too."

KENNY COOPER: We were pied pipers. We knew exactly what we needed to do to promote and pioneer the game. We served as goodwill ambassadors for soccer, and that could happen at any point and any time. If the phone rang and they said we needed to go the YMCA, a hospital visit, a speaking engagement at a Kiwanis Club or Rotary Club, then you just did it. Going into high schools, Roy and I both did that. In the later years Roy was working in the Tornado office as director of Community Relations. We refereed games, recruited parents to be coaches. As they say, "Shoe on leather." We hit the streets...

You'd put on your orange blazer, blue tie, shirt and black pants and go knock on doors the night before the game and hand out free tickets. Very often people wouldn't open the door and would question who we were and what we wanted. I'd say "I'm Kenny, we play for the Dallas Tornado and we're playing a soccer game tomorrow." They'd say, "Soccer? What are you talking about?" In those days people would say, "Soccer, that's another name for crap!" Some would open the door and some wouldn't. It was all part of our life.

We were grateful to live in America. In Dallas, Lamar was a great owner and you knew it was a solid franchise. You never had to worry about not getting a paycheck. The business prepared you for life after soccer. It was tough, it was hard, and you weren't paid the most money in the world. It made you a tough competitor. We've taken a lot of those things and applied it to our lives to this day.

You are a soccer player but you're also a traveling salesperson. You are selling the city that you represent. A lot of those guys that came out of Dallas had that same philosophy. It's hard work, but this country rewards success. Some people come over and don't realize the sky's the limit. If you want to be a millionaire you can be a millionaire...if you want to go bankrupt, you can go bankrupt. Nowhere in the world can you fail and then turn around and start over again. You always have a second chance here.

Indeed, Roy Turner would use those very same methods to grow the game in Wichita a few years later. In the late 1970s, with the arrival of Pele and other top players from around the world, the NASL began to become more and more competitive. In 1979, as German, other European, and South American players arrived into the league as a whole, and the Dallas Tornado in particular, tensions began to emerge between the "old guard" and some of the new arrivals.

ROY TURNER: Dallas had been a family and then they brought all these Germans and South Americans in and it basically created a split camp. That's mostly why Kevin left...that's why Steve Pecher left as well.

KENNY COOPER: It was a group of British guys that came in the late '60s and early '70s. Those guys were the heart and soul of the club. British people work as hard as you can, go out and spill your guts. We won a lot of games. We had a lot of British players who came in and could mentor the young American players...the Glenn Myernicks and Steve Pechers of the world. And it was a simple formula that worked. And then it all changed. I don't know why exactly, but then we brought in some South American players, who made more money than we'd been making. And then some German players came in. They were very different. It took time to get them all on the same page. I get along with everybody in the world, but what happened was that team started to change. Al Miller was very much on German and South American soccer. The old school [guys] kind of got moved on. It was a changing of the guard a little at a time.

I don't think the German and South American players realized the work ethic that was required to make the team a success...that the British and American players had, i.e. all the appearances and the commitment level. We had laid the groundwork for this team. Players started to get phased out. I was one of the last ones, but I knew I was being phased out. It's life though. It's evolution. Al started a changing of the guard, and we're still friends today. It's just part of life. All the British players sat down together one day and said, "It's going to be one of us a year until we're all gone." We could see what was happening. Francisco Marcos came in as Director of Personnel. He felt the game was going towards the South Americans. A lot of the guys stayed in Dallas and built lives there. Lamar Hunt and his family created that for us. I wouldn't have met my wife if I hadn't come there.

KEVIN KEWLEY: I wasn't very happy in Dallas by 1979. They brought in a bunch of new guys from Germany who weren't willing to do the things off the field that we were doing. The atmosphere completely changed. They didn't realize what they had. The team spirit went away.

AL MILLER: At that time we were at the stage where if you didn't have really top-class players you'd get murdered in that league. So I brought in some great German players: Wolfgang Rausch from Bayern Munich who was the replacement for Franz Beckenbauer. This guy had so much pressure from the media that he had a nervous breakdown; lost the hair on his head. He was dropped from the team and I found out about it, and went to Bayern Munich and bought him. I brought [over] about three other Germans and a Brazilian who played with Pele... Zequinha.

The old guard, the English guys, resented them. The Germans are the kind of guys who are very proud and very disciplined. The English are a little loosy-goosy and like to drink. But, it was the best team that Dallas ever had. It's true that the Germans weren't as willing to go into the community. They were big-timers, and weren't interested in going out and doing clinics. It was a tough thing for Kewley and Turner, who were guys who came from lower leagues and were sort of cast aside. I was responsible for that. But those were the best Dallas teams we ever had.

By the beginning of the 1977 season Turner had turned 34 years old. Al Miller's plan for the year included a faster pace on the pitch. Due to this change in style, he expressed concern that Turner might struggle coming forward during game-play. Miller even thought it was possible Turner might not make the active roster.[4] Although Turner did make the team and played in eight games in 1977, it was clear he was nearing the end of his career.[5] However, Turner wasn't quite finished living up to his reputation as "The Digger." In the opening game of the year, Turner had a masterful performance defending against Rodney Marsh, the Tampa Bay Rowdies' All-Star midfielder. On April 24th, the Tornado traveled to the Meadowlands in New Jersey to face the New York Cosmos. Coach Miller decided to use Turner to shadow the always dangerous Pele.[6] With 13,527 fans watching, Turner and the Tornado triumphed, defeating the Cosmos 2-1.[7] It is hard to imagine a better way to wind down a soccer career than to defeat, on the road no-less, the greatest player in the history of the game. Two months later,

Turner tore ligaments in his knee and was lost for the remainder of the 1977 season.[8] *The 1978 season would be Turner's last. He would play just one game during that final season.*[9] *In May of that year, he had knee surgery, effectively ending his playing career.*[10]

Turner accomplished a great deal in his long career. He played 131 straight games, earning him the "Iron Man" moniker. Dallas sportswriter Temple Pouncey added him, along with future Wings George Ley and Jimmy Ryan, to his All-Decade Team.[11] *Pouncey proclaimed him "the soul and bedrock of every Tornado team since 1969."*[12] *To honor his contributions to the team over the course of his long tenure in Dallas, July 8th, 1978 was proclaimed "Roy Turner Day." Turner was honored at that day's game against the Vancouver Whitecaps.*[13]

ROY TURNER: I had knee problems. Nobody knew it, but I had my knee drained every week so I could play. I eventually had enough of that and didn't have my knee done one morning and knew what would happen. I had knee surgery the next day and knew that was the end of it. I was 35 at the time. What I remember about that day was thinking, "What's next?" I wasn't scared...just excited.

DAVE PHILLIPS, WINGS RADIO ANNOUNCER, 1986-1993: He was a fierce, fierce competitor. One time when he came back to coach, he wanted me to understand what made him tick. "Do you know why I quit as a player in Dallas? I had so many knee injuries that I couldn't dominate anymore." It was too much for him to take to just be an average player.

ROY TURNER: [Lamar Hunt] had a special memorial night for me...He brought my parents over from England. Gave me a great send-off. I had no idea my parents would be there. Lamar's partner in the team was Bill McNutt. He owned a huge bakery/fruitcake company. As part of my mom and dad coming they got them a fancy hotel room and both picked them up in Lamar's Rolls-Royce and took them to dinner. My father was a breadman, and asked Bill what he did. "I'm in the bakery business." "So am I!" said my dad. "How big was your route?" dad asked [laughs]. Bill was so nice he continued to carry on the conversation.

AL MILLER: We had the pre-game ceremony and announced that Roy was retiring and we were going to retire his jersey. But then we had a limousine drive on the field, and his parents came out of it. He had no idea. It was one of my most wonderful nights as a coach. To be able to honor him in that way, all of which he deserved, was a great way for him to leave Dallas. I was so happy for him to end up in Wichita.

ROY TURNER: My parents used to come over and watch me play and realized how big it had become...and saw my success. They loved nothing more than coming and watching me play and coach. The game was maturing in this country so more opportunities were getting created. Lamar was very supportive of my retirement and tried to get me a job as a coach in the NASL. When I retired I was put in charge of community relations for the Tornado...Kenny Cooper and I left at the same time. He coached at Houston and Baltimore. I was the best man at his wedding. Our career paths were very similar.

KENNY COOPER: Between Ron Newman and Al Miller we had the two best coaches in the league. One who was a great motivator and one a great tactician.

By 1984 the NASL was dead. The league's demise was hastened by a rivalry with the upstart Major Indoor Soccer League (MISL). Several underlying problems might have sunk the NASL anyway, but the rivalry with the MISL certainly didn't help. Turner found three overarching reasons for the NASL's death...

ROY TURNER: [Reason #1] Overspending. In 1976, a NASL franchise cost $3 million...the New York Cosmos would get the best player from each country... not one country...each country. Other rich people in the league wanted to win as well, but there could only be one winner. So spending all that money to lose games made owners want to quit...There weren't enough people in the stands to pay their wages.

[Reason #2] The Players Union also led to its demise. They became quite strong and made things very expensive.

[Reason #3] I played in Soldier Field and the Rose Bowl...there were so few people at Soldier Field that one of the comedians on the team said we should shake hands with everyone in the crowd to thank them for coming. You can't create atmosphere with a few thousand people in an 80,000-person stadium.

KENNY COOPER: The NASL ran its course, and the MISL took over. The NASL expanded too quickly.

For Roy Turner, his career as a player was over, and he embraced his role as Director of Community Relations. However, his interest in coaching would soon bring him to Kansas, of all places. No one, including Turner, would ever have guessed how long he would stay.

CHAPTER 4

An Oral History

Hockey, Hold the Ice...

———

"Tom [Marshall] looked like a character from a Charles Dickens
book...like he was ten steps ahead of his next great idea."

- JACKIE KNAPP

*IN 1971, THE ST. LOUIS Stars invited Coach Ron Newman and the Dallas Tornado
to take part in a "Hock-Sock Tournament." It was to be the first professional indoor
soccer tournament in the history of the United States. The goals were only four feet
high and 16 feet wide, and the tournament was designed to help improve players'
passing skills for the outdoor game.[1] The NASL continued to hold indoor tournaments throughout the 1970s. Roy Turner played for the Tornado's indoor squad in
1975, 1976, and 1978. As he said in a 1978 interview, he was particularly effective
in the indoor game because "there's no place they can run to get away from me."[2]
Not including Turner, a whopping seven players from the 1978 Tornado indoor
team would go on to become Wichita Wings: Jimmy Ryan, Jeff Bourne, Kevin
Kewley, Freddie Garcia, Glenn Myernick, Chris Collins, and Carl Christensen.[3]*

*Meanwhile, on February 11th, 1974, the Red Army soccer team flew over the
Iron Curtain to play an indoor exhibition at The Spectrum against the Al Miller-
coached Philadelphia Atoms.[4] In the crowd that day were Ed Tepper and Earl*

Foreman. Foreman, a lawyer by trade, had previously owned the Virginia Squires in the American Basketball Association and now looked at this curious new sport with the eye of an entrepreneur.[5] *Together with Assistant Commissioner Tepper, Referee-in-Chief Joe Machnik, and Director of PR, Doug Verb, Commissioner Foreman would beat the NASL to the punch and form the first professional indoor soccer league in 1978. Their new creation, the Major Indoor Soccer League (MISL), began to sell the sport across the country, starting franchises in Cincinnati, Cleveland, Houston, New York, Philadelphia and Pittsburgh.*[6] *For indoor soccer, it has been a long and winding road since 1971.*

AL MILLER, HEAD COACH OF THE PHILADELPHIA ATOMS AND DALLAS TORNADO: I brought the Russians over to Philly at the Spectrum in February of 1974, with 15,000 people [in the stands]. An impresario from Portugal called me up because I was the general manager and coach and he said, "I've got a great idea...how about we play the Russian champions," who were the Red Army team, "against the US champions, the Philly Atoms?" I told him the problem is that it's February and there's snow on the ground and nobody wants to play outside now. So I said, "What about an indoor game?" He said, "We don't know anything about that, but our players do train indoors." I said, "Well, how about I send you the rules and you can run them by the coach and the players."

Earl Foreman and Ed Tepper came into the dressing room after the game and said, "What are you going to do with this sport?" I said, "I don't know, but the people really liked it, didn't they?" "Well, if you aren't going to [do anything], then we will." And that's how the MISL got started.

DOUG VERB, MISL EXECUTIVE, DIRECTOR OF PRESS AND PR: I was in a real fortunate position when I got involved with the MISL, having never kicked the ball before. I was a sportswriter. I worked for the *Washington Post* and covered, in the mid- to late-'70s, the wild times of the Cosmos...and a team in Philly for a while. Ed Tepper and [Earl] Foreman thought I knew something about soccer, which was funny. When I did go to work for him, Earl was a genius.

It was very important to keep the "brother-in-law effect" out of a new franchise, meaning when Earl and Ed would sell a franchise, and we were talking to a new owner, [Ed or Earl would] say things like, "Who's going to run the soccer end of things?" And they'd say things like, "Oh my cousin," or "My wife's cousin; he's been involved in youth soccer for years." And we were like, "No, no, no, this is PROFESSIONAL." What he would do to combat that is to send Joe Machnik and I out to live with a new franchise. It could be a week or two...I spent three months in one place...we would sit there and go over everything we needed to go over. To me, it was an incredible learning [experience]... it was a "bachelor's" in sports management, which they didn't have when I was in school. And it was a "master's" also, and I got my "doctorate" when I tried to run the team in Chicago. Because I was in so many of these franchises I had to do a lot of staffing. That was great. You'll hear from me often, "I gave him his first job."

Earl Foreman saw the MISL as the fifth major sport. You have to remember, in the late '70s and early '80s, in basketball, you weren't playing in the NBA if you didn't have what looked like sugar powder on your upper lip. The NHL always had the same problem: you can't watch it on television. We immediately seized on that. We outdrew the Blues in St. Louis; a lot of times we were outdrawing the Sabres with our Stallions [in Buffalo]. We were doing pretty well. When I got to Chicago, the Bulls didn't do much [marketing], so I used to say we outdrew both the Blackhawks and the Bulls. They had some guy named Jordan...I don't know what happened to him. To say we would be the fifth sport? Maybe? I think it was a good grandiose statement of a commissioner of a lower league. Did I believe we'd be successful? Absolutely, because the game was so exciting. I really thought it was going to be successful. I still think it could be.

We started Oct. 15th and played the first game December 22nd, 1978, with Pete Rose kicking out the ball. He was a 1/10th owner of the [Cincinnati] Kids. He was great. We had to figure everything out from October to December. I'd get a call from some owner and he'd say, "Hey, I can't find the memo, what's the size of the goal?" And of course, we hadn't made the decision yet, so I put him on hold and I went in to talk to Machnik and said, "Ok, is it going to be long and narrow, or tall and thin?" So we just made the decision and got back on the phone and said, "It's 6'6 by 12'." A lot of those things were just done like that.

Meanwhile, in Wichita, Kansas, more and more people discovered the joys of playing soccer. Several adult teams traveled throughout the region playing whatever competition they could find. The Wheathawks and the Soccer Club were the best of the local adult teams.

ALAN SHEPHERD, WHEATHAWKS CO-FOUNDER AND MISL REFEREE: I'm from England. My family moved back over in '64. I was nine. I lost my accent after a couple years. My dad got a job in Wichita as a pattern maker in the aircraft industry. There was a men's team called The Soccer Club that my dad played for. Those guys started a youth team that I was a part of. There were three youth teams back then. We had uniforms, but they were all #5 and #12. There was a Hispanic team from up north and a team from Derby. When I was 14 or 15 I played for the Soccer Club team. We'd go play KU and K-State or Kansas City teams. Matt Knoblauch and I and Bobby [Bribiesca] started a team called the Wheathawks. We played at Linwood Park. It was a great experience, a great team, and a good bunch of guys.

KEVIN HIMES, WHEATHAWK, RUGRAT, AND WINGS EMPLOYEE: Matt Knoblauch was one of the founders of the Wheathawks. My first game with the Wheathawks was a Kansas Cup final in KC. If you played for the Wheathawks, you didn't ever play for the Soccer Club. But there were some Soccer Club guys that did play for the Wheathawks. So that's the biggest men's rivalry in town.

Thanks to groups like the American Youth Soccer Organization (AYSO,) soccer was becoming accessible to kids throughout the Wichita metro area. In 1975, there were only 250 kids playing soccer in Wichita. But by 1978, that number had risen to 3,000.[7]

TOM MARSHALL, AYSO REGION 49 COMMISSIONER: I moved to Wichita from the Adirondack Mountains, near Keysville, NY. I was born and raised in Buffalo. I was an alcoholic and still am, but choose not to drink. Back then, when I drank, I used to solve my problems by backing a truck up and moving. I was in sales and moved to Wichita in about 1973.

We were hockey people, but my oldest son Tod was very small. On the west side, there was a rink across from the airport. They told us Tod wasn't going to play [because he was too small]. So we pursued soccer. My background [in soccer] is through my kids. Tod excelled at it and went on to play college soccer in Michigan. I got very involved in youth soccer because of them.

JACKIE KNAPP, AYSO VOLUNTEER: It's almost a laughable story. When I graduated from WSU, I must have had more majors than anyone on record because I worked in the Dean's office. I changed my major to journalism, signed off on it myself, and ended up with a journalism degree with an emphasis on sports writing. I was unemployed for six months and got involved with AYSO soccer when Tom Marshall was commissioner. My nephews were playing and my brother-in-law Gene Mandel had a soccer team full of what would become "the Rugrats." They were eight, nine, ten [years old] at the time. I would go to their games faithfully. I had never seen more soccer fields cropping up all over the city...never seen so much enthusiasm in youth sports. I plastered my old car with AYSO bumper stickers. That's how I got to know Tom and [Wings announcer] J.B. Johnson and all those founding fathers of youth soccer in Wichita.

Tom looked like a character from a Charles Dickens book. He had this black hair and round face. A short guy. These pale, Gene Wilder, wild blue eyes; always looking like he was ten steps ahead of his next great idea. The popularity [of soccer] seemed to come out of nowhere. I sought out books at the library. I read *Soccer in the United States*, written in 1969 about how Americans were starting to accept soccer.

The more I hung out with my sister, Mary Mandel, and brother-in-law, Gene, the more I'd see soccer folks stopping over at their house. Tom and Nancy would come over and smoke a cigarette or two and have a beer. That's how I got to know these people. I was beginning to have more of a PR interest than a pure sports interest. I would go to a few Wheathawks games. They scared the crap out of me because they acted more like rugby players. I wasn't a troll for athletes, so I didn't necessarily want to hang out with them.

KEVIN HIMES: I think that the soccer community in Wichita has been very close, even from back then. People on the west side knew people on the east side and we all worked together to promote the game.

TOM MARSHALL: AYSO Region 49 was already here at that time. The founders were Joe and Rose Behm...nobody had more passion for the game than

Joe. He'd go into the bad parts of town and bring kids to play soccer. He'd pay their enrollment fees as well. They moved to Texas, and I became commissioner. There was a basketball, football, and baseball mentality at the time. Soccer wasn't recognized like it is today. The main hub on the east side was Linwood Park. There was a little bar called the Soccer Club Inn across the street. Richard Brown ran that. He and Horst Hiller were promoting soccer on the adult level. Since Richard served beer, I became friends with him early on.

Larry Stockton formed the new AYSO Region 105, along with Bobby Bribiesca. We had a space problem...not enough fields. Some space opened up on East 13th. There were 23 acres that we were given. We formed the Kansas Friends of Soccer (KFOS) to try to secure playing fields on that land. It didn't go anywhere for awhile. Hunt Parker suggested I give Al Miller a call to have the Dallas Tornado put on an exhibition to raise funds to build our soccer complex.

The land for the new soccer complex had been an unused part of the Lakeview Gardens Cemetery at 13th and Greenwich, on the northeast side of Wichita. KFOS needed $35,000 to start the development of their dream complex. Marshall envisioned "a 3,000 spectator complex [and] enough playing fields to accommodate growth." [8]

JACKIE KNAPP: In 1978, Tom said, "I want to have a fundraiser for youth soccer of Wichita and I want it to be the Dallas Tornado vs. the Houston Hurricanes." I was like, "Oh, wow!" We'd have these guys in here from two pro soccer teams and they'd show us this new indoor game. I got really excited about that and told Tom I'd help with publicity. I would constantly churn out stuff on my old IBM Selectric and hand it to Tom, and he'd say, "This is great; I'll take it down to the Eagle." All I wanted was to see the games, I wasn't getting any money.

TOM MARSHALL: I flew down to Dallas in the summer of 1978 and spent the day with Al [Miller] and made arrangements to have this game. We had to pay $5,000 a team, plus airfare, lodging, and refs. [Tulsa] would loan us the carpet and we'd have to pay the shipping. I took this to the board of the [KFOS].

They approved and I used the kids as a marketing tool to make this happen. I had manila envelopes printed which we gave out to the teams. They had a deadline to sell as many tickets to this exhibition as they could. The kid who sold the most tickets won a free trip to Dallas to see the Tornado. The response was overwhelming. At 1:00 am I realized I had a pile of $30,000-$40,000 on my living room table. Then, I realized I had told about 200 people what the procedure would be to bring all this money to one meeting place. Then I got paranoid. I started hearing noises out of the garbage can...my imagination was running wild.

Then we turned around and started getting sponsors, like Coors of Kansas. This sponsorship led to other big leaguers. The game was a huge success... That's where I met Roy Turner. He was one heck of a PR guy. One of the local sports TV personalities asked Roy, "You know soccer is a very low scoring game, how will Americans enjoy this?" Roy rubbed his chin, and said, "Maybe we ought to just multiply each goal by 7?" The reporter's jaw dropped. Roy was a very talented individual. I was extremely impressed with him. That exhibition set the record, either first or second, for attendance in an exhibition game in the United States.

The exhibition was dubbed "The Sunflower Soccer Spectacular." The Tornado brought the Englishman Paul Child to town, on-loan from the San Jose Earthquakes. Child was considered one of the best indoor players in the NASL, and at the time was the second leading scorer in the history of the outdoor NASL. At 7:30 pm, on December 1st, 1978, the Dallas Tornado and the Houston Hurricane squared off at the Kansas Coliseum. Tickets could be had for just $7.50, or $5 for the cheap seats.[9]

JACKIE KNAPP: I saw Roy, and I watched him play and thought, "Wow, that guy must be 40, but he's everywhere on the field." Everybody who attended that first exhibition was just blown away.

ROY TURNER, DIRECTOR OF COMMUNITY RELATIONS, DALLAS TORNADO: 1979 was the first year I didn't play. It was awkward for me because I wanted to be on the field. We used to do exhibitions in those days and got a call from Wichita to do a game to raise money for the AYSO. I was in charge of setting it up. I came to Wichita for three days and even played in the game.

I had no intention of staying. The game drew 5,800. I got to know a lot of people in those three days and they were very nice to me. I met a couple people that would become guys I'd know for years: Jim O'Donnell and Horst Hiller. I went to a place on Seneca called the Soccer Club Inn and met the people on the amateur level and met the local soccer community.

AL MILLER, HEAD COACH, DALLAS TORNADO: I had a lot of respect for Roy, a wonderful guy to coach and a great human being. I came up with an idea that we could get some pre-season games sponsored by cities that didn't have pro teams. One of those ended up in Wichita. We had a game there and as I recall, the day before we had the game, the players, under Roy's supervision, went out and did clinics for the kids all over Wichita. That's how he got spotted and known by the people thinking about buying a franchise. It was a natural because Roy was at the end of his career and the league was getting much stronger....and we were having to phase out some of the older guys like Roy. It was a perfect fit for Roy to leave his playing career and go to Wichita to coach.

JACKIE KNAPP: The players were supposed to go back to the hotel in a bus from the Coliseum, but the bus broke down so that's why so many of us had to transport them back to the hotel. I remember volunteering to drive Paul Child and [some others] around. We drove out to a field out by the airport. My contact lenses were fogging over and I couldn't see very well, and the guys were complaining. So, I said, "If you guys don't like my driving then I'll let somebody else drive." So Paul drove my car and everyone was clinging to ashtrays and seatbelts. I thought "Jesus Christ, what have I done, he's going to kill us all." I don't know if he knew what side of the road to drive on or not...speeding down Kellogg in the winter at night.

The exhibition featured three periods, like a hockey game. The Tornado started Kenny Cooper in goal and triumphed 8-7, with all of the goals scored in the second and third periods. Three of the goals scored by Dallas came from future Wichita Wings: two by

Freddie Garcia and one by Caesar Cervin. Immediately after the game, both teams stayed on the field to sign autographs for the 5,800 fans in attendance.[10]

At the time it was just a fundraiser for AYSO. But it would open the door to much more. From the exhibition would ultimately sprout the Wichita Wings. And it wouldn't be the last time that youth soccer would go hand-in-hand with the professional indoor game. It was the first professional soccer game ever played in the state of Kansas. Not to reinforce any regional stereotypes, but it was played in a recently constructed big brown barn...with Tornados. Roy Turner, the Iron Man of the NASL, played his last professional game that night. Coincidentally, he ended his former career on the very pitch where his new one began. Though the game was a big success, it only whet Marshall's appetite.

JACKIE KNAPP: Tom said, "Wouldn't it be great to do this again?"

TOM MARSHALL: We used that money [from the first exhibition] to start grading the fields. I got a call from Barney Schwan of the Anheuser-Busch distributorship. He said, "Anything Coors can do, Budweiser can do better." He asked if we were interested in having another exhibition…

JACKIE KNAPP: The operations people from the respective pro teams laid the turf down and made it fit. They brought the turf with them. At the time the Coliseum was only being used for concerts and rodeos. The second [exhibition] game had a lot more clinics for youth players. Three or four pros would go and give demonstrations. The second exhibition didn't draw as many.

TOM MARSHALL: The second exhibition game involved Tulsa and Chicago. I was afraid of a complete catastrophe because I had previously sold almost all our tickets through the kids and had paid most of our costs through tradeouts with sponsors. Here it was February, with not much time to put this on. We had an ice storm, but still had about 4,000 people. The important thing was that soccer stayed in the news. We didn't make much money on that second game, but more contacts were made. Dr. Pepper was involved as a sponsor.

The Tulsa Roughnecks and Chicago Sting faced off at 7:35 pm on Friday, February 2nd, 1979. Tulsa featured future Wing, Laurie Abrahams. Fourteen members of the Roughnecks spent the week in Wichita giving clinics to youth players.[11] Though roughly 2,000 fewer people attended the second game; it was still considered a success. Now, Marshall set his sights even higher.

CHAPTER 5

An Oral History

Chasing Down the Dream

_____

"You can make this town big."

- ROY TURNER

JACKIE KNAPP, PUBLIC RELATIONS, WICHITA WINGS 1979-80:
Tom wanted to test the waters to see if interest was high enough for us to get a pro team.

KEVIN HIMES, WHEATHAWK, RUGRAT, AND WINGS EMPLOYEE:
You've got so many different points of view. There were countless people that were responsible for getting the Wings going. It wasn't just one person. Everyone deserves credit.

TOM MARSHALL, GENERAL MANAGER, WICHITA WINGS 1979:
That evening when I had the kitchen table filled with money I realized I should try to start a professional team. At that time, everything was about WSU basketball. But Wichita is such a family oriented and prideful area. I looked at Wichita as potentially being the Green Bay Packers of soccer. After the _Soccer America_ article came out about our success, Ed Tepper, MISL Commissioner, gave me a call. Then, Bob Cousy, the basketball star, who was commissioner of the American Soccer League (ASL), got involved. I went out to his office and was

very disappointed with their operation. They were talking about having a split season with indoor and outdoor. I liked that idea.

In April of 1979 it appeared that the new professional soccer franchise in Wichita would be associated with the ASL. This longstanding league had spent most of its existence as a regional outdoor league in the northeast United States. It sought to expand nationally and create both an indoor and outdoor presence. The Wichita franchise would need funding in the amount of $500,000 to $750,000 to get started. The plan was to operate in the Kansas Coliseum for indoor games and Cessna Stadium for outdoor games. Each season would have 14 home games and it was projected that it would take an average attendance of 3,000 to break even. Wichita would play in a newly created Midwest division along with Indianapolis, Cleveland, Columbus, and Las Vegas.[1]

TOM MARSHALL: I came back to Wichita [after meeting with the ASL], and met with Clarence Wesley of the Chamber of Commerce. He recommended Barry Hollie to help us get the money to start a team. [Hollie] was the biggest con man, flim-flam asshole that ever walked the face of the earth. He supposedly had a guy in San Antonio that was going to invest in the team. The good part of this is that it kept soccer in the paper. [*Wichita Eagle* reporter] Mal Elliott would follow the progress of it all and write articles about it, and it was probably important to making the Wings come along later. But all our questions to the potential investor were answered very ambiguously. Then I got a second call from Ed Tepper. After the disappointing visit to New York and listening to Hollie's stories about his plane crashing and having to crawl back to civilization, I was excited to hear from [Tepper]. Ed was a dynamite guy. He promoted an exhibition game with the [Red Army squad] earlier in the 1970s. It was the first indoor soccer game played in North America and was a tremendous success, which led to the MISL. They had a fairly successful first year and were looking at expansion out west. The bridge to the west was the Midwest. The way it was sold to investors was that it was a game for TV. I was tremendously impressed with Ed. He came to Wichita a couple times and helped me close out some investors later on down the road. I put together a pro forma [feasibility study]. John Frazier, the 7-Up bottler, said, "Look, you need to learn how to do a deal. I'm going to help you put this together."

JACKIE KNAPP: After [the exhibition] was over, Tom [Marshall] kept in touch with Al Miller and Timo Liekoski [coach of the NASL's Houston Hurricanes]. Tom said, "We could probably get a franchise here." I started working as a media relations person at Kansas Newman. I was kind of moonlighting with Tom doing the soccer stuff. Tom was talking to the American Soccer League folks AND the MISL. He was trying to drum up people who he could get to fund this thing. For the ASL, they wanted a $750,000 letter of credit.

In the summer of '79 I was offered a renewal of my contract at Newman, but I told them I was going to bow out and try to make the soccer team come to town. I had a little money after my aunt's death to live on. Indications were we were going to go with the ASL. There was this guy in KC who we were dealing with...Barry Hollie...He would never mention the name of his benefactor. He was bald, big, and you never saw his eyes because he'd wear sunglasses. He would come to town and drive us around and refer to "my man" who wanted this or that. We would sit around Tom's kitchen table and I'd talk about how this guy gave me the creeps. Tom thought he could get us the money. I can't remember how it went sour.

I know we took a trip to Tulsa and Al Miller was there. I was very quiet and I think Roy was there. Roy said he was ready to retire and would be interested in coaching indoor. I'm pretty sure it was still during the wooing of the ASL. We had gotten so far in our imaginations, we'd come with colors: violet, silver, and turquoise. A lot of people would probably go, "Jeez," at that now. I turned around and made a suit and blouse with those colors and wore it to the Tulsa game.

TOM MARSHALL: I talked to Jackie [Knapp] and she had just gotten a degree in marketing. She helped me put that pro forma together. We took it to Rob Wilkins at Smith-Barney and he got a cut-in for 5% to help us promote it. His brother Howard Wilkins came in as well. We met with him and Ed Tepper at the country club. [Howard Wilkins] kept saying, "This isn't gonna work," after I'd propose my plans for the new team. Every few minutes he'd say that. After about an hour of that, he said, "Well, this isn't going to work, but I'll go ahead and put in 30%." We were shooting for $1.5 million over time, with $750,000 up front. John Frazier also put in 30%. Don Slawson and [Gerry] O'Shaughnessy both also invested.

On June 29th the Wichita Eagle *reported that the ASL had officially approved Wichita's bid for a franchise after a $750,000 letter of credit was produced. Tom Marshall would become general manager and Roy Turner the head coach. Additionally, Marshall was attempting to sign Kenny Cooper as the team's goalkeeper. The franchise was to be called "The Wichita Wings." An official announcement and press conference was expected in two-and-a-half weeks.[2]*

In actuality, by July 8th the letter of credit was still yet to be posted. Barry Hollie was quoted in the Eagle as saying, "We will have the letter of credit before the end of July." Marshall praised Clarence Wesley of the Chamber of Commerce for his help: "...Wesley opened a lot of doors for me. He went out of his way to help us."[3]

By August 18th, 1979 everything had changed. The original letter of credit for $750,000 was never achieved and the ASL failed to find enough teams to start an indoor season. It appeared there would still be a Wichita Wings and Marshall would be the general manager, but it would be in the MISL, not the ASL.[4] Final permission from the MISL was anticipated to come during the league meetings a week later.

JACKIE KNAPP: All of a sudden, Barry Hollie stopped returning phone calls and evaporated. That's when Tom realized we'd better go with the MISL. When the ASL thing fell through, we had a change of colors. We decided to go with Orange, Yellow, White and Blue. All the stuff was pounded out at Tom's kitchen table. Tom was talking to people in the MISL and that's about the time [late June/early July] I started talking to some of the league PR people. Doug Verb was the main one. I was trying to figure out what we needed to do to get a franchise established. He said it would take a solid, committed owner and media coverage. That's what Tom was doing: going to lead after lead, meeting with some of Wichita's biggest businessmen, trying to get people to invest.

TOM MARSHALL: Rob Wilkins came across a guy who I'd never heard of: Bob Becker. Ed, Bob, and I all met together at Wichita Country Club. Then, Bob had a conference call with us and said he'd invest if he could have half...he had to be a managing partner for the other investors. Otherwise, he didn't feel like there would be tight enough reins on the money...Howard Wilkins agreed to lower his share. John [Frazier] backed off some as well. So, Becker became managing partner. John Frazier was named the alternate managing partner.

ROBERT H. "BOB" BECKER, OWNER, WICHITA WINGS 1979-80: I was born on May 19th, 1940 and was raised in Emporia and went to college at KU. I then spent three-and-a-half years in the Navy as a commissioned officer. Got out of the Navy, went to Emporia for a bit, and then worked in El Dorado and Wichita after that. Then I moved out to the West Coast. I was going to retire, and then found out I didn't have enough money to retire and live out there, at least not the way I wanted to live. I bought a big fancy house in Malibu and ceased to enjoy that. Then I moved back here in 1972. I got married and had a couple kids; a boy and a girl. I got divorced in 1979.

My dad was a German immigrant and he had played on a German team. He would explain it as a national team, but I think he was too young for that. He came when he was 16-years-old. So I had an introduction to soccer and that's how I got started. I had a few meetings with Tom Marshall. He was a nice young man, but he didn't have anything in the pot, and wanted to run the whole thing. He had never owned a sports team before.

I have no idea how Tom Marshall found me. I got a call from some other guy about it. My motivation was to go into a sports franchise that had a chance to grow into something...not realizing at the time how long it might take. I didn't know how long it would take compared to something like real estate development. I expected it to make money faster than it did. I thought it would be fun, but it wasn't so much that I just wanted to own a sports team, it was more about the financial consideration.

KEVIN KEWLEY, FORWARD, WICHITA WINGS: Bob Becker's [importance] was huge... He would party with the guys, especially after a big win. A great guy.

TOM MARSHALL: I am one of the most grandiose men to walk the face of the Earth. Bob Becker is probably the only person with a bigger ego.

JACKIE KNAPP: I had never met Becker until the league meetings. Tom had told me, "I think we have a bid from Great Plains Oil. Believe me, the guy has the money." Tom would take his excitement to these meetings with Becker and set the scene by talking about the roar of the crowd, and the Iron Man of the NASL, one of the most respected players as OUR coach, here in Wichita. I think that's what sold Becker. We never expected [Becker] to be a one-year wonder.

ROY TURNER, HEAD COACH, WICHITA WINGS: Tom Marshall and a bunch of his friends saw potential. [Marshall and Becker asked] "Would you be interested in coming up and coaching?" I basically said no...a few times. [Becker] then sent a jet down for me, brought me up and gave me the ol' dog and pony show. Took me to the Scotch and Sirloin and convinced me that this was the place. So I decided to give it a go. I didn't come up thinking this would be temporary or anything like that. I thought this was it. I bought a house within a month. They had a lot of issues and problems in that first year.

JACKIE KNAPP: We knew we wanted Roy to be our coach. Nancy Marshall and I said, "Oh, Roy is the best looking!" We would go back into their daughter Lorie's bedroom, and put Billy Joel's "Prelude/Angry Young Man" on full blast and would imagine the players coming out to that. I said, "We have Roy come out last." Tom would take on the role of each player and run into the bedroom and we'd announce him and their kids would be cheering and yelling.

...Nancy and I didn't hear anyone else's name after "Roy." He had that accent, and presented himself as such a gentleman. Except for one thing. Roy came to town to visit. It was the first time I'd met him as a prospective coach of our franchise. He was in a suit and in an atrium type setting. It might have been at the Wichita Royale. I walked in and the first course was a salad for me, and a cigarette and a salad for Tom. Roy ordered soup. They brought the soup and Roy picks the bowl up with both hands, his pinkies out, and drinks it [laughs]. I remember being speechless. He would make these slurping noises. He was on such a pedestal in my mind. I had gone to the library and read books that talked about him. It was such a funny first impression.

AL MILLER, HEAD COACH, DALLAS TORNADO: Roy and I were very tight and I told him I thought that his career as a player was coming to a close and asked him what he wanted to do. Like most guys, he wanted to play forever and I told him, "You have to start thinking about your future." As it turned out, that trip culminated in an offer to join the Wichita Wings. I'm 100% sure he got the job due to him being over there during those clinics. We gave him a great recommendation. It's guys like him that made the game work in this country.

KENNY COOPER, GOALKEEPER, DALLAS TORNADO: Both Roy and I were smart enough to realize the future was indoor soccer in 1979. The indoor game was like a hockey stick...it went up and up. We had satellite trucks broadcasting the games nationally. It was the right decision for us at the time. We both wanted to go into coaching. Roy asked me if I would be his player/assistant in Wichita, but I wanted to be a head coach.

DOUG VERB, MISL EXECUTIVE, DIRECTOR OF PRESS AND PR: When I think of Roy, the word "solid" comes to mind immediately. He was a real solid, strong guy. There were guys like Roy in every market...they saw something different. We knew we'd have an honorable guy, a guy of high integrity, and we thought he'd bring those kinds of players to it. We were fighting against the image of the pro athlete at the time. This was the era when players didn't want to mess around with fans, and we wanted our guys to do just the opposite. Seeing him at league meetings, I knew that guys like that...and Roy was always very thoughtful...I knew he had sat down and thought about the concept of doing something with the game that would make it better and exciting. We had extreme faith in him. I knew that if it didn't work out in Wichita we'd always find a place for him somewhere else.

JACKIE KNAPP: Did I ever expect Roy to spend the rest of his life in Wichita? Not on my life. I thought maybe he'd stay two years because this would be a stepping stone for him. It amazes me that Roy and Kewley stayed so long.

TOM MARSHALL: So we hopped on Becker's Learjet and flew to Hartford [Connecticut] for the league meeting in August. It was just a formality for the awarding of our franchise.

JACKIE KNAPP: Becker was a cold fish. He was 39 but he seemed like 60. He oozed money. He was polite, but he wasn't pleasant. I immediately felt my stature as a poor northeast-side person when he was in the room. I bought a whole new wardrobe for a three-day league meeting. [Becker] was haughty and carried himself with a confidence that bordered on arrogance. But the setting, going into league meetings, with all these heavy-lifters, you almost had to go in there with that chip on your shoulder. To somebody that wasn't real savvy about the world, it was intimidating.

I knew we had a deadline to get the line of credit signed, sealed, delivered, and approved by the MISL. I don't think we really knew for sure whether we were going to get a franchise until we went to the league meetings in Hartford in August of 1979. We went to the league meetings in Becker's Learjet. It was Tom, Becker, [and] me. It was surreal.

They had breakout meetings in Hartford. We didn't know at the time we had been included. All the team owners had to approve any new teams. I was in the meetings with the PR people. I learned what the guidelines were for these sports franchises. There were dinners and luncheons. I don't remember a lot about those meetings except I was completely overwhelmed thinking: "Shit is about to get real."

I don't remember the definitive moment when they introduced us an official franchise. There wasn't any time to catch your breath and think, "Oh, this is a monumental moment in my life." We went in there a little bit puffed up. I remember the league advising your city should have a population of 500,000+ to be considered. I remember taking a compass and laying out a city map and sticking the point in and drawing a circle that included Emporia and other outlying places [laughs]. We knew the 250,000 in Wichita-proper wouldn't fly. I said, "Let's see what the numbers look like if we include all these towns." I looked at the census numbers and got us to 500,000.

After the league meetings, Tom called me and said, "You've worked these past 10 weeks without a paycheck. I've got something for you." He handed me a $1,000 check for all the work I'd done to that point. It was like 10 Christmases. My salary for that year would end up being about $14,000.

Marshall, Becker, and Knapp returned from Hartford, Connecticut with an MISL franchise, approved by a unanimous vote from the league. The Wings would join the

Buffalo Stallions, Hartford Hellions, Detroit Lightning, and St. Louis Steamers as expansion teams in what would be a 32-game season. Becker would be the president of the club. Tom Marshall would be the general manager. Roy Turner was referred to as "one of the top candidates" for the head coaching position.[5] Outside of the soccer team, Becker ran the Great Plains Corporation, which was an oil marketing operation. Though he had no experience running a professional sports team, he had a great deal of experience in the business world.

For Wichita, August 21st of 1979 would be historic: on that day, the Wings became the first major league sports franchise in the history of Kansas.[6] This new indoor soccer league was designed to appeal to the American sports fan. There would be four periods with timeouts. Each side would field six players at a time and substitutes could come on and off the field as often as the team wanted. Most importantly, there would be plenty of goals. As a bonus, the dreaded and confusing offside rule from outdoor soccer would be scrapped. The game ball would be orange, making it easy to spot on television: a medium that the MISL hoped to fully utilize. Mal Elliott of The Wichita Eagle *described it as "a cross between ice hockey and basketball, complete with picks and screens and a goaltender."[7]*

The rules were clear, but as for the origin of the name "Wichita Wings"...

TOM MARSHALL: We came up with "The Wings" because Wichita was the aircraft capital of the world and "to take this idea and fly with it." Plus, I was a [Detroit] Red Wings hockey fan. It must not have been me who came up with the name, because if I did, I'd be the first to tell you about it. I think it was Jackie who came up with the name. She drew a plane with wings.

JACKIE KNAPP: I didn't like the name "The Wings" [laughs]. We were sitting around Tom's kitchen table trying to come up with ideas. It was obviously a tribute to the air capital of the world. We had a whole list of names. "The Plainsmen" came up. It had to be something that would appeal to the players so they could bond with the community.

So, the author of the team name has been lost to the sands of time. As for the logo, well...

TOM MARSHALL: There was this marketing agency...they had come up with the logo. Becker said, "This is great!" When Turner came into town, he said, "That's the Whataburger logo!" Becker looked at him like, "What???" Turner said, "Don't you have Whataburger in Wichita?"

JACKIE KNAPP: As soon as we knew we were signed, sealed, and delivered, [Bob Becker's] Great Plains Corporation went to our ad agency and came up with slick sheets of our new logo. They had to do that pretty quickly. It wasn't until our first trip to St. Louis for a game, we were in the team bus, and somebody goes, "Look at that Whataburger!" And I went, "Oh my God..." I'd never heard of Whataburger before.

The Wings were to play in the Britt Brown Arena in the newly-constructed Kansas Coliseum. Located north of Wichita, just off I-135, the Coliseum could fit just shy of 10,000 screaming Wings fans. The arena was owned and operated by Sedgwick County. Sam Fulco was the director of the facility and was a great help to the team over the years. It wasn't the fanciest or biggest arena in the league, but it was home.

TOM MARSHALL: I had been in contact with Sam Fulco at the Kansas Coliseum about the potential team playing there. We were the second tenant after Bob Hope! Sam was very laid back. I met him in his office when planning the exhibition game. He kept looking at me like I was crazy when I was planning that. He got a phone call while we were talking. He's on the phone and says, "You're going to do what?!? And you think people are going to pay for that?!" [Fulco turns to Marshall] "This is really my day, I just had a guy say he wants to fill my building with dirt and run trucks in it." Ironically, those two things probably kept that building open.

Back then, it seemed like the Coliseum was as far away as Grand Island, Nebraska...which is why we surprised people with our attendance at the exhibition games. Fulco really wanted hockey there. He brought in the 1980 Olympic team for an exhibition and eventually the [Wichita] Wind came. We officed out of the Coliseum as well. We thought it was imperative to be at the facility.

ROY TURNER: The Britt Brown Arena [Kansas Coliseum] was just being built then. It was likely meant more for rodeos than it was for soccer. I had the best lease of any team. I dealt with Sam Fulco and had a great relationship with the county. They knew our team's financials. They contributed to making it better for the owners.

BOB BECKER: I remember when Sam [Fulco] ran the Coliseum I brought him a case of Chivas one time and I'd come in an hour before each game and we'd have a little drink.

DOUG VERB: The Kansas Coliseum, until I got to work the Cow Palace in San Francisco, was the worst-smelling arena in the sport. It WAS small. It was a small market; we had hoped for the best. [But] because the [Coliseum] was smaller there weren't any bad seats.

NORMAN PIPER, FORWARD, WICHITA WINGS: We used to practice by the Coliseum next to the cattle!

On September 15th, 1979, the first Wings press conference was held at the Kansas Coliseum. Bob Becker, Tom Marshall, and Doug Verb were on hand to promote their exciting new franchise. Mike Limon of the Wichita Eagle *reported that "a giant video screen greeted visitors with highlights of the MISL's first championship game played in March." Becker was quoted as saying he wanted to win the championship in their first season.*[8]

TOM MARSHALL: So we contacted Turner and set up a press conference at the Coliseum to announce the franchise. We announced Turner either at that or the second press conference. We had logos on napkins and various things. We had very impressive press conferences. If you want the media, you have the best bar setup in town. I had a guy in a tuxedo and brought a whole spread. We never had trouble with [media] attendance.

On September 25th, Turner was announced as head coach of the Wings. In his remarks to the media he emphasized the American nature of indoor soccer and proclaimed that "I have been part of soccer since way back in 1966 and I have been asking when are we going to give the American boys a chance."[9] *Since the announcement of the franchise, the team and the league had been trumpeting the idea that this was an American game for American players. "We're making this sport for the American soccer player. You'll see an All-American lineup on the carpet faster than you will in the North American Soccer League," said MISL Commissioner Earl Foreman.*[10] *Although 11 of the 19 Wings in the media guide were American, the stars of that first season, and most of the Wings' subsequent seasons, would be players from overseas. This would eventually become controversial in some quarters.*

ROY TURNER: We could only have four foreign players.

KEVIN KEWLEY: I started out as a foreign player. But [in year two] Bill Kentling talked to somebody and I got a green card in like a week. If you had a green card you counted as an American. There was a rumor that if you were a citizen you'd get drafted to go to Afghanistan or something. I figured that if I just had a green card I'd be okay.

Roy Turner made an excellent impression during the first press conference. Wichita Beacon *columnist Steve Love sang his praises: "Were Roy Turner his advance man, even Jimmy Carter might win reelection...You're going to like Roy Turner...he is a little bit Sir Winston Churchill and a little bit Mary Poppins...He is the only coach whom the Wings wanted. And if you had listened to him Tuesday, you would have understood why...Roy Turner makes you believe in indoor soccer and in him."*[11]

Now that he was officially on board, it was time for Roy Turner to put together a real-life soccer team. He began to work his connections to try to find players to come play the indoor game in Wichita.

BOB BECKER: As soon as I decided to get involved with it, I met with Roy in Tulsa, picked him up and came back into Wichita. I probably paid him about $50,000. Roy has fantastic personal skills. It's probably what got him his job running the [Wichita Open] golf tour. He just has a great personality. I hadn't been with him for 15 minutes and I knew I'd hire him to be head coach and run the team. He had a great, positive attitude.

ROY TURNER: I tried to bring Kenny Cooper to Wichita to play, but he got an offer to coach in Houston.

KENNY COOPER: Roy is a builder; he built the Wichita Wings. I helped build the Baltimore franchise...He took guys like Kewley, Ryan, and Ley back to Wichita…guys who had character.

ROY TURNER: I worked really hard in that first year on recruiting. The first player I signed was Norman Piper. Mike Ivanow was second. The three of us spent a lot of time going to schools promoting the team. We'd go out at night and nobody knew who the hell we were yet. The rest of the players came in and spent a lot of time doing the same, getting to know the community.

Goalkeeper Mike Ivanow was SUPPOSED to be the first signee for the Wichita Wings. But when the contract arrived in Ivanow's mailbox, it was addressed to "Michael Ivhanov." The Wichita Eagle and Beacon reported it "was returned with the notation that there was nobody at that address by that name."[12] Thus, on October 9th, 1979, Norman Piper became the first Wichita Wing. Piper was a 5'7 multiple-position player from North Tawton, in Devonshire, England. He had played in the NASL with the Ft. Lauderdale Strikers, in the ASL with the Columbus Magic, and in the Second Division of the English League with Portsmouth FC. He planned to continue playing outdoor in Columbus for the other half of the year.[13]

The 6'4 Ivanow had been a talented goalie for the Seattle Sounders prior to coming to Wichita. At age 31, he had already accomplished a great deal, playing in both the 1968 and 1972 Olympics for Team USA. An accomplished baseball player, he turned down a major league contract and instead, played for the University of San Francisco. While there, he switched to soccer, and never looked back. As to the notion that goalkeepers are naturally insane, Ivanow said, "I don't think I'm crazy." "That," said Turner, "is what he thinks."[14]

Piper and Ivanow didn't waste any time getting themselves involved with the community. Within a couple weeks of signing, The Wichita Beacon's *Steve Love reported on a trip the duo made to Kensler Elementary, where they taught soccer skills to dozens of enthusiastic students.[15] This sort of community outreach had been the hallmark of Roy Turner's Tornado team. He would make sure the Wichita Wings continued this effort throughout his tenure with the team.*

(Don Marler/1981-82 Wings Yearbook) George Ley battles for the ball.

The Wings continued to sign players throughout the month of October. Defender George Ley and midfielder Frank Barton, both Englishmen, soon came on-board.

Barton had a long career in England before playing in the NASL for the Seattle Sounders.[16] *They were quickly followed by Kevin Kewley and Carl Christensen. Christensen was an American defender who had played for the University of Vermont prior to an NASL career with Dallas and San Jose.*[17] *Glenn Myernick, Jimmy Ryan, Freddie Garcia, Chris Collins, and Joe Howarth came next. All but Howarth had played with Turner in Dallas. Turner told* The Wichita Beacon *that Myernick "is without question, one of the best Americans in the game. He will be a leading light in the MISL..."*[18]

Prior to the first game, the roster was filled out with Portland Timber star Willie Anderson, Jamaican native Art Welch, Italian-born Peter Mannino, Dallas Tornado Caesar Cervin, MISL-veteran Keith Van Eron, Canadian phenom Garry Ayre, Mike Custer, and Keith Gehling. Custer was the first Kansan to play for the Wings. A raw talent from Ottawa University, he feared they signed him only to be the token local guy. Tom Marshall and Roy Turner assured him that was not the case. "Mike has an excellent attitude, a willingness to learn and great physical ability...Now he must learn when to run, how to run and how to improve his skills with the ball," Turner told Steve Love of The Beacon.[19] *Keith Gehling was the sole survivor of the 50 players who attended the November 3rd open tryouts at the original North Branch YMCA, located at the 3200 block of N. Hillside.*[20]

ALAN SHEPHERD, WHEATHAWKS CO-FOUNDER AND MISL REFEREE: I tried out for the Wings that first season, but didn't make it of course. Roy saw something I didn't [laughs]. It was at the north YMCA, way out there on Hillside. It was about as big as a living room and 40 guys in there trying out. A lot of us Wheathawks tried out. Of course, we didn't know the likes of the players they'd be bringing in. I remember Gehling being there. Most of us knew each other. I can still remember the drills Roy put us through...simple technical stuff. It was well-run for such a small area he had. Those players on that team were phenomenal players.

NORMAN PIPER: When I first came to Wichita, I was the first one signed. Then Mike Ivanow and Kevin [Kewley] came. We went out in the community and let them know what it was all about. The outcome of that was amazing. It was wonderful. Wichita itself was a small town...kind of a cowboy town. People were wonderful. The cost of living was fantastic. I remember getting gas at Quiktrip for $.89 a gallon!

ROY TURNER: When I accepted the job, I sat with Al Miller in his garden and picked his brain about who might be available to come with me to Wichita. I didn't think Kevin would be available, but it worked out. The Tornado were on the way down and the writing was on the wall.

JACKIE KNAPP: Roy used a lot of his contacts and we got a lot of those Dallas guys on the team that first year...Roy had so many favors to call in. Plus his charm helped.

KEVIN KEWLEY, DEFENDER, WICHITA WINGS: Roy asked me to come to Wichita and I decided to give it a shot. The NASL was on its way down at the time. It was time to try indoor, which was taking off. It was very individual, with goals galore and made for TV.

ROY TURNER: Initially the guys that came to Wichita were not going to be on a full-time basis. They were going to go back [in the off-season]. Then things changed down there and we were able to secure them. A lot of the NASL guys wanted to play in the MISL in the off-season. I had been involved with communities all my life. It's the thing I demanded right away. I had all kinds of NASL contacts of players I played with and knew about, not to mention I brought seven players from the Tornado with me...Jimmy Ryan, George Ley, Glenn Myernick, Freddie Garcia, Chris Collins, Kevin Kewley, [and Omar Gomez]. Kevin was the most important of that group. He was a great midfielder when I played with him. He played defense for us, but could do anything. I made him captain right away.

The NASL was about to "go under" and we had a lot of people who didn't want to leave America. I was then able to recruit what became four of the best known names in Wichita. This blend brought success. They knew they'd be out every day of the week, getting to know the people in Wichita and shaking hands. People knew these guys and knew them as people because of the relationships they had with the players. Jimmy Ryan and George Ley were both [NASL] All-Stars. I made Ley my assistant. Jimmy Ryan had been a Manchester United player and coach. He was a fantastic player. The three people I'll always think about from that group were Ley, Ryan, and Kewley.

I had my own drive when I brought them in...I wanted to show off Wichita a bit [to the new players]...I drove through College Hill. If I could get a car, I'd have a new car waiting for them in the driveway...[and] an apartment with a stocked fridge. It only cost me a few hundred dollars, but those guys would think, "This is it. This could be okay." You could make this town big...I sold Wichita that way...We'd have people decorate the apartment. The players lived in the Ponderosa Apartments that year.

KEVIN KEWLEY: I hadn't been to Wichita before I signed. George Ley and I came up here together. We had just played golf in Dallas and it was 80 degrees and we got up here and it was like 40. It was freezing! We had shorts on. We went to a place called The Hatch Cover and tried to get a drink and they wouldn't let us because we had to be a member. At that time you could hardly get a drink. I remember Glenn Myernick was pissed off because he couldn't take his wife for a meal because of the weird liquor laws.

JACKIE KNAPP: I remember driving Roy around, looking for condos. He didn't want a big fancy house, because he didn't know how long he'd stay there and didn't want the upkeep. I remember driving Roy by Comotara one evening. He'd bought his condo and near there in Tallgrass [Country Club], almost everybody lived within two or three doors of each other. It was like a cloistered environment those first couple months. They'd carpool up to the Coliseum for practice. It was a tight-knit group and there was no friction. I don't remember much bickering at all. There was a spirit of camaraderie. That fed into the whole mystique of the Wichita Wings.

ROY TURNER: We had two months prior to the season to put everything together. It was scary. We would go to the Friends University gym and the YMCA and would put tape on the wall to indicate where the goals were. We were practicing on hardwood. We did get fit though. The players were ready to go by the first game.

There was no doubt Roy Turner would have the players ready to face the New York Arrows on November 30th, 1979. However, within days of the first game, a shakeup in the front office would steal the headlines away from the players and put a spotlight on General Manager Tom Marshall and owner Bob Becker.

CHAPTER 6

An Oral History

Behind the Orange Curtain

———

"I bet everything on the team."

- Tom Marshall

DOUG VERB, MISL EXECUTIVE, DIRECTOR OF PRESS AND PR: I
was in Wichita from the beginning…We looked at the Wichita Wings as our
Green Bay Packers…We were at a point where the first year had a certain amount
of success to it. You have to remember a couple things: First of all, we had started
hearing for half a generation that soccer was the next biggest sport. "All these
kids are playing." To this day, they are still saying it. But, the truth is, that is
PARTICIPATION, which is different than spectators. Look at bowling, look at
swimming. We didn't know that at that time. We really thought we were on to
something. We were on to the idea of Americanizing the sport. More goals, a
little more physical. We built the game, LITERALLY, for television…in a two
hour window. So after our first year, it was new and it was different and it was also
coming off an era of all kinds of alphabet leagues that had folded. The ABA, the
WFL [World Football League], the WHA [World Hockey Association]. Here we
come, not only with a new league, but a new game bastardized from a game that
nobody liked anyway.

We had a little bit of success. One of the highlights of my career was
flying into Philadelphia the first game of the [1978-1979 MISL] season and

seeing a line outside the Spectrum and finding out it was for the Fever. They sold out the first game ever. The sad part was, it was all downhill from there. We somehow sold out 16,000- 17,000 and had some success in Cleveland and Pittsburgh. Not so much in Houston. In New York we had a great team, with the Babe Ruth and Wilt Chamberlain of the sport in Steve Zungul. We thought we'd do better there. We had some success, and people started finding out about us. St. Louis was a no-brainer. We all knew that St. Louis and Trenton, New Jersey were the hotbeds of American soccer. Of course, that was gonna be great. They were mostly American players. Buffalo, we had pretty good ownership there.

And Wichita came along, and, we said, "Well, if the check doesn't bounce... what the hell." They were playing in a 9,500 seat arena. "Let's take a chance... they'll be our Green Bay [Packers]." They seemed like good people, and Pizza Hut and the aircraft companies were there. We knew there was some money there. So, okay, let's do it. It actually turned out pretty well for us. The most amazing part was the influx of these English players, thanks to Roy, settling in the most mid-American place we had and making a go of it. It's an amazing story. Next to St. Louis it is our most amazing story. In St. Louis, out of 16 players, 12 were from St. Louis. That never happened anywhere else. The other guys were foreign guys, but were adopted by everybody else. They were good... and they were Americanizing the game. For me, what the Wings did, bringing in this group of English, Scottish, Irish guys...they were all nuts, and I know the beer consumption went up in those days. It was great.

I don't think anyone ever said, "How can you be a major league if you have Wichita in it?" Because you could always say, "How is the NFL major with Green Bay in it?" We were in most of the major markets most of the time. We never really, really made it in NY or LA. Chicago had a brand, mainly because of outdoor soccer. The rest of the markets, we had San Francisco, Kansas City, and Baltimore. Houston failed after a year. Cleveland became pretty big. Detroit was [short-lived]. Wichita fit in with everything.

Wichita was a small town and this would have to be an "Americana" story. Not only did no one know what a good indoor soccer player was, but the soccer players didn't want to be a part of this. This was a bastardized version. The USSF [United States Soccer Federation] wouldn't let the referees work this.

You'd have to have guys who had pioneering spirit. The players that came, came because it was a job and some money...

JACKIE KNAPP, PUBLIC RELATIONS, WICHITA WINGS 1979-80: We only had 10 weeks between the league meetings and the first game. That first staff were mostly people that Tom knew from AYSO. The [office staff] from Great Plains didn't know much about soccer. They'd sit around and look pretty and flirt with the players when they came in. They opened a ticket office downtown, but the whole first year my office was at the Kansas Coliseum. However, a lot of the day was spent in my car.

TOM MARSHALL, GENERAL MANAGER, WICHITA WINGS 1979: We became extremely obsessed with making sure the opening night had no mistakes, partly because we had a rookie staff. I intentionally scheduled our opening game against WSU's home opener. That was the grandiosity of my personality at the time. I looked at them as a competitor.

Our initial marketing was through the development of kid soccer players who would grab dad's hand and take them to a game, because we'd had success with that in the exhibition games. That was the thing that led to the final break up with me and the Wings, along with the "bottle." Provided we followed the business plan, which was building from the ground up, starting with youth players, we were confident we were going to succeed. We weren't going to spend an exorbitant amount of money on advertising. We would try to do things with tradeouts, like the Scholfield deal, apartment complexes, etc. It was a nice perk to help bring these guys to a place they might consider to be like Siberia.

That first season, every player on the team, and some staff members, drove a car from the Scholfield car dealership. Not a bad perk...

TOM MARSHALL: During that initial period, I was spending my time on marketing the team. I continued working with the youth leagues. I had a video put together by an Englishman from Hutchinson named Tony Nichols. That opening commercial was so well received that Becker gave the MISL permission to use that and add other teams to it. We had this flaming ball come across the

Coliseum on the screen. "The Wings have landed in Wichita," the commercial said.

JACKIE KNAPP: I don't think Becker realized what he was getting into. I don't think he understood the cost of operations.

BOB BECKER, OWNER, WICHITA WINGS 1979-1980: I had a guy that worked for me by the name of Ward Lawrence who was doing some real estate business for me and was a lawyer by trade. He had operated food franchises. I had gone to school with him. He was a fraternity brother of mine.

Tom Marshall wanted to spend money, and I wasn't very excited about that. I don't think he was very knowledgeable about the financial end of the business. I had a lot of faith and trust in Ward and I asked him to run it. I turned it over to him and let him run with it. I let him do pretty much whatever he thought necessary.

JACKIE KNAPP: I don't think Tom really knew how to budget. It's true what Becker said: that he knew how to spend money, but not necessarily budget it.

TOM MARSHALL: I made friends with Steve Walsh, the lead singer of Kansas. During the concert he shined the spotlight on me and talked about the Wings. That was the enthusiasm you had in the state of Kansas towards the sport. I was trying to negotiate a song by Billy Joel called "The Prelude to Angry Young Men." He wanted like $5,000 or $10,000 for it. I told Steve about this, and he immediately donated an instrumental to us. Becker didn't like it. Every little aspect, he tried to take over. He became even more than a micromanager. He'd send Ward into the office for everything.

JACKIE KNAPP: There was one time when Ward and Mary Lawrence took me to dinner at the country club to pick my brain on PR for the franchise. Becker wanted Ward around to make sure things were going well. This was prior to Tom's leaving. They told me this was something they were doing with members of the staff.

Ward was kind and gentle and soft-spoken. I never heard him raise his voice at any point. He was "quiet country club" in his persona. He wore a lot of v-neck sweaters, no tie. Very polished. Very "golly, gee-whiz." He was completely not savvy about soccer or our vision for the team. He was there to oversee the bottom line. I was not privy to some of the discussions that he and Tom had. Tom could be really stubborn. Once he got a vision, he wouldn't compromise. They had a local PR guy who was probably feeding Ward ideas about how we SHOULD be doing things. They said [this guy] was a local legend. He'd been in Wichita PR for all the major businesses since the '50s. He didn't know a lick about soccer or sports and how to sell it. Of course, I didn't either, but I was closer to it.

Originally, I was going to be director of PR and Marketing. But as my responsibilities became clearer, I realized there was no way I could do the marketing too. I answered to my Wings bosses and also to the league office. The media relations became huge. I had to reach out to the media people in opposing cities and plant stories. Everything was done by Telex and by mail. There is a picture of me kneeling on the office floor and stuffing 50 envelopes with media releases. I was working about 15 hours a day, seven days a week. They had me for a nickel an hour, it seemed.

It was hard work, having to learn the game, the players, the nuances, and Roy's personality. He had so many former colleagues and teammates and friends on that team. I can't imagine how hard it would be for him to coach them. I came out of my office in to the bench area during one practice. It was one of the few times I heard him drop the "F" word: "Jesus Christ, Jimmy [Ryan], you dribble the ball, you dribble the ball, you dribble the ball...you CAN'T dribble the ball. Shoot the f***ing ball!" Then he turned around, saw me, and went ten shades of bright red. He and the players probably had the same kind of relationship as teammates with the Tornado as he did with them as his players in Wichita. I don't think it was difficult for them to take direction from him.

As [Roy] built the team, as game-day approached, I demanded to travel with the team. I was the only female PR person in the league. It was half of my job to work with the media at opposing games. Roy called a meeting with the players and he pointed to me and said, "You see her? She is your sister. She is nothing else. If I hear of any fraternization or shenanigans or harassment, you'll have me to answer to." When that happened, a little part of me said, "Ahhh, I can't marry Kevin Kewley." [laughs] I really respected that about him. I remember being on a road trip and I was walking along the curb and he pushed me to the inside of the sidewalk, and said, "Rule number one, a gentleman always walks on the street-side with a lady." It was little things like that that showed the elegant, wiser-than-his-years side of him. I grew up real fast those first four or five years I worked for the league. But I never had to worry about shenanigans with the Wings players.

That first month, a lot of what we did was try to keep that bead of excitement going. We spent a lot of time going to schools in the city. We did a lot of soccer demonstrations. I had maps of Wichita and the directions we got from the principals were sometimes too difficult to understand. It was hotter than Hell. We were driving around and [goalkeeper Mike] Ivanow did not suffer fools. He was so impatient and I would get us lost every time. I pulled in front of a house and said, "I have no idea where the school is, I'll have to go up to the house." Norman [Piper] said, "Roll down the windows...listen." Mike said, "That's it! Follow the [sound of] children!" We'd do a gig in the morning and a gig in the afternoon.

DOUG VERB: Everybody was new to everything and they were young and inexperienced. For the most part, everybody worked more than they were being paid. We all had that pioneering spirit. Jackie was right up there. I remember making sure they were up to speed. I'll never forget on a conference call, and she had not gotten up to speed with something, and me searching desperately for some country reference. I said, "Jackie, you better put the pedal to the metal." She said, "You really hit me with that one." She was great. She opened up three markets. To do that is "yeoman's work." She wouldn't have been given the opportunity to do that if she wasn't good. She was good, she was thorough. She knew how to service the industry and to present stories, and she was a woman working in a man's game in the early '80s. Not easy...with a bunch of English blokes. I'm sure she kept them in line.

TOM MARSHALL: I practically didn't have an income for about eight months. I bet everything on the team.

It was a bet that would not pay off. Marshall and Becker would continue to clash over who would run the team, and how it would be run. This struggle for power defined the final weeks prior to the opening game.

JACKIE KNAPP: It's funny…when Ward started making himself a daily presence, I knew there was friction, but Tom and I never really talked about it. We didn't exactly know how to run a sports franchise, but they knew absolutely nothing about a sports franchise. We didn't give them any credit for the business knowledge about how to run a sports franchise. For us it was emotionally-driven and heart-driven. With Great Plains, it was all about the "business."

TOM MARSHALL: Almost immediately I had problems with Becker…We were $50,000 ahead of the proposal a couple weeks before I left. But Becker starts making these massive media buys. "We need to fill that arena," he would say. My drinking was really increasing at that time.

JACKIE KNAPP: I never saw [Marshall's] drinking get in the way of the job.

TOM MARSHALL: …So all of a sudden, all this money that was supposed to last, was gone in a minute…I was fired on my birthday. We called Ward Lawrence over and I said, "This needs to be done differently or I'm walking." So I got a phone call from Becker saying not to go near the Kansas Coliseum and to return my car by the next morning…

On November 23rd of 1979, just one week before the beginning of the Wings' season, Randy Brown of The Eagle and Beacon *reported that Marshall had offered his resignation and the team accepted it. Ward Lawrence, Vice President of Great Plains Corporation, would take over as Acting General Manager of the Wings. According to Brown, "Lawrence described the administrative shakeup as 'a basic disagreement over who and how to get things done.'"* [1]

Four other staff members, including Marshall's wife, Nancy, were also said to have resigned. However, the controversy continued. Marshall stated that neither he, nor the other four staff members did, in fact, resign. "We made a verbal statement that was misconstrued into resignations by Ward," said Marshall. [2] *Randy Brown quoted Lawrence as saying he specifically asked all five of the staff members, including Marshall, if they were resigning. "Those resignations were tendered and they were accepted…I'm very, very careful about that. There wasn't any question about it," said Lawrence.* [3]

The next day, Brown reported that "Lawrence...amplified the Wings' statement, saying that Marshall told him in a Wednesday night meeting that he (Marshall) would quit the team unless certain unnamed conditions were met. The Wings declined to meet the conditions and accepted Marshall's resignation on Thanksgiving Day."[4] Thus, it became known to some as the "Thanksgiving Day Massacre." Steve Love, of the Beacon, *cited an unnamed source as saying that "Marshall... perceived Lawrence as a threat. And as time passed, and Lawrence inserted himself more into the day-to-day operations, the threat grew more ominous."[5] The Eagle's Mike Limon reported that Ward Lawrence had been brought in because accounting and administrative control were not "running smoothly." Marshall contended that "there was no reason I could see for Great Plains coming in and taking control like that." Limon went on to say that "Marshall and Lawrence agree their dispute is basically personal."[6]*

TOM MARSHALL: I got a call from John Frazier, and he said, "Why didn't you tell me this was happening? I could have done something. Now I can't do anything."...The word "resentment" means to be keep refueling the anger. And that's what I did for many years. I just kept refueling it. The worst thing in the world was the fact that Wings went on and succeeded without me...because I'd absolutely convinced myself that couldn't happen. I'd say it was 50% my fault all that stuff happened. I took an offer I never should have taken [from Becker]. Instead, I wanted what I wanted now, and I paid for it later. I feel bad because I feel like the strengths of those other partners could have taken the Wings as far as they could go...

Such was the bitterness of the separation, that Tom Marshall would only attend one Wings game in person...and that was several years later in Kansas City.

ROY TURNER, HEAD COACH, WICHITA WINGS: My understanding was that Becker didn't like what was happening and sent Ward Lawrence in. I wasn't a part of it. I was practically the only one left after Tom Marshall was let go. It was a lonely office then. Ward Lawrence came in and brought [in operations director] Ray Denton. It was a week before the season was to start and hardly any tickets had been sold. [Becker] became a great friend of mine. Even after he sold the team he went to Denmark with me on a recruiting trip.

JACKIE KNAPP: I think Ward just showed up at my house on a Sunday. My mom was in her housecoat. I came out and was in jeans and a t-shirt. He said, "I need to sit down and talk with you for a few minutes." He told me that for all intents and purposes, the entire office staff had been let go: "resigned in lieu of termination." "But not you." There was never a meeting that I was a part of that was described in the newspaper. [Ward said:] "We want you to stay on." And I said, "But Tom...this is his dream, his vision." He asked me, "Are your loyalties with Tom or with the organization?" That was key, because it directed my conduct and behavior over the next few months. After spending literally a year of time with Tom, it got cut off. I never called him again or saw him again [that year]. I don't think they realized that Danny Bunker, the equipment manager, was Nancy Marshall's nephew. So, I would ask him about Tom every once in a while. I told Ward, "For the sake of all the work we've done, we need continuity, so somebody has to stay." Don't think that after every game if things weren't perfect, I was terrified he would say, "Oh, you aren't doing your job right, you're fired." I had given up a stable career at Newman University for this.

"I just tell them I think we are stronger than ever now, that we have a sense of management and leadership."[7] *According to the* Wichita Beacon, *that is what Jackie Knapp said. She disputes that.*

JACKIE KNAPP: Ward said, "I've already talked to *The Eagle's* sports editor, so you won't need to give any statements. Direct them to me on this subject." There was a quote from me in the paper. I was quoted as saying something like, "This is what's best for the team." I never said that. I never talked to anybody in the media about it. They had to have just made it up. I never would have disrespected Tom like that.

Fairly late in the season was when I talked to Tom again. I went out after a game to a bar, and there was Tom. He said, "Why the long face?" I said, "I feel so bad..." He replied, "I'm fine, don't feel bad. You've got a job to do and from what I understand, you are doing it well." I had survivor's guilt. And Ward had said, in not so many words, that he would appreciate it that I honor that I worked for them now.

I think getting rid of Tom was the wrong move. History would show that the team was like a cockroach. The rumors were it would die every year. But it had staying power. I think they could have kept Tom Marshall in some capacity. His energy and his gift of bullshit were tremendous. Even if they had said, "Tom, you do the promotions and we'll run the business side." They could have found a place for him. This all happened [a week] before the home opener. We thought we were doomed from the start. It was horrifying.

"Crapshoot" is the word for it. Every time I see one of those Judy Garland and Mickey Rooney movies on Turner Classic Movies, I think of Tom Marshall. That was the spirit of his organization…"Let's put on a show!" He didn't think things through, but just knew what he wanted to happen.

Though Ward Lawrence was well-equipped to handle the business aspects of the organization, the Wings brought in Ray Denton as a technical advisor for the operational aspect of running the team. Denton was an experienced event organizer and "fixer." If he were a baseball player, he would have been a utility man: able to play multiple positions. Eventually, his title would be upgraded to "Director of Operations."

RAY DENTON, DIRECTOR OF OPERATIONS, WICHITA WINGS 1979-1980: When I was hired, they got rid of everybody a few weeks before the opening. They only kept Jackie Knapp and one other person. She was left out there in the middle of nowhere, the only one they kept…and they were throwing everything at her.

I ran the Kansas Elks Charity Horse Show at the Coliseum. I got to know Sam Fulco [because of that]. When the Wings got in trouble: no ticket sales, nothing ready to go; they asked Fulco if he had anybody who could coordinate stuff. He said, "Ray's available." So Ward Lawrence came and talked to me. I didn't know anything about soccer. It was just "get 'r done." Whatever I needed to do, I'd get it done. I knew the Coliseum, I knew the lighting, I knew the union guys, and that was what they were missing: the operations stuff.

I never met Tom Marshall. He went out one day and I came in after that. If it hadn't been for Tom there wouldn't have been the Wings. But Becker was a business guy and he was saying, "Show me some figures." But there were no ticket sales. Tom was so excited about the game but it was a hard sell because people didn't know about soccer. We wound up, as they say in show business, "papering the house." We were giving away tickets just to get people to come, and then trying to sell the season tickets. We had the hardcore AYSO people...and it started building, but at the first it was tough.

Jackie was really upset. She'd worked so closely with Marshall. We had to convince Jackie to stay. If it hadn't been for Jackie I don't know what we'd have done. She was the only carryover from the original group, except for Roy. It was [Marshall's] baby and all of a sudden he was out. I was told by Ward there was some extreme tension right before I came. Ward inherited a basket of snakes, but he's a pretty solid guy and steered the ship.

Everybody was an "expert" on the Wings: all the way from people saying Turner had amassed one of the greatest teams of talent, to, "Oh, he just hired a bunch of his drinking buddies." You had "experts" everywhere analyzing everything that was done.

JACKIE KNAPP: [In the Wings movie] Ray Denton would be played by Dennis Hopper [laughs].

RAY DENTON: You just can't help but like Roy Turner. I think it was at that first meeting that I met him. [The players] idolized him; they'd do anything for him. [Roy] was more than a coach...he's smart...he's a promoter. He and I worked very closely together. I'd go to him with an idea and he'd figure out a way to make it happen. I really liked him.

I was totally new to soccer. It was embarrassing, I didn't know a thing. The goals weren't ready and we had to get those done. We had our first TV [appearance]. [Assistant Commissioner] Ed Tepper flew in and said, "Where's the logo in the middle of the field?" Nobody had said anything and nobody knew...so I had a week to get a logo down. I had been in the sign business before, so I called up a guy that I knew. I helped him make the logo, laid it out in the middle of the field, and made plywood templates and he painted it. It dried after a couple days,...but he put the wrong paint down. It was like steel. These guys slid and it just slit their legs open. So they had to get out there with wire brushes and strip it off and put it back on. That was the kind of stuff we were running into. It was the first time around and nobody knew what to do. Ed Tepper had come in to give briefings, but then Marshall left and all that was lost. The team logo was a league requirement [at the center of the pitch]; everybody had to have it.

Becker came in, gave a little speech about the way it was gonna be. "You can do anything you want, just don't spend any money. We're cutting staff down to nothing and we're gonna make it work." Just Jackie [was left]. Ward was joking that he was from real estate development and Becker tapped him to be general manager of a soccer team. We laughed back and forth to each other, like, "What are we doing here?" We didn't know soccer!

Ward Lawrence was super. He was a good business person and he let me go and get it done. He was the "outside guy," Becker's rep, and representative with the media, Turner took the players, and everything that was left, I did...he just said, "get 'r done...just don't spend any money." Which I understood.

JACKIE KNAPP: My brother-in-law Gene [Mandel] worked at Beech. In Ohio, before they moved to Kansas, he was a carpet installer. They would do big jobs at hotels and the like, until his knees gave out on him. He knew carpeting and knew how to keep it from sliding. When the exhibition games came to be, he told Tom he would lay it out and use the right kind of tape on the bottom to make it safe for the players.

We had bought the turf from Tulsa. When we went to play that first Wings game, Gene laid it out and we were shy a three-foot wide strip toward the end of one of the goals. He went out to a carpet place to buy some extra carpet to make it fit. He said you'd be able to tell. It was a slightly different color green. He said, "I don't know what happened because when we used it before for the exhibition games it fit perfectly." When they put the boards up for the real game it must have been a different size setup. Gene said he always got verbal kudos from refs and other coaches because the seams were nice and tight, and the carpet was laid properly.

Money being at a premium, any free labor donated to the team was much appreciated...even child labor. Rolling out and preparing the carpet for each game was a labor intensive activity. Thus, the "Rugrats" were born. An internal memo from Ray Denton to Ward Lawrence detailed the arrangement: the Rugrats would receive free soft drinks and donuts, plus seven tickets per game. There were even "substitute" Rugrats.

JACKIE KNAPP: Through Gene's affiliation with AYSO, he would pick kids to work as Rugrats. He'd give them free tickets to the games and food. Before the game they get the rolls of carpet out, which were numbered, and the Rugrats would roll it out and then walk on it to look for debris…making sure there were no staples or anything like that. Where the seams weren't perfect, they'd flip up the edge of the rug and use double-sided duct tape to make it perfect. The Rugrats would take a ball out and make sure the carpet was navigable. The problem was always TOO MANY Rugrat volunteers.

KEVIN HIMES, RUGRAT: Somehow we found out you could go after school to the soccer games and help lay carpet. So, myself and a couple of my friends from the south side would make that trip to the Coliseum and help lay the carpet and put up the banners on the dasherboards and do whatever else they told us, because we just loved being at the Coliseum that early.

So, I'm a Rugrat. It was all soccer kids, mainly boys…from 14 to 16. The first year my parents had to take me. They would go to Park City while I was doing that. The second year I had a friend that was old enough to drive. Once we got the turf down and the banners up, we went out to the Pavilion, where the practice field was, and played while the game was happening. I don't know if anyone from the Wings office knew we were out there playing soccer. It was a blast.

RAY DENTON: So we got the "Rugrats" to put out the carpet. Well the union came in and said, "Can't do it, get 'em off of there." "Why?" I asked. "They've got to be union members." "But they're kids!" "Well, safety problems." Finally they said, "Alright." Then we got the Heights band to come in to play. But a local union musician turned us in to ASCAP [The American Society of Composers, Authors, and Publishers] and said we couldn't play any of that music. I had picked [the] "Rocky" [theme song] because I thought it was neat. Marshall had gotten the rock group "Kansas" to do a song. But when we played it, it was like hard rock, heavy metal and nobody could identify with it. So Ward said, "Let's do Rocky." And it turned out to be a really inspiring thing with the fog machine and everything. But ASCAP said we couldn't do that. So we went to Ward and he says, "We've got to have music." So we went and got a temporary license to do the music. They were going to fine us $6,000 [for using it without permission], so it cost us $1,600 for a temporary permit. They backed off and said, "Ok, we'll let it go." Little things like that, we just had to dig it out...we didn't have the money to go first class.

(Author Photo) 1979-80 Wings uniform.

ROY TURNER: The jerseys came in short sleeves, but the league demanded they be long sleeve. We had to sew a yellow sleeve on. They were the ugliest things I'd ever seen.

RAY DENTON: Just before the first game the goals hadn't been completed. Nobody knew where they were. We had to track them down. They were being welded by a welder somewhere. There were league specifications obviously. They weren't ready and Ward said, "Give him a block of tickets," and so he was happy. When [MISL Assistant Commissioner Ed] Tepper came to town he said, "Make sure the flags are up." I said, "Flags?" "Yeah, the goal flags at the end." This was like two days before the first game. So we ran down to the bicycle shop and duct-taped them to the corners. Baling wire and chewing gum...a kiss and a promise, and we threw it together.

The need for labor was so great that some of the Rugrats were given additional stats-related duties...

RAY DENTON: Jackie had to do team stats for the league. They were throwing things at her...and she had to pull all that information together.

JACKIE KNAPP: Three or four Rugrats, as soon as they finished laying the carpet, I turned into my stats crew. All played soccer, and had been watching the indoor practices, and knew what to look for. Roy had a system of pluses and minuses and they would keep track of that. Whenever there was an assist, or pass that led to an assist, it was a plus. If they missed that pass, they'd get a minus. Roy insisted that he have this at halftime so he'd know who was on the mark.

Kevin Himes and my nephews [Mike and Sean Mandel] were involved in the Rugrats stats crew. Mike and Sean were 12 and 14 at the time. They'd take the stat sheet, make 30 copies and take one copy to the opposing locker room, and one copy for Roy, and then give the rest to the media. Even at that phase, there was a mom and pop vibe to the production.

Technology being what it was in 1979, a type of Telex machine called the TWX, pronounced "twix," was used to send the statistics off to the league and other franchises via telephone lines.

VIRGINIA CREAMER, ASSISTANT DIRECTOR OF OPERATIONS/ ANGELS COORDINATOR, WICHITA WINGS: We used TWX machines. When you were typing in the stats for the game, it would create this ticket tape that had holes punched in it as you typed. And you'd take this tape and put it in the TWX machine and you could send out the stats to all the other teams. They were big, huge things. We didn't even have faxes back then.

RAY DENTON: Right before the game we needed somebody to run the scoreboard. We were trying to get volunteers. We were told by the Coliseum we had to hire the union scoreboard guy. We had a guy who was willing to volunteer for the whole season. We had to win that battle. We did have to be very careful with the union. You couldn't touch anything electrical without them doing it. The union guys were pretty nice actually. They were kind of Wings supporters too. They would help us figure how to get it done...like they'd come and do something and if they had to go, they'd leave and let us finish it. They were accommodating. The league had a rule that the lights had to go out for the national anthem. We had mercury vapor lights and they took 15 minutes to get back on. We had to turn the lights off and turn the other lights on for them to practice, and we had to time it to make sure we knew when the national anthem would be over so [there would be lights] when the game started. Sometimes they'd get the timing wrong and the lights would come on before the anthem was quite over.

We were going to get the AYSO group to take the tickets. But there had been a church group who thought THEY had a contract for all the Coliseum activities. So they were fighting: AYSO vs. the church group. Again, Ward or Roy would get in the middle of it and say, "Hey guys, can you help us a little here?" Also, certain groups had always got to do concessions. We had to iron all that out.

JACKIE KNAPP: I barely remember that week. I clearly remember that first game. The electricity was humming. [Dallas Tornado star] Kyle Rote, Jr. called for Roy and we had this secretary from Great Plains with big hair and exotic eyeliner...She was getting a lot of personal calls for Roy from people from his past wanting to wish him well. She said, "I can't handle all these calls, and am going to deflect some of these to your number." Meanwhile, I am trying to handle all these calls about the game. Rote got sent over to my line and I asked to take a message. The other great phone call I got was from Bruce Jenner. "Hi, this is Bruce Jenner calling for Roy Turner." I told him Roy was out on the floor. "Here's my number," he said in this soft-spoken voice. That day was just wild. Media was wandering in and out as things were getting close to kickoff. I remember I made a bright orange velvet blazer. It was gross [laughs]. I wore it over a royal blue dress. It was horrible. I'm sure the dress was some kind of nylon knit. I remember putting all the press kits together with the player pronunciations and all the details. I spent a half-hour with J.B. on how to pronounce [some player's] name. That opening day...man, the stuff going on. There was a room in one of the corridors set up with beverages and sandwiches and stuff like that. I was trying to oversee that.

There were enough good articles in the paper about that first game that it gave a good buzz in the city. It was probably fuller than the 6,000 reported. We papered the house [i.e. gave away lots of free tickets]. There was a TV commercial as well. A 15 or 30 second spot. We did have media coverage that night and there was adequate hype building up to the game. There was a decent level of excitement. Did it catch fire that first game? Probably not, but it built up over the course of the season because of the somewhat surprising winning ways of the team. No one expected them to get to the playoffs.

Friday, November 30th, 1979: In the first game in the history of the franchise, the Wichita Wings faced the defending MISL champion New York Arrows. Led by "The Lord of All Indoors," Steve Zungul, the greatest indoor player of all-time, the Arrows were a tough first opponent. Aside from Zungul, the Arrows featured several future perennial MISL all-stars, including the "face" of American soccer, goalkeeper Shep Messing, and fellow Yugoslavian stars Branko Segota and Juli Veee. The team was coached by Don Popovic, who would become famous in Wichita a few years later as the nemesis of GM Bill Kentling.

KEVIN KEWLEY, FORWARD/MIDFIELDER, WICHITA WINGS: We were all apprehensive before the first game. We didn't know what to expect. [The game] made us realize what to expect. [Steve] Zungul was on that New York Arrows team.

ROY TURNER: Zungul was one of the best players to ever come out of Yugoslavia. He was one of the top players in Europe. He was the best guy to ever play indoor.

KEVIN KEWLEY: He was the best goal scorer. He had great pace, he was strong. He wasn't an Erik Rasmussen on the ball, but he was great overall.

JACKIE KNAPP: I remember Steve Zungul smelling like he hadn't bathed in years. He was a little cross-eyed. I remember meeting him and thinking, "That's the Lord of All-Indoors?" He looked like he was whacked with a skillet.

The first goal scored in a regular season MISL game at the Kansas Coliseum was by Arrow forward Damir Sutevski, assisted by Steve Zungul. Art Welch provided an assist to Norman Piper, who had the honor of scoring the first goal for the Wings. Welch would add his own goal in the third period, and Kevin Kewley would score twice that day. Unfortunately, it wasn't enough to defeat the Arrows. The Wings lost 6-4 in front of 6,334 fans.[8] *Thankfully, just two days later, the Wings recorded their first victory. They defeated the Detroit Lightning 4-3.*

The first year would provide many more big moments both on the field and behind the scenes. As the season progressed, the team would add more players, and just as importantly, more fans. Sex would sell tickets, and so would a wild man from California. The Coliseum would rock with excitement and the city would be shaken by bad news. It was going to be one wild ride...but worth every moment.

CHAPTER 7

An Oral History

Sex, George, and Soccer Balls

———

"It was about average-size, very suave European
guys running around in their underwear."

- DOUG VERB

(Don Marler/1982-83 Wings Yearbook) Wings Angel Dana Walker.

BASKETBALL AND FOOTBALL TEAMS HAD *them. Why not indoor soccer? On December 10th, 1979 the Wichita Wings conducted tryouts for a dance team dubbed "the Angels." At 7:30 pm at Wilner Auditorium, on the campus of Wichita State University, women between the ages of 18 and 28 were invited to try out for the squad. They had to bring a resume, a picture, and be prepared to demonstrate a minute-long dance routine. When the night arrived, 28 ladies showed up to audition.*[1] *Among others, Kathy Page, Rebecca Gentry, Cindy Harrison, Lisa Lindsay, Doreen Luke, Sarah Strunk, and Nancy Bogard were chosen to become Angels that year. Until the 1984-85 season, the Angels would be led by Virginia Creamer.*[2]

RAY DENTON, DIRECTOR OF OPERATIONS, WICHITA WINGS 1979-1980: Ward [Lawrence] said, "There's a lady who wants to [form a dance team]." I met with her. You talk about a bundle of energy. All these ideas. Ward said, "Yeah, go ahead and do it. Just don't spend any money." We got those young ladies to buy their own outfits and pay for their own mileage and all that. Virginia was always stirring up volunteers. She always wanted to do PR and promotions, so she used the Angels as a way of doing all the things she wanted to do.

VIRGINIA CREAMER, ASSISTANT DIRECTOR OF OPERATIONS/ ANGELS COORDINATOR, WICHITA WINGS: I had been an actress and a singer and dancer for most of my college career. I went to WSU. I had just finished a tour with the Nebraska Theater Caravan. It was based in Omaha and we traveled a four state area doing Shakespeare and musicals. I had just got home from that tour and had started working for *The Wichitan* [magazine]. I figured out that this new team was coming into town. They had a lot of promos: "The Wings are Coming." I remember seeing it one day and thought, "Hey, they might need a dance troupe." I interviewed the girls that put together the Dallas Cowboys cheerleaders and took some of their rules and ideas. One of the editors of *The Wichitan* was Pam Porvaznik. Her husband Paul was involved with them. I put together a budget, how many girls we'd hire, what they'd make, and how much it would cost us. I got a friend of mine to design what they'd be wearing. I came in and gave a presentation. I think I spoke in front of Ray and a couple other

people...Ward Lawrence too. Ray gave me a call and he said, "We want to do this, but we also want you to come on as my assistant as well." He was the Director of Operations, so I was the Assistant Director of Operations that year, in addition to choreographing and administrating the Angels. [I'd do] anything Ray asked me to do. I'd run errands. I liked Roy a lot...I was impressed with him. And then, the more we worked together, we got to be very good friends.

They had the Cherubs then too. They were there before the Angels. They were little girls, probably four or five-years-old that they put together as a little dance team. They were adorable. They were there for maybe two games. At one point the Angels did a routine with the Cherubs. After that the Cherubs went away because it was too hard to coordinate all these little girls and their mothers. They were really cute.

I never saw [the Angels] as cheerleaders. There wasn't any place for them to do that. They couldn't be on the sideline. I saw them as [being there] to entertain at pre-game and halftime, and to be community ambassadors. Our pet charity was the Special Olympics. [The Angels] did a ton of work with them. The kids just loved them. There was a lot of community development.

There were "Rules and Regulations" to being an Angel. According to an official Wings memo, Angels couldn't miss more than two rehearsals in a season, had to always be on-time, paid a $35 rental fee for the use of their uniform (which they would have to pay for if it became damaged), were required to attend activities to promote the team, and had to "act in a lady-like manner" during all public and social gatherings. Oh, and they couldn't gain more than eight pounds after their initial weigh-in...

VIRGINIA CREAMER: That [weight-gain rule] came right from the Dallas Cowboys cheerleaders.

But there were benefits as well. Each Angel was paid $15 per game (this would eventually be increased to $25 per game), would receive television exposure, and meet all kinds of interesting people...including the strapping lads of the Wichita Wings.

VIRGINIA CREAMER: I couldn't make the players do anything. They were gonna do whatever they wanted to do. There was a rule against fraternization, except during social events. It wasn't like they couldn't talk to them. It happened. We had several girls that were dating players. As long as the player was not married, I wasn't gonna worry too much about it.

At the very beginning I got some people thinking they were a little too scantily-clad. The first time Nancy Bogart sang the national anthem some people got upset because she was wearing her Angels uniform while she sang. Things like that. The gentlemen didn't seem to mind it so much.

The Angels all loved to perform and were all very athletic. One of the cutest things was that they were interviewing several of the Angels and one said, "Well, I just wasn't ready to hang up my pom-poms." I think a lot of them liked having these different connections to the community. I tried to do a lot of things for them. I had an agreement with a place where they got all their hair care and cosmetics provided for free. We had various other deals like that. Somewhere along the line we got involved with a balloon company. We came up with the idea of Angelgrams. They would pay me up-front and we'd get the balloons and the Angels would send them all out during the game. We ended up making money on the deal, even after paying the Angels. We'd get sponsorships too...they were the Bud Light Angels for a while, and the Arby's Angels... which helped balance the budget.

During the second season, several former Wichita State Shockettes joined the squad: Susan Ayesh, Angel Stuber, Dana Walker, Regine Clore, and Nancy Harrell. It was during the 1982-1983 season that the Angels partnered with Bonnie Coffey of Balloon Delights to provide the popular Angelgrams during home games. The next season saw them become "The Arby's Angels." According to Creamer, that was the first year they were able to completely pay for themselves. In the fall of 1984, Wings advertiser House of Schwan became the sponsor. Thus, they become the Bud Light Angels and toured the state in the Budvan along with several players. For many of the Angels, their time with the group had a big effect on their lives. "I started out a shy girl, afraid of her own shadow and I feel I developed into a mature person able to handle all kinds of people and situations," said former Angel Gayle Butts. [3]

VIRGINIA CREAMER: It was kind of my baby and I don't think anyone else had the desire to spend that much time on it. We rehearsed three to four nights a week and before each game. I did the choreography and then the girls would come up with a number. They got to be very good at that. It took a lot of time and I had to get the sponsorships myself…and do all the admin work too. I wrote scripts for every game so JB [Johnson] knew what he had to do, what the halftime would be like, what would happen pre-game, all that stuff. All the spotlight operators and sound folks had scripts as well, so everybody knew what was going on. If we had a special number, we'd rehearse the number with the spotlights before the game started.

I made a really bad decision one time. Muscular Dystrophy had a telethon and KAKE-TV asked the Angels to get involved. We went down there and had a kissing booth. You donate so much money and you get to kiss them. Well, they got these really gross guys that kept coming back and coming back. We had to shut down the whole thing because it became ridiculous. They had one guy they called the "Skoal Man." That was a bad decision on my part [laughs]. I'd say, "You know what girls? These are the types of things that build character."

Never once did I hear of anyone threatening them or stalking them. Nothing like that. I don't remember any weird stuff like that.

JACKIE KNAPP, PUBLIC RELATIONS, WICHITA WINGS 1979-80: I was not a fan of the Angels. We reached into the grassroots of this soccer community. They are coming to see soccer. We are not the Dallas Cowboys. I was overridden. As it turned out, the Angels were a huge draw. I said I wasn't going to be the PR person for the Angels. What cracked me up was the number of players that paired off with Angels. [We were told] we needed to play up the Angels. Sex sells. I remember going to Ward and saying, "Hey, I'm doing the media relations pursuant to the team and the players. Anything else, that's marketing's job. Operations can deal with the Angels."

Playing up the Angels figured to be a good way to receive free publicity. In an internal memo from December 19th, 1979, Mel Witrogen, a prominent figure in local public relations, and an advisor to the Wings, opined that editor Buzz Merritt and the Wichita Eagle would be more likely to give the team Page One press if they tied an announcement in with color photos of the Angels.

Undoubtedly, the Wings hoped the Angels would help their appeal with the male fan. But sex appeal wasn't limited to the Angels. In fact, it became clear from the beginning that females composed a larger percentage of the indoor soccer fan base than the audience for basketball or football...and they weren't just there to see the ball kicked around.

DOUG VERB, MISL EXECUTIVE, DIRECTOR OF PRESS AND PR: We were the ones that started with the big introductions with the lights and smoke and music and all of that. We got down on our knees to get people in to see it and once they saw it they loved it. We were the first league to crack 40% of our crowd being women. It wasn't about soccer moms. It was about average size, very suave European guys running around in their underwear. They were very approachable.

JACKIE KNAPP: I pooh-poohed it at the time, but there were A LOT of female fans. I'm not so sure that the women who showed up at the post-game parties actually went to the games. I would grit my teeth and turn up my nose, but the practical side of me knew that sex sells. Here are the three guys we wanted to put on the 6:00 news: Andy Chapman, Keith Gehling, and Kevin Kewley. We would push those guys constantly. We'd have them do spots, modeling; all that side stuff. I don't know how they did it with road trips and all the home games.

RAY DENTON: There was a little problem in that [the players] thought they were being used as sex symbols...and they were [laughs]. That's what brought the attendance.

The
Perfect
English
Gentleman

Kevin Kewley, who has been called Tiger for his aggressive style of play, tries for a new image in his portrayal of the perfect English gentleman. Thanks to Henry's and the Crown Uptown Theatre for supplying some of the articles. Photo by Howard Eastwood, Eastwood Studios.

(Howard Eastwood/Missile Magazine) Kevin Kewley truly was an English gentleman.

Like any new major league professional sports franchise, the Wichita Wings relied on the media to spread word about their team. Of course, most franchises competed in a sport already familiar to the public. Indoor soccer was brand new to the people of Kansas, and they would need positive coverage to help sell it. The Wings had an advantage over most of the MISL franchises: they were the biggest game in town. The teams in large cities often struggled to gain the attention of newspapers and television stations. But during Wichita's first season, The Eagle *and* Beacon *devoted an impressive amount of space to the team. In January of 1980, they published 31 articles about the Wings.*

The team was broadcast on the radio via KFH 1330 AM and KBRA 98 FM. Ken Softley became the "Voice of the Wings." Television coverage was spotty. An occasional game was broadcast nationally on the Madison Square Garden cable network, available in Wichita on channel 25. The first nationally-televised Wings game would be versus the New York Arrows on December 21st, 1979. The only other two games televised that year were blacked out locally.[4] The broadcast duo of Al Trautwig and Turner's old teammate, Kyle Rote Jr., would be the signature television voice of the MISL, including Wings games. They would continue that role even after the MISL signed a television contract with the USA network for the 1980-81 and 1981-82 seasons. Trautwig would go on to become a nationally recognized sportscaster for football, basketball, hockey, and Olympic gymnastics. Jim Karvellas, former voice of the NBA's Washington Bullets, and play-by-play man for the New York Cosmos, also called games for the network in Wichita.

RAY DENTON: Jackie had so much on her plate and she had to be absolutely right in everything she did. There was no room for error. I had as little contact with the media as possible. I had difficulty with them trying to put a slant on something that wasn't there. The media got on Ward like crazy. He said, "There are no good guys, no bad guys...just guys."

JACKIE KNAPP: The first couple weeks I thought I could do my job on the phone. Because I was so busy, I thought I'd mail out my press releases and do all this other stuff. I did not initially go door to door to all the radio stations and TV stations. I realized quickly that was a major flaw because they needed to know my name and face before the first game. So I mapped out a route and hand-delivered the media guides. The "Kingpin" was *The Eagle*, because without them we'd be lost. I dealt a lot with Mal Elliott. They assigned a beat writer named Mike Limon to travel with us. At first, he was very direct and kind of critical, kind of abrupt. But he started traveling with us and would stay away from the team. He and I went to the shore of Lake Erie on a road trip to Detroit. Then, Kevin and a couple of the other guys joined Mike and I up to Windsor, Ontario. But they didn't have their visas and we couldn't get back in. So we had to call Roy and he was pissed as hell.

We made a conscious decision to NOT try to compete with WSU or other entities in town. We had a lot of promotion nights and the marketing folks were in charge of that. I don't remember a bad relationship ever with *The Eagle-Beacon*, or them ever writing anything that was a misrepresentation. The only time I called "B.S." was after the Thanksgiving Day Massacre. There was not a meeting with Ward Lawrence, as the newspaper described. There were never resignations tendered, as reported. If it happened, I wasn't there.

We had a hard time getting TV coverage. Once a week I would go to the Big Three [TV stations] and have a new stack of press information. It wasn't until we had a winning record and were about to make the playoffs that they started giving us more coverage. I did a few radio interviews, and there was one fascinating interview we did at KPTS. It was about how Roy and the boys' lives had changed and how it appealed to men, women, and children. There was niche coverage. Some of the women's programs did feature some of the players and me. There were always interviews after the game with Roy. It started to build, but print came along a lot sooner than broadcast media. Ken Softley called the games on radio. He was a salty old, crusty character. He seemed genuinely interested in the game and built quite a bond with the team and Roy.

We got a lot out of Randy Brown. He was always questioning...especially after Great Plains divested itself. He was pretty brutal, but his brutality was successful because that helped fuel the "Save the Wings" campaign. *The Eagle's* Steve Love was the intellectual, "Doubting Thomas" counterpart to Mike Limon. We got to the point where we trusted each other and I could run things by him. It took months to develop that trust. I'll be the first to admit, I didn't know what I was doing when I got into it. The more I hung out with the players and the more games I attended, the more I learned. Doug Verb and the MISL staff helped a lot with learning about the job. They would check up on me and would give me feedback. They told me I was doing a great job and, "Just wait, the media coverage would get better and better." We all had to give out our home phone numbers in case the media needed to get ahold of us. It could be 1:00 or 2:00 am and I might get a call from another team with stats information. I had to lug the Telex [TWX] machine on road trips. And I was always wearing heels.

Now that I'm older and wiser I can look back and realize that I had a good relationship with local media. I think because I was a girl, Roy was savvy enough to know she needs to know about some things, but doesn't need to know about other things. I would sometimes take guys to the airport and if a subject came up that wasn't considered appropriate for me, "the girl," some-body would start a fake cough.

Bob Costas worked for a radio station in St. Louis called KMOX. He came with the St. Louis team. He was complaining about sitting right up against the glass, which was our press row. He said, "I've never been in a press row up against the glass like this." I explained that in the Coliseum, this is the best place for it. Then he said, "But I can't see over the table." Honest to God. "Do you have a taller chair that I can use?" I said, "No, but I'll be right back." I brought him two Wichita phone books and said, "This is the best I can do." He was furious. He didn't speak to me ever again. That was my celebrity mo-ment with Bob Costas.

Kyle Rote Jr. and Al Trautwig called the nationally-televised games...I re-ally liked working with Trautwig. He wasn't egotistical and sanctimonious. They would usually park the truck in the outer corridor of the Coliseum. I would give them a thicker press kit. I would type up a couple paragraphs on hot players...personal things as well. Give them plenty of fodder to talk about. They were good at calling those games, but it was so new back then that there were minutes you'd have to fill. They told me they always liked the "home touch" they got in Wichita. Years later Kyle Rote Jr. tracked me down and sent me a hand-written letter wishing me luck and thanking me for my years in the MISL. Every time Trautwig would see me he'd give me a hug and say, "How's my little sister doing?"

Jackie Knapp wasn't the only one with a lot on her plate. For Ray Denton and the staff, the work day had barely ended before it began once again. On game days, their schedule was even more hectic.

RAY DENTON: I'd go to work at 8:00 am, and get out of there at 1:00 am and be ready to go back the next day. It was one thing after another coming at you, things that nobody had attended to. I got to go on one road trip. Thank you Roy! I was working hard. He said, "You and your wife, we're taking you to Dallas this week." There were a handful of people in this huge stadium. And then you come back to Wichita and our attendance was almost packed.

Ward kept bumping up my pay because I kept doing stuff he didn't want to do. [He] first hired me as an "administrative assistant." When the "Saturday

Night Massacre" occurred, Ward named me "Director of Operations." When he resigned, I was General Manager for the last two weeks, tasked with "closing it down." But the "Save the Wings" campaign brought the Wings back for another year.

[On game day] we'd have the morning staff meeting to go through all the things we needed to correct. That was Jackie, Ward, me, and sometimes Roy...he was in-and-out depending on if it was player-related. Then we had all these ticket issues. We hired those salespeople and they were cycling in and out. [They were] recommended to us sometimes, but often...no production. So we'd have a ticket sales meeting, and a promotional meeting, and then Ward would say we've got a phone call or issue from the league to take care of. The league was televising the games and trying to standardize stuff. Coordination with AYSO, *The Eagle*, the advertisers, the VIPs... So we had to start building an agenda for the day of: when the lights come on and off, who is going to do the national anthem. All the myriad of details, even more so on the televised games.

We were constantly having to stroke people who were doing things for us. We had people wanting to do things we couldn't do. We had to be careful. [Ward's wife] Janie [Lawrence] would come in and say "I've got some people who want to do a show at halftime." "Ok, what is it?" "Well, I haven't seen them yet." So we'd have to send Virginia out to see if this was something we want or not. We had the legal issues: if you were going to have people out there [at halftime] they needed to have a medical release. What age groups could you have out there? I've never seen so many details that had to be attended to...and if you didn't do it, it would throw things off and people would say, "Why the hell didn't you think of that?" That's the way the day would go...to solve the problem before it would happen, to anticipate what we might run into.

We had people who started dancing [in the stands] when we played "Heard It On The Grapevine"...pretty soon, we had to decide, "Do we put the stoplight on them or not?" We had to have a meeting about it. "Are we creating a monster? Is someone going to fall? Will someone shoot them the bird when we put the camera on them?" I made up some orange-and-blue banners to put on the railings to make it look good on TV. Oh boy, after every game we had somebody assigned to get to those banners and get them back. The first night we lost half of them.

JACKIE KNAPP: On game day my sister Mary would make stuffed cabbage and stew and put it in the office in case anybody wandering through could eat. I was a bitch on game day. I was in a zone, and knew what I needed to do.

During that first season, some in the media accused the Wings of padding their attendance numbers. On December 20th, against St. Louis, the Wings report-ed an attendance of 7,098. Mike Limon of The Eagle and Beacon *reported that the turnstile count was only 5,444. Furthermore, he claimed that records showed that the Wings sold 4,506 tickets and gave away another 1,875.[5] An internal memo from the team shows that, in terms of season tickets, as of game six, 349 seats were complimentary: 79 for the players, 6 for Roy Turner, 44 for the Cherubs and their chaperones, 40 for Scholfield Pontiac, 40 for game officials, and the rest to various other sponsors, prize winners, and friends of the team.*

RAY DENTON: *The Eagle* got on us for lying about our attendance figures. There was no way [to do a count]. At one point they were going to get ticket counters. And it was just so cumbersome...the only way Fulco could do it was if it was a full house. But the last three rows held 20-30% of the total, so we did some estimations. It did get to be a joke. *The Eagle* asked, "How do you [count]?" We said, "Oh, we have a very scientific way of doing it." Well, Roy and Ward and I would go in there [look at the crowd] and say, "What do you think?" And then somebody would say, "No, it's about 200 more than that." [laughs] We had to because we didn't have time to count the tickets.

ROY TURNER, HEAD COACH, WICHITA WINGS: I would actually try to count how many fans were in the stands at the time. The players wanted to get to know the fans. The more people you have in there, the more fun we have.

Wichitans were able to support their team that first year thanks to very reasonable ticket rates. Season tickets cost only $4 per game for "Economy" seats. A "Coach" class seat was $5 a seat, while the most expensive seats were in the $6 "First Class" section. Kids could get in for $2.50. Individual game tickets were only $.75 more per ticket. Remarkably, by the 1987-88 season, season ticket prices had barely risen, with prices at $5, $6, $8, $10, and $15.

The crack front office staff came up with all kinds of good ideas for promotions at Wings games during Year One: Family Night, Bus Night, Government Employee Night, Wings Family of the Night, Balloon Pop, cash giveaways, Shriners Night, Argus [Tapes and Records] Night, Wichita State Fan Night, High School Night... and then there was Beer Night...

RAY DENTON: The security issue was always, "How many do we need?" If there was a big crowd somebody would say, "You need ten guys," another would say, "No you need five." We wound up with three guys [sheriff's deputies] for a crowd on "beer night." The beer sponsor wanted a 10 cent beer night. Oh my God. There were some people in the church group that didn't want that. The players and Ward were kind of against it. The crowd got very, very drunk. Afterwards there were fights. There was this poor deputy down in the south end. Four or five guys jumped him...really hurting him. I had to call the two guys out front who were trying to control the fights out there, to come back in. One of them came down and got him freed up. It was total chaos. They brought those teenage kids into the office. They gave them a talking-to. They could have hauled them to jail...but they let them go. And they said, "Look guys, you know you've had too much to drink. We don't know who started this, but you can't do this." It was really a neat scene. Some of them were crying. They started coming back to the games and these guys kind of turned them around. They could have jailed them that night.

Sponsors for the Wings in the 1979-80 season included: Scholfield Pontiac, Argus Tapes and Records, Admiral Uniforms, KFH Radio, AAA Auto Club, Henry's clothing store, the Wichita Racquet Club, American Athletic and Soccer Supply, SpaceAge Stereo Sales, BankTravel Agency, Chisholm Trail State Bank, Reffner's Sporting Goods, Steven Subaru, Comley-Neff Lumber Company, The Looking Glass restaurant, Waterbeds Unlimited, Jeanie's Beautiful People Place, Coca-Cola, Coors, and Sears.

JACKIE KNAPP: Everybody got a car that first year. Scholfield Pontiac was very generous. Henry's was a sponsor as well. I know the players got nice discounts on clothes.

Throughout the season, the Wings continued their grassroots marketing campaign all across the metro area. Roy Turner sent his players out into the community to sell the game of soccer to the men, women, and, most importantly, youth of Wichita.

RAY DENTON: An idea from Roy that really worked was player contact with the public. When they'd start going out doing these things with the kids at AYSO... some of these pro players were a little iffy on that, but he pushed them. He got them doing some modeling for local businesses, and then he started having them go to a local cocktail lounge. Now they liked THAT. But the intermingling with the fans...the women, with their kids playing soccer, picked up on it fast. I don't know how many guys said, "Soccer? What's that?" They started coming around later. Roy was a good PR person...people liked him. If he had only been a coach I don't know what would have happened.

There were only a few of them [that complained about doing public events]. Turner squashed that pretty quickly. He'd say, "This is what we do. This is also about entertainment, not just sports." George Ley, a peach of a guy...he was Turner's right-hand man. He was the one that kept all the guys in order. When they started to flare up he'd take them for a drink and calm them down. [Freddie Garcia] said, "I'm not going to do any more of those appearances." And then George Ley would take over and say, "Yeah, you are."

[Assistant MISL Commissioner] Ed Tepper came down here and said, "Where did you guys come from? This is the hottest bunch of people in the entire league. Your fan base is incredible. Where does that come from?" I said, "Roy and the promotions, etc." He was impressed...

JACKIE KNAPP: Wichita was an island unto itself. I think we were kind of the darling of the league. "Scrappy" was the word I heard either Ed Tepper or Doug Verb use...pulling the team together with a grassroots effort. It was a different vibe than any other franchise.

As the season progressed it became clear that something special was happening. As Alan Schroeder of The Wichita Eagle *reported, indoor soccer began to "become part of the local culture." Schroeder interviewed a number of fans at the Tuesday, January 15th game against the Detroit Lightning. He found fans of all stripes at the game: young, middle-aged, and old...blue-collar and white-collar. When first-time attendee Harlene Lipke was asked if the game was what she expected, she replied, "It's more than I was expecting...the excitement and fastness of the game surprised me." Pat Jennings stated, "I'm not much for organized sports, but this isn't bad." Schroeder described the arena atmosphere as "intimate," the game as having "ambience," and said the crowd's involvement "never wavers."*[6]

RAY DENTON: [The crowd that first year] started with the hardcore AYSO group, then mothers and business people with kids who played AYSO. We kept building...more and more guys. Once you got the family, the guys started to bring their friends. Then you got groups of single guys coming out. It became the place to go. Except for beer night, [the crowd was] always well-mannered and kind and good to the players. I made up a bunch of signs for fans to hold up (planted them with my friends in the crowd). The next week, fans brought their own and it exploded into a sea of creative signs.

We kept getting fears expressed by women: "Why bring a vanload of kids out there in the winter and my van won't start. If you had it downtown [this wouldn't be a problem]." I went and got a guy I knew in the wrecking business. "How many tickets would it take for you to jump-start cars after the game?" He told me, and we had plenty of tickets, so we did it. We advertised it and we got a story in *The Eagle*: "Free jumpstarts and tows if you get caught in the Coliseum in bad weather." Man, that was one of the smartest things we did. People kept coming to us and saying, "We're gonna bring a group out, we're not afraid anymore."

The Wings had many fans, most of whom were normal, average, ordinary people. But George Henderson was definitely not normal...nor average....and, in fact, quite extraordinary. "Krazy George" had built a reputation across the country as a top-notch "professional fan." The Kansas City Chiefs, Denver Nuggets, British Columbia Lions, and San Jose Earthquakes had all previously purchased his valuable services. Starting at San Jose State, where he attended college, Krazy George took his wild cheerleading routine and turned it into a career. Shockingly, he had once been a schoolteacher...which would have made for an interesting classroom.

His performance involved a drum, a lot of yelling, and a sense of humor. He used this to great effect for the Wichita Wings.[7]

RAY DENTON: Krazy George...the name applied. He was funny. He came in for $150 and a plane ticket. He really revved up the crowd and everybody loved him. At first I thought, "What is this?" It wasn't like a mascot; it was like a...crazy person. But it worked and people loved him. Then he wanted more money. I can't blame him because he was flying in from San Diego. We had to negotiate and I think a sponsor stepped up to pay half. We got him his tickets, but he didn't make all the games. One night, the assistant director at the Coliseum, Dave Rush, got an idea. "I have a lawn mower with no blade on it. Let's have Krazy George mow the 'green grass' [turf]." People in the crowd were like, "What the heck is this?" It was funny. So then the Wings Angels grabbed him and put him in a harness and sent him up to the ceiling. That was when we had the Riggers Union upset with us. He really did a good job. Something you wouldn't have planned: Let's get a bald-headed guy that's middle-aged and not too bright, that's crazy, and give him a drum and [have him] yell at people. I got to like him. He was a fun guy.

JACKIE KNAPP: Krazy George was a friend of Roy's. I had never heard of him. He had shorts, a Wings shirt, and his hair was wild. He never asked for much of anything. He just showed up with his drum, screamed, and the crowd loved it.

CHAPTER 8

An Oral History

The Lads

———

"You are who you are. You can't be someone you'd like to be. You just have to be yourself."

- ROY TURNER

THOUGH IT WOULD BE ROY Turner's first head coaching job, his journey was made easier by a familiarity with so many of the players. Building the team was an exciting challenge. Though growing into his own unique coaching style would take a little time and some experimentation, it would ultimately prove to be a smashing success.

ROY TURNER, HEAD COACH, WICHITA WINGS: I'm pretty good with people so a lot of becoming a coach was "man management." I would stay up the night before practice planning it out. I'd seen a lot of coaches, so I learned from that. In early days I thought maybe I should be more mad and intense. So one day during practice, I picked up a bottle of Gatorade, which I thought was empty, and threw it against the blackboard. Well, it wasn't empty, and it went all over the back of my shirt. All that did was make everybody laugh. You are who you are. You can't be someone you'd like to be. You just have to be yourself.

KEVIN KEWLEY, FORWARD/MIDFIELDER, WICHITA WINGS: It was an easy transition from being a fellow player with Roy to him being a coach.

ROY TURNER: The group of players accepted me. They could have made it difficult, but they didn't. I got great support from the guys every year, but especially the first year. The people I recruited wanted to win. They supported everything we did to try to win. They weren't here for a holiday...they were here to win.

KEVIN KEWLEY: You know the character of the players. You pick a certain kind of player. You didn't pick a guy who was an asshole even if he was talented.

ROY TURNER: You recruited not just ability, you recruited their personality. I didn't bring any problem personalities here. I could have brought the other entity of Dallas in...the guys in the other camp. But I didn't. One of the best players we ever had, [Omar] Gomez, wouldn't have thought of coming here if [those others] had come.

TOM MARSHALL, GENERAL MANAGER, WICHITA WINGS, 1979: Turner handled every bit of the player signings and was very good at it. He deserves 100% credit for all that.

ROY TURNER: Most of my career I did the contracts, which was stupid because usually the GM does the contracts. But we didn't have a general manager at the time. We had a budget and we had to stay within it. I don't know who the highest paid player was that first season...

KEVIN KEWLEY: It wasn't me [laughs]. I was on a six month contract. It was monthly. I made about $3,000 a month. They also gave me a car from Scholfield and an apartment. I was making good money.

ROY TURNER: In the first year, everybody signed for a partial-year contract, not for the whole year.

KEVIN KEWLEY: The second year we had year-long contracts.

ROY TURNER: We watched some tape of the 1978-79 season, but it was nowhere near the standard we were playing in the Wings first year. The NASL players weren't really there yet. There was no question the talent level shot up. The second and third seasons continued to see an improvement of play in the MISL as more and more of those NASL players came over. San Diego, Chicago, and [Golden Bay] came in and improved the league. That's when the league really got good. It became the number one league in America.

The 1979-80 Wichita Wings had assembled an impressive collection of talent. Despite this, they struggled to reach a winning record. After a 2-1 start to the season, with early December victories over the Detroit Lightning and the Cleveland Force, the Wings did not surpass .500 again until February 24th. On that day, an overtime victory over the Philadelphia Fever took them to 14-13. On and off the field, the Wichita Wings players were beginning to make their mark. They were getting to know Wichita, and Wichitans were getting to know them.

Scotsman Jimmy Ryan's success as a member of the European Cup-winning Manchester United team gave him legit soccer bona fides in Wichita. He would finish the season with a team-leading 26 goals and 29 assists, reaching the top ten in total points in the MISL. Turner praised not only his scoring ability, but his leadership: "Jim's got 20 years of experience and, believe me, he is always willing to share it with our younger players...Jim doesn't just find time to help his teammates. He makes time."[1]

Ryan's occasional resemblance to a famous punk rocker earned him the nickname, "Sid." But off the field, his habits were anything but "punk rock." He moved his wife Irene and their two elementary-age children to Wichita to live the "country" life. "Wichita reminds me a lot of my hometown, Stirling [Scotland]. We have a country atmosphere and I like the country. It is fun to play in front of the Wichita fans. There is good spirit here..."[2]

(Greg Fox/1985-86 Wings Yearbook) Norman Piper
and Jimmy Ryan celebrating a goal.

**RAY DENTON, DIRECTOR OF OPERATIONS, WICHITA WINGS
1979-1980:** My favorite player was Jimmy Ryan. Personable and hard-working.
He never went for the notoriety or attention.

ROY TURNER, HEAD COACH, WICHITA WINGS: Jimmy Ryan was a
great professional. He took care of his body. He had been great with Manchester
United, but he gave it his all here in Wichita as well. That's the kind of player he
was. He had been in the big arena and he was a great pro...a great veteran for me

when the team started. He came with George Ley, who quit too soon. Neither of them stayed long enough to see the greatness of the franchise we would build. It kept growing and getting better every year.

Ryan wasn't the only veteran leader. They had them in spades. Former Tornado George Ley brought his expertise to both the field, as a defender, and to the bench, where he acted as Turner's assistant. Ley had been playing professionally for 16 years and was beginning to struggle with the physical demands of the game. "There's not too many things going for you physically after you're 30. It's quite hard for me. During the season it's mostly playing and resting. The young boys can go out for all the late-night stuff and bounce back. I stopped all the late-night stuff. My body doesn't quite recover as well as it used to," he told Randy Brown of The Eagle.[3] *He would finish the season with 10 goals and 19 assists. Alas, he would NOT finish the season on Andy Chapman's list of most exciting players to bring to a party…*

ANDY CHAPMAN, FORWARD, WICHITA WINGS: You'd be surprised how many comedians we had. George Ley…GEORGE would admit that George was pretty boring. He was prettttttty borrrring. He didn't do too much or say too much. You'd be at a party and you'd see him in the corner practicing his golf swing [laughs], not talking to anybody. But I could get him laughing and it was so great because he did have a dry sense of humor. Most of the players, especially the ones from England, loved to have a laugh and joke and pull tricks on each other.

Kevin Kewley tied for the second highest number of total points on the team, with 20 goals and 21 assists. He also would channel his nickname, "Tiger," when it came to penalty minutes: he led the team with 24.

TOM SHINE, REPORTER/EDITOR, THE WICHITA EAGLE: Kevin Kewley is the nicest, most gentle family man, but during the games…he had a little bit of devil in him. He'd really go after people sometimes. He'd come unglued on occasion and kick the crap out of somebody.

In addition to Mike Ivanow, the Wings added a second American in goal: Keith Van Eron. The 6'1 Brooklyn native was signed to be the backup. But by the end of the season, he would end up playing more minutes in goal. However, through the first month of play, it was an extremely frustrating situation for Van Eron. "I don't consider myself a backup keeper, but that's the way it has worked out this season...I think I could start for any team in the league and help them...When I decided to come here, I thought we'd be switching off more."[4] Van Eron requested a trade to the Hartford Hellions, but it was rejected due to technical reasons involving his off-season NASL contract. "Once I got that out of my system and resigned myself to the fact that I'd be staying here, I decided to become the best backup keeper that I could possibly be...Besides, it's a long season. Anything can happen."[5] And something did happen. On February 1st, 1980, The Wichita Beacon *reported that Ivanow had left the team due to an accumulation of injuries over the course of the season.[6] He had played in 14 games and accumulated a 6-6 record. His Goals Against Average (GAA) of 5.23 was virtually the same as what Van Eron would average (5.08) over the rest of the season.[7] Van Eron would battle his own wrist and thumb injury problems throughout the season, but in February the job became his, and his alone.*

JACKIE KNAPP, PUBLIC RELATIONS, WICHITA WINGS 1979-80: Van Eron came before Christmas time. He established himself as a great goalkeeper. I never saw him with a hair out of place! Nice guy, very polite, very religious. Kind of a whiner. He would complain about the size of Wichita and the bad roads.

RAY DENTON: All the ladies loved Van Eron. Mike Ivanow, what a character. One night he didn't quite make it to a game.

JACKIE KNAPP: Ivanow was always surly.

TOM MARSHALL: I had a trade-out with Scholfield Pontiac at the time. They became one of the main sponsors and gave us a whole fleet of automobiles for both management and the team. I picked a Trans Am, which was stupid, because I had kids. It left Ivanow with a family car. We had a few drinks one night and decided to trade cars. I think he blew the transmission a week later.

ROY TURNER: That first Christmas the boys were all lonely because they were away from home, and I was like their dad, so I took them all to have a drink for Christmas.

KEVIN KEWLEY: Later that night, Mike Ivanow drove home and wiped out the phone box for the entire apartment complex.

ROY TURNER: There was a trail of tires, oil can, and telephone parts.

KEVIN KEWLEY: Nobody could call home for Christmas, so everybody was going crazy.

NORMAN PIPER, FORWARD/MIDFIELDER, WICHITA WINGS: Mike Ivanow was driving a yellow sports car. He went home one night and hit a fire hydrant or something. There was an oil slick all the way through the apartment complex parking lot.

JACKIE KNAPP: At Mike Ivanow's last game the Angels sang "What I Did For Love" from *A Chorus Line*, and did a choreographed dance. They had some kind of illumination with Mike's number on it.

Norman Piper was a rock for Roy Turner in 1979-80. He played in 30 of the 32 games, which tied for the most appearances on the squad. His 18 goals and 21 assists combined for the fourth highest total on the team.[8]

ROY TURNER: Norman Piper...I had watched him play for many years. I had played against him in Ft. Lauderdale in the NASL. He had played in the English League in Portsmouth in many games. I thought his play would suit the indoor game. He would never give away the ball. Great passer. Great player.

TERRY NICHOLL, MIDFIELDER, WICHITA WINGS: Norman could move gracefully...it was no effort for him to move around, look good, score and assist. Smooth.

NORMAN PIPER: [Roy and I] got along well. I think Roy was good at bonding players together, not just on the field, but off the field as well. We had some good times. These younger players were in Wichita by themselves, and they needed some comfort and Roy was good at that. Obviously, he was a good coach. And everybody played for him. But he wasn't very generous in buying us a drink [laughs]. We had to buy HIM a drink.

At 5'6 and 152 lbs., Piper was a miniature whirling dervish on the field. With his long, curly hair, and a trot that Randy Brown described as "swaggering," Piper brought a sense of flair and excitement to the field. "When you score, you should enjoy it. I like to show the crowd my appreciation. I get excited on the field. I get excited when the other guys score a goal. That's probably why they call me 'Stormin' Norman.' You have to enjoy the game to play well. That's the great thing about indoor soccer. The crowd is close to you. The crowd is more involved. The players love playing it," said Piper. Roy Turner described him as the team's "motor." According to Piper, "I'm just one of the engine-room boys, helping organize things at midfield." [9]

In December and January, Turner added players to the squad as necessary. Texas native Mike Hobgood would only play two games and would never put the ball in the back of the net. Argentine player Juan Carlos Michia performed a little better. In his four games he would score a goal and make an assist. [10] *Keith Gehling, the sole survivor of the open tryouts, would find a spot on the regular rotation. "He's shown us he can play, and play quite well," said Roy Turner. He appeared in 26 games, scoring three goals and making four assists. The highlight of his season was a return to his hometown of St. Louis to play in front of friends and family.* [11] *And, of course, Andy Chapman joined the squad. His impact would be delayed, but when he blossomed into the truly great indoor player he became, it had an enormous effect on the team. There will be much more about Chapman later...*

Up until the end of the December, Welshman Willie Anderson had been the Wings "most consistent offensive threat," according to Beacon columnist Steve Love. But an injury to his knee almost ended his Wings season. After returning to Portland to have exploratory surgery, Anderson discovered that "I had banged up me knee on top of an old injury I had about 12 years ago." Love speculated that a more cynical player would have stayed in Portland to rest up and heal, which no doubt his NASL Timbers outdoor team would have preferred. "I'm sure Portland wouldn't have minded me staying there...but the decision was mine. And it was an easy one....I couldn't let the lads down." [12] *By February he was back at it with the Wings. At the end of the 1979-80 campaign he would have 16 goals and six assists.* [13]

One of the most impactful late additions to the first year Wings was Turner's old Dallas comrade, Omar "El Indio" Gomez. Despite coming in the middle of January, Gomez scored 28 goals and made 13 assists, for a total of 41 points, which tied for second on the team. All this despite only playing in 18 of the team's 32 games.[14]

ROY TURNER: Omar Gomez...nobody realized how good he was. He was one of the best players to ever play here. He went on to play for the New York Arrows. He was a great outdoor player as well. I was surprised I got him to play in Wichita, but I was good friends with him and convinced him to come. He had great vision, great skill, and obviously was a wonderful goal finisher. He didn't speak English...though he could understand some. I remember Caesar Cervin doing the translation for him in the post-game interview one time live on TV. In the end, Caesar started answering the questions for Omar without bothering to translate them [laughs]. Omar really liked it here. He was on loan from Dallas and went back to play here. Omar was at his peak here in Wichita. He was definitely a key for our first year. He was a First Division player back in Argentina. He got on very well with the English players, but wasn't a big favorite of the German players back in Dallas.

I think the crowd appreciated him, but the players appreciated him even more because of the things he was doing on the pitch. I was very sad when he went to the Arrows. He went back to Dallas in the off-season and then the Arrows bought him from the Tornado and he won a championship there. We got him back in 1982 though. He liked the people here and the city. The former Tornado players treated him with great respect.

Life on the road...

JACKIE KNAPP: Roy wanted the boys to experience Niagara Falls. It was incredibly cold. I was wearing high heels as usual. The guys all walked down to the guardrail. It was so cold the falls were frozen. There was a foot-and-a-half of snow on the ground. So I took off my heels and plodded through in stocking feet. I didn't want to be considered a spoiled-sport.

One time in St Louis, I was walking among the catwalks above the arena carrying our telex machine. Roy and the guys were supposed to wait for me. So

I yelled, "God damn it, I'm lost and I'm up here!" Finally a janitor came and got me and led me down.

The All-Star game was a party. All the PR folks pitched in and helped out. I had a great rapport with the PR and Operations folks. Doug Verb was my PR boss and he had a couple of assistants. All the PR people were together...like college spring break. It was a party. I remember one of the league PR people ended up hooking up with [a player from another team].

ROY TURNER: In that first year, such was the weather then, we couldn't get the players to the airport, so we had to pick up every player from his apartment in a squad of 4x4s. When I returned from that road trip the path to my house was all cleaned up, the snow all gone. I thought, "How nice." But what had happened is that my house had been burglarized. They took everything. They must have cleared the path when they came in.

ANDY CHAPMAN: I can remember being up with the fans in St. Louis and we'd hang out and drink beers with them afterwards. We'd go to the pub and all start singing. I can remember singing in the lobby late one night with a whole bunch of people and the players and everyone was singing along. It was friggin' awesome.

ROY TURNER: We had celebrity in Dallas, but in Wichita we had a bunch of young, good looking guys. And they didn't stay in every night. So people got to know them REAL quick. They socialized a hell of a lot. Those post-game parties in the early '80s...we could hardly get a parking spot.

If you ask a member of the Wichita Wings about the good times they had in the 1980s, you are guaranteed to hear about The Hatch Cover...also known as "The Hatch." This bar and restaurant was just north of 13th and Rock Road, in a building that would one day become a couple different restaurants: Charley Brown's and, finally, Kwan Court. The original building no longer stands, and has been replaced by a dentist's office. The Hatch was the place to be after a game.

ROY TURNER: We had been known to "reopen" the pool behind The Hatch Cover. There was a pool behind that bar that we would sometimes use after-hours.

VIRGINIA CREAMER, ASSISTANT DIRECTOR OF OPERATIONS/ ANGELS COORDINATOR, WICHITA WINGS: [The Hatch Cover] was the place to be. Go to a Wings game, go to the Hatch Cover afterwards, and meet all the players. All of the press was there. Everybody that worked with us on television or the newspaper side were all there together. It was the in-crowd, the "in" place to be. It was great because you met the crème de la crème of Wichita at the time. We were all so close, the TV people and the print people. It was very exciting at the time. Everybody always had fun and had stories to tell.

ROY TURNER: I think their social lives ADDED to the team, didn't take away from it. They were great for the team. I would never complain about their social lives because it made everyone more interested in the team.

JACKIE KNAPP: I'm not a prude or anything, but I wasn't brought up that way. I didn't think the players would want to see me out on the dance floor [at the Hatch Cover]. I took the "no fraternization" rule seriously. On the road it was different. We'd all go out to dinner together. I'd sit at the bar with Roy, George Ley, and Kevin...a few of the more senior guys. Roy would get his Tanqueray and tonic and talk about the game and the opposing players. Shooting the bull.

Artificial turf, or "Astroturf," covered the floor of the Kansas Coliseum during Wings games. It was the standard playing surface in the MISL. There wasn't an alternative to it, but that didn't mean it was popular. Many of the players were used to playing on natural grass in the outdoor season, and they could tell the difference. "After I play a game on artificial turf, I'm sorer the next day than I would be if I played on grass. The artificial turf doesn't give as much when you cut and run. It allows you to push off harder and that puts more strain on your joints," said Wings defender Glenn Myernick.[15] Keith Van Eron concurred: "I separated a shoulder in a game once playing on artificial turf. I don't think it would have happened if I'd been playing on regular grass. Sometimes it's almost like diving on concrete, especially if the turf is worn down." However, Mike Ivanow felt that the turf gave goalkeepers an advantage. "It cuts down on what the (offensive player) can do. They can't chip the ball as easily as they can on real grass...You get a truer bounce. The ball comes at you quicker, but you get used to it."[16]

ROY TURNER: It was very difficult to play on Astroturf. It's like playing on concrete. The ball runs. When you move, your cleats stay where they are...the burns from the turf. It definitely changed the game.

KEVIN KEWLEY: My knees and ankles are shot now.

MIKE DOWLER, FUTURE GOALKEEPER, WICHITA WINGS: The indoor game is physically tough on all players, not just 'keepers. Sure, it was hard to have a soccer ball hit you at 70+ mph from close range; or to repeatedly dive on the playing surfaces that were HARD (especially those laid straight on top of ice); or to be clattered time and time again by players like [Don] Ebert. However, I would rather do all that than to play out of goal in a series of lung-bursting, two-minute shifts making slide-tackles on abrasive surfaces whilst wearing a pair of shorts skimpier than those that the Dallas Cowboys cheerleaders wear! On reflection, I did pick up my fair share of injuries but I am proud of my powers of recovery and fitness to have played as many games as I eventually did.

Not only was the turf unfamiliar to many players and coaches, so was the indoor game itself. Coaches would play multiple "lines" of players, borrowing from the world of hockey. One line would come on, and then it would come off. At least that was how it was supposed to work.

AL MILLER, HEAD COACH, DALLAS TORNADO, NASL: In the early days of the MISL everyone was still trying to figure out how to play the game. Ron Newman was way ahead of everyone in San Diego.

KEVIN KEWLEY: Indoor was a new thing for all of us. The biggest difference was going on and off. Roy said, "Go on for two minutes," but you'd think to yourself, "I can play more than that." You'd go out for five minutes instead and the next quarter you'd be dead. You'd feel like you hadn't gotten into a rhythm. Maybe you didn't even touch the ball during those two minutes. That was the biggest thing to get used to. I used to change with Norman Piper. We were pretty good about it. Other guys would have issues staying on too long. It would mess up the lineup.

ROY TURNER: There was a reason for the lines.

TOM SHINE: For a lot of these guys, they were outdoors guys; the first [indoor] game they ever saw was one they played in.

ROY TURNER: We really didn't use the boards much. We were very technical, very good with the ball. We learned so much about the indoor game just in three months. We had a lot of great players, and if they hadn't been so great I don't know if we would have picked it up so quickly.

KEVIN KEWLEY: We had to get in a different type of shape for indoor.

ROY TURNER: You train for two minutes. You pace yourself differently.

KEVIN KEWLEY: Power plays and that kind of stuff was all new for us. We would work on power plays and see someone else do it differently and we'd adjust based on that.

Occasionally, a newbie would revert to his outdoor experience. Like trying a throw-in...

RAY DENTON: I remember at one of the games, a player threw the ball clear across the field.

DOUG VERB, MISL EXECUTIVE, DIRECTOR OF PRESS AND PR: Guys like Roy Turner and Kenny Cooper, they went to their hockey guy and said, "Hey, how do I get out one door and in the other? How do I get these guys off the field?"

NORMAN PIPER: I think players can adapt quickly to the indoor game, especially a midfield player, which I was. I adapted to it very quickly. It was a new game and it was exciting for the fans, like a hockey game. That's what the American public wanted.

The Wings adjusted quickly to the new game, and came up with a strategy that suited the highly-skilled players Turner recruited. Their style of play showcased the finesse and beauty they brought to the sport of soccer.

KENNY COOPER, HEAD COACH, HOUSTON SUMMIT: Roy was big into possession of the ball...his teams were good at possession and passing. You'd go to Wichita and playing in front of the Orange Army was tough. He brought in experienced players and good passers. It was difficult to get the ball from them. When they were on, it was a long night. You'd try to keep the game close and hope to steal the game. Playing in Wichita was an emotional experience. It was a difficult building to play in. Very few teams had the "give and go" kind of tactics that Roy had. You can't go in there and play 100 mph, because you'd turn the ball over. Roy's teams played some of the finest indoor soccer I've ever seen. When you were on the receiving end of Roy's teams, it was hard. They were such great passing teams. Norman Piper very rarely gave the ball away. He had ball-winners and guys who could create.

CHAPTER 9

An Oral History

Disaster, Triumph...and a Savior

―――――

"The lights were out and we were feeling along the wall..."

- RAY DENTON

BY FEBRUARY 12TH, 1980, THE Detroit Lightning and the Wichita Wings were locked in a battle for the second and third playoff spots in the MISL's Central Division. Houston seemed to have the top spot all but locked up. The third place team would have to travel to the second place team's home arena for a one-game first round playoff game. This was something Roy Turner and the Wings very much wished to avoid. A 7-1 blowout of Detroit that night resulted in the Wings vaulting into second place.[1] At one point, it even seemed like first place might be possible. However, it wasn't meant to be. A loss to Houston, and a season-ending injury to 26-year-old Canadian defender, Garry Ayre, helped seal their fate.[2] Houston would ultimately finish four games ahead of the Wings.

But that was the least of their problems. On February 26th, with five games remaining in the regular season, Bob Becker and the Great Plains Corporation announced that as of the end of the 1979-80 campaign, they would no longer operate the Wichita Wings. According to the official press release, "Great Plains hopes... that the Wichita Wings soccer team will continue here next year, and far into the

107

future, and will do everything it can to help assure the continuation of the Wings in Wichita. Great Plains is committed to finishing the present season and the playoffs. It is our primary goal that the franchise will remain in Wichita, and we are actively seeking companies or individuals to take over the operations next year." According to Mike Limon, the team had lost around $1 million up to that point. In what was a previously unreported scoop, Limon revealed that in January, Becker had become "sole owner of the club...after five other partners dropped out because of the prospect of continuing losses."[3]

BOB BECKER, OWNER, WICHITA WINGS, 1979-80: Don Slawson was also involved in it that first year. John Frazier as well. I owned the controlling interest and when it was a matter of if the team was going to go away and stop playing, Don and John had recommended we stop playing. I bought their shares so [the Wings] could keep playing.

The Eagle listed Frazier, Don Slawson, Jerry Shawver, Gerry O'Shaughnessy, and C. Howard Wilkins as the five investors that Becker had bought out in January. Limon's article quoted Frazier as saying: "It was just that I (had) suffered all the losses I had wanted and just turned over my interest in the partnership to Mr. Becker. I said I would stand losses to a certain amount and quit at that point. All of the minority partners got out at the same time. Mr. Becker was very enthused (about the team) and said, 'Heck, my name is on the front of it...I'm willing to keep it going.' And we said, 'Fine, take it and run.'"[4]

The league, the city...virtually everyone was shocked by the news that Becker and Great Plains were pulling out at the end of the year.

RAY DENTON, DIRECTOR OF OPERATIONS, WICHITA WINGS 1979-1980: We were under constant pressure of paying bills. Ward [Lawrence] would hint that we were barely gonna make it [to the end of the season]. It was a hell of a shock [when Becker pulled out].

VIRGINIA CREAMER, ASSISTANT DIRECTOR OF OPERATIONS/ ANGELS COORDINATOR, WICHITA WINGS: While we were working they were taking out our typewriters, all the furniture. And everybody was kind of out of a job, except, I don't know why, but I had a written contract. So they kept me on till the very end of the season.

Roy Turner was left to deliver the bad news to his players. And what did he want from them? "I'm going to ask them to do the job they have been doing in recent weeks. Not just play in the playoffs but win the whole damn thing. We'll wait and see what the community reaction is and if the community gets behind us like I think they might. If some local interest comes out whereby they want to support the team and continue it here, then I definitely would give serious consideration to continuing my role with the Wings. I think all the players' hearts are into this franchise and this city." [5]

Many questioned the decision to make the announcement before season's end; and right after a well-attended, nationally televised game. MISL Commissioner Earl Foreman was quoted in The Eagle *as saying, "...what surprised me more than anything else, the timing of the announcement. I can see no logic or reason for him doing it now instead of at the end of the season. It makes it very difficult for all of us." [6]*

DOUG VERB, MISL EXECUTIVE, DIRECTOR OF PRESS AND PR: It was February...how could you do something like that? Lame duck. The team was good...what were they thinking? There was no reason to make that announcement at all. It was very troubling for us. Once something bush league like that happens, then this is like a minor league that has Wichita in it. It wasn't good for anybody... the players, the management...it was terrible. It wasn't good for [Becker]. It was a desperate...childish move. If they would have just stayed the course and kept winning and playing...would it have made any difference...?

What amazed me was that a lot of these owners actually thought they were going to make a profit right away. I don't know where they came up with that idea...I know we didn't tell them that.

To announce before the end of the season, or not to announce. That had been the question...

RAY DENTON: The lights were out and we were feeling along the wall...Mel Witrogen [the Wings PR consultant] and I met. He wrote out a press release on a napkin on what to do and how to say it. Should we or shouldn't we do it? Wait till the end of the season or not? Roy said, "I don't know...I don't know what that will do?" Ward thought we needed to do it and get some backers to come in and take things over. If we finish strong it might help us save the Wings. Witrogen jumped on it: "Absolutely. This is your one shot. All eyes will be on you. You've got a few games left. Imagine if you will at the end, the season is over and six weeks later there's a line in the paper that says: 'Oh by the way, the Wings aren't coming back.'"

Then the league got upset because there was a contractual thing about negative publicity. They couldn't understand why we did it either because it would reflect on the financial status of the league. Hindsight being perfect, [announcing it before the season ended] was the thing to do. [But at the time, some people called it] "The dumbest PR move in the history of the world."

Earl Foreman promised to do as much as he could to keep the Wings in Wichita. Meanwhile, Great Plains began to cull the staff. The Eagle *reported that "five of the nine staff members in the Wings' central office in the Kansas Coliseum have been fired, as were all three employees at the downtown ticket office. However, two of those workers at the downtown office came to work Tuesday, apparently without pay, to tend to a run on the ticket office by fans seeking seats for the Wings' final three home games of the regular season."*[7]

The MISL gave the people of Wichita till late April to come up with a new owner-ship group. "The board (made up of the league's team owners) decided that someone in Wichita should be given a chance to come forward with a proposal for keeping the team in Wichita. If they can regroup out there, I think the board is unanimous in wanting to keep the franchise in Wichita," said Earl Foreman.[8] *The community rallied to support the Wings. It wouldn't be the last time that happened.*

RAY DENTON: When they broke the news so many people came through. Frank Chappell from Channel [3] called and said, "What can I do?" They did a telethon. The Chamber of Commerce got a group together to try to fund it. Oh boy, we had people saying, "What can we do? We're buying tickets, we're bringing a crowd, and we're doing this and that." The momentum was at the peak when this [announcement] hit.

JACKIE KNAPP: They began to bang the drum for the team. They held rallies and screamed for the Wings.

RAY DENTON: *The Eagle* was very supportive to the last.

JACKIE KNAPP: I didn't believe the team would actually fold. I remember at a game after the announcement looking at Bob Becker and stared at him, sighed, and walked away...After that last game of the regular season, no one went to bed. The liquor was flowing. There were a handful of guys and everyone was depressed and worried because there wasn't a glimmer of ownership on the horizon. We were hoping and praying for playoffs because that would extend everybody's contracts for a bit. We were in a bar that overlooked the main lobby in whatever hotel we were in in St. Louis. Mike Hobgood and Mike Custer were there. They were the ones most concerned about their futures. Next thing I knew it was 5:00 am. I was fraught with anxiety about the future.

On several fronts, efforts were underway to save the Wings. Clarence Wesley and the Wichita Chamber of Commerce met with Wings representatives to determine how best they could help find new investors for the team.[9] The Wichita Beacon published an editorial calling on investors and the people of Wichita to keep supporting the team: "A lot of people who never got excited about any kind of sports have become avid Wings backers after watching just one home-game shootout here... The Wings have brought a new diversion with obvious growth potential to town, and given Kansans a sense of identity with a totally Kansas major league sports team...None of the problems now faced by the Wings are insurmountable. All of them can be overcome by means of strong, up-front community support."[10]

A 9-8 overtime victory at home over division-leading Houston showed the Wings still had fighting spirit. It was the second-to-last game of the year and the Wings had already clinched a home playoff game against Detroit. Despite the lack of stakes, they still fought hard...and so did their fans. The Beacon's Steve Love said it best: "... this game that meant nothing, meant everything. You could hear it in the throaty yet eloquent cries of the crowd of more than 8,000. You could see in the jut of the Wings' jaws, in the way they pursued what should have been a lost cause until it no longer was lost...If ever a crowd proved that a team belongs to it and that its concern can make a difference, it was this crowd."[11] *Roy Turner was clear about his feelings after the game: "I felt like crying after the game. But I'll really feel like crying if this team has to leave town after something like this."*[12]

While the community rallied to their cause, the Wings had little time to think about saving the team. They had a playoff game plan to prepare. The Detroit Lightning came to town on March 11th, 1980. It was a do-or-die moment for the Wings. If they won, they'd prove they belonged in a league filled with big cities. If they lost, momentum for the campaign to find a new owner would collapse.

The game was close throughout. Down one goal in the fourth quarter, Kevin Kewley tied the game with just 44 seconds remaining. Forty seconds later, a scrum in the front of the Detroit goal resulted in a succession of shots by Kewley. Steve Love related Omar Gomez's description of what happened next and his own reaction to it: "...Gomez hesitated before he said what he had to say in halting English. He told of how he stood in front of [Detroit backup goalkeeper Bart] Farley and his net and three times he took the rebounds of Kevin Kewley shots and tried to put them in. One, he struck with his foot. It failed. Another, he hit with his chest. It, too, failed. But the third shot, the shot that went in and ended Detroit's season at 15-18 and forced Houston to return to Wichita next Tuesday to begin the Central Division finals, that was something else again. 'I hit with my hand,' Gomez said, flicking his wrist in the air. 'Your hand?' someone said. 'But that's illegal.' 'Sorry,' Gomez said. Sorry? What's to be sorry about? Nothing could have been more perfect."[13]

"Our scripts are by Walt Disney. I think someone is trying to tell this team something," said Jimmy Ryan. "Fairy-tale stuff, that's what that is," agreed George Ley. "Tomorrow, they'll sweep out the popcorn and under it they'll find half a dozen old people who died of cardiac arrest while watching us," said Glenn Myernick.[14]

In the next few days the Wings would clarify that Omar Gomez had been misunderstood, and it was the goalkeeper's hand he was describing as touching the ball before it went into the net. Turner agreed, and stated that a viewing of the game tape confirmed this.[15]

ROY TURNER, HEAD COACH, WICHITA WINGS: In the first year playoffs against the Detroit Lightning...we won in overtime. Kevin scored to tie it up. It was great for me and Kevin because they were a bunch of guys we didn't care for from Dallas that ended up going [to Detroit]. Kevin didn't like them, Omar Gomez didn't like them. It was a key game. There was a gradual progression in attendance over the first year. Then it came to this big ending in Detroit. We were a pretty damn good team. The Detroit playoff game was huge.

KEVIN KEWLEY, FORWARD/MIDFIELDER, WICHITA WINGS: If we had lost to Detroit in the playoffs, we'd have been done.

ROY TURNER: Detroit was the big momentum to get new ownership...The success of the team and the way they played were the key to making year two a reality.

There was little time to celebrate...the team still needed to be saved. At 10:30 pm on Sunday, March 16th, KARD, the Wichita NBC affiliate, and precursor to KSN, staged a live telethon on the air...the "Wingathon." As part of the program, they also showed a replay of the Detroit game.[16] Meanwhile, Clarence Wesley and Bud Beren of the Chamber of Commerce, in an effort to woo potential owners, were working hard to get the people of Wichita to pledge to buy 4,000 season tickets for the 1980-81 season. As of March 15th, 2,000 pledges had been received. These pledges were the first part of the Chamber's five-phase campaign to save the Wings. The other four phases were: to sell large amounts of tickets to the home playoff game against Houston; go to large investors with the season ticket pledges; lobby the business community to buy blocks of season tickets; and seek additional smaller investors.[17]

VIRGINIA CREAMER: That's when they started the big Save the Wings campaign and Clarence Wesley and the Chamber were wonderful about giving us a big space to set up in, with a bank of phones. We had Orange Army people sitting on those phones taking pledges. It was pretty amazing. We still didn't have an owner.

Sadly, the Wings' season ended a few days later. Kenny Cooper's Houston Summit beat the Wings in Wichita on March 18th, and then in Houston on March 20th. The Wings lost both games by a single point. The Summit would go on to lose to the New York Arrows in the MISL Finals. The Wings' inaugural season was over and they had yet to find a new owner. The clock was ticking toward the April 15th deadline imposed by the MISL. 4,200 pledges had been received, completing Phase Two of the Chamber's campaign. Speculation had it that it would take $200,000 to buy the Wings' from Great Plains Corp.[18] Wichita businessmen Jim Hershberger and Buck Alley entered the mix by pledging $75,000 and $10,000 respectively. Their money would be payable once the future team reached profitability. Additionally, Dick Upton of the Chamber had already secured $50,000 in general partnership funds and $100,000 in limited partnership funds. This left about $760,000 more to raise in only a few weeks.[19]

VIRGINIA CREAMER: My friend was doing an off-Broadway show in New York and I went up to help her. While I was there, Randy Brown somehow tracked me down and called me. "Guess what, Frank Carney bought the Wings. My best friend is going to be the GM. He'd like you to come back to Wichita and interview." I came, met Billy [Kentling] and then he hired me. It was me, Steve Shaad, and Dave Bennett, all of us hired at the same time.

ROY TURNER: I may be the eternal optimist but I never worried about it. The chair of the Chamber of Commerce at the time became a regular fan of the team. He was instrumental in getting Frank Carney involved. They said, "Frank Carney wants to meet you."

On April 16th, 1980, The Wichita Eagle reported that an ownership group led by Frank Carney, co-founder of Pizza Hut, would be leading an effort to purchase the Wichita Wings and operate them going forward.[20] Thousands of Wings fans breathed a huge sigh of relief.

JACKIE KNAPP: It was announced that the Carney brothers would become the principal owners of the Wings. It was downtown and the room was pretty full. I got dressed up and trotted down there. Roy was there...not many others were there from the club. The media was there. It was a simple announcement.

Frank Carney would become the main executive. Nobody really talked to me. My understanding was that I'd have to reapply for my job. It was not going to be business as usual. I was sitting next to Frank Carney's wife and I didn't [even realize it].

I thought, "Ok, I can play with the big boys." But in the back of my mind I was thinking, "They don't know me from the man on the moon." All I could think of was, "This isn't gonna go well for me...this is out of my league." It was becoming a real, structured million dollar business.

BOB BECKER: I sold it for $175,000 to Frank Carney. He or one of his people approached me about buying it...I didn't regret getting out. It never made money. My regret was losing $500,000. That's a lot of goddamn money!

It was a volume equation of some sort. You have to have enough people in the neighborhood that are soccer fans. Wichita was too small a city, and the game of soccer wasn't that prominent yet in the US.

The general partners in the new ownership group were Frank Carney, real estate developer Sam Hardage, oilmen Jim Hershberger and Robert Beren, N.J. Abraham, Buck Alley, Rent-A-Center founders Tom Devlin and Frank Barton, and Michael and Jan Freeman. On May 19th, 1980, the ownership group announced that Hardage would serve as managing partner.[21] Three days later, at a press conference at the Fourth Financial Center in downtown Wichita, Pizza Hut executive Bill Kentling was introduced as the new general manager of the Wings. Hardage said the team "sought and had found an individual with knowledge of the Wichita marketplace, sports promotion and marketing excellence and a proven track record in business." Kentling had previously served as the Director of Corporate Communications for Pizza Hut and, prior to that, the Vice-President of the National Baseball Congress. His work with Pizza Hut included running their collegiate all-star basketball game. He didn't claim to be an expert on soccer. For that, he had Roy Turner. His role would geared towards promoting and marketing the team.[22]

BILL KENTLING, GENERAL MANAGER, WICHITA WINGS, 1980-86: In the winter of 1979-80 I was at Pizza Hut in a variety of roles. One day we had a meeting in which somebody in the room came to the realization that it appeared that Bob Becker was going to let the Wings go. I had not been to a Wings game and most of the people in the room hadn't either. There was some impetus in the room to look into this and see if this was something worth saving, in the same way you'd look at the Wichita Symphony or Wichita Art Museum. [We were trying to determine] if this was a community asset that we needed to look at. There were several meetings and about this time, concurrent to these discussions, Pepsico, which had acquired Pizza Hut, was making some decisions about the future of the food service piece [Pizza Hut, Taco Bell, and Kentucky Fried Chicken] of the Pepsico conglomerate. Pepsico decided to move in another direction and NOT have Frank Carney lead the food service division...which was the deal that had been struck when they bought Pizza Hut. Instead, they decided to have someone else head this up and Carney would report to this person. So, Frank made a decision to leave the company and I made the same decision, as did a few others. We set our departure date on or about April 1st, 1980. We continued to have these discussions about what we were going to do about the Wichita Wings. Finally the decision was to look at acquiring them.

I did know Bob Becker socially, but knew little about him and didn't do business with him. Several of the people who attended games thought it was a hoot and their kids loved it, so I had a positive feeling that it was something good to do, but just hadn't gone myself. The people who had gone had a positive vibe.

Carney makes the decision that he is going to acquire the Wings if he can get some other guys to come in with him. He set out to find some other general partners. He didn't want to be the sole owner of the team, but wanted it to be a community situation. So, Ken Wagnon, who was a prominent Pizza Hut franchisee, might have been the first person that said yes [to Carney's offer to be part-owner]. There was a guy named Sam Hardage that came on. A number of people, six or eight guys, stepped forward as general partners. So, I told Frank I'd come in as a limited liability partner. So we put together a group of general partners and a group of limited partners and went out and raised enough money to satisfy the league's demands as far as having enough reserve capital, and negotiated the lease at the Coliseum. We were still at Pizza Hut at that time.

Carney called me into his office and asked if I wanted to run the team. I told him I didn't know a lot about soccer, but sure, I would. So the decision was made as quickly as that, that I'd become the general manager. I met Roy

Turner and liked him very much. He filled in the blanks of what happened the first year, both good and bad. Don Slawson donated a space downtown as part of his involvement. The first place was at 2nd and Broadway on the 2nd floor. We were there very briefly and realized being on the 2nd floor was not going to work out. Slawson also had a property across the street at 114 South Broadway that was a storefront. That was the storefront that most people knew for years as the Wings office.

For Jackie Knapp, it was a summer filled with anxiety. While the rest of Wichita was celebrating the Wings return from death's door, Knapp was wondering whether she would be included in the new management team.

JACKIE KNAPP: At the first meeting [Kentling] wanted to know everything we had done...the relationship with *The Eagle-Beacon*, etc. Kentling being the PR person for Pizza Hut, and me in my third year of PR experience, was picking my brain. But he was also asking me questions to show me what I didn't know about doing PR. It wasn't a comfortable sit-down. It was a grilling. I remember saying, 'Have you talked to Doug Verb?' He said, "I don't need to talk to Doug Verb." I asked him when he'd make a decision on hiring me or not. He said it would be a couple weeks. When I got a call back I thought it would be a really good sign. We met face-to-face and he told me I wasn't going to be selected. He said he wanted to go with a "more Madison Avenue approach." Of course, I cried. There was no sympathy, no empathy. A few weeks later, I moved to Baltimore to work for the Blast. There were very few franchises that kept the same PR people more than one or two years in a row.

BILL KENTLING: [Regarding Jackie Knapp], I remember my thinking at the time: what I didn't want when hiring people was "fans." Because I didn't want people who would get too wrapped up in the team winning and losing. I wanted guys like Steve Shaad or Dave Bennett who would just focus on their job. The team had its own job to do. Sometimes fans get emotional and make emotional decisions. I already had an expert on soccer in Roy Turner. Don't get caught up in how the team is doing. You still have tickets or sponsorships to sell. If you do [get emotional] your head is in your hands for several days after a tough loss.

[Being emotionally uninvolved] is great in theory, and you can pull it off the first or second year, but after a while you do get intertwined in the fortunes of the team. First of all, they become your friends, you're at the games...in our case, road games were televised...so you are viewing or listening (or both) to the road games and it becomes part of your life. In the early stages, when you are setting your foundation it is better that you don't have fans involved.

JACKIE KNAPP: It was probably the best thing in the world to not be hired by Kentling. It forced me to leave home and peddle my wares elsewhere. I had never really lived anywhere else other than six months in Bloomington, IL. I was able to prove myself outside of the shadow of my hometown. My first trip back to Wichita was after my second season working in the league (in Baltimore.) I went home for Christmas and went to a Wings game. JB [Johnson] was there, and he saw me, and it was like old home week. They played that John Denver song about how it's great to be back home again. I just about lost it.

Director of Operations Ray Denton had already made his choice. A lucrative offer to work overseas in Saudi Arabia awaited. But his memories of that first year were nothing but fond.

RAY DENTON: It was probably one of the best jobs I ever had. It was constantly motivating. The number and complexities of decisions (political, legal, financial, personnel, scheduling, security, ticket sales, et. al.) that had to be made correctly the first year were staggering. *The Eagle* blasted us for inflating attendance, volunteers threatened to quit if we didn't pay mileage, some players were concerned they were being asked to do too many time-consuming "community appearances," Krazy George wanted his fee doubled, [and] we faced criticism for serving wine in the hospitality room before the games...But that first year of the Wings was really something to behold...

I remember Roy saying that, "If anybody had told me that a guy from Liverpool with a speech impediment would have wound up in Wichita running a professional soccer team, I'd have told them they were crazy." He never felt like he was a big shot. He just kept plugging away and plugging away.

Kentling came up to me and said, "I don't see how you guys could have lost $700,000 this year." I went overseas and worked in Saudi Arabia for two-and-a-half years, came back and went to a Wings game, and walked up to him. He remembered me and said, "Remember what I asked you?" I said, "Yeah." He said, "I now know how you can [lose that much money]." [laughs]

CHAPTER 10

An Oral History

Curve It Like Chapman

———

"I don't think we have enough time! You don't
have enough chapters in the book!"

- BILL KENTLING, ON ANDY CHAPMAN STORIES.

(Don Marler/Missile Magazine) Andy Chapman after one of his many goals.

ANDY CHAPMAN WAS THE BEST *Christmas present the Wings ever received. The 19-year-old Englishman, originally from the East End of London, left the ASL's California Sunshine and arrived in Wichita on December 25th, 1979, smack dab in the middle of the first season. Both the Wichita Wings and Andy Chapman would never be the same. His performance during the Wings first season was strong, achieving the sixth highest points total on the team. But Chapman's best years would be ahead of him. He would have an enormous impact on the pitch over the course of his career with the Wings, which spanned from 1980-85, and then again from 1988-90. Chapman would lead the team in goals scored in 1980-81, 1982-83, and 1983-84. He appears among the Wings all-time career leaders at fifth in goals scored, with 221, and third in game-winning goals, at 29.*[1]

TERRY NICHOLL, MIDFIELDER, WICHITA WINGS: Andy was a beautiful finisher. He could score with his left and his right...and his bicycle kicks were fantastic. He brought a special kind of goal to the team...

The impact of Chapman resonated just as strongly off the field. He could be seen in advertisements for local companies, hanging out at the Hatch Cover on the weekends, at grade schools demonstrating the game to the kids, and at youth clinics as well. Everyone loved him. But the ladies REALLY loved him. And his leather pants were legendary.

ROY TURNER, HEAD COACH, WICHITA WINGS: I knew about Andy Chapman from the California Sunshine in the ASL. [They were] one of the best ASL teams.

KEVIN KEWLEY, FORWARD/MIDFIELDER, WICHITA WINGS: Andy was very popular with the girls. And such a smart guy.

ROY TURNER: Smarter than everybody realized.

KEVIN KEWLEY: He was savvy in how he related to people. He played soccer the same way. Very smart and knew what he was doing. A great goal-scorer. He was always laughing and joking and didn't take life too seriously, which sometimes drove Roy mad. He was a great character to be around.

ROY TURNER: Andy's money took a big jump and he was very money savvy.

KEVIN KEWLEY: He didn't want to rent a house, he bought one. He didn't just put money in the bank; he bought houses that he could eventually maybe rent out if he ever left.

VIRGINIA CREAMER, ANGELS COORDINATOR, ASSISTANT DI-RECTOR OF OPERATIONS, WICHITA WINGS: Andy was very nice. He brought me back a book about the Diana-Charles wedding [from England]. The first time I met Andy Chapman was when we were in the old office that first year. He and Joe Howarth and Mike Custer came walking in. I asked somebody, "Who is that little kid?" Somebody said, "Oh, that's one of our new players." "Are you kidding me?" [laughs]

CHARLIE MINSHULL-FORD, EQUIPMENT MANAGER, WICHITA WINGS, 1982-85: Andy Chapman was a different character...he was funny. He dressed a little weird, but that was just Andy. He was just being himself. He was fun to be around at after-parties...he'd make everybody laugh. Kids liked him a lot. People really liked Andy. I know the ladies did.

TERRY NICHOLL: Andy Chapman...another unique character. I don't know how Roy did it. He seemed to blend these characters in. Andy was so "boy band"... he was like the lead singer of the biggest boy band. He could wear anything and look brilliant. He could have shaved his head bald and that would have been the new fashion. He was so in touch with fashion, music, London...He could talk... He had a silky tongue. He could converse and he was funny. He and Jeff Bourne were SO funny together. I'd just sit there and giggle. I was lucky to be around those lads.

Women would SWOON at him. He and Ian Anderson were chatting up this lady at the back of a plane. She was having a good time, mainly with Andy, and then we got to wherever we were going. This lady was met the airport by a famous wrestler. [laughs] They were coming off last, and we were hanging around, seeing if he managed to pull this lady...and have a date or something. We are all waiting, and saw this wrestler; he had long, curly blonde hair and was built like the side of a house. We were thinking, "Where's Andy?" Andy and Ian came off last, still chatting up this girl, and this huge mean wrestler was there, waiting. We didn't know. Suddenly they realized what was happening. Andy's face changed...from "boy band" and chatty...to "Oh my God, I've got to get out of here."

BRUCE HAERTL, WINGS PLAY-BY-PLAY ANNOUNCER, KFH RADIO: I've got a ton of Andy Chapman stories that I am not willing to share with you [laughs]. Andy loved people and people loved Andy. It didn't make any difference where we were or who we were with, Andy related to people on the most fundamental level. He had that little twinkle in his eye and devilish look. He enjoyed getting to know people and was not shy about it, that's for sure. Boy, I tell you what, a guy who could do it on both ends. He could be a lot of fun on one night and then the next night he was all about scoring goals. Andy loved to compete and loved to win. He was always one of those guys who showed up to play and play well. It really meant something to Andy Chapman. As probably as fun loving of an athlete as I've ever been around.

Sometimes, you just need to let a bloke from the East End tell his own story. No one else can tell it better...

ANDY CHAPMAN, FORWARD, WICHITA WINGS: I grew up in a council flat [public housing] in Dagenham, which is where the Ford plant was on the East End of London. My mum never drove a car, which was normal because none of my mate's moms did either. I wouldn't say we lived in poverty, but we didn't have a washer or dryer and we didn't have a telephone. You didn't think you were without because no one had stuff. My brother Nigel was seven years older. He was a good footballer. I used to play with him in pickup games on Sunday. All the dads used to come out. We'd throw down our sweaters and created a couple goals. I can remember being about four or five playing one Sunday and there's dads in their regular street clothes playing, an old guy was playing, a couple teenagers, there was a tomboy called Bobbi, she would play.

Nigel was very good...technically gifted. We thought he might go on to become a pro. I can remember him beating players and giving it to me in front of the goal where I used to score all the time, [even though I was] very young. Someone said, "Your brother's just a goal hanger," which means a "cherry picker." Nigel said, "Yeah, but he's really good at it." I always remember that. He used to work with me up against this brick building that used to house all the trash cans. The building used to smell, but it had a really lovely flat wall. We never had a leather ball, ever. Never had a new pair of football boots till I was 13. He would work on my left foot, and then my right foot. We'd do it and do it and do it. When I was on a club team he would drive the van. All these lads from the East End of London would go out and kick the asses of the teams in the suburbs because that's what you wanted to do. That was the motivation.

As we moved through I got to be 13 or 14...I had become identified and the top clubs were after me. At 15, I could have signed for any team that was in the First Division. I basically made my choice with no help.... my father never took an active role in my decisions only because he didn't have a father. You're considered older there because you leave school at 16. At 14 when your 'nan and granddad ask you what you want to be when you get older, you actually have to give them an answer...which might be, "Oh, I'm gonna be a bus driver, a train driver, a policeman, a plumber." Any kind of blue-collar work you thought you could do. At 14 you were supposed to have a friggin' answer. That was the mentality at the time. I signed with Arsenal at 15..."schoolboy forms" they called them, because I was still in school.

I graduated from school in July of 1976 and went straight to Arsenal as an apprentice professional. I [became] an apprentice professional with one of the clubs that had an incredible history. I turned pro at 17. I was thinking I was gonna have a career there. I was playing in the reserves. I was making 55 pounds a week, which is not a lot of money. There wasn't a ton of money in the game back then. Just to give you something to think about, that summer of 1977 Arsenal splashed out the largest transfer fee for a player. They bought Malcolm McDonald of Newcastle for 333,000 pounds. Now they go for 50 million pounds. I think he was making 200 pounds a week.

When you left school you lived at your mom and dad's. You paid to live at home. When I was 16 at Arsenal, as an apprentice, they were giving my mom and dad 12 pounds a week. The reason they paid that was so my parents could buy food so I could eat well...and to help in the household because they knew everybody struggled. I had to pay that out of the 50 pounds a week I made.

I was playing in the reserves in April of '78. I was playing on a very strong reserve team with international players because we'd got a new coach the year before and the coach of the first team wanted to offload the previous coach's players. I was one of the youngest on it. At that time, we knew that the older professional players in their 30s were getting the opportunity to come over to America. We had seen on TV what was going on in America with the New York Cosmos and Pele...the Seattle Sounders. It was big. A lot of older players wanted to go over in the off-season, which was summer.

I wasn't very happy at Arsenal. I felt like a foreigner. There were only three or four of us from London. The rest were Irish. It crossed my mind to play for the West Ham United...The Hammers! I was hoping I'd go there and continue and see if I could get into the first team there. I do remember a bit of advice I got from Bob McNabb, who was a left defender for Arsenal. He was older. You would hear these stories of older players who had retired and were driving taxi cabs or working in pubs. There was story after story of that. I went to Bob McNabb and told him I'd had the opportunity to go to America..."What do I do?" He said, "You go. Forget about this lot here. Go." This was a guy who'd been at Arsenal for 11 years, played 250+ matches, maybe more. Roger Thompson was the youth team coach at Arsenal, who I had played for. He told me to go. Bob McNabb ended up coaching at Tacoma, and I saw him at the Kansas Coliseum. Growing up and watching players, Charlie Cooke [future Wings coach] was a superstar at Chelsea. They were all in America. It was ironic that McNabb walked in with [Tacoma]; the last time I'd seen him I was thinking about going to America. Suddenly, being in America and making a name for myself and being considered a bit of a star. It was great, because it confirmed [all that].

We were playing one day and a guy [Derek Lawther] came up to me and asked to have a word with me. "Do you want to come and play in Los Angeles? I'll give you 100 pounds a week plus an apartment." You have to understand that my dad was making maybe 15 pounds a week at that time. I'd done an essay when I was 12 saying I wanted to be a professional footballer and my goal was to make 100 pounds a week, which seemed like a huge amount of money. 100 pounds a week was unthinkable. That essay always stayed in my memory...I still have it. Suddenly, when the guy said "100 pounds a week," I said, "Yeah, I'm coming." I went home on the train to see my mom and dad and I said, "I'm going to America." They asked, "When?" and I said, "In three days." I left on April 6th of 1978. I went off, and they were obviously worried, but at 18 at that time you felt like you were a man.

When I landed in America, culturally it was so different. In America, you weren't getting out of school till you're 21, which was the weirdest concept I could imagine, because we never had the opportunity for university, college, or further education. That wasn't an option for us where we came from. There was talk of Arsenal holding up my release. As it turned out I owned [my contract] and they had to pay ME off some money, which is how I got the money for that first condo I bought.

My goal was to make enough money [during that first summer in America] to pay a deposit to buy mum and dad a house, because I saved every penny. I sent home $3,000 in $100 bills one at a time. I sent it home each week to my parents. When I was making something like seven times what my dad made, it was just natural that you send the money home.

I thought I'd come back in September and continue my career at Arsenal. I was a changed person when I came back from America. I'd seen things I'd never dreamed existed. I always tell people the way it hit me was that one day we'd gone on a road trip: I had breakfast in New York, because we woke up from playing a game there, and had breakfast at the airport. The plane stopped in St. Louis and I had lunch there. And that night we landed in Los Angeles and I had dinner there. Now, a boy from the East End of London doing that... is unheard of. I was always thankful for that and always have been.

When I went home it hit me how bad things were in the East End. How gray it was, how desperate it seemed. How my mom and dad were living from week to week. I lived with a family that summer in Newport Beach, California: Bill and Jan Martin...Bill was a big oil exec. They lived in this sprawling house high up in the hills. Jan, she was a financial advisor. She asked about my parents money and I explained, "No, Jan, they don't have any money. They get paid on a Friday and it's gone by Wednesday of the following week just to pay their bills." Just a completely different world. So when I went back [to England] all that was magnified and I was changed. So, I couldn't wait to get back [to America].

My uncle, Stuart Underwood, was very big in non-league football. I was able to train with him, and he was David Beckham's first coach. He became quite famous [because of that] and had done an advertisement in the London Evening Standard, looking for all-star players. He went on to become famous because he was in Beckham's book. He and my Aunt Bettie were at Beckham's wedding. It was Stuart who I ended up training with all winter.

I came back to America in 1979, on March 1st, and I pretty much knew when I got on that plane that I wasn't coming back. I was coming to make my life in America. I was with the [ASL's] California Sunshine for two seasons. Bob Ridley, who Roy knew very well because they were together in Dallas, took over coaching in 1979 and we played at the El Camino College, where the [US] National Team played at that time. The World Cup was going on at the time and the only place you could see it was at the Rose Bowl on a big grainy screen. Ridley coached me that summer and may have had a conversation with Roy Turner about me, when Joe Howarth told him there was a guy who could score goals in California.

It's quite a unique story. I was playing outdoor soccer in California. I'd come over in 1978 and met Joe Howarth and was playing in Orange County. I was only 18 and Joe was older and helped me a little bit. I'd had a great summer and made the decision it was America I wanted to be in and continue my career. In the summer of '79, the word was spreading about that new indoor league, the MISL, that had just started, and had a few franchises. My goal by the end of the summer was to latch on to an indoor soccer team. Back then it was complicated because you had to have H1 visas in order to play and there were restrictions. So it was quite a complicated process of being able to sign on for a team. But Joe [Howarth] was an American citizen and at the end of that season (we were playing for the California Sunshine) he went off to Wichita and started to play for the new franchise that Roy Turner was heading. Roy had taken a bunch of guys from the Dallas Tornado and started the indoor team.

I hung around in California at the end of the [outdoor] season and in October, November, and December was working construction and playing some semi-pro ball and waiting to see if I would ever get a call. Their season had started and [the Wings] were struggling a little bit and [Howarth] told Roy about a 19-year-old back in California that had been a pro at Arsenal and he should take a look at me. I ended up flying into Wichita, KS on Christmas Day, 1979 and it was a complete culture shock for me.

I flew first-class, which was very nice. I sat next to Dyan Cannon, who was quite the famous actress at the time. We got to talking and I told her I was going to Wichita. I landed around 6:00 pm and Jackie Knapp picked me up. My America had been Los Angeles, and flying into glamorous cities like New York and San Francisco, and all the outdoor teams...I'd never been to Kansas and the Midwest. There I was, driving from a very small airport after coming from LAX and driving down Kellogg, and I can remember thinking: "What the heck am I doing here?" [laughs]

[Jackie] actually took me to a Christmas party, and I met Kevin Kewley and he was just fantastic. Obviously, there was an English connection there. I was only 19 and they were all a little bit older than that. Kevin was probably about 24 at the time. So, they made me feel really welcome and so did Jimmy Ryan. Jimmy was just fantastic...an older pro I'd heard of, who started off at Manchester United and played at Luton. The guys were great and I felt comfortable. I stayed in an apartment and was there for a tryout. I worked out all week and we trained the day after Christmas. The boys had taken a liking to me; I was a hard worker and wanted to impress. Basically, I was waiting to hear if they were going to sign me.

I can remember a sort of, defining moment in my life...[on whether I was] making the right decision to leave my family and coming to America. It was the days before all the technology that we have today. I can remember being in an apartment in Wichita on New Year's Eve and it was probably around 11:30 pm and there was no electricity because of the previous tenant, Mike Ivanow... somehow the bill hadn't got paid. So, there was no electricity, and I'm lying on the couch in this furnished apartment. Ivanow had gone back to San Francisco so I was just on my own, and was going from the 1970s to the 1980s, and was feeling a little bit sorry for myself...missing all my friends I had grown up with...and my family. I was laying there and suddenly I said, "Hey, stop feeling sorry for yourself, here! There are so many people in the world who would like to change positions with you right now."

I just woke up and it was the first day of the '80s, and I've got to say that the 1980s was probably the greatest decade that ever existed. They signed me the next day; I played in my first game in Detroit against the Detroit Lightning. It just started a journey that I could never dreamed how big it was going to get. I'll never forget that first season. I was very young and I had done quite well and the fans had taken to me. At the end of that season, I went to Cleveland to play outdoor, and I was delighted when Roy and Bill Kentling said, "We'd like to sign you again for the 1980-81 season."

At that time, it felt comfortable being around players, and Roy was a coach, so I was respectful, and he was like one of the guys. He'd been a player in Dallas and had been a part of a whole brigade of English and Scottish players that came in 1968 to start the soccer boom in America, just prior to Pele coming. There was a lot of respect there from me. And because of the age I was, I was respectful of older people. Back then (it's different now) we were all like a family, and he was like the dad. Wichita had become my home and the team had become my purpose.

...Kim [Roentved] and myself could relate to each other because we were the same age. There's a spot in my heart for Kim. There's a spot in my heart for Kevin and Roy. There truly is...Playing for Wichita was all I ever wanted to do. Being with all the players, the characters, Norman Piper, Jimmy Ryan, the Danish Connection [Jorgen Kristensen, Kim Roentved, etc.]...we would hang out together. We'd go training, you'd have the games, and then we'd hit the bars afterwards and there would always be a party. Roy was there with the guys...it's just how it was back then. Nowadays, with the technology [we have], [somebody] would take a photograph of a player in a bar that's had a few drinks and having a sing-song and it would be all over the internet with people saying, "Look how unprofessional they are!"

We were very professional on the field, but we used to like to let loose after the games. You have to understand, it was a unique situation because you are dealing with the early '80s, with a bunch of foreign players who were trying to promote the game of soccer. I truly and firmly believed that the indoor game was going to be the next big sport for sure. We were always a part of promoting the game and trying to spread the word. I did literally hundreds upon hundreds of appearances. Over the course of two years, I think I did 100 school assemblies. We were always doing appearances and meeting with the fans...things they are actually doing now back in England in the Premier League...just a copy of what was going on in the American soccer scene in the early 1980s. They've got a great product over there now, but a lot of the ideas they stole from the indoor game way back.

Part of that job of promoting the team is that there was an after-match party where all the fans and boosters wanted to touch the players and get autographs. I can remember being in the Barn [the Coliseum] and 7,000 people wanted autographs one night after the game. We had to stop it at midnight. We always had a great following. The time was just right. Wichita had never had a professional sports team to sink their teeth into. We got to know the fans by name. They got to know about your personal life, your families; it was just fantastic.

I never played [indoor] before. There was a game in England that was very popular called Five-a-Side. It was played on a small field, and I had always played [that], obviously without the boards. I had always been strong at it, so I felt very, very comfortable [indoors]. From a career standpoint, I had gone to play outdoor and scored 12 goals in 1978 in 23 games, which is a very good ratio. In 1979, I scored another 12 goals. In 1980, I increased it...scored maybe 15 or 16 (I had been injured part of the season as well). But in 1981...after playing three indoor seasons, where you have to be very sharp, and the goal is smaller, with a high concentration level....When I did that transition, and I did it for six seasons, the calendar year was me going from outdoor straight into indoor, straight into outdoor, etc...when I came to play [outdoor] for the Detroit Express, I scored 22 goals in 22 matches. So, it really sharpened me up for the outdoor game because it just seemed like I had acres of space. Because in indoor, space is at a premium, and you have to be a good player with great vision and anticipation to be a goal-scorer.

I really worked on my craft. I would stay behind at practice...first one there, last to leave. For a couple reasons: so I could get better as a player, and I had nothing else to do. Being a soccer player was my life. Why go home and sit on the couch and watch TV? I'd actually go workout in the afternoon. It was about becoming the best I could possibly be. I was in a zone. Also, I had a reputation as a single guy who liked to go out at night. I just wanted to make sure no one was saying, "Look, Andy is lazy because he's too busy being a party boy." So, it was to compensate. I was enjoying life as a 21-year-old outside the game, but I never stopped thinking about [soccer].

I was very fortunate to have such an excellent team, with Mike Dowler, and then Kim Roentved, and Jorgen Kristensen...I played on a line with Jorgen, who just loved to set up goals. There is nothing better for a goal-scorer. I could score individual goals that you can do because of some of the things that you work on, like receiving the ball at your feet and spinning and scoring. But there were also goals I scored where Jorgen would beat two or three guys and lay it to me. I had the simple job of tapping it in...but it's not a simple job because there are a lot of players that can't tap a ball in from three or four feet out in the heat of the game because it's a lot harder to do than people realize. Based on the players and how we were, it enabled me to turn those great chances into goals. With that comes confidence. My confidence was sky high. I never ever thought, when we went into overtime, that I WASN'T going to score the game-winning goal. In my head, I said "I'm going to score the goal." And a lot of times that happened. Not every time, but a few.

———

In my family it's still a standard joke: in one of the magazine [interviews] they asked, "What is your hobby?" I said, "Thinking." [laughs] "What were you thinking when you said that?" my family always asks. I said that because I used to love to think. I got that from my father. He left school at 13, grew up in poverty in the East End of London. He was a self-educated man. He was always making me think about things. I can remember so many sayings he used to tell me...and as I started growing older, they started to come true. My son, Dillon, is in Los Angeles, and was born in 1989 when I played in Wichita...He's a soccer player and I told him that everything I learned inside the lines [could be applied outside].

When you go into the arena and go onto the field, you are crossing the line and are there. And everything you have and is required of you, which is your responsibilities and duties on the field, your responsibilities to your teammates, being honest...all that I could apply outside the field. I used to bring Dillon up like that. Everything I learned outside the lines I learned inside the lines. I wouldn't say I was smart in the sense of a Rhodes Scholar. But I was very street smart. You had to be, growing in the East End. The main driving force in me, apart from soccer, was where I came from. I wanted to get out of that area.

Growing up on government property in the East End of London is not the most desirable thing you want to be able to do. That was the fuel in me to become better. When I was suddenly earning amounts of money that were way beyond whatever I thought I was gonna earn, all I did was save it and invest it. I purchased houses and stuff like that. I grew up in a government property. My mom had never driven a car. My brother and I grew up in a house with no heat. My dad would always point to a home that was owned by somebody and say, "See that house there? I could have purchased that for $1,000 and now it's worth $10,000." My brother and I would hear that all the time, so I always remembered that. So at 21 in California, I took every penny I'd saved, which was $12,000, and bought a condo in Anaheim Hills. 18% interest on a land contract. I didn't sleep for two days. Then, because I couldn't afford to live in it, I had to rent it out. That investment wiped out every single penny that I had. The reason I did it was because my dad used to say, "If I'd purchased that or done that..." And then I realized that I didn't care if I lost it all because at least I'd never have to say, "I should have done that...I should have purchased that."

So I did it and never looked back. I got into being motivated because we were a long way from our families and it WAS a big deal. The team was your family, but at times you felt alone. I always thought at the end of the season there's going to be a reason why I played that season and I'm going to save and purchase something as an investment so I can say that's why I was there. So in the '82-83 season the purpose of me playing that year and doing well was to save a lot of my salary to purchase a home in Michigan. So I can always look back at the home I have and go, "The '82-83 season purchased that home."

I lived with Jimmy Ryan on the west side in 1982. It was an incredible time in my life. His daughter Jane used to wake me up in the morning for Jimmy and I to "go to work." She'd bring a cup of tea in for me. I loved Jimmy, he ended up being best man at my wedding. My wife and I went back to see him in England and he was really struggling, selling sneakers...A few years later he became an assistant at Manchester United. You pretty much knew you were getting caught up in something exciting.

In 1983 I got a year-round contract. I would get phone calls from players who were back in England and they'd ask me to come back and play there. A guy called me and said, "I want you to come and play back in the football league." I asked how much, and it was like 4 times less than what I was making. I said, "I can't afford to [come to England]." There was still a part of me that wanted to say I'd played in the English League, for my brother. To say I'd played in the First Division, or won an FA Cup medal. The reality was I wasn't going to turn down all that money just to play in England. I'd established deep roots in the USA: With a place in California, and two places in Wichita; a condo on the west side, and a duplex with Joe Howarth and Don Tobin. I couldn't leave. Was there always that romantic notion of my school friends seeing me play for the Hammers? Yeah. But I remember saying in an interview, "It's not how many medals I've won, or how many league games I've played, it's how I've done for my family, financially. How have I maximized my career in something I've been blessed with." At the time it might have sounded mercenary, but that was not true. I was fed up with reading stories in the Sunday newspapers of ex-players, like Tony Curry, who played for England, who was a superstar, who was driving a cab. Or guys who were homeless. That wasn't going to happen to me.

I always respected Roy because back then he owned a house and had investments. I respected that. He seemed to be someone that had some depth. He was being smart with his money. They used to make fun of me...one year they had Subarus with the players' names on them. They asked, "Do you want one?" I said, "No way. Why would I want one of those? So they can look in the parking lot at the [store] and know I'm in there? I don't want that."

Those first few years at Wichita, I was piecing it together. There was the standard $2,500 a month with a car and an apartment. In 1981 I negotiated a great contract and now had the security of a two-year contract that was close to $50,000 per year. That was huge. I suddenly went to see Brian Begley at the car dealership, and he showed me a Jag XJS convertible. It was red. He said, "Get in it." It was everything I'd ever thought about. I'd never had a new car. I asked, "How much is it?" It was $29,000-30,000 and I COULD buy it. "You know what, there's no way I'll ever spend that kind of money on these flashy cars. One day I'll be in a position where I can buy two of these and I won't even skip a beat, but right now I can't invest that sort of [money in a car]...that's like half of a condo."

I ended up buying a used white Volkswagen convertible in mint condition. It was $4,750 and I paid cash for it. I drove it for like five years and I sold it for $4,500. These were the sort of things I would do. Someone had actually torn my convertible top at one point. I took it in and asked how much it would cost to fix, and the guy said, "Take my 12-year-old daughter to lunch, it will make her month." I said, "I can do that." That was something else the players loved doing. Because you were well known, we would go to the hospital and visit sick children and make people's days. I loved that part of being a professional footballer. When I looked down at those kids, I would think "I'm going to make a difference to that kid." I would get letters asking if I would call up their daughter because she's really not doing well in school and she's not doing her homework and if you called her I think it might help. I called her and asked, "How'd you like to come to a Wings game?" And she'd be screaming, and then I said, "Well, I'll get you tickets, but you need to do something for me. You've got to do your homework." They'd become part of my life. They'd write to me. That was a great part of being in the public eye.

When we were 15 and 16 back in England, fashion was really big. When you came from a poor area you might measure yourself by having a new pair of Levi's. I was just really into clothes. That was a big part. I'd go to a game and make sure my clothes were pressed...I'd put on a pair of leather pants. [laughs] We did a series of modeling jobs for Sheplers. Before there was Beckham, there was Chapman! Curve it like Chapman! Fashion was a big part of life. Nowadays I don't care about it one bit. Back then, a lot of the trendy players would put their gear on and hit the after-match party.

BILL KENTLING, GENERAL MANAGER, WICHITA WINGS, 1980-86:
[Andy Chapman stories:] I don't think we have enough time! You don't have enough chapters in the book! If you'd ever meet a guy willing to take a dare, it was Andy Chapman. He was a free spirit and a clever kid. You look at some of his actions and you think, "What a dolt." But he wasn't a dolt; he just was very independent of spirit. He believed that for two hours a week he'd give you everything he had in the game, and the rest of the time was his to behave as he chose. He saw America as a candy store...and he unwrapped a lot of candy. [laughs]

One of the things you could win was a trip to Kansas City with the team, because it was a bus ride. So we ran a contest through Mid-Kansas [Bank], and some little kid won the contest. And, oh my God he was thrilled. His parents brought him to the bus. We were riding to KC on the turnpike and [Don] Tobin and Chapman were chatting up the little kid. This kid's 12. He was saying that his sister was really gorgeous and was named the homecoming queen in her high school. So, Chapman says, "Hey, do you have any naked pictures of your sister?" The kid's embarrassed, and says, "Well, no." And Tobin says, "Do you want to see some?" True story.

CHRISTY ROBERTS, WINGS FAN: I was always an Andy Chapman fan. One evening my mom and I were at the old Garfield's restaurant and Andy was there and we got to talking about school stuff. He taught me how to remember the Great Lakes...H-O-M-E-S: Huron, Ontario, Michigan, Erie, Superior. I have never forgotten that.

ANDY CHAPMAN: H-O-M-E-S, Huron, Ontario, Michigan, Erie, and Superior!...I don't coach anymore, but when we used to scrimmage [with my youth teams], I said I was going to give the ball to the most intelligent team. I'd pick a country and ask, "What's the capital?" I had kids that learned every single capital. They started making me look in books for countries they didn't know about!

CHAPTER 11

An Oral History

Wings...Version 2.0

———

"I got a bonus one year for ONLY losing $200,000.
Nobody realizes how great these owners were.
Nobody made money at owning this team."

- ROY TURNER

TRUE TO FORM, NORMAN PIPER was, again, the first player signed by the new ownership group. Though the terms of his deal were not released, on June 24th The Eagle reported that he would likely make more than the league average of $2,500 a month. This was likely due to his appearance on the 1979-80 All-Star team, alongside Jimmy Ryan and George Ley. Unlike his first season, Piper would not be "on loan" from any other team. He would belong solely to the Wings.[1] Next, four days later, came Kevin Kewley, who had scored 20 goals, and assisted on 21 others during the Wings' first campaign.[2] Kewley spent part of that summer playing in the ASL for the Miami Americans.

KEVIN KEWLEY, MIDFIELDER, WICHITA WINGS: I went to play in Miami in the off-season for Ron Newman. After a month, I played two games and they ran into money trouble. I was their highest earner. They wanted me to take a pay cut. I said, "No," and they gave me a month's salary and I left.

Joe Howarth and Andy Chapman would be signed next. Both spent the summer playing for the Cleveland Cobras in the ASL.[3] Though many familiar names would be seen on the pitch that year, there was also quite a bit of turnover. Former Tornado players Chris Collins, Glenn Myernick, Freddie Garcia, Caesar Cervin, and Omar Gomez were among the 13 Wings that did not come back. Cervin and Collins would return to the Tornado. Myernick went back to the NASL as well, joining the Portland Timbers. Garcia retired upon leaving the Wings. Gomez would leave for two seasons but returned to Wichita in 1982.[4] Carl Christensen, Frank Barton, Art Welch, Willie Anderson, Garry Ayre, Juan Carlos Michia, Mike Ivanow, and Roland Sikinger also left the Wings after their first season.

There was also a great deal of change in the front office. Tom Marshall, Jackie Knapp, Ray Denton, Ward Lawrence, Bob Becker, and the Great Plains crew had all exited the stage. New GM Bill Kentling would quickly make his mark on the "new" Wings through his flair for the dramatic. He brought a more theatrical style of management to the team...and it worked. Due to the change in ownership, he was working with what could almost be described as a "blank slate." Kentling selected three Wichita State University graduates to lead his team. He named Steve Shaad as the director of media relations. Shaad had spent two years as the WSU women's sports information director. Dave Bennett, a former KAKE-TV sales rep, became the sales director. Lastly, there was the one familiar face: Virginia Creamer, who took on the role of director of operations.[5]

BILL KENTLING, GENERAL MANAGER, WICHITA WINGS, 1980-86:

There was no organization. It wasn't anything, because nobody had been signed. So one of the first things we did was to sign Roy. I was able to put together a front office staff of Steve Shaad, Dave Bennett, and Virginia Creamer...really a top-notch staff. We put them in that little storefront [on Broadway]. What I really learned from Roy was that there was an interest in the community. If marketed properly, and with ticket prices at a reasonable level, there was an opportunity for a lot of people to become interested in this. Roy had a vision of a lot of youth soccer, community involvement and youth soccer camps, and getting to the parents through the kids. I learned through Roy that Sam Fulco, who ran the

Kansas Coliseum, would be a willing partner in terms of working with us and not holding us up on rent. There were a lot of assets that could be picked up and put in place. In terms of the first year's operations, I don't have a clear recollection of it because I hadn't been to a game and wasn't intimate with the product. Typical of any first year organization, you're going to have mistakes, particularly with a sport as new as this.

You can ask any player from that era: We crossed every crick and shook every hand, doing those youth camps. That was the centerpiece of Roy's idea of how you'd grow a franchise. We did so many that we had a player who scheduled these youth camps...[they were] free camps. We also did a great deal of traditional marketing. But we understood that nobody had graduated from the "University of Wings," or the "University of the MISL," so we had no alumni base in the same way that WSU had. We had to BUILD our own alumni base and we did that through the kids.

There was never any doubt that Roy Turner would remain head coach under the new regime.

BILL KENTLING: I listened to a couple guys who I had respect for: Randy Brown was the sports editor of the paper and Ron Loewen was the general manager at KAKE. I leaned on them to tell me about the Wings. And they both knew Roy. They were very persuasive that a) The Wings were good for the community, and b) That Roy was the proper guy to have as the coach. A lot of times in life, you rely on the people whose judgments you trust.

Before the home opener could take place, change happened at the very top of the club. On November 21st, 1980, The Eagle reported that Sam Hardage would be stepping down as Chairman of the Wings, in favor of Frank Carney. Speculation centered on Hardage's possible nomination as Secretary of the Air Force.[6] Though he didn't join the Reagan administration, in 1982 Hardage won the Republican nomination for governor. He would lose to John Carlin, the popular incumbent Democrat.

The people who invested in the Wings in the early 1980s weren't small-timers. These were men and women with money, power, and influence. They were focused on *building up Wichita and dedicated their resources to doing so. Investing in the new team wasn't exactly a "sure bet." It was projected that the team would lose about $300,000 in the first year. Kentling explained to* The Eagle's *Randy Brown that "this is not a profit motive for this ownership...There is no reason to be in this. The only reason to be in it is to help the city begin to grow again."* [7]

BILL KENTLING: Carney puts together general partners, and we recruited limited partners. Because what we found was that there were people who were willing to go on the line as a general partner, guaranteeing losses. We found there was another group, folks like myself, who would write a check, but if there was gonna be a loss, wanted to limit those losses, but wanted to do it in sort of a Green Bay Packers kind of way. Then we found there was this third group who were willing to write a one-time check, and that was it..."Don't come see me again." Willard Garvey would have been in that last category. [He] wrote a $50,000 check and thought it was good for the community and wanted to help.

But were this third group of investors expecting to see this money again?

BILL KENTLING: Oh no. Trust me, this was like the art museum or the symphony. Nobody ever thinks they are going to make a profit at the end of the symphony season. Were there some guys who thought because Carney was involved it would make some money? It's possible, but I can't imagine who, because we sold it on the basis that we were doing this for the community.

Various local business luminaries chose to become general partners in the team.

BILL KENTLING: Ken Brasted was the head of Mid-Kansas Savings and Loan...he and his wife Sherry were great. Bud, Robert, and Joan Beren, who were in the oil business...Don Cordes was an attorney for Koch...James Remsberg, also oil. Dick Upton was the head of the Chamber of Commerce. Frank Barton and later his business partner [at Rent-a-Center] Tom Devlin came in.

DR. JAY PRICE, PROFESSOR OF HISTORY, WICHITA STATE UNIVERSITY: A couple of things are happening. We have to think of this almost generationally. If you think of a Frank Carney who has come of age in the 1950s, or

Tom Devlin, they're starting out in their businesses, Pizza Hut and Rent-a-Center. By the 1970s they are looking for new investments and new opportunities. Pizza Hut will become part of Pepsico. The Pizza Hut headquarters, which had been so central here, is now part of a larger corporation. Again, corporate decisions are now made elsewhere. Coleman, which had been a fixture of the Wichita economy since the turn of the century, is now part of Sunbeam. Again and again and again, what had been local corporations are now part of national chains.

In a lot of ways, the middle decades of the 20th century, the 1930s through the 1960s, are the Golden Age of the family business. The '70s see a dramatic shift. Some companies, like supermarkets, either grow and play with the big boys, or you retire and sell it. You have a generation of folks that come of age in the mid-20th century...Olive Ann Beech, Dwayne Wallace, the Farhas, the Ablahs...they are leaders in the community in the '50s and the '60s.

In many ways, we were a city where a handful of families got together at the Candle Club and made decisions...that's how things happened. That's not the case by the '70s...by then that generation is now senior management, and also on the verge of retirement. When they retire, at this level of income and activity, they don't just take up a hobby or play golf. Investment is their hobby. Investment in real estate or other ventures is a creative enterprise, every bit as much as gardening and model trains. Garvey is another perfect example. He's a little bit younger than the others. It's a creative outlet. They like investing. This is part of the mindset we are looking at.

ROY TURNER, HEAD COACH, WICHITA WINGS: I had a very special relationship with both Frank Carney and [future managing partner] Bill Oliver. I know that if I hadn't been there doing this, they might have got out. The Rolph family as well. They were the three major owners that I dealt with. Carney and Oliver both came to Jamaica for my wedding. They were very good to me and my family. Even as a coach they'd take me to the league meetings. We always had one owner that went. Kentling would represent Frank. [In later years] Bill Oliver started coming as well.

Carney got involved with the team because of the president of the Chamber of Commerce. He was convinced it was good for the community. Bill Oliver, Frank Carney, and Darrel Rolph, though Rolph loved soccer too, I would say unequivocally they were involved because it was a good thing for the community. I got a bonus one year for ONLY losing $200,000. Nobody realizes how great these owners were. Nobody made money at owning this team.

KEVIN KEWLEY: Back in the early days it was such a family thing. My wife joined an investment club with some of the owners' wives. That kind of stuff didn't happen later on. Those people would do anything for you and help you in any way possible.

BILL KENTLING: We started hiring and put together that staff. It was the single hottest summer in the history of Wichita, KS. Every day we got up and seemed like 100 degrees at dawn. We spent the summer selling smoke, in the form of sponsorships and season tickets, to play teams you've never heard of, with players you aren't familiar with.

One of the keys to success was finding local companies that would be willing to step up and sponsor the team. The business community did not disappoint...

BILL KENTLING: Kent Brasted was great...Mid-Kansas was huge. Bob Schwan at House of Schwan, at Budweiser, stepped up. The Coca-Cola guys stepped up. What we were really looking for were folks to buy signs and to sponsor games. Some of the things I was doing I copied from my time with Ray Dumont at the National Baseball Congress. One of the things I was interested in was for fans to be able to swing by Mid-Kansas Savings and Loan to pick up discounted tickets, and Mid-Kansas would advertise that in the newspaper or on radio/TV...to get discount tickets to fill up the [arena] because we owned the concessions, and if people weren't [in the arena] they couldn't eat those hot dogs and drink that pop.

Roy at this time, and assistant coach George Ley, were recruiting players. I wanted to get a true baseline on how many fans there were...I didn't want any fudge on attendance. We opened the season and everything on opening night was a full-paid ticket...on November 22nd against Chicago. We had about 3,000 people, which was not going to be enough. But almost all of those were season ticket holders, and we knew that was the key. We did an awful lot of research that first year. When we captured you as a season ticket holder we captured an awful lot of demographic and attitudinal information about you so we'd know the kind of folks who were drawn to the Wings. We just wanted to make sure we were always going to fish where the fish were biting. My first year was getting smart about our customer base.

TOM SHINE, REPORTER/EDITOR, THE WICHITA EAGLE: They went out in the parking lot and wrote down which county each tag was from. They had a cowbell on their front door and they'd know how well the week was going based on how much it rang. They did simple marketing stuff that Bill brought from Pizza Hut. They would get demographic data and go to advertisers and say, "Here's our season ticket base and here's our average income. Would you like to be in front of these people that make $75,000?"

BILL KENTLING: My relationship with Roy was a good relationship. Roy is cheap and that really helped. I say "cheap" in the most complimentary way. One of the things I explained to Roy early on: nobody in our group was named Steinbrenner. We did not have unlimited resources. So we could not make a lot of mistakes with our money because we aren't Chicago, New York, or LA. So Roy understood early on that the coaching decisions he made had to be good ones. In our six years together, Roy Turner and I never released a player once the season began. That's how precise he was. We learned that our first choices had to be our best choices and to make good deals as best we could. For Roy Turner to have achieved what he did on a limited player budget is phenomenal. It WAS phenomenal and still IS phenomenal.

ROY TURNER: By the second year our budget was behind the league average, and by the fourth year we were way behind. The highest budget we ever had was $1.2 million, in 1986. LA had $2 million.

KEVIN KEWLEY: My last year coaching the Wings, in 2000, the budget was $175,000.

ROY TURNER: We got through the first year, but it was so much more professional when Bill Kentling came in. Instead of starting two months before the season, we started the April before. I learned a lot from Bill Kentling. He knew nothing about soccer when he came on board, but he knew a hell of a lot about Wichita and media. He had been in charge of the Pizza Hut Classic [college basketball tournament] and knew everyone in this town. A very, very bright man. That was the beginning of the professional Wings. He never told me what to do when it came to being a coach. No one ever did. We spent nights and days together figuring out how to build a team. The Angels were huge. I'm not kidding. Those tryouts with all these great looking girls; they were famous in this town.

BILL KENTLING: My guess is that Norman Piper was our highest paid player at $35,000. Norman [was given] a car. [He] was a hell of a player and wildly popular. Every little kid who wasn't 6'5 and 250 wanted to be Stormin' Norman Piper. I worked out a deal with the Subaru dealer for six vehicles. We had a lot of international players who needed their own transportation.

While Tom Marshall viewed WSU basketball as a competitor, Kentling wanted to avoid the concept of WSU vs. the Wings.

BILL KENTLING: The community decided it was okay to be a Wings fan AND a WSU fan. I remember one year either three or four times the Shockers played at home on the same day as us and both sold out. I thought they all complemented [each other]. If you were a strong supporter of KU, WSU, or KSU and went to every game, we knew you weren't our target audience. One of the sad things was that it was tough for kids to go to the games. So we really tried to appeal to that unaffiliated fan who had two or three kids who wanted to go to the game. Most of the people on our board were WSU people, but they were big enough to know that if our community was going to grow we had to have more than one [team].

STEVE SHAAD, DIRECTOR OF MEDIA RELATIONS, WICHITA WINGS, 1980 85: I was working at WSU for the women's athletic department as an SID [Sports Information Director]. Bill Kentling was in charge of marketing for Pizza Hut. They sponsored a women's basketball tournament which was our showcase event of the year for women's athletics. I did that for two years. I had a

chance to work with Bill on that and he was impressed with the job I was doing creating crowds and introducing PA announcers and scoreboards. Before that they were playing in an open gym and that was it. I enjoyed Bill's personality and he liked me, so he approached me when he joined the Wings and asked me to come on-board.

The men's and women's programs were combining and I wanted to move on. I had never seen an indoor soccer game in my life. It was just Dave Bennett, Virginia Creamer and myself, with Larry Davis doing tickets…and that was about it. I came on around May of 1980. I was Director of Media Relations.

We didn't inherit a very good list of people who had attended games, so we had a very small database. We had 2,222 season tickets my first year. But it didn't seem like much when we had to fill 10,000 seats. Right off the bat we had a close-knit crew. Bill was very imaginative and Roy was very personable. It was a great atmosphere right off the bat.

I was doing the marketing. The game promotions were a group effort. Kentling taught us that you can't go wrong throwing free stuff to the crowd. No matter what happens you can always make a hit with the crowd. We had Bud Man throwing Frisbees and the Angels throwing mini-balls. I had previous relationships with the media that helped. I hand-delivered releases to the media and sat down with them and explained what we were trying to do. One of the most successful things we did was have the "Media Indoor Soccer League." On Saturday mornings, we'd invite the media out to the Coliseum to play a game. What it did was shut some of them up who thought this wasn't a real sport. They were huffing and puffing and then realized these guys were tremendous athletes.

Roy really took me under his wing. He educated me on the game so I wouldn't look like a fool when writing stories. I spent a lot of free time with Roy on the road. I am sure there are coaches who wouldn't have much to do with the PR director, but not Roy.

In the early years of the Wings, we traded tickets pretty freely…for cars, apartments, clothing, etc. When we got to near capacity, we still had a lot of "comp" tickets we wanted back but had already promised them in player agreements. We got caught in a bind.

Bill Kentling was marvelous…a genius. A good manager of people. Fun. He would encourage you and allow you to do your work….give you credit if you did a good job, and be there to defend you if you did a bad job. The simple promotions he thought up were always effective.

KEVIN HIMES, WHEATHAWK, RUGRAT, AND WINGS EMPLOYEE: If Steve Shaad needed something run across town or somebody picked up at the airport he had a network of people, my parents being just one, that would do anything to help the Wings cause and help keep this team in Wichita. Little things like picking up Krazy George from the airport. My mom and dad loved doing that. In the van, he was just a regular guy. He was very down to earth and very intelligent. He was great.

KEVIN KEWLEY: We'd do clinics in schools. We visited 48 of the 52 elementary schools in town. Kids always loved it. Bill Kentling was big on that. We'd give the kids a free ticket and of course then mom and dad would have to buy tickets to come with them. We'd have appearances. I wore a cowboy outfit for Sheplers!

I was called "The Tiger" and Steve Shaad wanted me to do a pose with the tiger at the zoo. I thought to myself, "There's no way I'm getting next to a live tiger." At the time there was a model on Sports Illustrated who was petting a tiger. He said, "That would be great if YOU did that!" No way. Shaad was brilliant with that stuff. That's the type of stuff we'd do to get attention. One time we did a calendar. We all had a month. I was November and they had me hold a pumpkin.

STEVE SHAAD: There was a new Ford dealer in town called Plains Ford Truck on the south side of town. I went down there and called on the general manager. I asked him to give away a Ford Bronco at a Wings game. [Fans] would come down to the dealership to register and we'd give them exposure at the games, driving the Bronco around the field. We would have a fan try to kick a ball through the window. All the dealer had to do was provide the insurance for the truck in case someone actually succeeded. I told him it would cost about $1,500. Every game we'd draw a name, and they would join the list of finalists. We had all our players attempt to kick it through the window just to see if it could be done.

It was almost time to give away the truck. I called the dealer and asked if he had bought the insurance yet. He said, "No I haven't got it yet." I called a second time less than two weeks before the event. He still hadn't got it. But the insurance company tells me that because it was less than two weeks before the event, Lloyds of London wouldn't let them write a policy. I talked to Larry Davis and another buddy in the front office, and we agreed to insure the truck personally. If the ball goes in, we agreed we'd make payments on the truck. We figured we'd make an easy $1,500. But the dealer says, "So, we've decided to self-insure it."

On the night of the event, I notice there are three members of the Bird family from Haysville on the list. People start kicking and nobody gets close. We get to number 16 on the list [and it's one of the Bird family]. He lines up and kicks it right through the window. I'm on the field and realize we'd just given away a $17,000 Ford Bronco. I talked to the kid afterwards. He went down to the dealer and measured the height and dimensions of the window and the distance to the truck and would practice every night. So, [the dealer] was out a $17,000 truck because of his decision to self-insure.

That wouldn't be the last time a halftime promotion involving a car would go slightly awry...

TERRY NICHOLL, MIDFIELDER, WICHITA WINGS: There was a halftime entertainment...they had this Subaru wagon parked in the middle of the field. There was a paper airplane in the program, and they'd have to throw it through the sunroof. They said, "It will take a couple of months at least." I remember coming out at halftime, the gliders were just barely missing. [Then] somebody banked it in, right into the Subaru. It was supposed to be there for two months. It lasted five or eight minutes. When we went to look at these gliders, they were so sophisticated. All these aircraft engineers building these paper planes.

Virginia Creamer stepped up her role with the Wings by moving up from being Ray Denton's assistant to taking over as the Director of Operations. She continued to run the Angels dance team, though she accepted help from all kinds of local luminaries to help judge the talent at tryouts. No one could deny her ability to coordinate a dance squad, but her experience running a soccer team and a business was limited. The Wings put on a great show game after game during Creamer's tenure. But, at the time, did she feel ready for such responsibility?

VIRGINIA CREAMER, ANGELS COORDINATOR, DIRECTOR OF OPERATIONS, WICHITA WINGS: No...no. I was a song and dance person. I was an actress. That's all I knew really. I told Billy [Kentling], "I don't have any business experience. Should I take a business class or something?" He said, "You know, Virginia, you just start working with me and you'll learn everything you need to know about business." And he was right, he taught me so much. We're still good friends today.

BILL KENTLING: One of the great hires we were able to effect was Virginia Creamer.

The 1980-81 Angels squad was composed of 18 women from the ages of 18 to 29. Among their number you could find college students, a legal secretary...even an electrocardiograph technician. From tryouts in August till the beginning of the season they practiced twice a week. That would increase once the season started. "The Angels wear royal blue leotards with gold jackets and white boots. For promotional work, they wear white slacks with a royal blue stripe up the sides." [8]

VIRGINIA CREAMER: The second year was the year that PM Magazine filmed the auditions. We had probably 50 or 60 girls audition. Billy got up and made a speech. Every year we had more and more girls audition. The girls had to re-audition every year. I think it was maybe the second year that I took myself out of the voting. I worked with them all, and I didn't want the fact that I liked them so much affect the decision. It was Kentling, sometimes Roy [judging], and media people...Randy Brown, Gene Rump. It was funny how many of the media people understood performance. They really understood if somebody had it. Anybody can see if somebody is not picking up a dance step.

The hallmark of the MISL was the over-the-top, show-stopping theatrics that happened each game, particularly during player introductions. Sports Illustrated, *the preeminent sports magazine of the 1980s, was forced to take notice of the MISL due to the attendance numbers and the theatrics. In 1983, the great sportswriter Frank Deford wrote a big feature article in SI about this new sport. For Wings fans, the "money" quote would be, "Wichita of all places is a valued franchise." Deford wrote about the particular importance of the first of the three S's (Show, Sex, and Suburbs) that were vital to the success of indoor soccer in the United States: "The Show in the formula is much more than the game. It takes in loud rock music, fireworks, all sorts of lighting effects (heavy on the lasers), introductions that would put even Merv Griffin to shame, and carefully orchestrated interaction between the players and the fans…The MISL [is] introducing to us what a fully integrated sports promotional effort will henceforth resemble."* [9]

As it turns out, Deford's words were prescient. The other major professional sports leagues would soon imitate the MISL's raucous ways. And as we all know, imitation is the sincerest form of flattery. The four Leiweke brothers, all MISL franchise owners, were at the forefront of much of the razzamatazz. Tracey Leiweke, who ran the Kansas City Comets, told Deford, "What we're trying to do with the Comets is to make them an experience. Everything about the club has to bolster the image. The theme has to be constant. You'll hear the same music on our radio commercials, for example, as you hear at the arena. People who dismiss us as simply being creative-marketing guys are missing the point. We're setting the whole tone." [10]

Deford describes a BBC broadcast of the theatrics at a Baltimore Blast game: "The British cameras carefully record the Blast's huge, simulated soccer ball, flashing and exploding as it descends from the roof of the Civic Center before each game, while rock music blares and laser lights speckle the full house of wide-eyed Baltimoreans. The ball lands, as it were, and splits open, emitting great clouds of steam, a staple of all indoor soccer introductions. The MISL could no more survive without steam than the U.S. Post Office could without [adhesive]. And then, from inside the great lighted ball, through the murk, come the players, one by one, garbed in neon citrus colors, all holding high red roses, which they will toss to lucky girls in the stands. There's a long pause from the BBC announcer. At last he speaks. 'Leeds versus Liverpool it is not' is what he says." [11]

BILL KENTLING: Every team in the MISL worth its salt had a different kind of introduction. Virginia was in charge of all of that. In St. Louis you came out through steam, and we had our mirror ball. The guys in the NBA will admit it: the NBA today has stolen a lot of stuff from the old MISL. There was a time when you introduced people and they just ran to center court, like they still do in college. We really made a production out of the opening.

TOM SHINE: You look at every single professional sporting event, they do big player intros. That started in the MISL. When the Chicago Bulls and Jordan were playing Alan Parsons [Project] to start their game, that was an MISL thing. Sports teams [before] then, their idea of marketing was like, "We've got a game at 7:00, and the gates will open at 6:45. It was true for the Royals and the Tigers. "You can come or not come." The Wings made it an event. Most people there didn't know much about soccer, but they knew it was fun and they could drink a beer, bring their kids and meet the players after. They marketed it as an event. Now everybody does that. Fireworks, dollar beer night, bobblehead day, etc. The [MISL] was way ahead of the game on that...the player intros, and making it an experience.

BILL KENTLING: We got people to sponsor the handing out of the roses, throwing those Mid-Kansas miniature balls in the stands. It was Virginia's idea to have the Wichita Wings Angels, sort of our Dallas Cowboys cheerleaders. We really tried to make it an experience when you went to the Coliseum, and also to intimidate the other team. We were never great on the road, but boy we were hard to beat in the Coliseum.

VIRGINIA CREAMER: I was on the headsets, talking to the spotlight operators the second year. I started backing up Bill and Roy administratively. I was with them for the next six years [after Kentling hired her back].

Creamer was in charge of the game-day production. It was a high-pressure job and things could get a little intense when trying to organize the intricate ballet that was a Wings game. Just ask Creamer's gopher, Kevin Himes, what his main job duty was...

KEVIN HIMES: I listened to Virginia Creamer scream [laughs]. I called for runners if something needed to be picked up at the PA booth. She'd tell them, "Go get this," and they'd go. She'd have me punch J.B. if he said something wrong.

Wings players and fans were subject to a new mascot in 1980-81. His name was "Wonder Wing" and he would not be long for this world. The Wichita Eagle described Wonder Wing as having the appearance of a "plucked relative of the San Diego Chicken," and said he would "entertain and pester fans."[12] Unfortunately, a mascot controversy erupted when Wonder Wing, played by Steve Olander, asked to be brought along to the playoff series in St. Louis. His request was refused and Krazy George was sent instead. This resulted in a Bob Getz column airing Wonder Wing's grievances in public. Though popular with children under six, Wonder Wing's appeal to adults was more difficult to discern. Eagle columnist Randy Brown labeled him a "turkey." Needless to say, Wonder Wing was never seen again at a Wings game.[13]

———

On the field, several role players returned from the previous year's team. Mike Hobgood, the lone survivor of season one tryouts, came back. However, he would appear in only a single game. Mike Custer saw his playing time increase substantially from only five game appearances in year one to 39 of the 40 games in the second season. Defenders Joe Howarth and Keith Gehling would also see an increase in action. They would play in 37 and 39 games, respectively, both becoming part of the regular rotation.[14]

Kevin Kewley, Jimmy Ryan, Norman Piper, George Ley, and Andy Chapman would return to their roles as the core talent on the team. Kewley continued as captain and for the second consecutive year would both score the second-highest point total, and lead the team in penalty minutes. Chapman would lead the team with 29 goals. Ryan would finish third in total points with 52.[15]

ROY TURNER: We had a great recruiting year, player-wise.

After losing 13 players from the first year's squad, the Wings were ready for new blood. Players from the Netherlands, Germany, Denmark, England, Wales, and the good ol' US of A would help fill in the gap. Roy Turner pursued and signed Helmet Dudek from West Germany. A First Division player in the German league, the 22-year-old Dudek had previously fled communist Poland for West Germany to be with his future wife. He came to the attention of Turner at a tryout for the NASL's Atlanta Chiefs. Though circumstances forced Dudek to return to West Germany before playing a game in the NASL, Turner was able to lure him back to the United States, and the Wings. "When Dudek returned to Germany, I decided to go after him for the Wings. His desire to come to America is one of the reasons we were able to negotiate a contract with him," Turner told The Eagle. *Dudek would play on defense for the Wings.*[16]

Dudek was joined by the wily Dutch-American veteran Hank Liotart. Liotart was 35 and had spent most of his life in America, having immigrated with his family as a teenager. The previous season, Liotart had played for and coached the MISL's Hartford Hellions through their first seven games. His 16 year playing career included stops in Cleveland, Dallas, and San Diego.[17] *While in Cleveland, he played with a certain Liverpudlian midfielder by the name of Turner. Liotart's impact on the stat sheets in Wichita would be modest. He only scored three points, off two assists and a goal. It wasn't much compared to Dudek's 23 goals and 7 assists, but Liotart added an important defensive presence during his 26 game appearances.*[18] *Moreover, Liotart did serve one important purpose on and off the field: as a German-Dutch-English translator...*

ROY TURNER: Don't forget we had Helmet Dudek just for that season. Boy, he could hit a ball. We communicated with him through Hank Liotart, who was Dutch but could speak German.

KEVIN KEWLEY: Helmut was brilliant at forward, but defensively, not as much.

ROY TURNER: He wasn't the fastest guy in town.

The first draft pick the Wings ever made, in the fall of 1979, was signed to play for the 1980-81 season. Rockhurst All-American Mike Powers would play for the Wings for three seasons, making his biggest impact in the team's second year. Of his four goals in 1980-81, one would be a game-winner.[19]

Newcomer Steve Earle would have a much bigger impact. The former English First Division player came to the Wings from the NASL's Tulsa Roughnecks, where he was one of the team's best indoor players. A native of Feltham, England, Earle spent years playing for top-level English soccer clubs Fulham and Leicester City before coming to America.[20] *He would have a big impact as a Wings forward, scoring 25 goals and making 9 assists in his lone year with the club.*[21]

Brian Tinnion, another NASL standout, would join the Wings midway through the season. A native of Workington, England, Tinnion had American residency, thus didn't count towards the limit on foreign players. Tinnion had starred along-side Pele on the New York Cosmos before playing for the Detroit Express.[22] *In Wichita, he would accumulate 15 points in his 21 games with the team.*[23]

The diffusion of talent from the NASL to the MISL was a major trend during the 1980-81 season. According to soccer historian David Litterer, "A new threat [to the NASL] was the resurgent Major Indoor Soccer League which was growing by leaps and bounds and entering into a serious bidding war with the NASL. This put more pressure on teams already in financial trouble, and was a serious damper on the NASL's fledgling indoor league. A number of international players already had commitments back home during the winter, and other NASL players were committed to the MISL during the indoor season; hence it was a diluted talent pool that remained with the NASL for the winter, and the results showed, with lackluster play and thin crowds."[24]

KEVIN KEWLEY: The whole league was upgrading that second year with the decline of the NASL.

ROY TURNER: There was a competition for players. There was a tension there. [By 1983] when San Diego and Chicago came into our league, we had more talent than the NASL. The second year I was here the NASL was starting to play indoor, but they weren't going to double the player's salary to play indoor as well as outdoor. Therefore, the outdoor players could make more money coming to the MISL than just playing for the NASL.

By 1984, the NASL would shut its doors, and many of the remaining players would migrate to the MISL and the Wichita Wings.

TOM SHINE: [The Wings eventually] had about six to eight ex-NASL guys on the team, all of whom were owed money still, and were in court over that money. They weren't gonna get it...because there was no money. That's the reason there was no league. They used to compare with each other, "How much do they owe you?" "That son of a bitch, he owes me $30,000."

The NASL wasn't the only source for new players. ASL All-Star, and former Andy Chapman teammate Don Tobin was lured by Roy Turner to Wichita from the California Sunshine. At the time of his signing, he was paid the highest salary in the history of the Wings. The 24-year-old Liverpudlian midfielder was owned exclusively by the Wings; there would be no shared contract with an outdoor team. It was Turner's goal to obtain exclusive rights to as many players as possible so as not to have to worry about losing them after their "loan" period was over. "I would like the people of Wichita to have their own players," said Turner.[25] Tobin's 14 points that season would be somewhat of a disappointment, especially considering that he was well-paid.[26] But off the field, in his two seasons with the Wings, Tobin would enjoy life in Wichita with his buddy Andy Chapman.

ANDY CHAPMAN, FORWARD, WICHITA WINGS: Me and Don, we were a famous duo. He was the first guy I met in California in '78. I was 18 and he was 22 or 23 at the time. We struck up a great relationship and were the wingmen for each other and were into fashion and would go out to nightclubs together. We both ended up in Wichita. We never stopped laughing.

(Don Marler/1981-82 Wings Yearbook) Don Tobin and his impressive mane.

ROY TURNER: He and Don Tobin were quite a duo on the social scene. Butch Cassidy and the Sundance Kid. You'd see them walking down the street in their leather pants and go "Woah!"

BILL KENTLING: [Andy Chapman] and Tobin were in a different league. Andy Chapman and Don Tobin could do things that other people couldn't figure how to physically arrange their bodies in that way.

On the field, Chapman became even more important during the 1980-81 season. His status as the "target forward" on the team became cemented over the course of the year. "My job is to form a target for the midfield players and defenders, to get the ball at my feet, shield it from the defense and give the others time to work off the ball. But my main job is to score goals. Scoring is what I like to do most," said Chapman.[27]

Chapman wouldn't be the only star to emerge in year two. Three new arrivals from Europe would make an enormous impact on both the team and the city for many years to come.

CHAPTER 12

An Oral History

Two Danes and a Welshman Walk

Into The Hatch Cover...

———

"Kim was 20 when he came...and became the basis of the team."

- ROY TURNER

BROODING...INTENSE...HOT-TEMPERED...UNCOMPROMISING. THESE were the sort of adjectives used to describe Jorgen Kristensen during his time with the Wings. In Denmark, he was known as Troldmanden, or "The Wizard." In Wichita, he became the "Magic Man." Kristensen had a long and storied career as a professional footballer. That career started in 1967 with the Danish club Koge. The next summer he found himself in Detroit, playing for the Cougars of the United Soccer Association (USA). But it was in the Netherlands and Germany that Kristensen made a name for himself. From late 1968 to 1972 he played in the top Dutch league for Sparta Rotterdam before moving to the team's cross-town rival, Feyenoord Rotterdam. At Feyenoord, Kristensen would start in the 1974 UEFA Cup Championship match where he was one of only two non-Dutch players that made an appearance. Kristensen and company would defeat the Tottenham Hotspur and capture the prestigious UEFA Cup, causing angry Spurs fans to rip out their seats and throw them at police before rampaging through the streets of Rotterdam.

In 1976, Kristensen moved to the Bundesliga, Germany's First Division, and spent a couple seasons in the midfield with Hertha BSC. He helped Hertha to a third place finish in 1976 and followed that up with a trip to the German Cup finals in 1977. He would be the only non-German to play for Hertha in the finals. Throughout the 1970s, Kristensen would star for the Danish national team, scoring three goals in his 19 international appearances. The Chicago Sting of the NASL brought Kristensen to America again in 1978. He set team records for assists in two of his three seasons with the Sting before leading the Tulsa Roughnecks to the 1980 NASL playoffs.[1] Kristensen was a three-time all-star in the NASL.

Signing such an accomplished player was a huge coup for Roy Turner. But the 33-year-old midfielder almost didn't make it to Wichita. In early November of 1980, a visa problem left Kristensen waiting in Copenhagen for a few days before he would make it to Kansas. According to The Eagle *the visa was cabled to Copenhagen from Washington D.C. "I called the embassy (in Copenhagen) and they told me it might have been held up because of the [1980 presidential] election or the [hostage] situation in Iran," said Kristensen. His wife, Solvej, and children, Benny, 14, and Karrin, 7, would join him a week later. Though his family came with him, his bar could not. Kristensen was the proud owner of The Golden Boot, a 70-seat drinking establishment in Copenhagen.[2] It is doubtful all that Carlsberg pilsner beer could have made it through customs.*

ROY TURNER, HEAD COACH, WICHITA WINGS: We got this guy called Jorgen Kristensen. We all knew who he was beforehand...he was a great player. He played in Chicago in the NASL. Jorgen lived in the Danish countryside in a thatched-roof house, which meant he was very at home in Kansas. I knew his agents because I dealt with them in Dallas. The agent came in and said he knew a young Danish player, Kim Roentved, that we should get. Jorgen was vital in bringing him in. When he came, he fit right in. The same agent got me Helmut Dudek.

(Don Marler/1982-83 Wings Yearbook) The Magic
Man, Jorgen Kristensen, handling the ball.

Though he had established his outdoor soccer bonafides, and had played a Danish version of the indoor game, with four players on each side, Kristensen had never played the American version of indoor soccer. "The game is completely new to me," said Kristensen.³ But luckily for the Wings, he turned out to be just as good at the MISL version of soccer as he was on the traditional pitch. How good? Kristensen would record over 50 assists in each of his first three seasons with the Wings. "I'm not that big a goal scorer. I'm the guy who sets the goals up," Kristensen remarked.⁴ Despite his modesty, he was quite good at scoring as well...

TOM SHINE, REPORTER/EDITOR, WICHITA EAGLE: I think Jorgen was making in the $50,000's or $60,000's at the height of his career. He was a great indoor soccer player. He scored a goal one night...he just took the ball and chipped it off the boards and went by the guy and headed it in. The [defender] never moved.

KEVIN KEWLEY, MIDFIELDER, WICHITA WINGS: Jorgen brought out the best in other players.

Wings goal-scorers surely salivated at the prospect of playing with a man who lived to pass. "I think that basically I'm born with the ability to handle the ball. But you can always make it better by practicing. When I was a kid, you know, we didn't have too many toys. So I got a soccer ball when I was pretty young and started playing with it. I played every day like a kid does. Once I got older, I started practicing. I really practiced on my skill. [Awareness of what's happening around you] is a natural born talent. It's something you just have and I'm pleased to have it, of course...I've always been a player who likes to pass the ball rather than shoot the ball in the goal. I don't know why. It's just the way I'm built, I guess. It seems to me I'm always in the position to pass the ball. To find the position and get the assist, again, it's just a gift you have. It's nothing I've been looking for," said Kristensen.[5]

ROY TURNER: You'd never see anybody work harder than Jorgen. He trained hard and also had a lively social life too. He was so serious about the game and he was a world-class player. That rubbed off on the other players. He still knew who the boss was and showed me that, but he had a temper that could erupt.

KEVIN KEWLEY: Everyone respected him despite his temper. If he was like that and wasn't very good he wouldn't have lasted five minutes.

ROY TURNER: He hated to lose. He didn't even want to lose a little five minute game during practice. He'd do anything to win. Jorgen is one of the reasons why we're all here. Was he easy to coach? No. Was he worth it? Yes.

CHARLIE MINSHULL-FORD, EQUIPMENT MANAGER, WICHITA WINGS, 1982-85: Jorgen Kristensen...off the field he would kid around a lot. More loose off the field. One season there was a woman chasing after Jorgen. She made a cake and left it in the locker room for him. It was terrible. "She's a psycho woman and she's chasing me." She'd come to every practice and sit in the same spot. Jorgen would sneak in and out trying to avoid her.

After a few Michelobs he'd be pretty funny. But on the field he was intense. When he was on the bench he wasn't afraid to tell other guys they were making mistakes...

TERRY NICHOLL, MIDFIELDER, WICHITA WINGS: Jorgen Kristensen found the secret to youth...it was to have three Budweisers for lunch every day and don't eat any food. He ran on beer and was fit as a fiddle. He wouldn't get injured. Here's me, I don't drink or smoke, and these other lads were much better than me! These lads lived hard.

BILL KENTLING, GENERAL MANAGER, WICHITA WINGS, 1980-86: I really liked Jorgen. We were the same age. Six years later I was six years older but Jorgen was still the same age...I never quite understood that [laughs]. He was a brilliant player, as precise a passer as you can imagine; a real technician. A good guy, but not overly popular...because he would call you out if you weren't precise. Sometimes those kind of guys are popular and sometimes they're not. Jorgen was never in great shape for the playoffs because he became a nervous wreck....literally gave himself hernias...but a good guy who could really play. If you were a coach and you came to a game, you could tell your kids, "Just watch that guy play for a while, that's what I want you to do."

TOM SHINE: Andy Chapman and Jorgen had a great relationship. [Andy] understood that if he wanted to score he had to get the ball from [Jorgen]. They were totally opposite. Jorgen was pretty dark...he had a little Hamlet in him.

ROY TURNER: Jorgen was a mentor for Andy [Chapman].

The Eagle's Randy Brown summarized the greatness of Jorgen Kristensen: "Indoors or out, Kristensen, 33, 5-feet-8, 160 pounds, is absolute magic with a soccer ball. He is pure guile and finesse. When Kristensen and an opponent go after a loose ball, Jorgen will take charge 9 times out of 10. Kristensen's style has been frustrating opponents in Europe and America for more than a decade...If Kristensen has a fault it is that he loves his skills so much that it is painful for him to take a shot on goal." Brown quotes Kristensen as saying, "I think that I should shoot more. It seems always when I decide to shoot I see someone in better position and I try to give the ball to him." Roy Turner could only echo Brown's sentiments: "'God, he is so unselfish sometimes, I don't know,' says Turner, shaking his head. 'It's one thing to tell him to shoot more. But soon he's going to realize that he's capable of making a lot of goals as well as making a lot of assists.'" [6]

Ronald Reagan's election and the return of the American hostages from Iran heralded the arrival of not just one Dane, but two. A young player named Kim Roentved tagged along as well.

ROY TURNER: Kim was 20 when he came...and became the basis of the team.

"The basis of the team" is no exaggeration. Roentved's impact on the team and the city would arguably be bigger than any other player over the course of the franchise's history. However, in 1980 he was just a shy 20 year old from Copenhagen. He was the "yin" to Kristensen's "yang": one Dane was dark and brooding, and the other shy and unassuming. There is little doubt that the Wings owe a debt of gratitude to Jorgen Kristensen for the introduction. "I had played against Jorgen in indoor tournaments in Denmark. He was back home on a vacation. Roy told him to look up a player over there in Denmark. Jorgen called me up one day. He had heard through a Danish reporter that my contract with Randers was finished. Jorgen asked me if I was interested in America and I said, 'Yeah, let me try that.' I didn't even know if they'd like me or whatever..." said Roentved.[7] As it turns out, the Wings did like him...a lot.

(Howard Eastwood/Missile Magazine) Danish superstar Kim "The Rocket" Roentved.

There was a lot to be said for leaving Denmark to play professionally. At the time, even the best players in the country couldn't support themselves on soccer alone. They were forced to work a second job to make ends meet. For Roentved it was accounting. "I hated it in the beginning but the more time I stayed there the more I realized how necessary it was for me. I grew up a lot then when I started right out of school. It was good for me. I'm very happy today that I did it," said Roentved.[8] According to Carol DeWoskin of Missile Magazine, *"During the 2 ½ years Kim worked as an accountant, he also attended school frequently from 8 to 10 in the evenings. The schooling was associated with his job. In addition to this, he practiced soccer in the evenings and played semi-pro and professional games on the weekends."[9]*

"I really don't like to sign players that I haven't seen, but Jorgen told me, 'I think I can get you the kind of player you've been looking for,'" said Turner.[10] Roentved's arrival in Wichita was unheralded since at that early stage in his career, he had little reputation as a soccer player. This athletic Dane was young and impressionable, and excited to be in America. He flew to Wichita with Kristensen and went right to work...after a few drinks at the Hatch Cover, of course.

KIM ROENTVED, DEFENDER, WICHITA WINGS: It was at the Wichita Royale [hotel]...Roy picked us up for practice. We practiced outdoors and Jorgen talked me into having steak and eggs an hour before we practiced. Later, I was puking that up. Roy came and picked us up. We had just flown in the night before and of course had gone to the Hatch Cover to have a few drinks. We had practice early the next morning. I saw Roy coming in his Oldsmobile and I thought "I'm REALLY in America." It was November. That was a Saturday. I remember Jorgen and I took a walk down Douglas from the Wichita Royale, where we were temporarily staying, and there was this little ice cream place and it was the first time I had a banana split. It was 75 degrees in November, and I thought to myself, "Thank God for America!" It might as well have been Hollywood Boulevard for me. A few days later we moved into our apartment complex down on South Seneca right by Circle Cinema [laughs].

VIRGINIA CREAMER, ANGELS COORDINATOR, DIRECTOR OF OPERATIONS, WICHITA WINGS: Kim Roentved became like a little brother to me. I thought he was the sweetest person in the world. The very first time he was in the US, Jorgen Kristensen brought him in to Wichita and I went to the airport to pick them up. It was Halloween and we were going down Kellogg and beside us pulls up a carload of girls dressed like Miss Piggy. Kim's eyes were as big as saucers. I said, "Jorgen, do you want to explain this to him? It's Halloween, this doesn't happen every day." He looked like he was thinking, "What have I gotten myself into!" That was my first encounter with him.

I went in to Quiktrip one night and Kim was there at the pinball machine by himself. "What are you doing?" So he came over to my apartment and we played *Supertramp* albums, because he really liked *Supertramp*. He didn't speak English very well, but we talked about how he missed his family and how homesick he was. I always had kittens back then and he'd come over and play with the kittens. He was kind of lonely back then, so I helped him out and he became like a brother to me.

KIM ROENTVED: It was exciting for me that first year, just being in America. I went back after the first season. Some say if I had stayed in Europe I would have been on the Danish national team, but it's water under the bridge. I just loved it here though. I could feel like I was growing; and why go play in the snow in Germany when I could stay here. Plus, the money was good. As a 21-year-old, I had a very nice contract.

Roentved didn't start his Wings career by lighting the pitch on fire. In his first five games he only scored a single goal and made one assist. This may have been due to an adjustment period related to playing indoor, living in a new country, or changing positions. Roentved had been accustomed to playing midfield or forward during his career. But Turner believed he could be a great defender. After those first five games, Roentved got the hang of the MISL. In games six and seven, he scored four goals and made two assists, which earned him MISL Player of the Week honors. Randy Brown called him "as unassuming a budding star as you could imagine." Turner said, "He can use force and he can use finesse. The best thing is, he can be so much better." Without a doubt, Turner's prophecy would be fulfilled over the next decade.[11]

ROY TURNER: Kim's impact was gradual. When he first came he was supposedly a center forward. That didn't last very long before we moved him back to defender. He was accepting of that and ended up enjoying the game from the back more than up front. He read the game brilliantly...as good as anybody who played the game. In indoor soccer there are certain times when you should take risks, and he chose those times perfectly. If something happens and we win the ball, he would take off. He was a great tactician, which made him a good coach. He can still play at 54. I asked him the other day, "How was practice?" He said, "I played for an hour."

Amazingly, Roentved would play one half of a real game in 2014 for the Wichita B-52s of the Major Arena Soccer League. Though his appearance had the whiff of a publicity stunt, it was a testament to Roentved's stamina and physical ability that he could take to the pitch in his 50s.

CHARLIE MINSHULL-FORD: [Kim] was an intense player and always would give 110%. He doesn't like to lose. Off the field he was a pretty mellow guy. He was never arrogant.

Though the transition was relatively smooth, sometimes an English accent and a Danish accent made for a bit of confusion...

KIM ROENTVED: The first time I didn't understand Roy...he had this drill where we couldn't pass it back to the goalkeeper, and the first thing I did was pass it back to the keeper. [Coach said] "Don't you f'ing understand what I'm saying?" I almost crapped my pants. There were times he was intimidating at the beginning. You have to go out there and prove yourself before you can start giving your opinions to the coach.

BILL KENTLING: By and large, it was a really decent bunch of guys. I go back to Kim Roentved...you talk about somebody who was really raised right. I'll tell you a story about Kim and it's all you need to know about him. We are on the road, and it is cold and a driving rainstorm. The bus pulls up to the hotel. It's a little bit of a walk from the bus to the hotel. [The trainer] Al Green is out wrasslin' the equipment while most of the players have been smart and run on in. I look back and Kim Roentved turns around and goes back in the freezing rain and helps Al carry in the equipment. You don't need to know any more than that story to know who he is.

BRUCE HAERTL, WINGS PLAY-BY-PLAY ANNOUNCER, KFH RADIO: Kim [Roentved]...one of the finest people I've ever known. Dependable, loyal, great fun to be with. He and I were of a similar age, young men...we were at least able to relate on that level. He had as much innate curiosity about America and how this country worked, and things that were important to Americans, as any player on that team. He became quickly ingrained in the whole American experience, including American sports. I'll never forget sitting down with him and teaching him about American football, baseball, and basketball. Trying to teach him at least enough that he could understand and appreciate what he was watching. He had a tremendous professional curiosity about other athletes and how they competed and got to know some of the Shocker basketball players, and enjoyed that.

Absolute jewel of a guy...probably could have been a kicker in the NFL. I remember seeing him kick the ball, and the absolute effortless nature of how the ball jumped off his foot. I would have loved to see him kick a football. He was such an incredible athlete. Such a tough, hard-playing defender, who was able to score moving forward. He's one of those guys, that no matter what it was, he could pick it up and start doing it. It was one reason he soaked up things when he was sitting there watching games. Kim would always ask questions. There were times when I'd say, "Shut up and watch the game." He was always asking questions about coaching, strategy, how things worked.

We were on a flight once with Scotty Bowman of the Detroit Red Wings. I remember a bunch of us sitting around discussing power plays with Scotty Bowman. To have that opportunity with an NHL Hall of Fame coach, who is picking the brains of indoor soccer players because the concept is the same: same number of players, an extra man, the whole 9 yards. I will never forget that whole give-and-take with Scotty Bowman. I don't think the team was on the flight, but he was. Kim reveled in that kind of thing. He loved learning about new things.

KEVIN HIMES, WHEATHAWK, RUGRAT, AND WINGS EMPLOYEE: I'm the locker room boy, picking up the dirty laundry. We had just lost to Tacoma in the playoffs. We lost in overtime. It was as quiet as a mouse in the locker room. I kicked all the clothes in the center. Roentved says, "Hey Kevin," and throws me his uniform. "Put that in your bag."...It was like a Coke commercial.

Roentved's impact on the field and in the locker room was matched by the connection he made with the community. Over the years, he would become one of the most beloved Wichita Wings that ever stepped on the pitch at the Kansas Coliseum. On and off the field, he became a fan favorite.

DAVID WEBER, WINGS FAN: As a young defender, Kim Roentved was the player I most wanted to be like. I just didn't quite have the flowing locks of hair but I enjoyed his effort and skill on the pitch. I was also blessed with a cannon of a leg as well.

ERIC SCRIVEN, WINGS FAN: ...I've had the opportunity to talk to Kim on numerous occasions. Even better than that, my daughter Chloe has had the same chance. He greets her every time with a huge smile and a hug and says, "Hello beautiful." He always asks her how school is going, and tells her that comes first, even before soccer. Getting to share one of my childhood heroes with my daughter is more than I could have ever asked for.

MARK WEDDLE, WINGS FAN: My sister took me to Camelot Music in Towne East to meet three of the Wings. I recall Kim Roentved and Jorgen Kristensen being two of them. To me, Wings players were larger than life and the prospect of meeting them was utterly nerve-wracking. All I really remember about my interaction with them is that their accents were so thick I barely understood a word either of them said!

Of course, in between inspiring youth and scoring goals, there was fun to be had...

NORMAN PIPER, FORWARD/MIDFIELDER, WICHITA WINGS: We used to play golf up by Wichita State...Kim Roentved, Roy, and I. There was one hole...near a liquor store. We'd jump the fence and get a 12-pack of beer and throw it back over, and [off] we'd go [laughs].

―――

Alone among the previous year's goalkeepers, Wings veteran Keith Van Eron returned to the team for the 1980-81 campaign. After a series of nagging ailments in year one, he was determined to have an injury-free season. He no longer would have to worry about sharing goalkeeping duties with Mike Ivanow, who had moved on to the NASL's Seattle Sounders indoor team. However, Canadian goalkeeper Brad Higgs emerged from the tryouts to make the squad. Higgs had no professional experience, but would have been on the Canadian Olympic team, had it not been for the boycott of the Moscow games by the Canadian government.[12] Before the season began, it was unclear whether it would be similar to the first season, when the two goalkeepers shared playing time, or whether a clear starter would emerge. "I don't think I'm No. 1. I think we'll both be good goalkeepers. We play 40 games. One guy is not going to play all 40," Van Eron told The Eagle.[13]

Just a few days after making that statement, Van Eron hurt his knee in practice. He was faced with a choice: repair the cartilage and have a functional knee, but miss most of the season and possibly give up being a professional athlete; or have the cartilage removed and return to action in a few weeks. Van Eron elected to have it removed because he did not wish to miss a huge chunk of the season. Team physician Dr. Charles Henning opposed removal of the cartilage because it risked causing arthritis later on in life. Van Eron elected to go to the University of Cincinnati Hospital and have an arthroscopic meniscectomy to remove the cartilage, possibly allowing him to return to action by the first game on November 23rd. The loss of Van Eron left the Wings with Higgs as their only goalkeeper.[14]

Though Van Eron's surgery was successful, his status was still uncertain for the first game, and Turner needed a second active goalie. Fortuitously, George Ley had recently scouted a 23-year-old goalkeeper in Wales named Mike Dowler. Though only 5'9, considered short for his position, the Welshman had skill and determination in spades. So, on November 12th, 1980, after several days of negotiations, the Wings signed their third goalkeeper of the season.[15]

Mike Dowler grew up alongside two sisters in Caldicot, a small town in southern Wales. After graduating high school at 16, he became a soccer apprentice with Hereford United, a team in the lower divisions of English football. Dowler quickly discovered being an apprentice wasn't easy. "Basically it was a 9 to 5 job. At one time there were eight apprentices with Hereford United, which is quite a lot. We all had a certain number, say three or four, professional players assigned to us to look after. We had to clean their boots and clean their kit. We also did all the laundry - the folding and drying. We cleaned the floors, cleaned the dressing rooms every day, cleaned the showers. Also the terraces (the playing grounds and stands) had to be cleaned after every game. It was hard work but a lot of guys would have given their right arm to do what I was doing - playing football. I was doing something I enjoyed rather than working in a shop or an office," said Dowler. For all this, he received free lodging and 10 pounds spending money a week.[16]

Under the apprentice system, at the age of 18, a player was either signed on as a pro, or released. Unfortunately for Dowler, the team chose to let him go. However, he caught on at Newport County AFC in his hometown and played there for five years.[17] And then he came to Wichita...

MIKE DOWLER, GOALKEEPER, WICHITA WINGS: After being let go by my team in the UK (Newport County), I had to make a snap decision on my future and that turned out to be with the Wings. I knew nothing about the league, the city, or any of the players...Quite literally, nothing, except that it was indoor football. "Good," I thought: as I am not that tall there would no crosses to deal with!

I realize that Wichita is a long way down the list in terms of size in the US but compared to most British cities, it was a huge, sprawling, urban town bursting at the seams with fast-food restaurants, cars, and bars.

Dowler would start against the New York Arrows in the first game of the season on November 16th, losing 7-2. Six days later, the home opener against the expansion team the Chicago Horizon would feature both Higgs and Van Eron in a 5-4 overtime victory. Van Eron would start the first half of the game. At the next home game, on November 28th, against the Denver Avalanche, Van Eron would play three-quarters of the game. It seemed to be a trend of increasing playing time.[18]

MIKE DOWLER: While I was the third goalkeeper to arrive in camp, I did not view myself as [the] third choice.

Through the first nine games of the season, Van Eron had the edge: playing in six games in comparison to three each for Dowler and Higgs. Furthermore, his Goals Against Average (GAA) of 4.21 and record of 4-1 bested Dowler's 5.33 and 1-2, respectively. Higgs brought up the rear with 6.15.[19] However, in the next couple weeks, Dowler would surge to the top of the MISL goalkeeper statistics with a league-leading 3.55 GAA.[20]

MIKE DOWLER: To be honest, while I felt that while Keith was more experienced than me playing indoors, I was learning the game quickly. However, due to the rules regarding the number of overseas players that could be named in the playing squad, Roy was often left with the difficult decision of playing me in goal and limiting his outfield options or going with Keith, who was already an established 'keeper, and freeing up his choices for however the game panned out.

(*Howard Eastwood/Missile Magazine*) "Iron" Mike Dowler with his son James.

Then, in a two game stretch, Dowler would make the position his to lose. On December 28th, Dowler would achieve a shutout against the San Francisco Fog in an 8-0 drubbing. In the next game, on January 2nd, 1981, he would shut out the Cleveland Force 10-0. Any shutout in indoor soccer is a great achievement. But to do it two games in a row against the kind of talent present in the MISL was nothing short of amazing, and an MISL record. The previous MISL record for consecutive shutout minutes had been 81:35. Dowler shattered that record with 140 minutes and 31 seconds of shutout time. Of the six shutouts in MISL history at that time, Dowler now claimed two of them. "I was really privileged to get the first shutout. I thought that would be my quota for the rest of my days with the Wings, or with anyone else indoors. I just can't believe it," Dowler told The Eagle. *In the second shutout, Cleveland took 63 shots on goal. Dowler stopped every single one.*[21]

But Keith Van Eron wasn't quite ready to give up his job. Since a poor performance on December 19th against Buffalo, Van Eron had been "missing in action." However, he returned with a masterful performance against the Stallions on January 12th.[22] *Unfortunately for Van Eron, it was too little, too late. The writing was on the wall, and on January 20th, it was reported that he had asked permission "to shop for another team." The Philadelphia Fever bought him for an undisclosed amount. For Van Eron, there were sour grapes. "The situation in Wichita was ideal, except for my relationship with Roy Turner. He just didn't believe in my ability as much as (Fever coach) Lenny (Bilous) does," he told* The Eagle's *Steve Love.*[23]

For Turner, it was simply a matter of unfortunate circumstances for one player leading to an unplanned opportunity for another. "Before Van Eron's injury, there was no way we intended to bring Mike [Dowler] in. It took me two months last summer to sign Keith. Before his injury he was certain to be the goaltender," said Turner.[24] *The verbal sparring continued, with Van Eron claiming Turner had not praised him after his excellent performance against Buffalo. "I can't go and tell each one every day how I feel about him. I knew Keith needed a lot of personal attention, but I couldn't forsake the other 19 just to give it to him," said Turner. Van Eron also stated that he believed Turner would have eventually found some excuse to replace him because he didn't really believe in his ability. "It was just a matter of time before Roy brought in another 'keeper," said Van Eron. Wings GM Bill Kentling summed it up: "Dowler has accomplished in half a season something that no one else has ever accomplished in the Major Indoor Soccer League - two shutouts - and though he is younger and less experienced than Van Eron, he already is statistically superior."*[25]

BILL KENTLING: Keith Van Eron had been the goalkeeper the first year before I came. We brought in Mike from Wales, really to be the number two. He turned out to be good, despite his small size. Keith got hurt, and Mike ended up playing more than Roy anticipated. Mike became the number one and Keith went on to [Philadelphia and Baltimore].

[Dowler was] solid, had a calming effect on the team. He worked very hard to overcome his physical abilities. Slobo could out-athletic you. Mike couldn't. He had to outwork and outthink everybody else. We had a group at the north end [of the Kansas Coliseum] that became "Dowler's Towelers." I can't tell you how many of those "Dowler Saves" license plates we sold.

ROY TURNER: Mike Dowler, I only paid $5,000 for. He was a bargain basement player. He was only 5'9, so he didn't have as much value for outdoor teams...No one ever really equaled Mike Dowler as a goalkeeper.

MIKE DOWLER: As the coach, Roy had to make the big decisions regarding who to recruit, who played, how we played and what tactical changes to make if things were not going so well. As a player, I may or may not have agreed with all of those decisions but respected them once they had been made.

For both Dowler and Van Eron, it would be a happy ending. After a stint in Philadelphia, Van Eron would eventually end up starring for the Baltimore Blast, where he would win a championship ring in 1984 and the 1986 MISL Goalkeeper of the Year Award. Dowler would continue his excellent play throughout the 1980-81 season, eventually finishing the season as the MISL's best goalkeeper, with a season record 4.12 GAA.[26]

CHAPTER 13

An Oral History

The Fog of War, The Agony of Defeat

———

"I won't watch the tape. We got screwed."

- KEVIN KEWLEY

THE OUTLOOK FOR THE WINGS *seemed bright at the beginning of year two: the 1980-81 season. A playoff run the previous year and an upgrade in talent had Roy Turner excited about the possibility of going all the way. In regards to the defending champion New York Arrows, Turner was hopeful: "I honestly feel that we can beat them."*[1] *Wichita was now part of the MISL's newly created Western Division. They were joined by two expansion teams in the Denver Avalanche and the Phoenix Inferno, and a Detroit Lightning team that had moved to San Francisco and become the "Fog." Turner picked the Wings to win the division, followed by Phoenix, San Francisco, and Denver.*[2] *He would be right about the first two, but San Francisco would end up underperforming throughout the season. Despite their eventual 11-29 record, they would make a significant impression in Wichita in December...especially on Jorgen Kristensen.*

In the Central Division, Turner predicted Cleveland would win, with St. Louis coming in third. Unfortunately for the Wings, the Steamers would win the division, setting up a fateful playoff game with Wichita. In the Atlantic,

Turner's predictions were precisely correct: New York would win the division, his old friend Kenny Cooper would lead the Baltimore Blast to second, and Philadelphia and Hartford would bring up the rear.[3] Cooper and Turner's bond from their Tornado years did not fade as they moved into coaching. Though they would be rivals on the field, their personal connection allowed them to set that aside after each game. Plus, they had a common purpose: to build up the MISL.

KENNY COOPER, HEAD COACH, BALTIMORE BLAST: We were always living on the edge in those early days...trying to build media relations, and build investors. [Roy] asked me to come help promote the game in Wichita. So we went to Wichita early and did a TV campaign and both teams did a lot of events. We explained how we needed Wichita to stay in the league. Then we went out on Saturday and would take chunks out of each other. We got blown out and I didn't want to even be around Roy. The reverse happened in Baltimore. Somebody had to win and somebody had to lose. It's difficult, but invariably we'd talk on the phone afterwards.

The two teams would play three games that year, twice in Wichita and once in Baltimore. Each team would win at home.[4]

KENNY COOPER: Sometimes the phone would ring at 3:00am and it was Roy, and we'd talk about how the teams were doing and our troubles on the field. You are the figurehead of the franchise...with that comes a lot of pressure. Our careers have been very similar.

For Roy and I, failure was not an option. We would find a way to make it a success. In any business you are only as strong as your weakest link, so you have to have desire to win. You have to be strong to survive. It taught us great character.

The Wings received national television exposure several times during the season. An early December game against the San Francisco Fog was featured as the MISL Friday night game of the week. The game could be watched across the country, but not in Wichita, thanks to a local TV blackout. The Wings needed 8,500 fans to break the blackout.[5] They didn't get it. In fact, there was a great deal of worrying around town about the attendance numbers. An Eagle *editorial lamented the disappointingly dismal attendance at a Tuesday night game on December 2nd: "Surely there are more than 2,282 people who like to see a big-city, powerhouse, defending national champion sports team get its sails trimmed by an up-and-coming small town club. But that's all that turned out to watch the Wichita Wings indoor soccer team stun the twice-champion New York Arrows..."*[6]

Wings fan Al Villegas wrote a letter-to-the-editor to The Eagle exhorting the people of Wichita to step up to the plate: "O.K. Wichita, last March, April, and so-on, we were all running around saying, save our Wings, save our Wings. Through a lot of hard work, a lot of people put up a lot of money to keep the Wings here. So the Wings are here, so where are you? Come on Wichita, let's not just be all talk - let's get off our butts and support this team."[7] *Unfortunately, the people of Wichita didn't heed Villegas' call that night. According to Rich Paschette's meticulously detailed book about the MISL,* Hot Winter Nights, *only 3,178 fans showed up for that Sunday afternoon game.*

An Eagle *editorial speculated that the near-simultaneous seasons of the new minor-league hockey team, the Wichita Wind, and the Wings might be unsustainable in the Wichita market. Additionally, they worried that the $6 and $7 ticket prices for most Wings tickets were too high in such economically uncertain times. "Economic realities for most Wichitans, coupled with the relative newness of both sports to the area, translate into reduced numbers of people making the still somewhat unfamiliar trip to the Kansas Coliseum."*[8] *To combat the lagging numbers, Dick Upton and the Wichita Chamber of Commerce, so vital in saving the Wings the previous season, stepped up to sponsor $2 tickets for the December 28th game against the San Francisco Fog. It would be a fortuitous choice...for that game would go down in Wings history as one of the most pivotal in creating the rising tide of orange that would engulf south central Kansas over the next decade.*[9]

On December 28th, 1980, the San Francisco Fog swept into town to play the Wings. Though the Wings had appeared on nationally-broadcast USA Network games of the week, no local channels had produced a game that season. KAKE-TV decided to make the Fog game the first. However, instead of showing it live,

they would re-broadcast it at 10:30 pm that same evening. KAKE executive
Ron Loewen had seen the previous televised MISL games and thought he could
do better. "It seems to me that indoor soccer is a game that should play well
on TV. But most of the games I've seen have been very antiseptic. The action
should translate to TV, but you never get the feel of the ball crashing around
in the goal area or the bodies colliding," Loewen said to The Eagle's Randy
Brown. His solution? "We're going to put mikes everywhere. We're going to
mike the goals; that's never been done before. We're going to use directional
mikes to pick up sounds away from the ball. We're going to mike the referees.
And we're going to try to mike one of the goalies."[10]

*Ironically, in that same pre-game article, Randy Brown described the Fog as a
physical team and said the Wings "had best watch for forward Mike Mancini."[11]
Unfortunately for Jorgen Kristensen, they didn't watch closely enough.*

ROY TURNER, HEAD COACH, WICHITA WINGS: There was one
incident in Wings history that took this franchise to the next level. We had a
game versus the San Francisco Fog in Wichita. They had a player named Mancini.
We won 8-0. He thought Jorgen Kristensen had flipped him off. None of us saw
it. Mancini punched him and gave him a black eye and laid him out. I remember
chasing Mancini around the field. His brother was a professional boxer. I'm glad
I never caught him! [laughs] The whole stadium went berserk. This was at the
conclusion of the game.

*Prior to the violence, Mancini had been sent to the box for a two-minute tripping
penalty. During his time in the box he was seen gesturing threateningly to Kristensen.
In the audio from the game videotape, you can clearly hear Mancini threaten violence
upon Kristensen while in the presence of a referee, who warns Mancini that if he fol-
lows through on his threat he'll likely be banned for the season.*

The Eagle *describes what followed: "As players from both teams milled around midfield shaking hands after the game, Mancini burst into the group. He shook his finger
in Kristensen's face several times, then slugged the Danish star in the left eye. Kristensen,
who was apparently knocked cold, went down, and Wings Coach Roy Turner went after*

Mancini. As a series of pushing and shoving matches broke out, Coliseum security personnel, as well as police and officials from both teams, rushed onto the playing surface to calm the melee. Then, as Fog players were being escorted off the floor, a fan reached from the safety of the stands and hit San Francisco goalkeeper Roy Messing. Mancini's blow opened a nasty gash just over Kristensen's eye, and club physician Dr. Chuck Henning said it would require at least five stitches to close the wound."[12]

The 6'4, 185 pound Mancini had been undefeated in his 10 amateur boxing bouts. After December 28th, he would be a very unofficial 11-0. Wichita's 5'8, 160 pound Dane was no match for the San Francisco Slugger. Virtually everyone associated with the Wings was incensed. "I want him out of the league for life," said GM Bill Kentling. Roy Turner added, "If I see him again, I will be very, very upset. I want to know if the league wants to see the skills of a Jorgen Kristensen, or the street-fighting tactics of some other programs. If they go along with the street-fighting mentality, then I'll quit." A woozy Kristensen, about to leave for the hospital, stated, "The (bleeping) guy shouldn't be allowed to play in the first place. He can't play. They should suspend him for life."[13]

The next day, the MISL levied a one-week suspension on Mike Mancini. Needless to say, the Wings were disappointed at what they saw as a slap on the wrist. "I don't want to see Mancini in a MISL uniform again. I'm getting tired of some of the teams in this league bringing in guys as hatchet men. I've been giving some thought to signing some guy like Roger Carpenter (a local karate instructor) or Ned Hallacy (a local pro fighter). Maybe it's time to see how tough these San Francisco guys really are," said Kentling.[14]

Though Fog officials had, at first, condemned Mancini's actions, GM Dick Berg (formerly with the Dallas Tornado) said, "We are asking the league to examine the provocation as well as the incident, including Kristensen's obscene gestures and comments to Mancini throughout the game." Kristensen denied all of it: "Suddenly he came at me...the guy was completely crazy."[15]

ROY TURNER: That punch...that fight... it was in the newspaper. Right after that, home attendance skyrocketed...It was a real game-changer. The passion from the fans and the players was amazing. All that happened that day was passion.

While we don't want to see violence, it's part of sport. It shows how much it meant to everyone. In those days, the Wings were their lives. I didn't realize at the time how much it meant to the fans. It meant that much to the players as well.

STEVE SHAAD, DIRECTOR OF MEDIA RELATIONS, WICHITA WINGS, 1980-85: I remember Bill Kentling [tried to get] a court order from a judge banning Mike Mancini from returning to Wichita after he punched out Jorgen Kristensen.

Bill Kentling approached the district attorney in order to determine if any civil or criminal charges could be filed against Mancini. After getting stitches, Kristensen complained of a headache, stiff-neck, and flu-like symptoms. Despite his temporary pain, there were no lingering injuries from the fight. Thus, charges never materialized.[16]

BILL KENTLING, GENERAL MANAGER, WICHITA WINGS: So much of that stuff we did was staged. I don't want to say "staged," but it was staged. We just took advantage of opportunities that came along. There's no question that Mike Mancini sold me a lot of tickets.

...7,842 to be exact. That was how many showed up for the Wings next game. It was a season-high attendance record, but it wouldn't even last a week.[17] *The next game, versus Baltimore, was a sell-out crowd at 9,637.*[18] *Was this sudden rise in attendance connected to the fight? "I feel quite sure that the incidents have made the public more aware of the team," said Turner.*[19]

"Does violence appeal to soccer fans? I don't know enough psychology to give a definitive answer. I guess it would be easy to say it helped our attendance, but I think there were other factors, more important factors. I don't think parents want to bring their children to a game to watch adults - or alleged adults - fight," Kentling told The Eagle.[20] *With a wink and a smile for sure.*

A war of words between GMs continued as the Wings traveled to San Francisco on January 23rd. Prior to their arrival, Dick Berg wrote a letter to The Wichita Eagle: *"It's time, perhaps, to put the "Mancini Massacre" in perspective. It appears that you and seemingly all of Wichita have been duped by a small-town hype campaign into believing that a mad maniacal villain is still plying his trade in the MISL and wearing a FOG uniform. Since small issues can rally small minds in small towns, here's hoping the truth won't wreck Mr. Kentling's ticket-selling campaign..." Bill Kentling wasn't impressed. He retorted, "I don't know whether that is serious, or like some of Dick's players, a joke. If he is totally serious, I would be disappointed."*[21]

The Wings would come away with a precious road win in the city by the bay. Later that season, Mancini would return to Wichita, without any fireworks, criminal charges, or assorted craziness. Much to the delight of Frank Carney, Roy Turner, Bill Kentling, the Chamber of Commerce, the Wings players, and the people of Wichita, the increased ticket sales would continue, in large part thanks to the hullabaloo resulting from the Mancini incident.

———

Throughout their existence, the Wichita Wings almost always thrived at home and were just as lousy on the road. Season two was no exception. They would end the year having won a whopping 90 percent of their home games, with only two losses at the Coliseum. On the road, they would lose 75 percent of their matches; going 5-15.[22] *The raucous and exciting home atmosphere that helped the Wings achieve such a notable home record wouldn't have been possible without the assistance of their beloved announcer, J.B. Johnson.*

BILL KENTLING: There are people that have really gone unsung, like J.B. Johnson.

CHRIS JOHNSON, SON OF J.B. JOHNSON: He was born in Lincoln, Nebraska...He helped start AYSO here in 1974...At first I don't think [the Wings] could afford to pay him. He was doing it for the love of the game.

By day, an elementary school principal in the Wichita Public School system, Johnson would be a fixture at Wings games throughout the MISL era. He started out playing soccer as a youngster growing up in Seattle, Washington. After settling down in Kansas, he coached and refereed kids when the AYSO came to Wichita in 1974. Even at work he would extol the virtues of soccer, organizing games for his students at Arkansas Avenue, Ingalls, Kelly, and Waco elementary schools. Johnson believed academics and soccer went hand-in-hand. "Soccer develops gross and fine motor skills. It's been proved that those skills are tied closely with good reading skills," he told The Eagle *in a 1981 interview.*[23]

An extrovert, Johnson had no professional training as an announcer. However, his natural skill at public speaking had been noticed by a district administrator who witnessed Johnson give a speech at a NEA (National Education Association) event. This led to his promotion from teacher to assistant principal, and later principal. For fun, he would announce at city league fast-pitch softball games. From there, he went straight to the MISL...a pretty big leap. But, as The Eagle *reported, "Johnson's voice is rich and is easy to understand."*[24]

CHRIS JOHNSON: There were a few times he got in trouble for saying stuff over the PA. He made a smart-aleck reference about Stan Stamenkovic. [Stamenkovic] wasn't real happy about it. Dad would joke around like that all the time...I remember people coming up to him and [dad] signing Wings banners and shirts. They'd come down to the PA booth afterwards.

"And now Wichita, are...you...ready?!?!" *These words would become Johnson's trademark opening to each game, followed by the sounds of "Gonna Fly Now" by Bill Conti. Most would recognize it as the theme song to* Rocky. *The Wings would have no cheerleader more loyal than J.B. Johnson. His blood, like the blood of Roy Turner, would forever run orange.*

CHRIS JOHNSON: I know he did it for 15 or 20 years...He missed maybe one game over the years.

Apparently, orange was less popular around the league that year, based on the All-Star roster. The selections, voted on by MISL players in January, were highly disappointing to Wings GM Bill Kentling and Eagle *columnist Randy Brown. "Three*

Wings were selected in the voting...One of them has been traded (Keith Van Eron, to Philly), one is injured (Norman Piper), and one (George Ley) will play in the game as a Wichita representative," said Brown in a February column.[25]

Strangely, since Van Eron had been selected as a Wing, he would play for the West team, while his Philadelphia brethren would play for the East team. Kim Roentved would also join the squad as an additional selection by Pat McBride, coach of both the Steamers and the West squad. "I am confused and concerned about the selections. I find it hard to believe that none of the three people considered to be maybe the top three goalies in the league were selected...We're the leader of the Western division and we've got two people in the game. St. Louis is the leader in the Central division, and it is going to have eight people in the game," said Kentling. For evidence of the MISL's growing importance, the game would be aired live from Madison Square Garden on the USA Network, and then on CBS on tape-delay a week-and-a-half later.[26]

With Turner as his assistant coach, McBride would lead the West squad to an 8-5 victory. The two coaches would see a lot of each other that year. Though it was the Steamers first season in the league, the rivalry between the two Midwestern cities would grow red-hot very quickly. Without a doubt, the Steamers and the Wings grew to hate each other because of the events that transpired during the playoffs of the 1980-81 season. For many years thereafter, few Wings fans would be able to utter the words "St. Louis" or "Steamers" without a note of contempt in their voice... and vice-versa.

BILL KENTLING: Clearly, the St. Louis Steamers were the big geographic rivals.

The rivalry had to start somewhere. That somewhere was St. Louis, MO, on January 4th, 1981. The Wings had just come off two Mike Dowler shutouts and were riding high atop the Western Division standings. The Steamers were just as hot, leading the Central Division with a 14-3 record. They met in front of 12,622 fans at the old Checkerdome. It wasn't even close. The Wings were crushed 11-2.[27]

Fourteen days later, the Wings returned to St. Louis, looking for payback. They wouldn't get it. Despite a first period lead, they lost 8-5.[28] On January 30th, the Wings finally got a chance to play St. Louis in the friendly confines of the Kansas Coliseum, in what would be their last regular season match with the Steamers. St. Louis came out hot, opening up a 6-1 lead by halftime. Though the Wings made a game of it, they were embarrassed by the number of times the Steamers were able to beat their defense and end up with fast break opportunities. "St. Louis' last goal in the first half was a real bummer for the Wings. MISL rookie Don Ebert, a St. Louis native, broke down the floor while the Wings players were complaining to the referee about a possible foul, and punched a shot past Dowler," reported The Eagle's *Lonnie Crider. Of all the teams the Wings played in the 1980-81 regular season, they beat each at least once...except for the Steamers.[29]*

But still, the rivalry had yet to heat up. The Wings entered the playoffs with a first-round, best-of-three series with the Chicago Horizon. They had clinched the division and first-round home field advantage by defeating the Phoenix Inferno at home on February 27th. Wichita followed that up by winning their last three games of the regular season. The series with Chicago would begin on March 12th in Illinois, followed by a second game in Wichita, and, if necessary, a third game also at the Coliseum.[30]

After a 4-3 loss in game one, the Wings had their back to the wall. But everyone in the league knew that the Wings were almost impossible to beat at home. Indeed, the Coliseum crowd would save their necks. In game two, Andy Chapman scored five goals; the last two of which were courtesy of assists from the always reliable Jorgen Kristensen.[31] Four days later, the Wings would close out the series in front of 7,753 orange soldiers. The 8-6 victory gave the Wings a Quarterfinals victory and advancement to the Final Four in St. Louis.[32]

The format for the playoffs that year was highly controversial. The top four teams would travel to St. Louis and each play a semifinal game, with the winners meeting in the final to determine the MISL champion. It was a huge advantage for the Steamers, who were guaranteed to play every game at home. "It's ludicrous," said

Bill Kentling.[33] *Randy Brown called the format "silly" and "fraudulent."*[34] *St. Louis reporter and author Dave Lange offered the reasoning behind the decision: "The host of the championship series was picked by MISL team representatives before the season. St. Louis seemed the logical choice. The Steamers had averaged over 14,000 fans in 1979-80. Although the format favored the host team, no one figured the Steamers would go that far. In 1979-80 they had stumbled to a 12-20 record. Thus, the MISL believed St. Louis offered the ideal location: one that would guarantee good crowds and yet would be a neutral site."*[35] *If the league WERE to have this format, Kentling believed St. Louis made the most sense as the location...*

BILL KENTLING: I thought that of all of the communities that we could have held an event, that St. Louis was ideal. It had a fervent fan base, centrally located, easy to get to. And I thought it was an excellent place to have it. Remember that one of our primary league and team sponsors was Anheuser Busch. In fact, I don't even know what my second choice would have been.

There were 25 great players in the league, 20 of them played for NY. It was a wonderful array of talent, starting with Zungul. After that, the league really did achieve some balance, particularly when the NASL teams came in. And so it would be very difficult to give up that home advantage and you really didn't know who would be in it. We all get greedy. We want to have the home games at our place. We weren't the NFL; you couldn't have a neutral site and expect to have a sellout crowd. You needed one of the teams to be the host, which in effect, takes away the neutrality of it.

The bad news for Wichita was that they had to play St. Louis first. The good news was they were flying high and full of confidence. In the postgame locker room after the quarterfinals victory, Randy Brown described the Wings as "howling and jumping around like a bunch of college kids." Luis Dabo, coach of the Horizons, felt the Wings were more talented than the Steamers. "If Wichita doesn't yield to the pressure, they're a better team than St. Louis. They have great players. The question is whether they can handle the pressure on the road," he told The Eagle. *For Randy Brown, the question was, "Can the Wings get their minds ready?"*[36]

What no one could question was the coaching skill of the four men who led their teams to the Final Four. Don Popovic of the New York Arrows had won the previous two MISL championships. Kenny Cooper had taken his team to the playoffs two years in a row, previously when the squad was based in Houston. Roy Turner brought his beautiful, European style of play to the Checkerdome, his Wings showcasing some of the most skillful players in the league. The Steamers' Pat McBride took a team many people thought would be mediocre and turned them into a championship-caliber squad that prided themselves on playing a mostly American lineup. This theme of Americans versus foreigners was always a subtext throughout the Wings/Steamers rivalry.

STEVE PECHER, DEFENDER, ST. LOUIS STEAMERS: Our team was 80% American, the majority from St. Louis, and Wichita had a lot of foreign players. People looked at it as Americans versus foreigners every time we stepped on the field. We felt that. Both sides felt like they had something to prove, probably more on our end. A lot of the players on the Steamers were former national team players, so this America versus Europe thing came into play every time we played.

Most Wings fans would watch the semifinal game on KAKE. All MISL Final Four games were also broadcast nationally on the USA network. But 700 lucky fans snatched up the Wings' ticket allotment and would travel with the team to St. Louis...Krazy George would be foremost among them.[37] The Steamers were a very athletic and very physical team that liked to run. The Wings were considered to play more of a "finesse" type of soccer. These contrasting styles would become obvious during the game.

(Author Photo) A ticket to the MISL's greatest game: Wichita vs. St. Louis.

STEVE PECHER: If you look at that playoff game in 1981 as a whole, you can summarize the style of play with that. Wichita came out and was pinging the ball around, everywhere they wanted to go. We wanted to play a more physical game, getting the ball to the corners. But they were just taking it to us. That was a typical type of game, style-wise. They always had at least 60% possession percentages, and we'd have 40%. The games were always close, nobody ever got blown out. They were physical games. Once we could get them into the physical part of the game, we could take over. I didn't feel like they could play like that with us. Then again, if they successfully would ping it around, it was hard for us to get into the game.

What made the Steamers particularly dangerous was the athleticism and skill of their goalkeeper, Slobo Ilijevski. The Yugoslavian-born keeper would consistently finish at or near the top of the goalkeeper stat sheet every year. Over his seven seasons with the Steamers, he would twice be named MISL Goalkeeper of the Year.

MIKE DOWLER, GOALKEEPER, WICHITA WINGS: ...There were a lot of fine 'keepers who played in the old MISL but the one who I respected the most was, no surprise, Slobo Ilijevski. A terrific all-around goalkeeper. He had the lot: reflexes, bravery, consistency, good hands, and he was probably the first goalie to understand the importance of being able to be comfortable with the ball at your feet, rather than just in your hands. I believe that he became so proficient at this that he even scored a couple of times in his career. Indeed, I recall one game at the Britt Brown Arena where I had to make a last ditch, sliding tackle on him just outside my penalty box to prevent him scoring against us (read – me!) Oh, and a nice guy too.

The traces of the rivalry to come began to form before the game began. The Eagle *passed along a local St. Louis paper's report that Steamer rookie Don Ebert reportedly believed "the Wings might be too old to give his club a lot of difficulty."*[38] *That rivalry's intensity would race from 5 mph to 100 mph within minutes of the game's end. Years of bad feelings would be born on March 27th, 1981. It would become known as the greatest indoor game ever played.*

In the first ten minutes of the game, the Wings would score three times: Brian Tinnion at 4:41, and Kevin Kewley twice, with a deflection off Slobo Ilijevski at 9:57, and a shot between his legs at 10:23. It only got worse for the Steamers in the 2nd quarter, with Andy Chapman and Kim Roentved extending the Wings' lead to 5-0. Television announcer Terry Leiweke stated, "This is a film on how to play indoor soccer, folks." A goal just before halftime by St. Louis midfielder Ty Keough made it 5-1.[39]

The third quarter brought more bad news for the Steamers in the form of a Jorgen Kristensen goal. With a 6-1 lead, it seemed a Wings win was inevitable. However, the game had become very physical, which favored the Steamers. Referee Artie Wachter, along with the sideline official, Anatol Popovich, only called two penalties during the entire game. Both of these penalties occurred on the same play: concurrent violations by Helmut Dudek and Don Ebert. During the fourth quarter, the Steamers made their move. Lange quotes Mike Dowler as saying, "They came at us in waves." One of those waves resulted in a Keough goal. "We kind of looked at each other and said, 'It's possible,'" Ebert told Lange.[40]

With a little under five minutes left in the game, St. Louis had clawed their way back to a two goal deficit, at 7-5. And then it happened. According to Lange's 1985 article: "As the ball came off the back wall, Dowler tried to clear the ball with a right-footed kick instead of falling on it. Ebert rushed in a split-second later and thrust his left leg in a vain effort to stop the ball. Momentum carried Ebert into Dowler's right knee, and the resulting injury forced Dowler from the game. Ebert denies deliberately running into Dowler...Compounding the incident was the judgment of the referees, who did not penalize Ebert. Privately, at least one high ranking MISL official says today that a penalty should have been called."[41]

KEVIN KEWLEY, MIDFIELDER, WICHITA WINGS: Losing Mike Dowler was huge.

KIM ROENTVED, DEFENDER, WICHITA WINGS: I don't remember that Don Ebert did that on purpose, though I've heard that from others. I would like to think that he didn't do it intentionally. It's a historic game by itself.

STEVE SHAAD: I think the situation that put Dowler out was clearly a foul.

ANDY CHAPMAN, FORWARD, WICHITA WINGS: Did Don Ebert intentionally take Mike Dowler out? No, I don't think so. I think he went in a bit harder than he normally would. I don't think he intentionally took him out of the game.

As for Dowler, what does he remember from the game?

MIKE DOWLER: The raucous crowd, the incredible atmosphere, the pressure the Steamers put us under in the last quarter, the pain in my right shin after Ebert tackled me, my decision to try to chip a pass to Andy Chapman that was intercepted by one of their players that ended up with them scoring another goal on the play, the many chances we had to win the game in overtime, the huge disappointment of blowing the chance to get to the final. Apart from that, I never give it a thought!

Reserve keeper Brad Higgs came in the game to replace Dowler. Within a couple minutes, he was scored on by Yilmaz Orhan. The Steamers now had a minute-and-a-half to tie the game. And they would succeed in doing so. "...[Sam] Bick shot at the glass above the back wall. The rebound came to Pecher at Higgs' right. Pecher angled the ball off the glass above the goal. The ball rebounded to Ebert, unmarked at the edge of the net to Higgs' left. Ebert headed the ball into the open side with 1:09 left in regulation. Pandemonium broke loose. As cups, programs, and rolls of paper rained on the floor, Ebert sprinted to the side, leaped on the ledge separating the wood from the glass and waved his arms as delirious spectators reached over and clapped him on the back."[42]

STEVE PECHER: If you watch the tying goal we scored at the end of the game, never, ever will a goal be scored like that again. I think we touched the ball three or four times without it hitting the ground before we put it in. It was such a fluke to get that tied up.

Thus, the game went to overtime. Though the Wings shot six more times than the Steamers in the overtime period, they were unable to score. Pecher's head stopped one of the Wings' best attempts to score.

STEVE PECHER: The Wings had a good chance in overtime. If the ball hadn't hit me in the face, the Wings would have won.

St. Louis failed to put the ball in the goal as well. Lange believes the Wings had a couple opportunities for power plays in the overtime period, but the referees did not blow their whistle on "Pecher for hitting Roentved from behind and Ilijevski for handling the ball outside the penalty area." At the end of overtime the score was still tied 7-7, so the game went to a shootout. "In the shootout, the ball rested at the attacking red line and a player received five seconds to score one-on-one against the goalkeeper. The Steamers and Wings alternated five shootouts apiece."[43]

After three rounds, the Steamers had a 2-1 lead off goals by Keough and Tony Glavin. Roentved missed on his fourth round attempt, meaning that the Steamers only had to score once more to win the game. And then the Steamers brought out their next shooter, the Nigerian-born Emilio John: "...John pushed the ball to his left as Higgs sprinted out to cut down the angle. John followed the ball and Higgs dove, arms flung straight out, blocking John from the ball. Referees whistled Higgs for tripping in the penalty area and awarded a penalty kick to John." [44]

Lange describes what happened next: "[Higgs] stationed himself inches away from the post to his right, giving John the entire left side to shoot at. To this day, Turner doesn't know why. 'I think he was trying to outsmart John. I just think it was a gamble,' Turner said. After 60 minutes of regulation, 15 minutes of scoreless sudden death, and 3 ½ rounds of a shootout, John lined up as thousands of cheering voices implored him to complete the Steamers' miraculous comeback. It was 12:30 am. Given the entire side to his right to shoot at, John put the ball there. Higgs didn't have a chance. The Steamers raced off the bench and buried John with bear hugs. The greatest game in MISL history was over." [45]

ANDY CHAPMAN: The backup keeper that came in, I used to room with him a few times. I knew we were in trouble because he was very raw back then. It's not like nowadays [in the MLS] when you have two great, great keepers, who go back and forth vying for their position. I mean, we had Mike Dowler and then it dropped off with Brad Higgs. He was just not experienced; played in college, and all of a sudden, BOOM, there he was in goal. On reflection, back then maybe a greater signing would to have had two great goalkeepers, but there's a lot of financial dynamics that go into that. And then as the game wore on, from a Wichita standpoint, it's getting dramatic, they're getting the next goal, and then suddenly they've got three and they've got four. The place is rockin', and when you have that sort of fan support, you feel like you can shift mountains...you can do anything. We just got caught up in a tidal wave and that was it. The African rookie went round Brad and Brad pulled him down and it was a penalty. Brad Higgs in practice, when he'd take a penalty shot, he'd decide to stand to one side of the goal and encourage the guy to shoot on the other side. He was standing there and I can remember being on the bench saying, "What the heck is he doing? Now he has NO chance." The fella just ran up and piled it into the right corner. And that was it.

BILL KENTLING: Maybe the best thing that happened to the franchise and the worst thing that happened to the franchise, happened my first year: Getting Kim Roentved as a teenager from Denmark, who left an indelible mark on the franchise; and that sincere screwing we took on March 27th, 1981 in St. Louis… but who's hanging on to anything…[laughs]. I understand that it was in the best interests of the league for that first world series to [involve] St. Louis. But that doesn't mean it wasn't a "screwing."

I believe that crowds can influence play and officiating. I think it's hard to go into another guy's hometown and win. I think there is a psychological factor involved. Do I believe the commissioner of the league went into the ref's dressing room and said, "We want the finals to be NY vs. St. Louis"? No, I don't think that happened at all. But clearly, without New York or St. Louis in the finals, it's probably, from a league standpoint, less of a championship game than Wichita versus somebody else. That's just the reality of it.

KEVIN KEWLEY: I won't watch the tape. We got screwed. In the last 20 seconds, I kicked the ball off a St. Louis player and it goes out of bounds and they give it to St. Louis. I was going berserk. The ref saw it and then said "St. Louis ball." We were killing them until Mike went down. If the ref got that call right we would have won the game.

ROY TURNER: The league must have been involved in those decisions.

KEVIN KEWLEY: No one in the league wanted to see Wichita versus the [Arrows]. They wanted St. Louis to win.

ROY TURNER: In the finals, I went to the reception in New York and their owner introduced me and said, "We all know what happened," i.e. cheated. It was robbery. It was nice to see St. Louis lose.

Roy Turner didn't pull any punches in his post-game interview with KAKE-TV's Mark Allan. He risked a hefty fine from the MISL in order to give his opinion about the officiating on that March evening. "A team playing like and then getting beaten just amazes me. I don't care what it costs me; I haven't seen officiating like that in my life. I've never seen anything like it. We're not a physical team. Maybe I should hire some boxers or something. I think that so many things were let go tonight. It's not an excuse, congratulations St. Louis, good luck in the final. But I think they know and these guys know, it's the Wichita Wings that should be in the final," said a disgusted Turner.

KEVIN KEWLEY: We wanted to take on New York. We thought we could beat them. But it didn't happen. I do think the league had something to do with what happened in St. Louis…Earl Foreman told the refs to "let them play" at the half. That gave St. Louis an advantage. We shouldn't have let it slip away though. You have to give credit to St. Louis for coming back.

STEVE SHAAD: We did have a feeling the league was trying to push us out. We were a minor league city in a major league. We used that as part of our David versus Goliath type of marketing. I got the same feeling from the MISL marketing people. They weren't as willing to promote us as they were for other teams.

STEVE PECHER: Of course they are still sore about it. Every time I see them I remind them we won the game [laughs]. I would agree with most of what they say; not the part about the league wanting us in the finals. We still had to score goals; the league couldn't control that part of it. But we came out in the second half and started playing a real physical game. I've watched the game 100 times and I almost think that Wichita got to the point where they were knocking it around so well that they couldn't adapt to any other type of game at that point. We started playing physical. Did we get away with some stuff? Probably. Now, who was or wasn't making the calls, I can't answer that question. But we really came out and started playing physical. When Ebert runs into Dowler and broke his nose; that changed the game around.

There were opportunities for them to win. In my opinion, they stopped going forward after halftime, and didn't attack like they did in the first half. If you watch the game, Roy comes out with a jacket, nice shirt, and tie. He looks sharp. As the game gets later in the fourth quarter, his jacket come off. The next shot of him you see his tie is undone. The next time, the tie is off, then the shirt is undone. Oh my God, it was pretty funny. I couldn't tell you if that referee threw the game or not. I've never heard that they did. But I can tell you that in my opinion it was the best indoor game of all time.

The stories locally that came out of that game afterwards...people were driving home who pulled over to listen to the game. People trying to get back into the arena because they could hear the crowd going crazy. I swear 50,000 people were there that night because everybody in St. Louis comes up to me to say they saw it.

NORMAN PIPER, FORWARD, WICHITA WINGS: I know we were up 7-2. I remember Jimmy Ryan in the shootout hitting the post. I don't like excuses...we should have won the game. Maybe the foul on Dowler, the guy should have got a red card. But to be up 7-2 and lose the game, there had to be something wrong. If you can't defend that then you don't deserve to win. It was a credit to St. Louis. They did their job.

STEVE SHAAD: I thought it was the best game in MISL history. I was calling it with Bruce Haertl. I thought we had it in the icebox at 7-2 and what an unbelievable comeback.

ANDY CHAPMAN: I still remember that night...one of the most dramatic events in Wichita Wings history. They say it was the greatest indoor game ever played...where we lost in the semi-final. I remember it vividly even though I was very young. I've only cried once in my life...really cried...it was after that game. After midnight...I couldn't go in the locker room, and hid behind the Zamboni machine and I [cried] my heart [out] for like five minutes. The emotion of playing in that game...we SO wanted to get in that final for the people of Wichita because of all the stuff the Orange Army had done keeping it afloat. And there were times when we thought the ownership wouldn't be there, and someone would step in and Bill Kentling would be raising money.

191

Each time the season ended a part of you died. The way that it died that night...I still remember it to this day. I don't think anybody knew I cried my heart out. There was silence. It was awful. I don't think there was any conspiracy. On reflection, it summed up all the great reasons why the indoor game was so special. It summed up why people were coming to watch...because it could turn on the flip of a coin. We were cruisin', and they came back and scored the goals.

BRUCE HAERTL, WINGS PLAY-BY-PLAY ANNOUNCER, KFH RADIO: I bet he wasn't the only one [crying]. There was no question those guys burned at a very hot level of competitive intensity.

After the playoff game, the rivalry became a full-throttled hate fest between Steamers' and Wings' fans. For the players, it was often just as intense...perhaps even more so. For years the two teams would battle for supremacy. Each side thought the other was the ultimate "bad guy" and bemoaned the opposing fans as classless and crude.

STEVE PECHER: The Wings facility was always very packed, very vocal; and then they'd come to St. Louis and we had 17,000 people in the old arena and everybody is sitting on top of you and the atmosphere is twofold what it was in Wichita...just because of the number of people. Both places had an atmosphere that fueled the rivalry.

We enjoyed playing in Wichita because of the rivalry. We would get introduced and would get batteries thrown at us...whatever people had in their hands. Our rivalry was based on bad blood. We had a rivalry with the Arrows, but there wasn't the bitterness. The Wichita rivalry took a different turn.

TOM SHINE, REPORTER/EDITOR, THE WICHITA EAGLE: If you thought our crowds were vile, they'd really get after it in St. Louis. People were fearful getting in and out of the arena, a little bit. A little drunk, a little crazy. There'd be a few more security present when the Wings went to St. Louis. It would get a little crazy.

KIM ROENTVED: From the first game I played in St. Louis there was this one fan in the stands, who was already old then, he would always say "f*** you, Roentved!"

and give me the middle-finger. He was always sitting five or six rows up and a little to the side. I could always hear him. EVERY GAME...I hadn't even done anything yet! 14 years later, I saw the guy at a restaurant in St. Louis and he was REALLY old then. I recognized him and went up and introduced myself. I had the best conversation with him. We became good friends. He would never flip me off after that. We got pretty close...it was so ironic. The St. Louis fans could be nasty. Some would call Andy Chapman "faggot" because of his short shorts. But, I think it also came from the way we treated them when they came to Wichita. How would you like running around on the field with a cowbell in your ear?

ANDY CHAPMAN: That rivalry with ST. Louis was a great rivalry in the early '80s. I loved playing against Steve Pecher...I loved Ilijevski, who has since passed away. Things did get intense. The fans would get a little crazy. There was a particular fan who used to be at the Checkerdome and he would lean over and just be shouting with the veins popping out of his neck, at Jorgen and the boys and myself. At the time, Terry Nicholl had purchased a tanning salon in Wichita and we all went tanning...and basically we all looked like friggin' movie stars. Back then, because you were playing on the turf, you'd put some heat on your legs and dilute it with baby oil. You'd go out there and be all glistening. This guy would rip us...."With your fake tans, you look like girly boys." I remember I got traded to Cleveland and we were there and he obviously did it to all the teams. We were walking off and he was leaning over the glass, the same guy, and I said to Keith Furphy, "Man, I hate that fella, he drives me nuts." He screamed to Furph, "You big girl!" We were one of the last two to leave the bench. Keith was drinking a big ol' cup of Gatorade and he reaches around me and threw it right in his face. The guy tried to climb the glass and get at us. In fact, he waited after the game still wanting to have a piece of us.

According to Turner, "The devastation lasted for months."[46] *While the Wings wallowed in misery, the Steamers went on to the final, which they lost to the Arrows in a narrow one point defeat. The Steamers' appearance in the final on their home pitch helped put a permanent end to the Final Four format. In the future, the playoffs would take place over multiple games at each team's home arena.*

A temporary comedic interlude to the Sturm und Drang of the playoffs was pro-
vided by English Leather cologne and their 10 ½ award. As a Bob Getz column in
The Eagle *noted, their commercials showed a woman exclaiming that "my men*
wear English Leather, or they wear nothing at all." In this case, he wore number
"7." Now, Stormin' Norman Piper was officially the sexiest player in the MISL.
Not a bad gig. When Getz asked him whether this would lead to him meeting more
women, he replied, "I hope so." [47]

NORMAN PIPER: It must have been my hair.

But the real legacy of the 1980-81 Wichita Wings would not be ignominious
playoff defeat or an award for sex appeal. Something beautiful was created that
season: The Orange Army, as named by Roy Turner.

ROY TURNER: At that St. Louis game I said, "We've got the Orange Army
coming up I-70," which is what started that phrase.

STEVE SHAAD: The people who called themselves the Orange Army were
much greater than the people who came to the meetings. It grew tremendously
after about 300 of them drove to St. Louis for that famous game. We did a good
job of marketing the color orange and various orange gear. We really pushed
the orange as a way to identify yourself as a Wings fan. I went to Orange Army
meetings and we created a cooler with Coleman. We sold merchandise that had
"Orange Army" on it. It was fun for them to feel like they were a valuable part of
the team...and they were. I give a lot of credit to them.

MARK WEDDLE, WINGS FAN: As a Wichita born and bred child of the
'70s and '80s, I was primed for Wings fandom! I'm uncertain when I went to
my first game, it might have been 1979 but it was probably in the early '80s. I
was immediately obsessed with all things Wings and MISL, so much so that I
had a fantasy league in my head with imaginary rosters, schedules and stats all
hand-written on paper. I begged my parents to take me to every home game and
when I wasn't there, or the Wings were on the road, I dutifully followed along
on the radio or TV. As a kid, the Kansas Coliseum was a magical place and the

atmosphere at games was positively electric. While I'll never forget the feeling of being there, in the moment, some of my fondest Wings memories took place elsewhere.

My grandfather's farm was near Valley Center just down the road from the Coliseum. We'd visit my grandparents every Sunday. It was heartbreaking to be stuck there when the Wings happened to have a home game at the same time. On those days, I'd be out in the yard kicking my orange and black soccer ball around while listening to the game on the radio. When the Wings would score, I'd hear the actual sound of the crowd roaring from a mile away at the Coliseum before it came through on the radio!

LOUIS MCCLUER, WINGS FAN: My family's first time going to see a Wichita Wings game in 1980 was actually a mistake. I thought there was a Wichita Wind game: the then hockey team. My sister and I went to the game, only to find out it was an indoor soccer game instead. Even though neither of us had ever attended a game, we were hooked from the time we walked into the Kansas Coliseum. From that first game on, we took our parents, who to our surprise, actually fell in love with the Wings and the game [of soccer] as well. Another soccer, and die-hard Wichita Wings fan family, was born.

Many Orange Army soldiers were created that year. And very soon they would be called upon to show their support for what Frank Carney and company were trying to build.

CHAPTER 14

An Oral History

Save the Wings

———

"Where were you going to find standings [for anything] where
you have Wichita AND New York together? That was our
biggest selling point...this put us in the Big Leagues."

- BILL OLIVER, PART-OWNER, WICHITA WINGS.

*SEASON TWO PROVIDED EVIDENCE THAT the Wings were capable of making a playoff
run. But it also showed how difficult it was to make money at professional indoor
soccer. In April of 1981, Frank Carney announced that the team had taken in
$700,000 that season. Unfortunately, they had spent $1.3 million. That $600,000
deficit helped convince Carney and his 31 junior partners that it might be necessary
to expand the ownership group in order to bring in more money. Another way to
raise more revenue was to increase ticket receipts. The most expensive seats near the
middle of the field would go from $7 to $8 for the 1981-82 season.*[1]

ROY TURNER, HEAD COACH, WICHITA WINGS: We FLEW to Kansas
City to play...and we stayed the night...at the Hyatt! What a waste of money.
Those are the things you look back and wonder, "Why did we do that?" Nobody
thought about saving money. Everybody knew how to spend it though. In 1981
we went to Madison Square Garden for the All-Star game and stayed at the
Waldorf-Astoria.

BILL KENTLING, GENERAL MANAGER, WICHITA WINGS, 1980-86:
History had shown that no one had ever made money on professional soccer in
the United States. So we knew that expenses would outstrip income. We were
prepared to take a loss. The question was: how big a loss? It's easy to paper a house,
but I don't know who it is you are fooling...certainly not your own accountant.

*Money, or the lack thereof, was not only a concern for the Wichita Wings. The
people of Wichita and the surrounding communities were feeling the effects of a
difficult economy. The glory years of economic growth were over. The economy was
changing and it was affecting the quality of people's lives.*

**DR. JAY PRICE, PROFESSOR OF HISTORY, WICHITA STATE
UNIVERSITY:** Wichita's economy is in a transition period. We had come out
of World War II having almost lost aviation and then things dramatically change
in a number of ways. With aviation in particular you have the Cold War and the
creation of the bomber programs and things of that nature coming into play.
You really have the [aircraft companies] all paying decent wages and investing
a lot in the community. There are issues related to that. There are going to be
fluctuations. There are going to be times where one company will layoff and
[those employees] will go over to the other company. But there's always the sense
these big companies will remain a presence in the community. They don't just
fund wages. They are sponsoring institutions and entities. That's starting to
change as the post-war boom gives way to a lot more fluid and uncertain time.

Meanwhile, some of our other core industries, oil for example, remain important but are now shifting to western Kansas. People are starting to think,
"How prominent ARE we in the oil industry?" Certainly by this time El
Dorado has faded. The meatpacking industry, which had been a bedrock of
our community since the 1880s, with the stockyards and so forth, is being re-
constituted out in western Kansas, where the feedlots are. Rather than shipping
cows to the stockyards to go to the Dold and Cudahy meatpacking plants [in
Wichita], they are moved out to western Kansas. If you went up on 21st Street
in the 1930s-1960s, you had these big meatpacking establishments. By the late
'70s they were gone. The stockyards closed.

Now we are increasingly beholden to an international dynamic. In the aviation industry, these had really been, with Beech and Cessna, local companies.

A lot of changes are going on there. Dwayne Wallace and Olive Ann Beech who had run these two companies since the 1950s, they were emerging into the senior level of society and they are starting to look around about how you pass this to the next generation. Dwayne Wallace was off the board of Cessna by 1983 and eventually these companies become part of global conglomerates. Cessna becomes part of General Dynamics in 1986. Beech is acquired by Raytheon in 1979. Learjet, a promising upstart in the 1960s, became part of Bombardier eventually. So the decisions that had once been very, very local are now being made by corporate offices on the other side of the country.

From 1979 to 1983, the unemployment rate in Kansas more than doubled, going from 3.1% to 6.8%.[2]

DR. JAY PRICE: Of course this is a time of stagflation in the national economy: high inflation, high tax rates. The energy crisis is hitting...We have this recession. Aviation employment goes from 18,000 in 1979 to 13,000 in 1981 in Wichita. That's a huge drop. That's one of the first of the big declines in the aviation industry which had been seen as resilient before this, and then wasn't anymore. There was always a sense that we are having a cycle [of ups and downs], you just lay low, because aviation will come back, because it always comes back. But what if it doesn't? It's not just economic, but cultural. Wichita is wrenched with cultural changes, like civil rights and the desegregation issues. The city has just celebrated its centennial in 1970, but behind that are the riots on 21st Street, the Herman Hill riot, the shooter downtown, BTK, so there's a lot of anxiety...and a lot of opportunity at the same time.

Despite the franchise's money woes, the Wings managed to keep the seats behind the goals at a rate that was affordable for almost everyone. For $4, it was possible to be part of the fun. In 2015 dollars, that was about $10.50 a ticket, still a relatively low price even today. It allowed the Wings to appeal to Wichitans of all income levels. Thanks to reasonable ticket prices, much of the fan base of the team had a strong blue-collar flavor. For a sport that should theoretically appeal to upper middle class suburbanites, the indoor soccer fans in Wichita were a lunch pail kind of crowd. You could find the average Joe at a game...and just down the aisle there might be a member of the city's upper crust. It took all kinds to build an Orange Army.

And then, without warning, it appeared that Wings fans might not have an opportunity to buy those $4 tickets, or any tickets at all. On June 16th, Frank Carney and Bill Kentling announced that without an infusion of $400,000 by June 27th, the Wings would either fold or move out of town. The team wasn't looking for small investors. They were happy with the 2,500 season tickets that had been sold to that point. "The public has responded magnificently...Now we want eight $50,000 shooters to step up," Kentling told The Eagle.[3] *"I'm still in a state of shock...As far as I'm concerned, it would take a miracle for [the Wings] to stay, a miracle that could only happen in Wichita," said Roy Turner.[4]*

On Sunday, June 21st, 3,000 members of the Orange Army came to Lawrence-Dumont Stadium to show their support for the Wings. Roy Turner, Bill Kentling, and several players were on-hand to rile up the crowd.[5] The Eagle's Randy Brown said, "...I've seen lots of sports fans. And I'm telling you, folks. I've never seen sports fans who were close to the Wings fans. Their enthusiasm is unequal in my experience, their loyalty unshakeable, their intensity constant, and their sportsmanship and class unquestioned in the league."[6] It was a massive show of support, and one that made an impression on Wings management.

BILL KENTLING: We did an awful lot of marketing around trying to gauge what the level of interest was in the community. It's easy to give lip service and it's another thing to write a check or give me your cash. The owners also wanted to see it. I remember on [Father's] Day we had a huge gathering at Lawrence-Dumont Stadium. We weren't going to do something the community didn't want. There was a lot of educating ourselves on the wants and needs of the community.

One of the difficulties the Wings faced was that some of the big-time general partnership money from the last season had been lost. Sam Hardage's $50,000 investment would not be repeated. Since the announcement, only three parties had come forward to help. Local businessmen Howard Sherwood, Roger McCoy, and Steven and Connie Acker each invested $10,000.[7] The Wings would need a lot more.

By June 27th, the search for large investors, or general partners, had born little fruit. The Wings announced they would extend the drive till July 13th. However, now, they were looking for a grand total of $650,000. But there was good news on *several fronts. Ken Brasted of Mid-Kansas Federal Savings and Loan was leading a campaign to increase advertising revenue, starting with an additional $20,000 from his company. He expected to be able to get another $150,000 to $300,000 from other advertisers. Grandy's restaurants were donating 10% of a month's worth of sales to the Wings, which would generate about $25,000. The National Baseball Congress (NBC) would donate 100% of one day's revenues (about $5,000-$6,000) to the Wings. Businessman, oil tycoon, athlete, and local celebrity Jim Hershberger would throw in another $50,000, adding to his previous investment. Also, 100 new season ticket holders were found between the announcement and June 27th. Finally, the Orange Army would attempt to raise funds as well.*[8]

By July 12th, a mystery investor had come forward with about $25,000. Meanwhile, the House of Schwan beer distributor and Burger King were pledging more support, and Pizza Hut, Coleman, Fourth National Bank, Town and Country Markets, and Mid-Continent Fire and Safety brought another $100,000 in total advertising revenue to the table.[9]

On July 13th, Frank Carney called a press conference to announce the verdict. The crowd of onlookers erupted in applause when they learned the Wings would be back, despite, falling short by about $115,000. The new donors and investors included: Horst Hiller, a longtime local soccer booster, would join as a new investor; Cessna and Learjet committed money to the team; The Wichita City Commission would donate money from hotel tax revenue; The Sedgwick County Commission donated a new carpet, worth $35,000; $62,500 from the Orange Army; and additional contributions came from Wichita State Bank, National Bank of Wichita, United American Bank, Multi-Vest Corporation, and the Wichita Aeros minor league baseball team.[10] *Additionally, KARD-TV (which would soon become KSN-TV) and KFH radio teamed up to put on a Wings "Block Party" outside the KARD studios on the 800 block of North Main Street. The block party raised an impressive $103,000 for the Wings.*[11]

Interestingly, the management and front office look back on that time NOT as desperate, but as an opportunity for the people of Wichita to prove the team could be viable going forward.

ROY TURNER: I think that "Save the Wings" campaign was just about a show of support, not about the team really possibly leaving the city...The Save the Wings campaigns were draining but also motivating because at the end of the process, I'd think about how much the people of Wichita really cared.

KEVIN KEWLEY, MIDFIELDER/DEFENDER, WICHITA WINGS: The players weren't worried about the team going away that year.

BILL KENTLING: This ownership group was willing to stay involved if that's what the community wanted. I wish to hell WSU had done the same thing before it dropped football. The overwhelming response was, "Hell yeah we want [the Wings]."

All the meetings were very calm and businesslike. We approached it unemotionally. If the community wanted it, we'd find the people to put up the money to produce it. Things were expensive because you do have a lot of player contracts. We didn't own our building so we were entering into a lease agreement with a county-owned facility. There were real expenses tied to it. So the decision was a simple one: If we see a show of faith on the part of the community, we'll do it again.

We thought that our hardcore fans, the Orange Army, if you will, were so pissed off after the St. Louis playoff loss in 1981 that they were fired up to come back again. In fact, the Orange Army that second year probably sold as many season tickets as our wonderful staff did...and we sold a lot of season tickets. Clearly there was momentum. We had that sort of Green Bay mentality. If you look at the landscape of the NFL, how in the world can you explain that Green Bay, Wisconsin is in the NFL? We took on that same attitude and continued to sell more and more season tickets each year. We clearly had the correct ownership group, staff, the right coach, right players, and we had real support...the Orange Army was not a cliché. It was made up of real human beings. These were people who went out and pounded on doors and did what was necessary. Win or lose, these people would be at the airport to welcome us back.

DOUG VERB, MISL EXECUTIVE, DIRECTOR OF PRESS AND PR: "Oh, they're having a cookie sale on the corner so they'll have another season."

We said that admiringly because it seemed like somehow they kept pulling it together, and they always had good teams and it was a tough place to play. Solid guys, solid people. To us, it was always something very special because of that. It was against all odds.

It wasn't the first, and it wouldn't be the last "Save the Wings" campaign. To some, these campaigns were an opportunity for the people of Wichita to come together and show their support for a local professional team that figured prominently in their lives. For others, the campaigns are looked back on with a roll of the eyes. For the skeptics, these fund raising drives figure TOO prominently in their memories of the Wings. Did these campaigns sully the Wings' good name over the long-haul?

BILL KENTLING: No, the team went on for a long time. I don't think there's anything wrong with asking people, "Listen, we're thinking about having a party, would you like to attend?" If there is some long-term negative impact, someone would have to show it to me. I do think there are people who are not going to embrace indoor soccer in the way [others do]. In the 1983-84 season we sold out 19 of 24. Shocker basketball plays, Wings play, and both sold out. If people are looking for some reason to not love indoor soccer, "Save the Wings" is as good as anything.

Throughout their tenure in the MISL, the Wings would fight to remain a part of a league in which they were the smallest of potatoes. During its third season, in 1981-82, Wichita would be the only city in the league, other than the Memphis Americans, that did NOT have either a NBA, MLB, NFL, or NHL franchise. In fact, all but three cities, Memphis, Phoenix, and Wichita, had at least two teams in those leagues. The people of Wichita were well aware of their image as the hick town in a league full of big-time cities.

DR. JAY PRICE: We're in the middle of an agricultural state. We always had a love-hate relationship with agriculture...There's this love-hate relationship because rural is seen as "yokel." This is a city that is deathly afraid of that image...By the '80s you see this discussion of us being part of the "Midwest." But the Midwest is a rural heartland and has a connotation of being small-town and country. At its best it is folksy: Prairie Home Companion. At its worst it is Hee-Haw. Now we are starting to be associated with being a backwater. It doesn't help that we have liquor laws that reinforce this idea that Wichita is backwater and yokel.

ROY TURNER: When I was on the plane [coming to Wichita for the first time] I crossed the state line and they took my beer away from me. I said, "Where the hell am I going?" [laughs]

The people who invested in the Wings wanted to promote Wichita as a city on the rise. They believed Wichita could compete with larger markets and considered it a public relations coup to have the Peerless Princess of the Plains associated with the biggest cities in the country.

BILL OLIVER, GENERAL PARTNER (PART-OWNER), WICHITA WINGS, 1981-86: The most important thing to me was that we play teams from New York, Chicago, Los Angeles, Cleveland, and Dallas. That put us in the big leagues and I thought that was important for Wichita. It was WICHITA I was more concerned about than anything. Where were you going to find standings [for anything] where you have Wichita AND New York together? That was our biggest selling point...this put us in the Big Leagues. That's what we tried to sell [when presenting to potential investors].

One key to being considered a Big League team was an expanded presence on television and radio. The 1981-82 season saw the Wings step up their broadcast presence. The team announced that KARD-TV, Channel 3, would broadcast at least eight games live on television. They would also produce a weekly coach's show with Roy Turner and 60-second "Wingtips" highlighting the intricacies of the game of indoor soccer. KFH Radio agreed to broaden their coverage of the Wings to include every game. Future KWCH-TV sports director, Bruce Haertl, would be their play-by-play man.[12]

ROY TURNER: In the [third] season they started televising more games and we started doing a coach's show. We negotiated a contract and got paid for our games. These were away games. We had great ratings...a 13-share one time. Dave Armstrong called those games.

We made Bruce Haertl. We were his first sports gig. He did our radio. He got big by being controversial. He had a loyalty to the old Wings. He did a call-in show pre-game and a post-game show as well. The broadcasts became so successful that KFH put our logo on their van to help promote their station. "The Voice of the Wings" they called themselves. I hated those post-game shows after losses.

KARD, which became KSN in 1982, would continue to televise the Wings through the 1985-86 season. The Wings became a sought after commodity in the local media market.

ROY TURNER: KSN paid us about $10,000 for the privilege of televising us. That's how big it was.

STEVE SHAAD, DIRECTOR OF MEDIA RELATIONS, WICHITA WINGS, 1980-85: It's a fast-paced game and is very exciting. We had the cooperation of the media as well. We were on TV quite a bit over the years. When we were on KSN they did like 10 road games and four home games. The fans saw stuff like that Steamers playoff game in 1981. That game converted a lot of fans... For one of our playoff games, we had higher Nielsen TV ratings than any other local network for that night.

TOM SHINE, REPORTER/EDITOR, THE WICHITA EAGLE: They always had a local TV contract [in the 1980s]. I don't know if they made money on it, but it was worth it to get the exposure. They felt they had to get the product out.

National TV coverage on the USA network gave the MISL a larger stage to show-case their new game. Al Trautwig and Kyle Rote Jr. continued to anchor many of those games. The Wings would be featured on the USA game of the week four times that year: against St. Louis, Pittsburgh, Cleveland, and Phoenix. The St. Louis game was their home and season opener at the Coliseum.[13]

BILL KENTLING: USA network was the best. Al Trautwig and Kyle Rote Jr. really did a nice job.

TOM SHINE: Al Trautwig did the game of the week; he's become a big announcer. Kyle Rote Jr. did announcing as well. During the All-Star Weekend, we had a media game. Rote is playing and he's being nice because he's so much better. So I'm young and fairly athletic, and I think, "I'm gonna go take the ball from Kyle Rote." Boy, BAM! Right to my ribs. "Okay, I won't be doing that."

The Wings didn't just upgrade their media presence. A new practice facility was built at the Coliseum. Though it was much appreciated by the players and staff, the facility would sometimes be used for other purposes when the rodeo and circus came to town, creating a humorous and stinky situation. "I can't wait till the ball is kicked out of bounds and lands in some bull's stall," said Turner. "We forgot to tell our rookies who goes after the ball when we signed them."[14]

ROY TURNER: In year [three], the ownership tried to build me a training facility in what was called the Barn at the Coliseum. They put soil down and Astroturf on top. It was better than anything else we had at the time. They didn't check the schedule very well though. At our first practice the circus was in town. All the animals were stored at our practice facility. We walked in and there were elephants and tigers everywhere and it smelled like crap...welcome to Wichita, you know. It was a great gesture, but next time we hoped they'd check the schedule.

The landscape of the MISL changed during the 1981-82 season. Most notably, and quite humorously, the CHRISTIAN group Athletes in Action bought the HELLIONS and, for obvious reasons, promptly changed their name. According to the Wichita Wings 1998-99 Yearbook: "...The Chicago Horizon folded. They were replaced by the New Jersey Rockets, who were added as an expansion franchise before the season begun. The Hartford Hellions moved to Memphis and renamed themselves the Americans, the San Francisco Fog relocated to Kansas City as the Comets, and the Pittsburgh Spirit rejoined the league under new ownership. With 13 franchises now, the MISL went back to a two-division format, with Wichita joining natural rivals Kansas City and St. Louis, along with Memphis, Denver, and Phoenix in the Western Division."[15]

Seven Wings players departed from the previous season. Brad Higgs returned to Canada, no doubt haunted by the Steamers' playoff-winning goal. Mike Custer was sold to the newly-formed Kansas City Comets, but was soon cut from their roster. Helmut Dudek and Hank Liotart were sold to the Memphis Americans.[16] *Brian Tinnion left for the Detroit Express in the ASL. Steve Earle went to Tulsa to coach the Roughnecks in the NASL. Mike Hobgood also did not return.*

(Don Marler/1981-82 Wings Yearbook) Frank "The Danish Cowboy" Rasmussen on the attack.

Though the Wings had one of the smallest player budgets in the MISL, at just under $500,000, they were able to add nine new players over the course of the 1981-82 season.[17] Three of those men, Terry Nicholl, Frank Rasmussen, and Jeff Bourne, would become household names in the city of Wichita. Ian Wood, a 33-year-old with many years of English Second Division experience, would prove to be a solid presence on defense for the Wings. Scouted by George Ley over the summer, he would play in 40 of their 44 games. Also added on defense was Steve Westbrook, the Wings' 1980 third round draft choice. John Cutbush, an English defender, would win a roster spot thanks to an impressive performance at tryouts. He would play in 39 games and accumulate 12 total points. Rich Reice, a 25-year-old forward from Penn State, would score four goals in limited action in his only season with the Wings. Frank Rasmussen was discovered on Roy Turner's summer scouting trip to Denmark. He would play in all 44 games and become an important component of the Wings' offense at the forward position.[18]

"The Danish Cowboy" received his nickname not because he was a fan of John Wayne or the Old West...but because he was known to frequent a popular '80s Wichita nightclub. "It was my first year and I was living alone. I went with Jorgen [Kristensen] a few times down to the Cowboy Club. I kind of liked it because of the way they were dancing down there. They are nice people at the Cowboy. One day J.B. (Johnson the Wings announcer) came to Jorgen and said we need to give Frank a nickname. Then Jorgen said, 'Call him Cowboy,'" said Frank.[19]

Like most Danish professional players, he had a second job while playing for B-93, his Danish club. "I was helping the doctors and nurses...I learned a lot because I worked with older people. Most of them were about 60 years old. They had broken legs and such and we tried to get them to walk again..." It was a relief for Frank that in Wichita he could concentrate on playing soccer. However, there was a learning curve for the American indoor game. "The indoor game in Denmark is a lot different. It's played with only four people on each side. It is played on a handball field which is close to 40 meters by 20 meters - about the size of a tennis court," said Frank.[20]

There was one player who would most definitely NOT be playing for the Wings. In a cruel twist of fate, Mike Mancini, who knocked out Jorgen Kristensen just the season before, was out of a job. And who did he want to play for? That's right, the boys in orange. Apparently, the Comets general manager, Tracey Leiweke, passed word to Bill Kentling that Mancini was interested in a tryout. Needless to say, it did not come to pass. "'We weren't successful in getting him banned,' cracked Kentling, 'but it looks like his talent got him banned.'" [21]

(Don Marler/Missile Magazine) Terry "The General"
Nicholl drives the ball downfield.

Terry "The General" Nicholl was perhaps the most important of the team's new additions. Roy Turner told The Eagle's *Randy Brown that "when we signed him, two other MISL teams wanted him, not to mention five other clubs in England and elsewhere. His honesty on the field is just tremendous." Randy Brown translated the English soccer term "honesty" as meaning Nicholl "gives you 110%."*[22]

Nicholl hailed from England's industrial north, in Cheshire County, and came from good soccer stock. According to Nicholl, "My dad was a good soccer player. He was a part-time professional player in Northern Ireland, where he was born and brought up." Nicholl's older brother, Chris, was a professional player as well. As for Nicholl, he started out as a student with a bright future in mechanical engineering. But then the soccer bug bit. When he played for Sheffield United in England, he managed to score the winning goal against the world-class Liverpool team (no doubt to the chagrin of former Liverpool FC player Kevin Kewley), breaking their 35-game win streak in front of 55,000 Liverpool fans.[23]

In Wichita, Nicholl became a fan favorite over the years. He eventually gained his own fan club. As reported in Missile Magazine, *"Another dimension has recently been added to the lives of the Nicholl family. They are now busy getting acquainted with a group of fans called Terry's Troops. A car rally, picnics, and a day at FantaSea [water park] are a few of the activities that have been planned to bring the General, his family, and his fans closer together."*[24]

ROY TURNER: George Ley had a relationship with a team in England called Gillingham. Terry wanted to come to America, so we purchased him from Gillingham. We told him he'd do an awful lot of work. His work allowed others to do what they did. He was a wonderful, personable guy.

TERRY NICHOLL, MIDFIELDER, WICHITA WINGS: George Ley had been an excellent player, a left-footed fullback. George had played for Gillingham FC in the English Second and Third divisions...and I had played there as well. He talked to me after a game and said, "If you ever want to go to America, I'd recommend the Wichita Wings." The only time I'd heard of Wichita was when I heard about its great aero industry. I fell out with the manager and I was told if I wanted to leave, I could. George followed up and he got me to the Wichita Wings, and I was so glad. I wished I had gone and played there earlier in my career… "Why don't we give America a try?" All I was gonna do was come out for a five-month season.

When I got there and I started to talk to Roy, he said, "We do appearances. Do you want to take the appearance job? If you want to work towards a green card, it's another way to have a positive bullet point in your application…" It helped me because I'd go out to all these schools, and they'd bring the kids into the auditorium and I'd bring another player and we'd be juggling the ball. We had it down pat. I was a very average player but I got great support because I was one of the faces of the Wings, in front of all the kids. Sometimes we'd play volleyball but use a soccer ball and our feet, and we'd be diving around trying to keep the ball up. We were like "Disciples" going out there.

I think [Terry's Troops came about] because I made all those appearances. [It] was a little club of people who wanted to know more about me. We did do some neat things. We went on a few little day trips. We had some cookouts. We did some treasure hunts. It was an excuse to get Wings people together. I wasn't shy and didn't mind putting myself forward. We'd go to the hospitals; at Christmas we'd take gifts for the kids. We were prepared to give back our time as well.

Of course, Wichita, KS was a big change from merry, old England in one respect…

TERRY NICHOLL: I always described the weather in Wichita as "very"…and that's it. Very cold, very hot, very windy, very rainy. Very. The winter was a whole new experience for me. Although it snowed a lot, it was always bright. Blue sky. We'd go get sweaty and play hard and didn't really notice the bad weather. The tornados were the most traumatic. We got hit with the F5 and I lived half a mile from the airbase, but it just turned away. It was only a half a mile from my house. There was a house there…and next door, rubble.

Wichita became home for Nicholl. He would be impressed with the kind of people he met around his neighborhood.

TERRY NICHOLL: On my street in Wichita, there was a commercial pilot, and Air Force Pilot, an engineer who was expert on crash sites, a Boeing engineer…the most sophisticated street in the world! They were geniuses.

ALAN SHEPHERD, MISL REFEREE: Terry Nicholl was an awesome guy...a complete gentleman.

KEVIN HIMES, RUGRAT, AND WINGS EMPLOYEE: Terry Nicholl was a mentor, and a genuine good-hearted gentleman.

BILL KENTLING: We had some guys that performed better than their physical ability. They did what was necessary...Joe Howarth and Terry Nicholl...that just became valuable members of the community. You need organization players. I remember Joe Howarth in the second half of a game against Buffalo, won the game with his defense. The first night Terry Nicholl got here he scored three goals. Guys like that become a part of the fabric of the community even though they're not going to be leading players.

KEVIN KEWLEY: Jorgen was always on with Terry Nicholl because Nicholl could play great defense.

ROY TURNER: One year he bought a sun tanning business. You've never seen a browner team in your life. All our players used to go there REGULARLY.

TERRY NICHOLL: All the lads got free tans. Jorgen loved going in there. We at least looked better with our tans.

Mike Dowler was now the undisputed first string goalkeeper. However, with the departure of Brad Higgs, the Wings were in search of a backup. Just two days prior to the first game, they finally found their man, or so they thought. Former Dallas Tornado keeper Billy Phillips agreed to a contract with the Wings.[25] *As it turned out, he would only be a temporary solution. In mid-March, after starting four games in places of an injured Mike Dowler, he would leave the team, to be replaced by a player who would settle in Wichita for the long-haul.*

Kevin Kewley returned to the Wings as captain, but with a new position on the field. He would move from the midfield to defense. Roy Turner told Randy Brown, "We've got to have some goals from our fullbacks, and Kevin's record the last two years would indicate he can score them for us."[26]

KEVIN KEWLEY: I was still playing midfield at that point and then [Kim Roentved and I] switched. It seemed so natural for him because he could do both.

ROY TURNER: If at the beginning I had told Kevin he was going to eventually play fullback, he wouldn't have stood for it. But eventually he realized that you could score as much from there, at least the way we played the game.

KEVIN KEWLEY: I think I scored more goals from defense. That all happened by accident.

Meanwhile, the team was desperately trying to get Andy Chapman back to America. Problems with Chapman's visa were threatening to delay his budding young career.

ANDY CHAPMAN, FORWARD, WICHITA WINGS: We had all become quite versed in immigration and visas and all that. Getting married got you a green card. You knew everything to do with that. In 1980-81 that was part of the negotiation I did with Roy, to get a green card. We negotiated that. There's a process you do and basically you get letters from local police chiefs...I think I got a letter from Bob Dole's wife, or maybe even Bob Dole. We pretty much had it nailed down. Virginia Creamer and I flew in a Cessna to the embassy to get this green card. Along the way of putting it all together, we discovered that in 1980 at Cleveland, they hadn't got my H1 Visa for me to play and earn money. We made the decision that we didn't want to hide that. I didn't know at the time...not that that's an excuse, I was told later. It was illegal what I'd done. We told them in the interview process...revealed everything. I was nervous that I'd be declined.

Virginia was wonderful. The guy said to me, "Okay, that's no excuse." He said I had to go back to London and wait for an interview there. They couldn't tell you when you would get it. I told him I had a contract signed to play in Detroit. I asked if I could wait till the outdoor season was done and he agreed. When the Detroit season ended, I flew to London. I signed a two-year contract with Bill Kentling, starting in October. I'd done well for myself. So I fly off to London and I'm waiting. [My girlfriend] Patti came to London and we had a week together, and she flew back to America in September. I was waiting for this interview.

Someone in politics wrote a letter asking what's going on. While I'm waiting, Ronald Reagan gave political asylum to 100,000 Cubans in a Miami Stadium. Meanwhile, I'm stuck in London...a stand-up guy in the community waiting to be told if I'm good enough to get back to America. October 1st came and went...October 15th came and went...we got into November. The opening game was on the 27th. Nine weeks after arriving in London, I finally got an interview. I went up there nervous and shaking. My whole future depended upon this really. I was granted the green card, jumped on the plane, went through Chicago, landed [in Wichita] and played in the opening game. I remember after the game sitting in the dressing room thinking, "What the heck just happened?"

As if the Wings needed any more pressure to succeed, the opening game of the season was at home against the hated Steamers. The wounds from the playoffs had yet to heal. However, Roy Turner smartly attempted to lower the stakes: "It means a lot just because it's St. Louis. But win or lose, we must realize there are 43 games behind this one. We don't want to let our fans down, and we want to win it for the fans, but the whole season is not riding on this game." [27]

9,302 fans showed up to cheer on their Wings. Unfortunately, Slobo Ilijevski was there too. The 25 shots he stopped made the difference, as the Wings fell 4-2. Andy Chapman was off his game, after having just arrived in the country after his visa debacle. "He only needs a week or two. He's just not match fit yet," Turner told The Eagle. [28] *The tradition of losing to the Steamers would continue throughout the 1981-82 season. The losing streak would end at 10 in a row in April, when the Wings finally prevailed. The home crowd at the Coliseum let out a sigh of relief that could be heard from Oklahoma.*

The beginning of the season was marred by a nasty losing streak. The Wings lost seven of their first eleven games. Much of their initial trouble could be traced to the injury bug. Don Tobin and Terry Nicholl had sprained ankles, Mike Dowler battled a painful thigh bruise, Jimmy Ryan's hamstring was hurting, Norman Piper had a sprained knee, and John Cutbush and Rich Reice also battled injuries.

The bright spot amidst the early season losses was an MISL-record third career shutout by Mike Dowler, this time against the Denver Avalanche. It was the first 1-0 shutout in the history of the MISL, which to that point had only recorded eight total shutouts in its first four seasons. What was particularly remarkable was the fact that Denver outshot the Wings 45-27. Dowler stopped them all. "A kid asked me yesterday, 'You gonna shutout Denver?' I told him I didn't think I'd ever get a shutout again...I'm just thankful for any shutouts that come my way. It's a team effort; I can't stress that enough. We were breaking up shots, really hustling," said Dowler.[29]

By the end of December of 1981, the Wings record stood at 4-7. They needed more offensive punch. Luckily for them, they found it in another former Dallas Tornado. Jeff Bourne, originally from England, was one of the top 10 scorers in NASL history. The 33-year-old forward had most recently led the Seattle Sounders indoor team in scoring. Prior to that, he had put up an impressive 51 points with Atlanta in 1979.[30]

The Wings would win six straight games in January, and Bourne played no small part. During the January 14th game against Memphis, Bourne scored a hat trick in their 6-5 victory. "I said Jeff Bourne would score goals. This is just the tip of the iceberg. Wait until our players get used to him," opined Roy Turner. "I like to get around the goal. My game is really knocking it off and going toward the goal. I try and sneak around the back post on the other side. The goalies watch the ball and by the time the ball comes to you they don't have time to turn and stop it," said Bourne.[31] The Wings won five of the first six games Bourne played. During that span, he scored 10 goals and made two assists. Those 10 goals were made on only 27 shots. Randy Brown described him as an "instinctive athlete" and a "classic forward" who liked to "lurk around the goal."[32]

(Don Marler/1981-82 Wings Yearbook) Jeff Bourne on the attack.

Originally from a coal-mining region of the English Midlands, Bourne seemed destined to follow his father into the mines. In fact, he did. From age 16 to 17 he worked at the top of the mine and later hauled supplies down to the bottom. Then, a lucky break led to a tryout with English First Division team Derby County. Improbably, he made the team and eventually led them to a First Division title. Bourne's time with the Wings would be highly productive. As Bill Kentling told Missile Magazine: *"I think Jeff spoils you. He does what he does so well and so quietly that you don't remember until you're driving home exactly what he did to help win the game. He's just a very solid player."*[55]

ROY TURNER: Bourne was a full-time player. He wanted to be around his teammates all the time on and off the field. I played with him in Dallas as well.

He was one of the stars in Dallas. He was a prolific goal scorer...being in the right place at the right time. He invented standing in the far-post.

BILL KENTLING: Positioned at that back post, I can't tell you how many goals he stole. He made a real contribution to the Wings.

But it wasn't just on the field that Jeff Bourne made a positive impression. His teammates loved him, even when he would play one of his many practical jokes. His sense of humor was legendary. "I think it helps the team a lot. Jeff is just a very funny man and his timing is excellent. He's very intelligent about his use of humor," said Bill Kentling. Trainer Al Green agreed: "His humor is right off the top of his head and it really keeps the team's spirits up while they are traveling. He's a real clown."[34]

KIM ROENTVED, DEFENDER, WICHITA WINGS: Jeff Bourne was one of my favorite people. He was a real teddy bear...I loved talking with him, playing golf together...he could hit it a long way. I was his roommate as well. We had played outdoor together. We became good friends and I just loved that I could find him at the back post [which] made me look good too!

What a prankster. Another player lived at Rockborough [Apartments] with him. They were leaving and I was coming in. He had this golf club in his car. There was a tiny bit of mud on it. [Bourne asked] "Did you know that could totally screw up the flight of the ball?" I said, "Of course." I was getting ready to go to the pro shop to have [mine] cleaned before he stopped me [laughs].

KEVIN KEWLEY: Jeff Bourne was a great joker. I played in Dallas with him as well...he smoked and drank like it was going out of style. He could score goals. We used to make fun of him because J.B. called him the Jet, but he wasn't the quickest. All he wanted to do was play the game, have some drinks and a smoke. He didn't have a malicious bone in his body. A great guy.

CHARLIE MINSHULL-FORD, EQUIPMENT MANAGER, WICHITA WINGS, 1982-85: Jeff Bourne would play practical jokes on the Danes all the time.

BRUCE HAERTL, WINGS PLAY-BY-PLAY ANNOUNCER, KFH RADIO: "Bourney" was such a funny sonuvabitch. The most wonderfully sarcastic guy that maybe I've ever been around, but never in a way that made you feel uncomfortable or cynical. It was always funny, insightful, reflective, ironic, and sarcastic. Jeff Bourne paid me the highest compliment I've ever had as a broadcaster. He'd broken his leg or an ankle. After surgery, he was left to listen to the games. He pulled me aside and said, "Haertl, brilliant." And that's all he said. I didn't know my ass from my elbow when it came to soccer, but I found a level of enthusiasm and energy and tried to express that as best I could. For him to pull me aside and look at me with that look he had, and say that, was the finest compliment I ever got from a player...That's the kind of person you are glad to have known.

BILL KENTLING: I don't know what it was about those English guys…not so much the Scots or the Welsh, but those English guys never met a prank they wouldn't pull on somebody.

CHARLIE MINSHULL-FORD: One practice Jeff Bourne switched everybody's shoes around. He took Roy's shoes and switched them with an extra small pair. Roy came to me and said, "Are you playing a joke?" He was dead serious. "Why did you give me these small shoes?" Then Jeff Bourne said, "Hey Roy, how do those shoes fit?"

ANDY CHAPMAN: Jeff Bourne and myself got along so well. Both working class guys. He loved smoking his cigarettes, as all the professional players did in the '50s and '60s. Obviously times have changed. He loved his pint of beer at night. His kids were great. Fantastic soccer player...different physique. He wasn't into getting as fit as you possibly can. I loved Jeff. He meant a lot to me.

By the halfway point in the season the Wings had overcome their slow start and achieved a 13-9 record. Just as important, the Orange Army had grown throughout the season. Home attendance averaged 6,500, a thousand-fan increase since 1980-81. Next door in Missouri, the Steamers were breaking all kinds of records. Their nearly 18,000 fan average was not only highest in the MISL, but more than any NBA team.[35]

A few days later, a familiar face returned to face the Wings. Keith Van Eron, former Wings goalkeeper and critic of Roy Turner, welcomed the Wings to Baltimore with an 8-3 drubbing. Old wounds were reopened when Van Eron appeared unimpressed with his team's performance. "I was a little disappointed. They shouldn't have had two goals in the first half and I'm just thankful that my defense played so well," said Van Eron. The Eagle *reported, "Turner fired back with a simple 'congratulations' for his ex-goalie. 'I said last year that if anyone didn't want to play for me, they could leave. Van Eron is a good goalie but I've got no complaints with my goalkeeping now.'"*[36]

On February 21st, Baltimore traveled to Wichita for a rematch. Though hurting, Van Eron would play. And the Wings were glad for it. According to Kevin Kewley, there had been some taunting coming from the Blast's goalie: "He was making fun of us when they were winning. That's not very nice. I don't think any athlete should do that to another athlete...He felt he should have been starting [last year] instead of Mike...I don't think he's as good as Mike Dowler, so what can you say?"[37] *As it turned out, the return of Van Eron was not triumphant. The Wings won 6-5. "If Keith had won today, I'm sure he would have said that it's great to beat Wichita, so I'm going to say it's great to beat Baltimore," said Turner.*[38] *Ironically, beating Baltimore meant beating one of Roy Turner's best friends: Coach Kenny Cooper. But the bad feelings between Van Eron and Turner couldn't affect the strong friendship between the two coaches.*

KENNY COOPER, HEAD COACH, BALTIMORE BLAST: We competed like hell against other as coaches, but at the end of the day there was a deep respect and love for each other. He was the best man at my wedding.

In a bright note for the Wings, they had four players selected to the Western Division All-Star team: Jorgen Kristensen, Norman Piper, Mike Dowler, and Kevin Kewley. On February 23rd, 1982 the Western and Eastern squads squared off in Buffalo,

New York. Kewley would score two goals in a winning effort. The Wings would fol-low up this individual effort with a huge victory on the road against the defending champion New York Arrows.

As the season began to approach playoff time, the Wings sold backup goalie Billy Phillips to the NASL's San Jose Earthquake. In his place, they signed Cliff Brown. The Tacoma, Washington native had previously had a stellar stint with the Cleveland Force. But after a rift with management, Brown found himself without a job. He had an offer from the Wings at the beginning of the season, but passed in hopes of a better paying contract. His bad luck continued as he struggled to find a roster spot on an MISL team. As bills started to pile up, he began work in an auto repair shop doing valve jobs. So when Roy Turner called with an offer, Cliff Brown didn't hesitate. "Cylinder heads aren't my thing. Soccer is," Brown told The Eagle.[39] *In April, he made two straight starts and achieved two victories, cementing his role as a reliable backup to Dowler.*

As the playoffs approached, the Wings were still beset by their Steamers curse. It seemed the long drought would continue forever. However, an uncharacteristic seven game losing streak by St. Louis put first place up for grabs with only a few weeks left in the season. The Wings not only might be able to beat the Steamers, but they might just be able to steal the top spot in the playoffs. On April 17th, 1982, the Steamers hosted the Wings in St. Louis. Wichita was only two games behind in the Western Conference standings and the Steamers seemed ripe for an upset. Except they weren't. The Wings lost 5-4 in overtime, after giving up a 4-2 lead at half. The win was the Steamers' tenth straight over Wichita. And then, in the last game of the regular season, assured of a second place finish, and having been mathematically eliminated from first place contention, the Wings finally beat St. Louis. It was a 6-5 triumph. In true Wings-Steamers tradition, the Wings narrowly avoided turn-ing their 4-0 lead into another comeback victory for the Steamers.

STEVE SHAAD: During the 1981-82 season, the front office members all grew a beard until we beat the Steamers. We beat them, and I go into the clubhouse to congratulate the team. I walk up to Roy and congratulate him. He didn't think we played well. So I determined since he wasn't completely pleased, I only shaved half the beard...as in one side of my face. I'd turn one way...had a beard...another way...no beard. That half-beard didn't last long.

The Wings finished the regular season with an impressive 27-17 record, including a 12-10 record in away games. This was a huge improvement on their 5-15 road record the previous season. Roy Turner and the lads were now faced with a best-of-three quarterfinal series with the Memphis Americans. Though Memphis had a significantly worse record, at 20-24, they had evenly split their six games with the Wings during the regular season.[40]

Though the Wings lost the first game at home, they would win the road game and close out the series at the Coliseum with a win, advancing to the semi-finals against the Steamers. However, this quarterfinal series would be remembered for something entirely different than the actual outcome. "Having been ill for a week and not playing well in the first half, [Jorgen] Kristensen was told by Turner that he wouldn't be on a regular shift in the second half. Turner asked Kristensen to sit on the bench and be prepared to go in if another player were injured. But Kristensen refused to return to the field and remained in the locker room," reported The Eagle's *Casey Scott.*[41]

Scott continued: "When the Wings arrived...in Wichita for the deciding game of the series, Turner and Wings General Manager Bill Kentling met with Kristensen and informed him that he was suspended for the game. It was then that Kristensen told the Wings he wanted to go home." Kristensen believed that he shouldn't have been suspended for his actions, and if the team were going to follow through with the suspension then he just wanted to go back to Denmark. The result was his release by the team.[42]

Kevin Kewley expressed the players' disappointment: "This is all very sad and unfortunate. It was a silly situation to start off with. Jorgen was very sick and shouldn't have played in the first place. I'm sure there were other alternatives open for Kristensen to return, but Roy made that decision and we've just got to get on with it."[43]

ROY TURNER: In the 1982 playoffs in Memphis, Jorgen wasn't performing. I think he was on medication. He was sick...and not himself. When I kept him on the bench after halftime, he said, "I'm not going back out." After the game, I said, "That's it." I sent him back to Denmark. It was such a difficult decision. We won that game and had to play Memphis [again] and he wasn't there. All the publicity was about him. We got back at 1:00 or 2:00 am and there was still a line out the back of the Wings office for the next day's tickets. I would never change that decision. It was the right decision. There was a lot of criticism, but not from our front office. They were 100% behind me. The players too. You can only do one thing in that kind of situation.

BILL KENTLING: Roy was headstrong, young and had not been through every situation. Jorgen certainly was headstrong. He was a coach on the field at the time. I didn't think either of them handled it the way they might of a year or two later in their maturity. But it was an ironic situation. We released Jorgen and sent him home. I was the last person to talk to him…I took him to the airport…he understood exactly why it had to happen, why there had to be discipline. And we made a deal that he'd be back the next season. So it's just one of those unusual things…I'm certainly going to back up my coach in his decision and Jorgen knew he had pressed it too far and Roy did the only thing available to him. Sometimes that stuff happens inside a team, and never gets out. But it does happen, particularly among professionals. He wanted to win so bad that he literally made himself sick in the playoffs.

The semifinal series with the Steamers had many of the usual themes of the rivalry: the Wings' finesse vs. the Steamers' physicality; bad blood between opposing players; Wings players angry at the refs for letting the game get too physical; come-from-behind victories; and, sadly, a loss for the Wings. After a game one defeat in St. Louis, the Wings returned to Wichita on May 9th, 1982 for a shot at redemption. It was an epic 7-6 comeback victory in front of their largest paid home crowd to that point: 9,643 screaming fans. The Wings came back after having been down 5-1. Jimmy Ryan tied it with 32 seconds to go and Chapman won it 39 seconds into OT, thus prolonging the series one more game. Randy Brown called it "the sweetest [victory] in the franchise's three year history."[44]

The Steamers would finish off the series at the Checkerdome a couple days later, winning two games to one in the best of three series. Due to a knee injury to

Mike Dowler, Cliff Brown started all six of the Wings' playoff games that season. Jorgen Kristensen was gone as well. It was a testament to the Wings' fortitude and the solid play of Cliff Brown that they performed so well despite the loss of two All-Stars. But with their game two victory, the Wings proved they could beat the Steamers in a playoff game...setting the stage for triumph in 1983.

And then, in a strange twist of fate, there existed a moment when the Minnesota Wings might have come into existence. The ownership of the Minnesota North Stars NHL hockey team offered to buy the Wichita Wings for $1 million and move them to Minneapolis.

BILL KENTLING: The Gund Brothers out of Cleveland owned the Minnesota North Stars. The Gund Brothers representative flew me to Minnesota, put a million dollars on the table, and made an offer to purchase the team. It was a legitimate offer. We didn't have ONE owner even remotely interested in being the one to cause Wichita to lose the Wings. But it was a REAL deal.

The Wings then produced shirts for sale that read, "We wouldn't take a million for our Wings."

BILL KENTLING: We tried to make a profit off of everything that happened.

The 1981-82 season saw progress on several fronts. The Wings decreased their financial loss from $600,000 the previous season to just under $300,000 in 1981-82.[45] Average home attendance rose from 5,825 to 7,301.[46] The team's .614 winning percentage would be the highest in the history of the franchise, and this would be the third year in a row they had made the playoffs. Most importantly, the team was on solid enough financial footing that it would be years before another "Save the Wings" campaign would be necessary.

For George Ley, the 1981-82 season would be the end of the road for his long and distinguished playing career in England, Dallas, and finally Wichita. The team had announced in April that Ley would retire at the end of the season and look for full-time coaching opportunities. The 36-year-old defender had been an MISL

All-Star in two of his three seasons. His position as assistant coach would be taken over by Norman Piper. "George Ley typifies what Roy Turner has tried to bring to the club. Not only did George bring us great skills, but a lot of class as well," said Bill Kentling.[47]

Ley would be honored at George Ley Appreciation Night on April 29th, 1982, during the first game of the quarterfinals against Memphis. "The basic thing is that the people [of Wichita] are good. It's like when I arrived at the arena last Sunday. I saw the people waiting outside and the cars lining up in the lot. And the atmosphere inside...I know there must be cities somewhere that would be on their hands and knees to get something similar to this," Ley told The Eagle.[48]

On the field, there were many fine individual performances in 1981-82. The only two Wings to play all 44 games were team captain Kevin Kewley and the "Danish Cowboy," Frank Rasmussen. Jorgen Kristensen led the team in assists with 51. Kewley's 30 assists were the second highest on the team. With 33 goals, Norman Piper was the Wings' most prolific scorer. Kim Roentved and Andy Chapman tied for second most goals, with 28 each. Kristensen was the total points leader with 65, followed by Kewley's 53, Piper's 44, Roentved's 43, Chapman's 40, and Rasmussen's 39. Kewley led the Wings with four game-winning goals...and also unfortunately dominated in penalty minutes, with 31; more than twice any other Wings player. Roentved led the team in power play goals with nine, with Jimmy Ryan coming in second with eight. Both the Wings' goalies had solid years, with Dowler accumulating a 22-14 record and 4.52 GAA, and Brown going 3-0 while maintaining a 3.33 GAA.[49]

An Oral History

The View from the Press Box

———

BRUCE HAERTL WOULD BE THE dominant television sports personality in Wichita from the latter decades of the millennium right up through to the publication of this book. As Sports Director at KWCH-TV, television play-by-play announcer for Wichita State basketball, and through a myriad of other broadcasting endeavors, Haertl would establish a national reputation as a sports journalist. Of course, everybody has to start somewhere...

BRUCE HAERTL: I was interning at KFH radio in the summer of 1980 and trying to finish up at Wichita State where I was playing baseball...or attempting to play baseball. Ken Softley left...I went from an intern to Sports Director in one fell swoop of a pen, with absolutely no idea of what I was getting into. Sports and Director were two words put together that I didn't have the faintest notion of what it meant or what the job entailed. But it sounded good and was a paying job and meant I didn't have to immediately go back to school...all of which was very attractive to me at that point.

The Wings were looking for a radio partner. At that particular point, KFH was being run by a GM named Barry Gaston and then Jason Drake, their program director. They're the ones that made me sports director. The natural progression, once they decided to do the Wings, was to find a play-by-play guy. I had done absolutely no play-by-play. I had no real aspirations of doing play-by-play...certainly didn't know my ass from a soccer ball, but was more than willing to try at the age of 20. It sounded pretty good once I got the job description: traveling around with a soccer team going to New York, Chicago, and San Francisco; and doing it with a per diem and all my stuff taken care of. It sounded like a pretty good deal and I took it without any sort of experience.

The great thing about it was that there was so little understanding of what play-by-play was supposed to sound like for indoor soccer at that particular time, because the game was so new, that I had kind of a blank canvas...So [Wings Media Relations Director] Steve Shaad and I, Klaus Kollmai as well at home, kind of learned as we went. Klaus was the soccer coach at Wichita South and was a very good soccer guy and I learned a lot of things from him in particular. I spent more and more time around the team and got a sense of what had to be done and how it needed to be described...and just kind of waded into it and created a style that seemed to work. Although, to be frank, I'm not sure that anybody would have known the difference anyway.

Even as a young broadcaster, I was relatively prepared and had a sense of what I wanted to do. I had talked with Roy [Turner] enough to know what they were trying to do, at least on a rudimentary basis. I tried to work my way into it and solicited feedback from people because I knew I needed to get [feedback] as to how it sounded: was it making sense, could they envision where the ball was on the pitch, conveying the proper sense of energy and enthusiasm, and was I too editorial. I trusted people to be candid with me, got good feedback, and I think developed a fairly acceptable style about halfway through the season.

I was an athlete and I was an American athlete and there were precious few Americans on that team. There was a very different kind of mentality from the European competitiveness as to what American competitiveness was. It took me a while to appreciate the way those guys competed. They were guys who were very interested in the entertainment value by which they played. That shouldn't have been mistaken for lack of competitiveness and desire to win; because they certainly had that. But, whereas with American athletes, it was ALL about winning and that was it period, these guys were very different in that they were very concerned about providing a very entertaining product. That was a very new concept for me but it was one I grew to appreciate and respect.

I had at least seen a couple of games, seen maybe some video, or on television, but not much. Not much. I tried to get to practices, pay attention, and listen. As an athlete, I understood listening to coaching and authority; I could at least relate to it on that level, even if I couldn't relate to the skill sets they possessed. When I say a "blank canvas" I mean it. There was no one I learned it from or heard that I could emulate. It was a "from the bottom up" kind of broadcast. It's not like I took a tape recorder out and worked on it at an exhibition game or something and listened to it. When I hit the air for the first time, I really hit the air for the first time.

I do think there was commonality from Bill [Kentling] as GM, Shaad running the media, Roy with the players...although Roy had some indoor experience in Dallas. He adapted to it the quickest. Everyone was kind of cutting their teeth. It's probably one of the reasons there wasn't much pushback to what I was doing (if there were people listening that didn't like it) because everyone was so worried about doing their own job and trying to figure out how to do it that they weren't concerned about what I was doing. There was pushback sometimes. I'd hear from a player or something through the backdoor that I was too critical.

There was one time that summed up my experience with the Wings. I don't know if I was an acquired taste, but at that point in my career, as a young man, probably with a fair dose of arrogance, certainly with a large dose of confidence, that people could have taken exception to. I'll never forget coming off the plane from a game in St. Louis. They, of course, were our nemesis, and they had the upper hand on us, and it would infuriate most of the guys, simply because that St. Louis team was mostly Americans. They were an outstanding team, and clearly our main rivalry. Back in the day, people would show up at the airport when we'd come back in...It was a hard fought close game, and I walked through the airport and, as God as my witness, someone said, "Haertl, it's not your place to second guess the coaching staff and these players." I said, "Thank you, I appreciate that." I walked another 20 feet (it was a game that the Wings had lost) and another guy said, "Haertl, stop sugarcoating things. We can take the truth." I'll never forget the yin and yang of those 20 feet at Wichita Mid-Continent Airport and the whole perception and reality of things that 30-some-years later stays with me in broadcasting to this day. One man's silk is another man's burlap. Interpretation is a really funny thing. I am sure, and I wouldn't know this, but I would imagine that when people look back at the contributions I made to the Wings, I don't think there were a lot of people in the middle. There were people that really liked what I did and people that couldn't stand it. And you know what? That's ok with me.

The development was twofold: it was the Wings and myself...and I apologize for the selfish bent, but I was recognizing that at the same time the Wings were becoming a force in Wichita, I was kind of developing, and I don't want to say becoming a force in broadcasting, because that probably occurred when I moved to television. But the spark was being lit for me as a broadcaster. And I've been doing this now for 35-36 years, and it all started with the Wichita Wings. Everything I do now, from broadcasting games in the SEC, BIG 12, and Missouri Valley, that flame was lit doing the Wichita Wings. I look back on those years in glowing terms. The friendships that you make: I ask the question to people all the time, how many really good friends do you have in your life? For me, I can do it on one hand. Part of it is the pace of life, part of it is the way we are wired. But I still see, catch up, and enjoy the friendship of Kim Roentved all of these years later. I have a longtime relationship with Steve Shaad, and Roy Turner of course...a very warm relationship with Roy. There are very few people who I respect more than those three guys.

Roy could not have been more patient with me. Especially now as a more mature person, I appreciate the patience he had with me as a young broadcaster. There were probably times when he was ready to string me up. But he always was positive with me. He was always very encouraging to me, which I really appreciated. I owe him for that because he taught me the importance of giving that back, and giving young, impetuous people leeway. It's interesting where you get your lessons in life. Sometimes you don't know about them until later. He was always good with me and very supportive. He was a pleasure to be around and an extremely good coach who knew what he was doing. The fact that the language they all speak could be very different, but through soccer they had the commonality and understanding and what he did with that was remarkable.

I know it probably dug at him a little bit that they were a very successful franchise in terms of wins and losses, but it never equated to a championship and I know there were times the personnel on the team was good enough to do it. But for whatever reason they couldn't. I think that bothered Roy because that's an incredibly competitive guy who played the game internationally at the highest level. I love Roy, and I'm not afraid to admit it. In fact, I embrace it. All you need to know about Roy Turner is, when hasn't he been successful? He was successful bringing this team out of nowhere and this sport no one had ever heard of...building this into a very viable entertainment value and an important part of the community...and then reinvents himself later as the president and tournament director of the [Air Capital Classic] and all the success he's had on the Nationwide, Web.com, and Nike Tours. All the man is, is a winner.

Bill Kentling took a chance on me, sight unseen. For that I'm forever indebted and very appreciative. While there weren't a lot of other options, he could have gone for someone else. I got that experience because Bill signed off on me. He was innovative and incredibly creative. He understood that he had to find a way to relate to meat and potato American sports fans this very different kind of athlete menu coming in. I thought he did a tremendous job from an administrative standpoint in being able to relate the importance of community to the guys that came, who to their credit, all caught on to it. A lot of those directives were right from Bill. He really understood what he had to do to quickly ingratiate himself. You also had the Wichita Wind, which was a high level...essentially AAA hockey. They had guys who went on to win Stanley Cups in Edmonton. The market was fractured...you had the Shockers, the baseball team, the Wind, and the Wings all vying for the next piece of the pie. He was remarkably successful because of his willingness to think outside the box as it related to a brand new sport which no one had any preconceived notions about. They were at their best with Bill Kentling in the front office.

After three years broadcasting Wings games for KFH, the Wings decided to go in a different direction for their play-by-play man in 1984...

BRUCE HAERTL: They were not going to have me back, which was fine. It was time for them to move on, and time for me to move on. I don't know if there was one particular reason or event or moment that precipitated that. But shortly after that, my first news director at then KTVH, about to become KWCH, Steve Ramsey, God rest his soul, contacted me and asked if that's what I wanted to do. Essentially, I went right from the Wings into television. I'm sure some of the

Wings people were counting on me to fade away, and then I became an even stronger factor in Wichita media from that point forward. I had run my course and they were ready to go a different direction. I was fine with it. It's not that it had soured; it had just run its course. I might not have liked me very much, or all of the time, at that age too. They were golden times and had great results for me. I'm very grateful for my time with the Wings.

CHAPTER 15

An Oral History

A Head of Steam

———

"So, St. Louis became the so-called 'American Team'...I would just say to them, 'How many of YOU played for the USA?'"

- ROY TURNER

THE 1982-83 SEASON SAW MORE changes to the MISL's team lineup. "...The MISL 'borrowed' three teams from the North American Soccer League: the San Diego Sockers, Golden Bay Earthquakes, and Chicago Sting. Among the new teams, San Diego and Chicago instantly became two of the top teams in the league..."[1] The Sockers were the 1982 NASL Indoor Champions and were a force to be reckoned with. Meanwhile, the New Jersey Rockets and the Philadelphia Fever folded, while the Denver Avalanche went dormant for a year.

Wings' GM Bill Kentling unsuccessfully opposed the Los Angeles Lazers joining the league. The Eagle's *Randy Brown laid out some of Kentling's reasons: "Dr. Jerry Buss is the money man behind a Los Angeles franchise, and that could be the end of the MISL as we know it. Buss' reign as the owner of the Los Angeles Lakers of the National Basketball Association and the Los Angeles Kings of the NHL has been most notable for its spending excesses, specifically Buss' penchant for giving athletes outrageous contracts. All the four-year-old and still shaky MISL needs is for some high-roller to come in and distort the salary scale even more than it already is."[2]*

The addition of three NASL teams, who came to play in the MISL during their off-season, was seen by many as the first step towards a merger between the two leagues. Kentling saw little positive in this possibility. "While there are some excellent people in the NASL, and I'd love to have rivalries with Tulsa and Chicago, I have not seen any evidence of the NASL's ability to market its product. They have more problems than we do with their players' contract. The MISL's TV contract with the USA network is much better than the NASL's contract with ESPN. I just don't know what it is that the NASL has that we would want," said Kentling. Kentling believed in building the MISL slowly and methodically, unlike the frenetic expansion that many believed had doomed the NASL.[3]

The league now had a team in the three largest markets: New York, Los Angeles, and Chicago. The Wings would have ten gameday opportunities that season to receive media exposure in those cities. It made the owners and the community proud that the city of Wichita's name was alongside the largest cities in the country. Wichita had hit the big time. But along with change came new challenges. The Wings would now have to face San Diego's deadly scorer, "Triple E" Juli Veee. Veee, Hungarian by birth, previously led the NASL's indoor league in scoring and would be a difficult opponent in 1982-83.

Back in Wichita, as usual, there were changes in the cast of characters. Ian Wood returned to England and George Ley retired. In a surprise move, Jimmy Ryan announced in August that he would be returning to Scotland and most likely retiring from soccer. The 37-year-old Ryan, the leading all-time scorer for the team as of 1982, was one of the original Wings. "I just want to thank all the fans in Wichita who made my stay here so good," he told The Eagle.[4]

Joe Howarth, another original Wing, would retire as well. Howarth had not only been a stalwart defender, but had also run the Wings summer soccer camps and been in charge of community relations. In a sense, he had been for the Wings what Roy Turner had been for the Dallas Tornado during his last couple seasons. Fans would see him on KSN doing color commentary for Wings games for the next couple years.[5] Don Tobin would leave his partner-in-crime, Andy Chapman, and sign with the Los Angeles Lazers. Keith Gehling and Rich Reice would also depart the team. But, Jorgen Kristensen, the one man who some might have thought would NOT return, was back in Wings' orange for the new season.

Of course, there were additions as well. Tony Peszneker was a young Canadian player from Calgary who excelled in both hockey and soccer as a boy. After a successful stint with the NASL's Minnesota Kicks, he was left without a team when they folded. He impressed Roy Turner at tryouts, but because of other available players, wasn't signed. But the Wings weren't done with him yet. Turner asked him to play in the Wings' exhibition games to see how he'd respond during actual game play. He played well enough to earn a starting job on defense. "When you select a team and train individuals, you're looking for the right blend and the player's various strengths. Tony's strength is defensively a lot more than going forward," said Turner. "The way I play comes from hockey. You don't let someone stand in front of your net in hockey and you can't do it in soccer. There are some similarities," Peszneker told The Eagle's Tom Shine.[6]

CHARLIE MINSHULL-FORD, EQUIPMENT MANAGER, WICHITA WINGS, 1982-85: I got Tony Peszneker some ice time for the Wichita Wind. Roy was not happy about that. His dad had played hockey in Hungary. Tony probably could have played professionally.

Ray Vigliotti was signed to play midfield and would appear in 14 games for the Wings in his only season with the club. Jimmy O'Neill became the first player from the Wheathawks to sign with the Wings. O'Neill had previously played for Rockhurst before coming to Wichita. Though he was told from the beginning by Roy Turner that he would only suit up if the team roster fell below the league minimum of 16, O'Neill's signing showed that the Wheathawks could produce an accomplished player. Unfortunately for O'Neill, those conditions were never met over the course of the season.[7]

A more impactful signing was that of Gregg Willin. A graduate of Jacksonville University, Willin made the ASL All-Star Team while playing for the Georgia Generals in the summer of 1982. Though he had a reputation as a physical defender, he wasn't foul-prone. "That's my style. If there's a 50-50 ball, I'm going to end up winning it," Willin told The Eagle's *Tom Shine. "We just don't have the room for errors in the Major Indoor Soccer League because you get punished. But Gregg has the confidence that he won't make any errors. And when he makes errors, he's very coachable," said Roy Turner.[8] Willin would become a regular contributor over his initial three year stint with the Wings. He would play in 43 of the Wings' 48 games that season, accumulating 13 points and 40 blocks.[9]*

TOM SHINE, REPORTER/EDITOR, THE WICHITA EAGLE: They had big travel bags for the road and [trainer] Al Green would drop them off at the airport [on the way back to Wichita]. And he'd always pick up Gregg's bag and [groan] because it would weigh like 400 lbs. Gregg had taken every Coca-Cola and beer in the locker room and put it in his bag to take home from the road.

His wife lived here full-time. She wanted the same amount of money as Kim Roentved, because her logic was that [Gregg] was playing with Roentved so they should make the same amount of money. Bill Kentling was like, "No." She said, "Well, we'll have to start looking somewhere else." And Bill said, "Here's a list of all the other GMs, go ahead and call them."

CHARLIE MINSHULL-FORD: Gregg Willin was a good American defender, but it didn't mesh with the flare the Wings had. His wife Anna cornered Roy and berated him because Gregg wasn't getting enough playing time. She was from Miami but wasn't stuck up or anything. I think Gregg would have fit in if this had been an American team.

In a major coup, the Wings added one more Roentved to their roster on October 26th, 1982. Kim's older brother Per Roentved came to Wichita ready to contribute on defense. At 6'2 and 180 pounds, he could bring a level of physicality some of the smaller players couldn't muster. What made him particularly valuable was his experience against top-level competition. "I've never had an opportunity to sign a player of his caliber," Roy Turner told The Eagle. *"Roy thought one Roentved on the back line was good, two would be great," added Bill Kentling.[10]*

Per was considered a national treasure amongst Danish soccer fans. He had played in a record 75 international games for Denmark and spent almost ten years as captain of the national team. He defeated the Italian national team prior to their World Cup victory, even scoring a goal in the game. In 1972, Per was named the Danish Player of the Year and played for the Danish Olympic team in the infamous Munich games. He even traveled across the Iron Curtain to play in East Germany and the Soviet Union. His experience in Moscow was enlightening. "The hotels are a lot different...When you go in you have to show before you enter that you are living there. When you take the elevators up they check and when you come off to the floor where you are living they look again. They are sitting there watching every step... That's the way they do it over there," said Per.[11]

(Don Marler/Missile Magazine) Wichita Wing and
Danish national team captain Per Roentved.

For Per, playing in Wichita was almost like a vacation. After he left the German Bundesliga and returned to play in Denmark, he was busy running his sporting goods store, playing soccer, and conducting speaking engagements around Copenhagen. "To have a store, to practice four times a week, and to make the match Sunday and sometimes travel Saturday...My family didn't see me anymore...I was going mad. I wanted to concentrate fully on soccer. Not 8 a.m. in the store, 6 p.m. on the soccer field, and 10 p.m. back in the store," said Per.[12] *In addition to scoring 16 goals and assisting in 14 more, he would lead the team in blocks that year, with an astounding total of 72.*[13]

Like most players, Per brought his family with him to Wichita. In his case it was his wife Janne and their two children, Christina and Thomas. Roy Turner was a firm believer in players keeping their families together.

ROY TURNER: We brought a player's wife and children here. It was wonderful for their kids to get an experience at an American school. All of the families loved living in America. It was a bad idea to leave the family at home. When players came over with their family, the wife would get homesick. But then they go home for a month and realize they want to come back to America. The guys who stay long-term would send their kids home in the summer for a month or two to get it out of their system. A lot of wives hung out together. The Danish wives would hang together; the English wives would do the same. They'd sit together at the games and socialize together. They also would meet American families that would be nice to him.

The most important addition during the 1982-83 season was a blast from the Wings' past. Omar Gomez had left after the Wings' first season to return to the Dallas Tornado and then followed that up with a highly successful stint alongside Steve Zungul with the New York Arrows. But Wings management was a little nervous about signing an Argentinian to play alongside a bunch of Englishmen just months after the Falkland Islands War. According to Randy Brown, "First, Turner talked to several English players: Captain Kevin Kewley, assistant coach Norman Piper, Terry Nicholl, John Cutbush, Joe Howarth, and Mike Dowler..." "To a man, they said, 'Get him,'" said Bill Kentling. "Then Roy asked El Indio if he objected to playing with the British players, and he said, 'No.' He was anxious to get here."[14]

KEVIN KEWLEY, DEFENDER, WICHITA WINGS: Bill Kentling asked me if we'd have a problem with signing Omar Gomez, because of the Falkland Islands War going on.

BILL KENTLING, GENERAL MANAGER, WICHITA WINGS, 1980-86: We were gonna bring back Omar Gomez in 1982. Great Britain and Argentina are at war...Omar was an Argentinian and we had five or six Brits. So we asked the English players, "Will this be a problem if we bring Omar back, as an

Argentinian?" And Norman Piper said, "No, let's bring him back. Hell, what do we have to worry about...we won!" The Brits were so happy to have beaten somebody without help! Norman was pretty proud.

The exuberant and emotional Gomez added a spark to the Wings right away. "When we first brought Omar here in 1979, it was because of his ability, and he did perform. When we brought him back from New York, he became truly happy for the first time in the United States because of his love for Wichita and his performance improved even more. He is a real asset to the team and the entire franchise," said Roy Turner. "Omar has an understanding of the indoor game that's almost frightening. His overview of the game is absolutely brilliant. He desperately wants to be a champion and that desire is very infectious," added Bill Kentling.[15]

"We want to be a contender and it's going to take the likes of Gomez to keep us a contender. We were looking for someone to help us score us more goals and, without question, Omar's record proves he can do it," said Turner. There was no doubting that, considering the 76 points he had scored the previous season in New York. "I am happy because I go to Wichita. That's all I think about now. I am very excited. I will try very hard to score many goals because I love the people in Wichita," said Gomez, in his characteristic broken-English.[16]

As it turned out, he loved his teammates just as much as they loved him. He formed an odd couple with English midfielder Terry Nicholl. Though each player's homeland was on opposite sides of a short, but bloody war in the South Atlantic Ocean, the two men got along famously as roommates on the road. "It raised a lot of eyebrows. A lot of people couldn't believe he put a Briton and an Argentine together," explained Nicholl. "Omar is a great character. I was very fortunate Roy put us together on the road. He's easy to get along with. I know Omar and I get along better than some of the other Argentine and Britons who play together." Omar agreed: "Me and Terry are very good friends. We're roommates. We spend a lot of time together...I don't feel anything against the English people...I'm not worried about the Malvinas [the Argentine name for the Falkland Islands]. It's not my problem. It's a political problem."[17]

(Don Marler/Missile Magazine) 1982-83 Wings MVP, Omar Gomez.

TERRY NICHOLL, MIDFIELDER, WICHITA WINGS: We went to the Falklands and won the right to keep them. During that time I was Omar Gomez's roommate. They thought we'd change roommates because our countries were at war. We were happy to be roommates. I was his defensive back-up. There were no worries. Our countries were at war but we weren't. Being Wings teammates was more important to us than our countries being at war...

Gomez would continue his stellar MISL career that year, most definitely earning what was speculated to be a salary in the $40,000-$50,000 range; a number likely *exceeded by only Jorgen Kristensen.*[18] *By season's end, he would accumulate a team leading 86 points off 37 goals and 49 assists. He would also lead the Wings in power play goals with 10. But his fiery temper contributed to his 37 penalty minutes, almost twice as many as any other Wing.*[19] *That temper led to a one game-suspension at the beginning of the 1982-83 season, resulting from a fight during the previous year's Arrows-Steamers playoff series. This reputation would follow him throughout the season. He would receive two red cards that year, and miss four games due to suspension. "They say Omar Gomez is making trouble every game. I can say anything and get two minutes or a yellow card," said Gomez.*[20] *He wouldn't be the only Wing to complain about the officiating that season. More about THAT later.*

The season began with a bang during a match against the Memphis Americans. Kevin Kewley was given a two-minute penalty for tripping the great Yugoslavian player and 1983 MISL Pass-Master, Stan Stamenkovic. But there was more to come. "...after Kewley's first penalty, he and Stamenkovic traded a volley of elbows and kicks and were both ejected from the game after much pushing and shoving by members of both teams. During the argument following the flare-up, which was punctuated by Stamenkovic sneaking in a kick to Kewley's behind while Kewley was being restrained by his teammates, Omar Gomez was given a two-minute for dissent."[21]

KEVIN KEWLEY: Stamenkovic and I got sent off when we had a fight in Memphis. He elbowed me in the face so I smacked him and there was a big melee. The guys were joking after the game, "It was a great trade-off for Stamenkovic."...I remember at the All-Star game, Stamenkovic said, "You knocked my tooth out." I felt bad because he was a great guy.

ANDY CHAPMAN, FORWARD, WICHITA WINGS: Soccer players from England usually came from working class areas, from rough areas. It's different than it is in America where it's a suburban sport, where you pay to play. Most of the people from Europe and South America are from rough areas. These are hardworking guys who won't back down from a fight.

For the second year in a row, the Wings started their season in a slump, losing four of their first five games. Uncharacteristically, they struggled at home, starting out 2-4 in what should have been the friendly confines of the Kansas Coliseum. "At home they're playing with emotion and trying to win the game too hard. Impatient is the word. I think they're trying to please too much. The crowd is wonderful and I don't want them to stop. We're playing too much with emotion and not enough with brains," said Roy Turner.[22]

Thankfully, the Wings began to turn things around in late December and early January. They could thank Mike Dowler's play for much of that success. Roy Turner believed that Dowler's 26 save performance in an overtime victory against the Steamers on December 27th was one of the best games of his career. "As the team plays together more, we get to know our style of play. It's become evident now. Teams are having to work hard to score on us," Dowler told The Eagle.[23]

When looking at the playing time and performance of the members of the 1982-83 Wings, the dominant performers were men from Denmark, England, Wales, Argentina, and, even Canada. Save Gregg Willin, Americans were absent from the equation. Some Wings fans noticed, and did not approve. One fan wrote this letter to The Eagle: "I would like to know why Coach Roy Turner will not give the American players the same opportunity to play as he does the foreign players on the Wichita Wings...It almost seems like Coach Turner is afraid the American players will perform well and some of the foreign players will not get as much playing time...I feel if the American players had been given the same opportunity to play this year they would be playing just as well and the Wings would not be any worse off in the standings."[24] *Various people had been making this argument since the first season. Roy Turner had addressed the issue in 1980 during an interview with The Eagle: "If I could find 18 Americans who could give us a competitive team I would sign them. But my priority is not Americanization, then Wichita. It's Wichita, then Americanization. As long as coaches in this league are hired and fired according to their won-lost record instead of how good their Americanization is, the Americans will continue to have trouble coming to the front..."*[25] *It was a controversy that wouldn't die.*

RAY DENTON, DIRECTOR OF OPERATIONS, WICHITA WINGS, 1979-1980: There were people criticizing Roy about too many English guys.

CHARLIE MINSHULL-FORD: Roy liked foreign players better than the American guys.

TOM MARSHALL, GENERAL MANAGER, WICHITA WINGS, 1979:
There is still a lie that the American player is ten years away from catching up
with the foreign player. I feel it's a con job and has been going on for a long time.
We kick butt around the world at the under-16 teams and then they go overseas
and are automatically put in the back. It's a shame. That was part of the premise
when we started the Wings: we'd revolutionize the game here in the US. That's
what [Assistant Commissioner] Ed Tepper preached. That all immediately fell
by the wayside...Not only did St. Louis continually spoil Wichita's seasons, they
did it with a core of American players, many of which were local.

...I contend that there were an ample amount of American players equal
to the Second Division and aged English players. To find them and develop
them would require work and effort when the European player acquisition
required only connections. The league paid great lip service to the American
player. In its first year, they rode the back of the Arrows local goalie, Shep
Messing. In Dallas, the NASL was promoting their forward, Kyle Rote, Jr...
but all this effort fell by the wayside quickly on a national basis.

*As a former player for Team USA, Roy Turner was a bit irked by the accusations of
an anti-American bias...*

ROY TURNER, HEAD COACH, WICHITA WINGS: St. Louis was THE
hotbed of developing soccer players in this country. Before the MISL started the
St. Louis players were playing all over the NASL. When they started the Steamers,
all those guys wanted to go back and play there. Pecher and those guys didn't care
about the NASL anymore once the Steamers started. So, St. Louis became the
so-called "American Team." They kind of marketed it as, "We are going to beat
the crap out of these foreigners." I would just say to them, "How many of YOU
played for the USA?" We did what was best for this community, which was to
bring in guys from other places to play. The way they played the game and the
way we played the game were totally different. They played a much more physical
game. We were more finesse. That style of play is one of the reasons why the
Wings were successful.

ALAN SHEPHERD, MISL REFEREE: I think Roy Turner has an eye for
talent. He brought in some pretty darn good players. I think Roy would have

given an American a shot if he could blend in with the team and were good enough to play. I think Roy did what he had to do to make the Wings successful. Today it may be completely different.

BILL KENTLING: I don't think there is any question that in our first year together [Roy Turner] went with known quantities. The known quantities to him were European players. He came with a contingent of European players to the NASL, and they were better than the American kids. Remember, this was 1980, not 2015. Leaving Kyle Rote, Jr. out of it for the moment, the level of play of the American kid in those days didn't compare. The worst kid in Buenos Aires was as good as the best kid in Kansas City. Now, there were pockets of American players. St. Louis was clearly a pocket. Dallas was clearly a pocket. But the first year, there's no question we leaned heavily on Europeans players because they could play that entertaining style. I'm well aware of the [criticism] and I thought it got overblown as the years went on because Roy was given no credit for Mike Fox or Chico Borja. He was given no credit for Dale Ervine. He didn't ever get any credit for the American players that played well. I thought that early on it was strictly Europeans but gained real balance as we went along...because the American kids got better! I credit the NASL for what they did, I credit the MISL...everybody played a part in [developing American players]. Guys like Roy Turner really did a wonderful job in the markets where they were located.

CHARLIE MINSHULL-FORD: The American players felt jilted sometimes. Steve Westbrook said "We've Gotta Get Out of This Place" [by The Animals] was his theme song. He wanted to go back to St. Louis.

TOM SHINE: If guys got hurt they got put on "school duty," or, if you were an American. Normally, they weren't as good [on the field]. They were good ATHLETES. Jimmy O'Neil was a very good baseball player. Steve Westbrook played football. He was a very good athlete. They had to go around and do school assemblies all over town.

KEVIN KEWLEY: I was captain at the time, and we had a few people write in to the paper that they shouldn't let a foreigner be captain of the team! I was at a union meeting once, and someone stood up and said everyone should do what

St. Louis is doing. "Wichita should have all American players." But it wouldn't have worked in Wichita. One of Roy's best qualities was getting the best players for the money he had.

It's hard to deny that having foreign players with exotic accents in a place like Wichita, Kansas was part of the appeal of the Wichita Wings...

ROY TURNER: The personality of the players was one of the reasons we were so successful. The accents were important in creating a buzz in town. Our "foreignness" was part of our success.

KEVIN KEWLEY: We were different and that made it interesting.

ANDY CHAPMAN: So, you get that mix in there of all those different nationalities; it is a lovely concoction. And the fans got to see it. That was the unique appeal that everyone in the stadium watching the game was from Kansas and they were all the same. It wasn't a diverse crowd. But they were getting to watch foreign players from South America, Scotland, England, Poland, Germany, you name the European country. It's not every day back then that you could go to something and see that. That was part of its intrigue.

───────

On January 15th, 1983, the Wings met the Pittsburgh Spirit in Pennsylvania in what turned out to be a night at the fights. "Just as time ran out [in the first half] Kevin Kewley kicked Stan Terlecki, Spirit's top scorer, and Terlecki retaliated by kicking the ball at the Wings as they headed for their dressing room. Wichita Coach Roy Turned charged Terlecki, then Gomez took a run at him. But Child came to Terlecki's rescue and then the cavalry arrived in the person of Civic Arena security. Gomez and Terlecki both received unsportsmanlike conduct penalties to start the second half." [26]

"Then it began to get rough. [Terry] Nicholl and Bob Ramsey were sent off for unsportsmanlike conduct. Kim Roentved went off for pushing and 16 seconds

after that, Steve Buttle went to the penalty box for tripping. Paul Toomey was penalized for holding...and when Child followed him...the Wings had a two-man advantage...Just 1:41 remained in the game when [Omar] Gomez and [Dave] MacKenzie were sent off with unsportsmanlike conduct penalties. Shortly after they got in the box, Gomez hit MacKenzie in the head with a water bottle, inciting both MacKenzie and the fans. MacKenzie tried to climb into the other half of the box to get at Gomez, but was restrained by Paul Child, who was serving the last seconds of a tripping penalty. Meanwhile, Wichita's Gregg Willin tried to get over the glass at some of the fans who were attempting to throw punches at Gomez. Gomez and MacKenzie were ejected... The 30 minutes in penalties for both teams set a record for a game involving the Wings..." Wichita lost 6-4.[27]

But Roy Turner and the Wings were angry with the Pittsburgh Spirit following the game. They blamed the referees for the brawl. "The people who are supposed to control and protect either side are the referees. I think our game is a game of beauty and the officials who don't control it are just going to make the game along the same lines as Philadelphia (Flyers, the Broad Street Bullies) used to be in the NHL. Players make mistakes. I get punished for making mistakes and doing wrong in a game. I think it's time the officials got the same treatment," said Turner. "I witnessed the opposing coach literally pushing, literally pushing (the referee) backward, making statements." Bill Kentling asked Commissioner Earl Foreman and referee-in-chief Dr. Joe Machnik to review the game-tape to determine whether the referees, Don Wynschenk and Anatol Popovich should be sanctioned for not being proactive in stopping the conflict before it boiled over.[28]

It wasn't easy being a referee in the MISL...

KEVIN KEWLEY: I had the most penalty minutes of anybody on the team, and I built up a bit of reputation with the refs over time. Some of the refs would try to tease you or wind you up and give you a bad call to see how you'd react. I remember a guy named Sarkisian who told me that putting my hands up in frustration was "dissent" and that I'd get a card if I did it again. The refs in the early years were awful. We got some calls here in Wichita, but on the road the refs were against you. Roy would say, "We'll have to fight through the refs." I'd say, "Screw the refs, let's beat them anyway." Most refs wouldn't listen.

After a couple years the refs improved. I think partly because the owners demanded it. At first, guys would never explain their decision. I liked the guys that would explain. Marty Templin would explain…Emmanuel Rossi, in the later years. Gino D'ippolito got better. At first he was just an ass. If he knew you he would start talking to you. Jeff Mantel was pretty decent. Herb Silva had some great games and some bad games. The league had regular guys and then some local guys to supplement them. The local guys on the road would miss stuff off the ball. There was a learning curve over the years on how to call an indoor soccer game. It would drive you crazy when a ref would call a penalty when you had a chance to score. They didn't understand you'd rather have that opportunity than the foul. It wasn't that they got better refs; it was that the refs eventually got better over time. They flew Gino D'ippolito in to my retirement party.

In Wichita, local soccer refs like Bobby Bribiesca and Alan Shepherd went from calling local college games to flying around the country refereeing MISL matches.

ALAN SHEPHERD: I started as a goal judge. My dad started as a statistician up in the bleacher area at Wings games from the first year. I was involved, if it wasn't the first year, it was the second. I'd sit behind the goal and decide if it was a goal or not. We were paid in the form of complimentary tickets, which was a huge deal back then because everyone wanted to be a part of it. The referees would come into town and we'd take them to dinner after the game and it was like a mini-referee clinic while you were eating dinner. It was awesome to listen to the likes of Gino D'ippolito and Herb Silva talk about the game.

I learned so much from all of them. They all had different styles. Some you could talk to, others would just put a guy in the box. They were all mentors to me as a referee. I'm talking about local and full-time guys. Gino D'ippolito was one of the best. Herb Silva was one of the best…Billy Maxwell was one of the best…Esse Baharmast was one of the best. He refereed a World Cup game. All those guys were good referees. Herb was a dentist.

When you are a local official, you do goal judge or penalty box, and work your way up to be an assistant referee, and then to being a floor referee. We went to dinner after every home game. You get to know the floor referees, the full-timers... you listen to them and get to know them. It's like any other job...pretty soon, maybe somebody doesn't show up as an assistant referee and they put you in there. If you do a good job, you get another game and work your way up. Being in the right place at the right time and getting to know people. Some of them came from the NASL or high-level college games. Most of us were doing college games in our area. When the Wings came to town it was an awesome opportunity for us local guys to take an advantage of getting involved as much as we could.

For the referees, integrity was vital. They couldn't let external factors affect their judgment.

ALAN SHEPHERD: I don't think a good referee will let [game atmosphere] affect their mindset. They are there to call a game equally. There might be calls you don't want to call, but you do. Referees instinctively make the call. I think something you learn from the top refs is to read how the players are going to play in the first few minutes. They'll either want to play or not want to play. In big games, most players will want to play and accept the calls and play within the parameters of the game. There are some games you can let them play and some where you have to tighten up and control the match a little bit more.

The Wings players were always gentlemen, to me at least. I don't know if that stems from me being a local guy and having to see me the next day. I did camps with them too. To me they were really competitive guys, if they weren't they wouldn't be at that level. They'd say stuff, but weren't guys who'd curse at you. I can't remember anybody in the league that really came at me. As far as being vicious, I can't think of anything egregious.

I think assistant referees got $50 and four tickets. Local guys like me that did local games and traveled got maybe $200. After a while they picked five or six full-time guys who did nothing else. They might do three games in a weekend. Then they'd use guys like me and Bobby Bribiesca as well. When I traveled, I went all over St. Louis, Dallas, Tacoma, and Cleveland. They'd pay airfare and put us up, plus the game fee.

Criticism from players and coaches was one thing, but to be criticized in the newspaper was beyond the pale in Shepherd's opinion...

ALAN SHEPHERD: I think it's a one-sided perspective. If you have two teams playing, one team's newspaper will say negative things, and the other team's paper won't mention the refs. As a ref, you can't win. I think it's overstated. There were some pretty critical editorials at the time. I thought they were not warranted. Referees are human and will make mistakes...at every level. It's okay to be critical of referees, but not in public or in the paper.

As Charlie Minshull-Ford remembered, the refs' focus wasn't ALWAYS on the game at hand...

CHARLIE MINSHULL-FORD: The ref Toros Kibritjian wanted to fire us all because the beer in the cooler wasn't cold enough. The ball boys had put warm beer in there. "I want cold beer!" he yelled out from the locker room.

———

Jorgen Kristensen and Kim Roentved were among the players named to the West All-Star team in 1983. It would take place in Kansas City on February 22nd and be televised by the USA Network, making it accessible to both casual fans and the most rabid Orange Army members. "We've got something to play for. We've won three in a row and want to do it again," said Roentved. Playing alongside both Steve Zungul and Juli Veee surely must have given the pair of Danes a boost of confidence. In overtime, the game-winning goal was the product of a Kristensen corner kick out to Roentved, who punched it home.[29] *But the most impressive play of the game came from one of Stan Stamenkovic's four goals for the East squad...*

BILL KENTLING: Roentved was on the wrong end of, in my opinion, the greatest goal scored in the history of indoor soccer. The All-Star Game at Kemper [Arena] when Stamenkovic puts him down, puts Zungul down, and gets it past Slobo, all within six feet of each other. It was magic. Oh my God, it's like you cannot do that!

One of the more unusual games of the 1982-83 season was on March 27th against the New York Arrows at the Coliseum. Coached by former referee-in-chief Joe Machnik, the Arrows took advantage of a little know codicil in the MISL rulebook to try to slow the game down. After tying the game in the third quarter, Arrows goalie Shep Messing took the ball just outside the penalty box and stood stationary, holding the ball with his foot, attempting to delay the game. Jorgen Kristensen took offense, charged Messing, and knocked him down. "Shep was within his rights to hold the ball outside the box. It's the home team's job to entertain the crowd. We just wanted to bring Wichita to us and open up some space behind them. We're trying to introduce some tactics into the game," said Machnik after the game. In the end, the tactics failed and the Wings won 4-2.[30]

As usual, the St. Louis Steamers guest-starred in the story of the Wings that season. To start, St. Louis ruined the Wings' home opener with a 7-4 victory. "If we want to win the division and not just make the playoffs, then we have to beat St. Louis," Roy Turner told The Eagle.[31]

But after that victory, the Steamers began to sputter. The Wings traveled to the Checkerdome on December 27th to face a Steamers squad that had limped to a 4-7 record. The Wings nine game losing streak in St. Louis ended that night with a Terry Nicholl goal in sudden death overtime. "We wanted to prove something in this game. We haven't deserved to lose nine straight," said Turner.[32]

On March 17th the Steamers got their revenge back in Wichita, with a 3-2 overtime win in what both sides called a great game. In what would be a fairly regular occurrence, a subplot involving Steamer defender Tony Bellinger stirred the metaphorical pot in a rivalry that already threatened to boil over on a regular basis. Bellinger wore a cast in what the Steamers called a precautionary measure to protect his weakened forearm. The Wings thought it was a cleverly disguised weapon. "If he has to wear it, there must be a medical reason. You know what that is and you know what it can do. It seems strange (the MISL) allowed it for so long," said a suspicious Turner.[33]

BILL KENTLING: Every time Tony Bellinger would show up in a cast we'd make some remarks about how that arm had been hurt for four seasons.

After opening the regular season with a loss to the Steamers, the Wings managed to do the same in the last game as well. But despite this downer, the Wings were now in the driver's seat in their playoff series with the Steamers. For the first time,

Wichita had won home field advantage against St. Louis by finishing second in the Western Division with a 27-21 record...just one game better than the third place Steamers.[34] *"I'm very proud of what myself, the team, and the Wings have accomplished in four years. Nothing irks me more than (that question), 'Why does St. Louis have your number?' It's time we put that to rest," said Turner.*[35]

Turner and the Wings went a long way toward achieving that goal by winning the first game in the best-of-three series. This overtime victory on April 19th featured a hat trick by Jeff Bourne and a game-winner by Andy Chapman. For Roy Turner, the game had personal significance: it was his 100th career coaching victory. The Wings went to St. Louis confident they might be able to steal a victory and reach the MISL semifinals for the fourth season in a row.[36] *Unfortunately, the Wings were steamrolled 8-3 at the Checkerdome, meaning that they would now need to win at home to advance. When answering questions from the* St. Louis Post-Dispatch, *Steamers star Don Ebert decided to let the Wings, and the world, know what he really thought... "[Wichita is] the worst town there is. But we've got to get back there and beat them. Call it a business trip...We're going to hammer them."*[37]

In front of 9,875 screaming Wings fans, Don Ebert would be proved wrong. The Wings had a three goal lead twice in the game, but the Steamers clawed their way back both times. The game featured two famous goals: A 125-foot short-handed goal by Per Roentved, and a 100-foot header by his brother Kim that sailed over a helpless Slobo Ilijevski. The Wings would win 9-7. "I wouldn't have missed the game for my wedding. This is the greatest, absolutely the greatest," said one female fan. The Eagle's Brian Settle set the scene: "At last, after 2 ½ hours of intensely emotional soccer, the Wings had beaten the hated St. Louis Steamers...The 9,875 fans packed into the steambath called the Kansas Coliseum stood cheering for several minutes after the game...In the stands, everyone hugged everyone. Behind the goal, General Manager Bill Kentling hugged Wings Coach Roy Turner."[38]

TERRY NICHOLL: I remember Kim's header...he headed it in from over the halfway line. It was absolutely outrageous. Slobo was watching it go over his head. It was brilliant. After the game, we were talking about how it was a whole year's highlight video in one game. We couldn't stop talking about it.

CHARLIE MINSHULL-FORD: The 1983 Steamers win was like winning the World Series.

BILL KENTLING: Any win against the Steamers was going to be a good win. Our fans needed it. The team needed it. The community needed it.

MIKE DOWLER, GOALKEEPER, WICHITA WINGS: The game and the atmosphere were intense.

BRUCE HAERTL, WINGS PLAY-BY-PLAY ANNOUNCER, KFH RADIO: I just remember how contentious the game was. I remember how desperate the Wings were to win in that situation. For so long, the shoe had been on the other foot. The Steamers had kind of owned that rivalry and it frustrated so tremendously those guys. It was the greatest source of angst they had. Their attitude to the Steamers was: "Their game is crap." There was nothing stylistic about it, nothing pretty about it, nothing beautiful about the type of game they played. They played a rough, physical, intimidating kind of soccer. So, to finally get them and win that game, in a game where they kind of forced Pecher to lose his patience and his cool, was probably the finest win that I've been associated with covering that team.

The Steamers were CLEARLY the rivals. I spend a ton of time in St. Louis, and inevitably the Steamers come up. It's funny how that whole thing comes up and you can talk with people in St. Louis about that day and how hot they were. I just remember the joy [the Wings] had...and almost the relief...and I'm not sure they weren't more relieved to have finally beaten them. In an odd kind of competitive way, it was a validation for how the Wings played the game because they were so diametrically opposed. At their core [the Steamers] were the great, young American bad asses. For the Wings to have finally won, that game, that day, in that locale, with what was at stake, was the finest moment I had in the three years with the team.

KIM ROENTVED, DEFENDER, WICHITA WINGS: I scored three goals in that game and made a great header. Slobo [Ilijevski] was a little outside of his goal and he was trying to chip it. The more years that go, by the further out I was.

A couple years from now I will have headed it in from the tunnel. He's outside the box and tries to chip it over me, and I saw it and said, "Shit, why not?" and hit it in with my head. It was perfect timing. He read it wrong and it worked out perfect for me.

Almost as memorable as the game itself was the infamous fight between Steve Pecher and a Wings fan named Dave Hull. In the first quarter, Pecher had been sent to the penalty box...just in front of Hull's seat. "We were cheering and kind of motioning at him. The next thing I knew, he walked to the glass and pushed me and then hit me," Hull told The Eagle.[39] *Both Pecher and Hull were ejected from the game.*

STEVE PECHER, DEFENDER, ST. LOUIS STEAMERS: I go walking over to the penalty box, unusual for me [laughs], and a guy behind the glass dumps a beer on me. I don't know if I was mad that he wasted the beer and didn't offer me any, or what [laughs]. I decided to take this into my own hands. There was a little bench [that I stood up on] and I took a swing at the guy. And then it was over, because I got tossed...although the ref never asked what happened or who started it. The policeman who came over to me asked if I wanted to press charges, and I said, "No, I'm not worried about it." I have a picture of me punching the guy.

BILL KENTLING: All the Steamer games we tried our best to rile up the fans. Several times I'd buy a beat-up car and put it out in front and everybody could sledgehammer it for a dollar...it was the SteamerMobile. We did our best to stir the pot and were pretty successful at it. There was always a lot of emotion in those games. Our guys got what we were doing, and hell, the Steamers got what we were doing too. It got a fan base riled up and certainly built the rivalry. I was a little surprised that Pecher went in the stands. But I thought it was wonderful. I couldn't have paid him enough to have done it. Thank you Steve! I owe you a beer.

ALAN SHEPHERD: At the Pecher game I was either assistant referee or the reserve official, who was behind the assistant. I can remember looking to my left and Pecher was going over the glass, going after a fan. That was quite a show.

MIKE DOWLER: Although we won, I am a little fuzzy on the game details... but I think that it was a tight affair until Pecher was sent off for fighting with a fan after being sent to the sin-bin for a two-minute violation. Thank you to that fan, whoever it was?

KEVIN KEWLEY: Controversy always helped promote the team.

KIM ROENTVED: Pecher is a super nice guy and we talked about that game. The guy threw a drink at him. It was a normal reaction from Pecher to fight him. In Pittsburgh, Omar Gomez had water bottles thrown at him while he was in the box.

STEVE SHAAD, DIRECTOR OF MEDIA RELATIONS, WICHITA WINGS, 1980-85: That was a great game for attendance. The altercation definitely helped with marketing...good vs. evil. Pecher was the embodiment of evil. He and Ebert were our two best friends because they were easy to market against. They weren't shy about their disdain for Wichita and the foreign players. Those sorts of things help create rivalries.

After all the tears of joy, the parties, and the good times, the Wings now had to face Juli Veee and the San Diego Sockers in the best-of-five semifinal series. Though every game was close, the Wings lost the first two in San Diego, and then came back to Wichita only to lose at home as well.

BILL KENTLING: Friggin' Juli Veee could really play.

Despite the sad ending, the season was a very successful one for the Wings. The Steamers monkey was finally off their back, which was an important accomplishment and confidence booster. Average attendance rose 1,000 per game to 8,341, a team record to that point. It was a breakout year for Andy Chapman, who was the only player to appear in all 48 games. He led the Wings in both goals scored, at exactly one per game, and game-winning goals, with six. Jorgen Kristensen led the team with 56 assists, his third year in a row with over 50. Omar Gomez was the total points leader with 86. Jeff Bourne shined with 43 goals and 23 assists; also managing to accumulate exactly zero penalty minutes despite playing 46 games. With four successful years completed, the Wings now looked to take the team to the next level...the MISL finals.[40]

CHAPTER 16

An Oral History

A Year to Remember

─────

"I don't much like 'em."

- BILL KENTLING, ON THE ST. LOUIS STEAMERS.

By the 1983-84 season, it had become more than clear that the people of Wichita had developed a legitimate passion for the Wings. Wichitans embraced their only major league professional sports franchise as a surrogate member of the family...one that often spoke Danish, Spanish, or English, with a Liverpudlian accent.

"And like the team they scream and howl for, the Orange Army is known throughout the United States, wherever there are indoor soccer teams and fans to cheer them, because the Orange Army soldiers are the mightiest cheerleaders of all. They have been named the No. 1 boosters in the league by the cable television network that carries the Major Indoor Soccer League games," wrote The Eagle's *PJ Rader.[1]*

The Wings fanatics agreed: "There's a magic here...We're the Green Bay of indoor soccer. For the first time, we're not following the big cities. We're the ones setting the trend. We're the ones leading the league. We aren't waiting for the east coast or the west coast," said Larry Emmel, food machine vendor. "If there's a game, nothing else matters," said Paul Jones, a Beech engineer. "Nothing, nothing comes between you and the Wings," agreed teacher Patsy Harrison. "The Wings are easy to love. Because of the way the franchise developed, people feel they own part of the team," noted Wichita State professor Greg Buell.[2]

Superfan Jim Hill, who dressed up as a giant soccer ball named Captain Kick, became a fan immediately after watching his first game. "That's why I went, to find out what it was all about. It's the perfection of those guys on the field that got me involved." For Pam Farnham, it was the personal touch that made it special. "For me, the relationship the players have with the fans is the key to the team's popularity. It's a unique closeness. They make you feel like you're a part of them. They're interested in you. The guys are down-to-earth, neat people, not big-headed jocks." In the middle of a mob of fans on the field after a game, Larry Emmel had a similar experience: "And in the middle of that, Jeff Bourne looked up and saw me and said, 'Hi Larry.' I'm just one of the fans but he had met me and remembered me. And that's flattering, to know a professional athlete, someone like that, remembers your name."[3]

"They're great athletes, they're gentlemen and they set high standards for themselves. And you know you have it made when the KISS poster comes down in your kid's room and the Wings poster goes up," said Lynn Hill, Captain Kick's wife. "Other athletes are Supermen, 250 pounds or 6 foot 9. We're the blokes next door, Mr. and Mrs. Normal. We don't make astronomical salaries. They befriend us and we befriend them. When we rub shoulders off the field, they feel it when we're kicked on the field," said Wings midfielder Terry Nicholl.[4]

In a Wings promotional video, fans at a game were interviewed about why they loved the team. They spoke eloquently about what it meant to them: "Why should the Wichita community support the Wings? I don't know, it's kind of hard to say. All they've done is give us heart failure!...It's not a part of something else, it's a part of us. I was born here, lived here, and will die here...and the Wings are a part of me. They're not Roy's team or Wichita's team, they're MY team. I love 'em," opined one fan. "My son has been to soccer camps the Wings have helped coach. They are involved in almost every phase of community activity I can think of. The fans have open access to the players and the players reciprocate the warm friendship. It's a give-and-take thing. We have a real good relationship," added a mustachioed man wearing a Wings cap.[5]

A mother talked about what the Wings meant to her two kids: "I feel like the players help in any way they can. They have been to both of my children's schools. I have two children who have participated in soccer camps and have come away feeling like they were the king and queen of the whole world and received a lot of individual attention. When they see the kids later they always know them by name and want to know how they're doing." For another fan, hometown pride was a huge part of the Wings experience: "It's very different to go to a schoolyard. It used to be that all your heroes were in New York, Miami; anywhere else in the world but here. And now you go out there and everyone wants to be Jimmy Ryan, Norman Piper, Mike Dowler...somebody that plays right here in their hometown."[6]

The fans showed their support by setting all kinds of attendance records. There were over 5,000 season ticket holders in 1983-84, with a total of 250,000 attendees over the course of the season. "That averaged out to 9,391 per game, an amazing 97% of the capacity of the Kansas Coliseum! In 27 home games (regular season and play-offs), the Wings had 12 sellouts, and 5 more crowds of more than 9,200." A home game against the Steamers set the all-time Wings record for highest attendance ever, at 9,891.[7]

ROY TURNER, HEAD COACH, WICHITA WINGS: I was once nearly late to the game. I'm not the most punctual person in the world, but there were so many people going to the game [on I-135] that I could hardly get there.

KENNY COOPER, HEAD COACH, BALTIMORE BLAST: Only St. Louis and San Diego could match the atmosphere they had in Wichita.

TOM SHINE, REPORTER/EDITOR, WICHITA EAGLE: The Coliseum, when you get 8,500 people in there, it's pretty damn loud. It holds the sound in. All the seats were pretty good. There were no bad seats. It would really get hoppin'.

TERRY NICHOLL, MIDFIELDER, WICHITA WINGS:: Every player, and anybody connected to the Wings, talked about the Kansas Coliseum's atmosphere. It was a magnificent place to play...it seemed the perfect size, just under 10,000, all cheering under the roof on a cold winter's night. It was warm inside because of the atmosphere and the energy. It was like a furnace. Outside it would be bitterly cold and the wind was whistling. But inside people were buzzing around and usually we'd play good soccer and there was a good response from the people. I think the players all got addicted to it. When we'd go to Tacoma, they were pulling 13,000 to 14,000 people in there, but it didn't seem as good as Wichita. Wichita seemed to get it right, with the fans, the connections between the fans and players. I may put it down to the Save the Wings campaigns. I think that people felt they were playing their part, instead of some rich owner...it meant that people and the people's energy kept the team there and they felt more a part of it.

KEVIN KEWLEY, DEFENDER, WICHITA WINGS: One of the most amazing things about the fans was how many people showed up at the airport. Hundreds. You didn't know what to do exactly. You signed autographs. Roy would sometimes stop and give a little speech.

ROY TURNER: Ward Lawrence started those airport gatherings...We had so many public appearances. That made it special to play for the Wings. Guys in a big city like Chicago wouldn't get that kind of personal attention. This community was behind the team, and kept it alive. It was the oldest professional indoor team in the country when it shut down in 2001.

KEVIN KEWLEY: [Being in the public eye] wasn't ever problematic, but sometimes it was awkward. Some people wouldn't have a clue who you were and other people thought you were a god. My daughters would wonder, "Why does everyone know who dad is?" People would try to get my daughter to play on their soccer team just so they could have me as coach.

DAVID WEBER, WINGS FAN: Being part of the Orange Army and my mother being bigger than life in many ways (being in a wheelchair), the staff and players always went out of their way at events to say hi to my mom. And I got to meet many idols and guys I looked up to because of it.

CHICO BORJA, MIDFIELDER, WICHITA WINGS: One of the things I remember is the fan club doing the most amazing Christmas party. They'd give trophies out to the players. It was the greatest feeling...we felt like superstars. Everybody had suits on. They were beautiful parties.

ANDY CHAPMAN, FORWARD, WICHITA WINGS: I was 19 when I landed...it just impacted my future and everything. The kindness and making it feel like it was my family. I still consider in my heart, Roy, Kim, Norman, Jorgen, Don [Tobin], Jeff [Bourne]...we were family. The people of Wichita, I don't even want to refer to them as fans. They were part of our extended family. You got to know about them and their kids.

VIRGINIA CREAMER, DIRECTOR OF OPERATIONS/ANGELS COORDINATOR: They decided they wanted to do a song. Roy was really into that. He always wanted me to play "Nobody Does It Better" at the end of games. I had a friend named Robin Salem. Her brother John had a sound studio and he said he'd put it together for us. We had the Orange Army guys singing "Go Wings!" as backup singers. We made a bunch of copies and sold it at games.

"Go For It!" became the official song of the Wings that year. Though catchy, it didn't capture the fans' imagination like the Rocky *Theme Song, which became so inexorably associated with the Wings. After each win, the Wings' production crew would play "Another One Bites The Dust" by* Queen. *You'd think* Queen *WAS in the building when 9,800 fans rocked to that song after an emotional win. It was like the music playing during the credits at the end of an awesome movie.*

TOM SHINE: They were part of the community. Kevin Kewley married a local girl and raised a family here. Roy Turner married a local woman and raised a family here. The AAA baseball team played here and then they all left. Then they were all different the next year. WSU basketball players played and then they went home for the summer and then were gone in three or four years. The Wings were part of the community. You'd see them at Dillons and they'd talk to you. Then they had kids and their kids started playing soccer and you'd see them at soccer games. They were a community asset. They provided entertainment. They were an event to go to...they provided dates at a publicly-owned facility and helped keep that open. They were pretty good at it, and had pretty good teams. When we finally beat St. Louis they were giddy. We did not ever come back from a road trip...and I mean never... come back and there weren't people there waiting for us at the airport.

Steve Westbrook, Mike Powers, Ray Vigliotti, and Jimmy O'Neill departed from Wichita prior to the 1983-84 season. All four men had played limited minutes the season before, with Westbrook playing the most games, at 22. Westbrook would go on to play for the Dallas Americans in the ASL. The New York Arrows snatched up Vigliotti in what would be their final season in the MISL. Powers would eventually become a longtime Dallas Sidekick.

BILL KENTLING, GENERAL MANAGER, WICHITA WINGS, 1980-1986: Mike Powers turned out to be a great defender in Dallas. He thought he was a forward when he was with us. But what he WAS was a great defender, and he figured that out in Dallas.

John Cutbush retired from soccer after what had been a distinguished career in both England and Wichita. Cliff Brown played for the Tacoma Stars and Kansas City Comets after leaving Wichita after the 1982-83 season. He would play for a number of other clubs in his long career, but eventually made a name for himself as a coach, leading Newman University's men's team since 1988.

As usual, the Wings had one of the smallest player budgets in the league; with a total of about $625,000 to spend.[8] David Pierce joined the Wings as a defender for 1983-84. The former snow skier and defender for the ASL's Carolina Lightnin' impressed enough during the Orange-Blue scrimmage and Kansas

City exhibition game to make the squad.[9] *However, he failed to make much of an impact, only appearing in two games during the regular season.*

Miguel Filardo came to Wichita hoping to make a mark at the forward position. Filardo had played for Quilmes in Argentina, the same team as Omar Gomez, who served as Filardo's translator in Wichita. Prior to coming to Wichita, Filardo had scored three goals in three games against the Wings while playing for Chicago, Kansas City, and Baltimore. Filardo's sense of humor and reputation as a bit of a klutz led to him being dubbed "FoFo," a famous Argentine clown. While in Chicago his unfamiliarity with Coke machines (which were uncommon in Argentina) led to him to deposit two quarters and then say to the machine, "Give me a Coke! Give me a Coke!"[10] *Unfortunately, Filardo's success AGAINST the Wings couldn't be followed up with success on their side. He only appeared in 13 games and ended up with more penalty minutes than total points, at four to two.*[11]

ROY TURNER: I brought in another Argentinian to make [Omar Gomez] happy...Miguel Filardo. We played him at forward. He only came in for one season and his game wasn't what it needed to be.

Throughout the Wings' history, the language barrier would sometimes result in moments of comedy. However, was the lack of English comprehension ever an obstacle to success?

ROY TURNER: No. Look at the best league in the world right now, the English Premier League...some of those guys don't speak a word of English. Same thing in Spain.

VIRGINIA CREAMER: Omar Gomez was stuck in Argentina and we can't get him back in the country and the season is about to start. So I'm working really, really hard trying to get his visa in order so I can get him into the country. I had to call his house in Buenos Aires. I get his mother, and I'm thinking, "Well, I had four years of Spanish, I can handle this." I said, "Omar Gomez, esta aqui?" And she said, "No, Omar Gomez esta aqui." I went: "No, Omar Gomez, esta aqui?"

She said, "No, no, no, Omar Gomez esta AQUI." I was saying, "Omar Gomez is here." And she was saying, "No, Omar Gomez is here." We went through this a couple of times. I finally got him on the phone. His first day back, he came to my cubicle and said, "My mother wanted me to tell you, you speak lousy Spanish." [laughs]

Newcomer Clyde Watson, a midfielder from British Guyana in South America, failed to achieve much on the field. Watson's struggles were mostly related to injury problems, which led to him only playing in 21 games for the Wings. He contributed four total points and five blocks on the field in 1983-84.[12]

Fellow midfielder, Jan Van Der Veen, a native of the Netherlands, had better success. Van Der Veen had a long career in Europe, playing for famous teams like Sparta Rotterdam and FC Antwerp. In fact, he had played games in every European country with the exception of the Soviet Union and Finland. He learned from some of the best. "It was a very hard school but I'm glad I had it. It forms and builds your character. I was able to listen to the older players and learn. If you are smart enough you listen to them. If you're not, you won't make it," Van Der Veen told Missile Magazine.[13]

Van Der Veen earned the praise of his coach and teammates due to his contributions on the field. "He's so competitive and wants to win so badly. It just naturally rubs off on the people around him. And anyone that has seen him perform on the pitch is immediately aware of his great skill," said Roy Turner. Jeff Bourne agreed: "I really enjoy playing with Jan. He certainly set a few nice shots for me. He defends, he gets assists, he gets goals. I guess he does it all now, doesn't he?"[14] *Van Der Veen would end the season with 16 goals, 18 assists, 20 blocks, and six power play goals in his 40 appearances.*[15]

The Wings also added a fun-loving, humorous, and very talented Scotsman to their lineup in 1983-84. Ian Anderson was a native of Edinburgh who had played for Dundee in the Scottish First Division before moving to the United States to play for the Tampa Bay Rowdies in the NASL. Anderson then made his way around the MISL, playing for Houston, Cleveland, New Jersey, and St. Louis. He quipped,

"I've had more clubs than Arnold Palmer." It wasn't like Anderson moved around a lot because of a lack of talent. He was a three-time selection to the All-MISL First Team.[16]

Anderson always had the habit of being highly quotable. Being a Scotsman, Anderson enjoyed ribbing his English teammates. "The best thing to come out of England was the road to Scotland," he declared. On his time with the Steamers: "[It was said] I had too many brains to play with St. Louis. All St. Louis wanted to do was play Atari or pinball soccer." On the Wings chances in 1983-84: "The ingredients are right. It's just a case of baking the right cake." On the importance of his golf game: "I have a feeling that when I get my golf game together, we will win the championship. Better tell Roy I need more practice on my golf game!"[17]

(Howard Eastwood/Missile Magazine) The proud Scotsman, Ian Anderson.

TOM MARSHALL, GENERAL MANAGER, WICHITA WINGS, 1979:

My favorite player was Ian Anderson. He was a hoot. He was more fun that anybody you could imagine. He was a very dedicated soccer guy. He used to take a quart of vodka, fill a water glass with it, drink it, and then go play the game of his life. It was amazing. I met him at the exhibition game when he played for Houston.

I built a bar in Arena East and we hired Ian Anderson to be the bartender. That wasn't the best idea. I got so mad at him. We built the bar and we'd show videotape of the adult games to their participants after they had played. It seemed like every drink was "on the house."

ALAN SHEPHERD, MISL REFEREE: Ian Anderson was a funny, funny guy. I remember doing an [indoor] clinic with him. I showed up 8:00 am. He was already there at the bar with a pitcher.

With the departure of Cliff Brown, the Wings needed a backup for Mike Dowler. It was the bad luck of Mark Snell and Jan Madsen that they happened to come on board during one of his finest seasons. Dowler would win all 25 of the Wings' regular season games that year, and all three playoff games. He led the MISL in wins and set records for minutes, games, and shots faced. He would earn the Wings' MVP award and came in third for MISL MVP.[18]

Snell was drafted out of college by the NASL's Edmonton Drillers and went on to play Third Division soccer in Germany before heading to the Buffalo Stallions of the MISL. He arrived in Wichita with dreams of soccer stardom and making a million dollars by age 30. "My ultimate goal is to become a millionaire through real estate," said Snell.[19] But his welcome to Wichita wasn't exactly out of the Lifestyles of the Rich and Famous...

CHARLIE MINSHULL-FORD, EQUIPMENT MANAGER, WICHITA WINGS, 1982-85: One time I was supposed to meet Mark Snell and a couple guys at the airport to pick them up. Well, my van broke down, and it was their first time to Wichita. What a great first impression. I would point out all the local attractions and had to apologize that I couldn't go any faster because only one of my fan belts was working.

Meanwhile, Jan Madsen traveled from Denmark to Wichita, leaving behind his "large ancestral home" and thriving English soccer memorabilia mail-order business. Madsen had gone to school with Per Roentved and would eventually appear in over 400 games in Denmark's professional league. He and his Danish club Hvidovre would face soccer powerhouse Juventus and manage to tie them 4-4 in front of a raucous crowd of 70,000 rock-throwing Italian fans.[20] However, his stay in Wichita was short. He would leave after just one season. He would appear in only three games, compiling a 0-1 record while accumulating an 8.57 GAA.[21]

CHARLIE MINSHULL-FORD: Jan Madsen came in and it was hard to transition from outdoor to indoor, plus the language barrier. He could play but he had to beat out Mike Dowler, which was a challenge. Jan Madsen wanted to leave because he wasn't playing and wasn't well-liked.

ROY TURNER: Sometimes I recruit from a recommendation. Jan Madsen didn't live up to the hype.

Snell had no better luck dislodging Mike Dowler from his starting position. He would go 0-1, playing in only two games.[22]

Perhaps the most memorable signing of the 1983-84 season wasn't because of what the player accomplished, but what he did NOT accomplish. Oscar Ortiz had played for the 1978 World Cup-winning Argentine national team along with a distinguished career for several top Argentine and Brazilian clubs. The arrival of the 30-year-old midfielder had Roy Turner excited. "He looks very much like Omar Gomez when Omar first started," said Turner.[23]

Wings GM Bill Kentling brilliantly tells the story of Oscar Ortiz in an article for the Wings' 10th Anniversary Yearbook, called the Orange and Blue Review: *"It was good old Omar who first introduced the concept of Oscar Ortiz. You see, Oscar was a world-class player...the story went that Oscar wanted to finish his great career in America (shades of Pele) and bring a championship to Wichita. Well, the more we thought about it the more convinced we were that we had found the secret weapon...we are convinced that he is the best player to ever come into the league...we watched him at half-speed [in practice], and are even more convinced that we've stolen one. Mike Dowler, who doesn't start many conversations, came in after practice and told us Oscar has the hardest shot he has seen; Omar and Miguel Filardo are ecstatic. Even Jorgen acknowledges this guy has all the moves...The first day, the first damned day we arrive [on Ortiz's first road trip], Roy takes the players for a leisurely run in sunny Southern California. Within 400 yards Oscar has pulled a muscle. The wheels fell off after that...To finish this once and for all time, Oscar tripped on the carpet in his home debut [during his] first shift."* [24]

ROY TURNER: Oscar Ortiz joined the team for a while. He had played for the Argentine national team, and I thought if you could play at that level, you could be good for the Wings. But he couldn't...[laughs]. He certainly didn't live up to his resume. I hadn't seen him play in person. He was a real bomb. I've seen some of the biggest duds come to this country to try to play indoor. A lot of them were past their prime, and the game had become more physical, with a lot of speed. It was a young man's sport. It's hard for older players to compete.

KEVIN KEWLEY: I remember [him] because we'd heard he'd played for Team Argentina. I think he came to practice twice and then got hurt. I think they thought he was gonna be another Omar Gomez. Kentling wasn't too thrilled about that. That happens...you take a chance on a guy. Omar was happy to have another Argentinian.

CHARLIE MINSHULL-FORD: There was a language barrier, but he played for the Argentine National Team, so everybody was excited. But when he came in, he didn't really stand out.

BILL KENTLING: Oscar Ortiz had been a winger on the Argentine national team...had been a real international player. Omar brought him in. He played some practices with us. You can ask Mike Dowler today, he hit a ball unlike anyone else. His ball whistled and moved as it came through the air. We really thought we had something. Unfortunately, when Roy would say "hombre y hombre" [man on man] he didn't get that. He didn't get the defensive part of it. He just thought it would be 6-on-5 and he'd wait and play offense. A wonderful offensive player. Mainly, I just remember what he could have been on offense and that he absolutely refused to play defense.

Listen, pulled muscles are a part of anytime you don't want to play...grabbing the back of your hamstring. I don't know if he pulled a muscle or just grabbed the back of his hamstring. As I recall, it happened after three or four steps. My recollection is that we paid him $6,000-$8,000 to come. I remember we didn't get our money's worth. Three games, no goals, no assists, 2 penalty minutes.

TERRY NICHOLL: Oscar Ortiz...first day of practice, and Roy was all excited we had this Argentinian. "What are we doing first, Roy?" "Tag," he said. It was a warm-up drill. We were trying to teach this Argentinian the game of tag. We'd say, "Ok, I am 'it'." He'd say, "It? You are 'it'?" [The lads]: "I tag you and you become 'it'." [Oscar Ortiz]: "You tag me and I become 'it'?" We were trying to explain it and he didn't speak English. The game started, and he just stood there in the middle. Someone tagged him and he just stood there. I don't think the lad lasted very long. If he couldn't play tag, he wasn't any use to us [laughs].

Change didn't just come in the form of personnel moves. A big change in 1983-84 also occurred off-the-field for Roy Turner. In an interview with The Wichitan *magazine, Turner talked about his personal life with writer Dave Kratzer. According to Kratzer: "Friends anxious for the new season to begin talk of a 'New Roy Turner,' a coach free of some nagging personal problems, ready and determined to seize that elusive MISL championship. They say he's got his mind on that, and virtually nothing else. Lately he's even warmed a few church pews, they say. 'The New Roy Turner' is probably a stone (14 pounds) lighter, gets up an hour or two earlier and is certainly a better dancer because of [Body by] Schliebe."*[25]

A chance encounter at Body by Schliebe would change Turner's life...

(Dan Moore/The Wichitan) Roy Turner at the Kansas Coliseum.

DR. TAMARA PRYOR, CLINICAL PSYCHOLOGIST: I'm originally from a small town in Illinois...Quincy, Illinois. I grew up there and left to go to college and moved around quite a bit for that... I got a PhD. in Clinical Psychology at Southern Illinois University...I came to Wichita in the fall of 1983...I thought I was going to the wild, wild West. But as it turned out, I loved Wichita. It's a well-kept secret; a great community.

I was introduced to Roy at Body by Schliebe. I was doing my pre-doctoral internship at KU Med School and came to do a one-year internship in the Department of Psychiatry. I didn't know who he was. I went there for the first time to work out. He actually held the door for me when I walked in. He said, "Here, let me hold this for you, love," which I thought was a little forward [laughs]. I said, "I've got the door myself, and I'm not 'your love.'" That was my very first encounter. I wasn't very impressed with him.

After I worked out there a few times, Frank Carney told Roy about me. I think maybe I'd worked out next to Frank. He thought of me and thought that Roy should ask me out. It was funny...the way he asked me out was that he asked me to a game. But of course he was coaching. So he had a friend of his, [KAKE-TV station manager] Ron Loewen, sort of fill in for him as a date. Only Roy would do this. I end up getting taken to the game by Ron Loewen. I spent a whole evening with Ron, who was delightful. Then Roy shows up late to the party after the game; and, of course, was the man of the hour. I don't think Roy and I said more than 15 words to each other on our first date [laughs].

In fact, I look back at it now, I really think I got the whole gang: I didn't just date Roy Turner, I dated Ron Loewen, Joe Howarth, Billy Kentling, and [KAKE-TV host] Gene Rump. They had this group that called themselves "Only the Lonely," who were all married and then divorced. Because Roy was on the road so much, I ended up spending my time with this whole group of his friends, doing everything with them. It was sort of like collective dating [laughs]. I always had a fun, interesting clever group of his friends to spend time with. I was in a field where you don't share anything about work because I was practicing as a therapist. And Roy's world was so out in the open. I think it worked well in those early years because I didn't want or need to compete with him for any limelight...

ROY TURNER: I went through quite a change in life in those years...had a turn around. And got married a couple years later. However, I'm positive my social life was positive for the team. I actually worried that my lack of a social life after I got married might HURT the team. You've got to keep a grip on your personal life. I took it upon myself to change my life in 1983. There was a lot of pressure going on. I sometimes wonder did it suffer because I slowed down my lifestyle? It would have suffered at the beginning if I hadn't had been so social.

While Roy Turner's social life may have been slowing down, the players and much of the staff were still living it up. And quite often, the nightspot of choice was The Hatch Cover, north of 13th, on Rock Road. This bar was usually filled to the rim with single ladies...and more than a few Wichita Wings.

KEVIN KEWLEY: The Hatch Cover was jam-packed every night.

BOB BECKER, OWNER, WICHITA WINGS, 1979-80: The Hatch Cover was a good spot. The building was owned by Howard Sherwood. It was built to be the Hatch Cover.

BRUCE HAERTL, WINGS PLAY-BY-PLAY ANNOUNCER, KFH RADIO: The Hatch Cover was a notorious launching pad for "fill in the blank."

I will leave it to people's imaginations. There were a lot of things "hatched" at the Hatch Cover...appropriately enough. The Hatch Cover was notorious...it was a great place. I get a chuckle because it's a dental office now. Without getting into too much graphic detail...suffice to say, anything that you can imagine would have happened in a place like that in the early '80s, did happen there in the early '80s.

VIRGINIA CREAMER: We spent a lot of time at the Hatch Cover. Per and Kim's parents were visiting us. They came over from Denmark. Their dad was a lounge singer. There were a bunch of us around the piano and he was singing old Frank Sinatra songs. It was a magical evening. His family were the nicest people.

STEVE SHAAD, DIRECTOR OF MEDIA RELATIONS, WICHITA WINGS: Our players were very accessible to the public. We'd go to the Hatch Cover after the game and all the players showed up to get their two free drinks. The players picked up on girls, kissed old ladies, had more than their two free drinks and developed a personal relationship with the fans.

CHARLIE MINSHULL-FORD: [Trainer] Al Green was great...he'd have a Grand Marnier and a cigar at the post-game parties.

TOM MARSHALL: The last time I saw Mike Ivanow, he was swinging on a chandelier at the Hatch Cover.

KEVIN HIMES, RUGRAT, AND WINGS EMPLOYEE: We were on our way to the Hatch and I pull up and opened my door and there's money on the ground. It was two $100 bills. I went straight in there and bought drinks for all the players.

Over the years, the Hatch Cover wasn't the only place for hijinks. You also could find good times in the Wings' office...

TERRY NICHOLL: A neighbor of mine had this trick. It was a cage within a cage...it had a little water jug and this tail sticking out. We said it was a weasel. I'd take it around to show people. When you pressed the trigger, the tail would flick up and frighten people. Steve Shaad was on crutches, and I thought I'd frighten him and the ladies. "My neighbor has gone out of town and given me this weasel to look after. It's not drinking its water; does anyone know anything about it? I've got to make it better." So, I brought it in, and said, "He's very, very nervous, so keep quiet." I was building it up to be this nasty thing. Shaad said, "You need to mix in some milk with some water." As he leaned over I flipped the switch, and the tail hit his face and he fell over. We were all laughing because it was so funny. All the office people were all around. I knew they'd get me back for this. They put a stuffed rattlesnake on the passenger seat of my car. I was kind of ready for it though.

I used to play cricket in the corridor at the office. It would drive Roy mad. I wanted to show all the American lads the game of cricket. Roy would be thinking, "What the bloody hell are they doing playing cricket in the office?"

The Hatch Cover didn't have a monopoly on nicknames; just about every Wings player of that era had one. Jeff Bourne was "The Jet" because of speed...or lack thereof. Andy Chapman was sometimes "Chappy" to his teammates. However, Kevin Kewley and Mike Dowler called him "Bud." "He's just a little flower," said Kewley. "He hasn't grown up," opined Dowler. Though Jorgen Kristensen was "the Magic Man" in Wichita, Per Roentved revealed that in Denmark he was known as "Little Spot" because, as a man of small stature, that was all the space he took up. Per himself was sometimes called "Sikma" due to his resemblance to the Seattle Supersonics player.[26]

The roster of MISL teams changed once again during the 1983-84 season. The three NASL teams that joined the previous season, Golden Bay, San Diego, and Chicago, all "took a break" from the league. The Denver Avalanche were resurrected as "The Stars" and relocated to Tacoma, Washington. They would become something of a rival for the Wings in the years to come. The Phoenix Inferno didn't go anywhere, but their name did. They became the Phoenix Pride after a bankruptcy resulted in new ownership.

On television, there was hope that the limited contract with CBS from the previous year would continue into the future. "I think that NBC has a serious interest in us. I think CBS's interest is renewed. For the first time ever, I think that national commercial television is a possibility. Not a probability, but a possibility. They are now aware of the fact that our ratings on CBS last year, while not great, were significantly better than most of the NBC or CBS feature college basketball games. They are beginning to realize that there is something out there. We will be working with CBS this year, and there is a possibility for something as soon as '84-'85..." said GM Bill Kentling.[27]

The question was, could major broadcast networks make enough money on advertising when televising MISL games? The answer wasn't clear, but evidence clearly existed that the MISL could sell tickets. The 1983-84 Wings averaged higher attendance than the NBA's Atlanta Hawks, Chicago Bulls, Cleveland Cavaliers, Golden State Warriors, Kansas City Kings, San Antonio Spurs, San Diego Clippers, and Washington Bullets.[28]

As it turned out, the MISL would get some national and regional coverage that year. A fledgling, short-lived sports network called Sports Time would televise some games toward the end of the season. Broadcasting in fifteen states, mostly in the Midwest, Sports Time would only last for one year, from April of 1984 to March of 1985. A national audience would be reached when CBS broadcast game four of the 1984 MISL Championship series.[29]

It was another slow start for the Wings in 1983-84. The team started off 1-4, with all but one of those games taking place on the road, a place where the Wings never flourished. However, they then won six straight against the likes of old rival St. Louis and new rival Kansas City. Three of those wins would come in overtime, including a triumph against the Steamers at the Coliseum. Deprived of San Diego, now back in the NASL, the Wings and Steamers continued their tradition of battling for the top spot in the Western Division. However, it would be a tight race in the West till the very end. Only four games would separate the eventual division-winning Steamers from the fifth place Tacoma Stars.[30]

The St. Louis Steamers finished on top in the West at 26-22, closely followed by the Wings at 25-23. The Los Angeles Lazers and Kansas City Comets would follow at 24-24 and 23-25, respectively. All four teams made the playoffs, with Wichita facing the Lazers and St. Louis against Kansas City in the two quarterfinals series. The Wings won their best-of-five quarterfinal series 3-1 and, for the fourth consecutive year, would meet the Steamers in the next round of the playoffs.[31]

The rivalry wasn't dead. Far from it. "We pretty much hate Wichita's guys - professionally, not personally..." said St. Louis defender Sam Bick. Steamer Neil Cohen had been "fined and suspended by the MISL for kicking Andy Chapman in the head" during one game that season.[32] *"St. Louis can get carried away when they are in their arena, and our fans spur us on, and this tends to make players a little bit braver, a little bit faster, and they tend to try to do things they wouldn't usually do. That is when you have incidents," said Kevin Kewley.*[33]

"I'd like to think that I'm professional enough that every game matters, and I'm sure everyone in the locker room would say the same, but I'd be a liar to say that there aren't some games you get cold chills thinking about. And St. Louis is one of them...the intensity, the emotions run very high," added Andy Chapman. Per usual, Bill Kentling said it best: "[The Steamers] still do a lot of things that I find tiresome. I get tired of Slobo [Ilijevski] boarding himself. I get tired of Steve Pecher sort of whacking his way through the league. I don't much like 'em."[34]

It was an anticlimactic series, with the Wings losing in three straight, including one at home. Each game was decided by just one goal. Unfortunately, the Wings were without Jorgen Kristensen for much of the playoffs. When he was available, he was too hobbled to be effective. Meanwhile, Jeff Bourne would miss the entire playoffs.[35]

It had been an injury-filled season for the Wings; even more than usual. Kevin Kewley had missed 15 games, while Per Roentved missed 25. Omar Gomez and Jorgen Kristensen were out for 18 and nine, respectively. But worst of all was the loss of Jeff Bourne on April 7th, 1984 against Tacoma. He would hurt his knee so badly that it would end not only his season, but his soccer career. Bourne was having a stellar year, with 46 goals and 12 assists, making his loss not only a devastating one for Bourne personally, but also for the team's playoff chances.[36]

In the long-term, the events that followed his injury would end friendships and cause hurt feelings for years to come.

KIM ROENTVED, DEFENDER, WICHITA WINGS: [Bourne] tore his ACL and we knew it right away.

KEVIN KEWLEY: He had a bad deal because of his knee right near the end of the season.

KIM ROENTVED: Nowadays, that piece of filet mignon they put in your leg is stronger than the old piece, and he could have come back, but not back then.

ANDY CHAPMAN: I remember going to the hospital after his injury...nowadays they might be able to do something. There were certain injuries back then that you never returned from and nowadays you can. It was difficult for Jeff. I know the players were a little upset about it.

ROY TURNER: I can't say that if we had Jeff Bourne we would have won that playoff series, but it certainly made a difference. In those days an ACL injury meant your career was over. His contract was up, and they paid him the remainder of that and he was done.

BILL KENTLING: Jeff Bourne could do the thing that Zungul could do...play and score from the back post; and could teach other players how to do that. Jeff had signed a two-year deal and he was in the second year of that two-year contract, when very late in the regular season, he had a season-ending injury. Obviously his contract paid him to the end of the contract. In consultation with Dr. Henning and the rest of the staff [we determined] that this was, in all probability, a career-ending injury. I brought Jeff in and we talked about it. I asked him what he wanted to do. If it was a career-ending injury, the union contract called for a player to receive $25,000 or $30,000 and then he wouldn't play anymore.

My recollection is, in having this conversation with Jeff, I said that we obviously aren't going to sign an injured player contemplating a career-ending injury [clause] to a new contract. But we could sign you to a minimum contract, which I think was $12,000 year. His choice was to go for the career-ending injury. We filed the paperwork. That was it for him and he got his $25,000 or $30,000. But I think he had buyer's remorse after that….wanted the money but also wanted to keep playing. There was a waiting period of 60 or 90 days so that you couldn't get hurt on a Tuesday and claim your money on a Thursday. He needed two physicians to attest that it was career-ending. There was a whole procedure that had to be administered.

Bourne would struggle to deal with the idea that he could no longer play profes-sional soccer. Wings' team physician, Dr. Charles Henning, had warned Bourne to never play again or he'd risk crippling, long-term damage to his knee. Bourne would continue to harbor bitterness and resentment towards Roy Turner and Bill Kentling for what he felt was unfair treatment in the days following the injury. "I've probably lost more sleep over it than anything we've ever done on the club. I don't know the right way or wrong way to handle it," said Turner.[37]

Though the end of Bourne's career was tragic, it would have paled in comparison to the tragedy that almost happened six days before his injury…

VIRGINIA CREAMER: We had decided we'd have all these kids [at a game] modeling clothes we had for sale in the Wings' office. I had choreographed these girls for a little marching thing. We had this rehearsal. I sent them back to the dressing room and told them we'd let them know when halftime starts. I was standing [on the field], I think with Steve Shaad, by the sound booth, talking to JB [Johnson]. We hear something funny and look over, and the scoreboard dropped. We dove into the penalty box and glass went flying everywhere. It was the scariest thing that ever happened to me. I had just gotten all those kids off the playing field when it dropped. The emergency brake failed. It took hours to get it up off the ground and the glass cleaned up. The game was vastly delayed. I always thought about how lucky we were.

Though the Wings had lost in the semifinals to the Steamers, Bill Kentling believed there was a great deal to celebrate about their fifth season in the MISL. In fact, he made a case in the 1989 Orange and Blue Review *that 1983-84 could be considered the best season ever for the Wings. Kim Roentved had a stellar year from the back with 27 goals and 33 assists. His overall play garnered him the MISL Defender of the Year award. Andy Chapman became the first Wing to break the 50 goal barrier, with a total of 53 scores plus another 21 assists. He also led the MISL in hat tricks with six. The MISL rewarded him with a spot alongside Roentved on the First Team All-Select squad. Both the man-advantage and man-down power play teams were second best in the league. The team played beautiful soccer that season, only committing 180 total minutes of penalties. Mike Dowler beat out Roentved and Chapman as the Wings' MVP. He led the league in wins and set records for games, minutes, and shots faced. Not a bad year at all.*[38]

An Oral History

A Wizard's Spell

———

"Erik [Rasmussen] could do things at a level different
than others...at a Stamenkovic, Zungul, Tatu level."

- BILL KENTLING.

*FOR EVERY STALWART DEFENDER OF the legitimacy of indoor soccer, there were a score of
naysayers who questioned the sport. Some fans of traditional American sports derided
the game as insufficiently manly, while many traditional soccer fans looked down their
noses at such a vulgar bastardization of their "beautiful game." So when the United
States of America hosted the 1984 Summer Olympics in Los Angeles, the MISL saw
their chance to shine. As the host country, Team USA earned an automatic berth in the
tournament. Of the 17 members of that team, 15 were current or future MISL players.
Four of those players would eventually play for the Wichita Wings.*

*Future Wichita Wing Dale Ervine was excited to represent his country when se-
lected to be part of Team USA's Olympic pool. He, along with a number of amateur
players, were slated to be on the squad. Things didn't quite work out that way...*

DALE ERVINE, FORWARD, WICHITA WINGS: I was on the US youth
team that played on the World Cup team in 1983 in Mexico. After that they
brought four of us from the youth team into the Olympic team in November

of 1983 in Honduras. I'd only been part of that Olympic development team for probably six months and I was still a junior at UCLA at the time. But in March [1984] they passed a rule where they could use professionals for the first time in the Olympics, so that's when guys like Chico Borja, Ricky Davis, Kevin Crow and all these guys who weren't part of the Olympic pool [joined the team]. US Soccer decided to go that route and they got rid of all the amateurs. That was my only experience with the Olympic team. So, three months before the Olympics started they got rid of all the amateurs and brought all the professionals in. That's unfortunately how that Olympic thing ended.

Mike Fox made it but he was part of that Olympic pool for three or four years. [Not playing] was disappointing for sure since it was three months away, but I hadn't invested the time that say Mike Fox had done or for that matter, even my brother. My brother Glen was in the Olympic pool for three years. They were in Malaysia, they were in China, they were everywhere. I was more disappointed for him. He had put years into the Olympic team, I had only put six months into it. I was only part of it because a few of us from the youth team were asked to come and [join] the more senior team.

I guess the most frustrating part of it all was even though they brought in the professionals they still didn't get out of the first round. If you're part of that pool for say two or three years and they don't get out of the first round, you say to yourself, "Well shit, WE could have done that!" And there was probably more continuity with those guys just because they had been together for years. You had that closeness or that camaraderie that was built. But it was probably a stronger team because they were all professionals.

The naysayers thought that the MISL players would be embarrassed because: "(a) Playing indoors affected the style for outdoor play. (b) The stamina required for 90 minutes would not be there. (c) MISL players wouldn't know what to do if there was no wall to bounce the ball off." As it turned out, the MISL players acquitted themselves quite well, despite not advancing past the first round. The American team defeated Costa Rica 3-0, lost narrowly to Italy's world-class team (who would go on to lose in the bronze medal match) 1-0, and tied Egypt 1-1.[1]

Future Wings Chico Borja, Jean Willrich, David Brcic, and Mike Fox played on the 1984 US Olympic team. In their opening game against Egypt, St. Louis

Steamers sensation Ricky Davis would score twice. The third goal would be added at the 35 minute mark by starting forward Willrich, who would play for the Wings from 1987 to 1989. Borja, who joined the Wings just one year later, would start all three games. So would 1984-85 Wings backup goalkeeper Brcic. Fox, who came to Wichita at the same time as Borja, came off the bench against Costa Rica and Italy, and started against Egypt in their final match.[2]

CHICO BORJA, MIDFIELDER, WICHITA WINGS: It was a great experience. For me, it was the greatest to represent our country and represent a lot of the Latin American people in this country. It was my greatest [achievement] as a soccer player.

——————

The impending collapse of the North American Soccer League brought several teams to the MISL for the 1984-85 season. The San Diego Sockers and Chicago Sting had been down this road before, playing in the MISL during the 1982-83 season. However, two MISL virgins, the New York Cosmos and Minnesota Strikers, added depth to the Eastern Division. The Cosmos replaced the now-defunct New York Arrows. Meanwhile, both the Buffalo and Phoenix franchises folded before the season began.[3]

Norman Piper had announced his retirement in the off-season. It had been a historic run from the curly-haired dynamo from Devonshire, England. Originally, he had been brought to America to play in Ft. Lauderdale for the legendary Ron Newman (Roy Turner's first coach in Dallas.) Piper had been the first player signed to the Wings in 1979 and would be the first player in team history to have his jersey retired. For most of his five seasons with the club, he was a consistent goal-scorer, leading the team with 33 goals in 1982. As he aged, he became more defensive-oriented, but remained very fit throughout his storied career with the Wings. After his retirement, Roy Turner made him the team's full-time assistant coach, a role he was accustomed to.[4]

Like many professional players, Piper wasn't fully committed to the idea of a permanent retirement from the game he loved. "I want to get across to the people that the Wings are just retiring my jersey and not Norman Piper. If I feel that I'm fit enough to play soccer again, then I will..." said Piper. According to Missile Magazine, *"... [Piper] was told he could not expect to play for the Wings in the 1984-85 season, as Turner tried to bring a younger look to the Wings." Piper added, "I felt that if we had gone all the way, beaten St. Louis, gone to the finals, Norman Piper would still be playing for the Wings this year." In the end, Piper greatly enjoyed his time playing for the Wings. "The people have been fabulous here in Wichita. They've helped me enormously. That's why I've made my home here in Wichita..." said Piper.[5]*

For another talented Wing the offseason would bring disaster. Per Roentved suffered a debilitating stroke that temporarily robbed him of his sight, speech, and the use of much of the left side of his body. The speech and sight soon returned and he left his wheelchair behind within a few months. However, his long and storied career would be at an end.[6] In addition to his European and international career, he contributed two solid years to the Wings on defense, accumulating a total of 98 blocks.[7] The Danish presence on the Wings would continue to grow, but it would no longer include two Roentveds.

There were other departures as well. Oscar Ortiz wouldn't return after his injury-filled stint with the Wings. Though on the roster, Clyde Watson would play no games during the 1984-85 season. He would soon retire. Both Miguel Filardo and Jan Madsen's MISL careers would end after their brief stints with the club. Jan Van Der Veen would return to the Netherlands to play one more season of soccer before hanging up his cleats. David Pierce would also leave the Wings.

The sting of the departures was healed with the salve of new talent. The team's only rookie was 1983 draftee Steve McLean. A Scotsman by birth, he moved to America at the age of nine, settling in New Jersey. Prior to joining the Wings, McLean toured the globe as a member of the US Junior National Team. Of course, the MISL was a wholly different beast. "...the pace of the game is totally different. Outdoors it's a big field and the dimensions are totally different and you can slow the game down. In here, there's no such thing. The game's bang, bang, two minutes on, two minutes off..." McLean told Missile Magazine.[8] *Though he would only play in two games in 1984-85, McLean stuck with the Wings for the next season. He became a regular contributor on defense in 1985-86, accumulating 21 blocks in 17 games.[9]*

Steve Wegerle would also play two seasons for the Wings, arriving in Wichita from his native South Africa by way of the Tampa Bay Rowdies of the NASL. Wegerle played both midfielder and forward for the Wings in his 39 games with the club in 1984-85. He would accumulate ten goals, three assists, and 11 blocks that year; the better of his two years in Wichita.[10] *As a South African, Wegerle couldn't play in international soccer games because of the apartheid boycott that FIFA and various countries enforced throughout the 1970s and 80s. "One time...when I was with [the] New York [Cosmos] in the Trans-Atlantic Cup competition, a Russian team was due to be one of the four teams. When they found out I was South African they issued an ultimatum. If I was allowed to play then they were not coming. New York, of course, turned around immediately and said, 'Alright, don't come...'" Wegerle told* Missile Magazine.[11] *Ironically, Wegerle was part of the first multi-racial South African National Team. However, it too was banned from international play.*[12]

(Don Marler/Missile Magazine) Englishman Barry Wallace had a powerful left foot.

Croatian forward Drago Dumbovic spent 12 games with the Wings in 1984-85 before being traded to the Minnesota Strikers in late January. Dumbovic would go on to have a lengthy indoor career, playing through the late 1990s for various squads in various leagues. In return for Dumbovic, the Strikers sent the Wings a Londoner named Barry Wallace. He was glad to get out of Minnesota. "Yeah, I'm a warm weather man. I'm not a winter man at all. I like the sunshine. I'll get up a lot happier and I'll do things a lot more efficiently when the sun is shining and it's warm. I can handle normal winter, but [the Minnesota winter] was just too much..." Wallace told Missile Magazine.[13]

In 1982, Wallace had briefly played with Kim Roentved for the Tulsa Roughnecks of the NASL. That bond had lasted. "He helped make it a lot easier for me. Being a player that's been here for a while and a well-respected player, just showing me around and quietly but surely showing me the way to go...it's difficult when you come to a new team sometimes to know where to tread, where not to tread..." Like many of the Wings, Wallace had grown up in a working-class English family. There was food on the table and his dad was always employed, but it wasn't a luxurious existence. The Queens Park Rangers were his ticket out of that life. He would play three seasons of English First Division soccer before coming to America.[14]

Wallace would accumulate seven goals in 18 games before his season was cut short by a knee injury. Over his three seasons with the MISL's Wings (he came back for a second stint during the National Professional Soccer League [NPSL] version of the Wings in 1994) Wallace's powerful left foot would leave its mark. He increased his goals scored to 13 and then 25 over the next two seasons.[15]

In July of 1984, Roy Turner took a trip that would bring a top-notch young player to Wichita for many years...

ROY TURNER, HEAD COACH, WICHITA WINGS: I had a connection at Arsenal in England, and ran a complete tryout with 20 players there. Terry Rowe came from that. These 20 [English] League players wanted to come to America. We conducted it at Arsenal's stadium. Myself and Norman Piper ran the session on a Saturday.

'the Gambler'

Terry Rowe chose to portray a high stakes gambler to symbolize his daring style on and off the field.

(Howard Eastwood/Missile Magazine) Terry Rowe would
be a mainstay on defense for many years.

*Terry Rowe would become a defensive mainstay for the Wings from 1984 to
1992, with an encore performance from 1997 to 1999. Originally from London's
west side, Rowe had played professionally for Brentford in the English Third
Division from the age of 15, making their top level squad by age 17. Valued for
both his speed and aggressive style of play, Rowe had considered a professional career
in cricket, but luckily for the Wings, he took to the pitch.*[16]

*Rowe's accomplishments over his career would be impressive. He placed third in all-
time games played, with 349, only trailing Kevin Kewley and Kim Roentved. Rowe
placed second behind Roentved on the all-time blocked shots list. During the 1990-91*

season, his 87 blocked shots became the second highest single-season total in Wings history.[17] *But like so many of the Wings, he was much more than a pile of statistical figures. For a high-school-aged Kevin Himes, Rowe became a friend and a mentor.*

KEVIN HIMES, RUGRAT, AND WINGS EMPLOYEE: We were at the Grape, me and Terry Rowe and Steve McLean. Terry asked me, "Have you ever been to England?" Terry had a stutter and he was very difficult to understand. He always said, "Don't hesitate to tell me if you can't understand me. Don't act like you got it if you didn't get it." He asked me if I wanted to go to England with him for a month in the summer. I said, "Yeah!" I was 17, and I went home to ask my parents. They looked up Brentford, where he was from. There were race riots going on, so they said it probably wasn't the best idea. I'm sure he would have kept me safe. I thought that would have been so cool.

In addition to Terry Rowe, the tryout at Arsenal also produced Tommy O'Neill. Though small at 5'7, 158 pounds, O'Neill never stopped moving once he hit the pitch. He would be voted the Wings Most Inspirational Player during the first of his two years with the club.[18] *Originally from Scotland, O'Neill had played in the English Second Division with the Cambridge United. His best year with the Wings would be his second and final one, 1985-86, when he made 28 blocks in his 28 games played.*[19]

There would be two new Danish players on the roster in 1984-85. Karsten Christensen was a physical specimen at 6'0, 182 pounds. He would score six goals and make five assists in 41 games at the forward position during his only season with the Wings.[20] *In Denmark he played outdoors for AGF, one of the top teams in the country. "A season is 30 games. I didn't make under 10 goals any season. I'd make between 10 and 15 goals every year," he told* Missile Magazine. *The transition to indoor was difficult. "...it takes some time to learn [the indoor game]. I can see that because I am a typical outdoor player. I have to learn some of the things," said Christensen.*[21]

TOM SHINE, REPORTER/EDITOR, THE WICHITA EAGLE: Karsten Christensen...We were in Los Angeles one time. Roy was good about mixing it up in practice and keeping things loose and light...it was a nice day and they went to play an outdoor game in this park. They put some trash cans out to mark the boundaries. I played goalie. Karsten was unstoppable. No one could guard him. He was great with the ball. He was a big guy and he could run a little bit. He was good with both feet. He scored all day. I said to Roy, "Holy shit." He said, "It doesn't translate to the indoor game." But outdoors, he was unbelievably good. He didn't play much and got kind of down on himself.

And then, there was the other Danish addition to the team. The Wizard. Erik Rasmussen.

ROY TURNER: When I went to scout in Denmark, I saw a team called Koge play. A Friday night game...Jorgen said, "Watch him." I saw [Erik] do what he did with the ball and the crowd loved it. He was just incredible. I stayed up all night and by the time I got to the airport I convinced him to commit. Erik was the type of person who was always seeking adventure in new places. It was a great opportunity for him. He had been studying law at the University of Copenhagen before that. It was a real coup...a hell of a sign.

BILL KENTLING, GENERAL MANAGER, WICHITA WINGS, 1980-86: Rasmussen came out of Denmark, so highly recommended by the Danish players and our guys in Europe. I think Jorgen was involved. Per Roentved may also have been involved [in his signing].

It was a momentous signing and everyone knew it. According to The Eagle's *Tom Shine: "Roy Turner never got too excited when he talked about a new player...But every time Turner talked about this Danish player the Wings had just signed, a guy named Erik Rasmussen, he just about hyperventilated. He began every discussion with, 'I may be wrong, but...' and then launched into a glowing account of Rasmussen's skills - 'an entertainer', 'superior dribbling skills' - before finishing with the assessment that Rasmussen might, just might, be a superstar in the MISL."*[22]

And he was. In his first season, he set what was then a Wings record with 55 goals. Not only does he own the Wings record for most goals in a season (75 in 1998-99) but he has the second highest season goal total (67 in 1985-86) as well. He is both first (57 in 1987-88) and third (54 in 1998-99) on the list of all-time season lead-ers in assists. The Wizard is tied with Chico Borja for most game-winning goals in a season (nine in 1985-86) and has the top two highest season totals for power play goals (16 in both 1985-86 and 1987-88).[23]

(Don Marler/Missile Magazine) 1987-88 MISL MVP Erik Rasmussen.

You can find Erik Rasmussen's name all over the list of Wings All-Time Career Leaders: He is first in goals scored, with 358; first in game-winning goals, at 39; and first in power play goals, with 68. He is also fourth in assists, just below Jorgen Kristensen, with a total of 256.[24] *In 1985-86, Rasmussen led the MISL in goals scored and came in second in total points on his way to being named First Team All-MISL. In the 1987-88 season he was the league scoring champion and was named the MISL's Most Valuable Player. In 1988-89 he was named to the Second Team All-MISL squad while placing fourth in goals scored and third in assists. By any measure, he must be counted as one of the greatest scoring forwards in MISL history.*[25]

Of course, no one knew this on November 15th, 1984, when the Wings opened their season in Los Angeles. Rasmussen was unknown to the rest of the MISL. But not for long.

ROY TURNER: We played in Los Angeles, and our guys had seen what he could do in practice, but the guys from LA were looking at each other wondering, "Where did this guy come from?"

The season-opening road trip next took the Wings to Tacoma. Tom Shine wrote: "Even though he didn't score, you could tell he was going to be great. He screwed Tacoma defender Ralph Black into the carpet on consecutive trips down the pitch. It must have been like watching Babe Ruth take his first couple at-bats. You knew you were watching the beginning of something special. After the Tacoma game, Turner said, 'I think the people back home are in for a surprise.' A pleasant one. Rasmussen scored four goals in his home debut and the rest, as they say, is history." [26]

ROY TURNER: Our players will always have Erik right next to Zungul in terms of talent. He wasn't a show business kind of guy, except when he had the ball. He wasn't a showboater at all. He'd score a goal and just walk away. EVERYBODY looked up to him. He was a very clever man...Some of the things he did on the field were incredible. He could make other players look bad...His quick release of the ball was amazing: a very short backswing and into the goal.

I would never ask Erik to work back defensively. It sometimes left us short-handed, but it was worth it when he could get ahead on offense. Our players literally would crack up at practice at what he'd do. When he'd score a goal in a game, sometimes they just couldn't believe what he had done. These guys realized he was a real talent. He was a magician...they called him the Wizard. Kim may have been the best all-around, but Erik was the best in a different way...the most effective player.

CHICO BORJA: I believe Erik is in the same [category] as Preki and [Stan] Stamenkovic. They had unbelievable talent. I didn't belong in the same category as those three because I was not a goal scorer. [Erik] was a goal scorer. They scored goals left and right.

TERRY NICHOLL, MIDFIELDER, WICHITA WINGS: He was just was an absolute gem, wasn't he? You look at the highlight films...some of these goals, there'd be three or four people's bums on the pitch...Erik was beautiful because he just put his arm up. "By the way everyone, you might have just seen one of the best goals in indoor soccer, but I'm just going to put my arm up and run off." [laughs]

CHARLIE MINSHULL-FORD, EQUIPMENT MANAGER, WICHITA WINGS, 1982-85: He was one of the most level-headed players. Off the field he was a regular guy. He was nice, not arrogant. Erik was a family man. He could do so much with the ball.

BILL OLIVER, MANAGING GENERAL PARTNER, 1986-92: Erik really cared about the team, not only wanted to win but make sure we survived and got the players we needed. He was a good guy.

BILL KENTLING: Erik could do things at a level different than others... at a Stamenkovic, Zungul, Tatu level. His only real problem [on the field] was he didn't know how to dive. It was a manhood thing to him. He wouldn't go down. It was lucky he didn't get killed. If most players get hit on the ankle, they go down; a foul is called and you play on. But he took pride in never going down. He could really, really play.

Erik's skill was going forward, and Andy was very much a back-to-the-basket player and was gonna hold the ball in turn. When you have guys like Kristensen, Gomez, and Piper feeding you, you're going to get plenty of op-portunities to score.

Missile Magazine *described his game this way: "Rasmussen's style, protecting the ball with his body as he dribbles into a cluster of opposing players, then ripping a shot off with his quick release, is as entertaining as it is effective." The real question was: How do you stop Erik Rasmussen? "I don't know, it's hard to say...Maybe you have to play physically hard, sometimes," said Rasmussen.*[27]

ROY TURNER: I saw him go through a physical beating because other teams couldn't stop him...so they'd try to bully him. It led to a big melee in the [1987] Tacoma series.

Prior to coming to Wichita, Rasmussen had played for Koge, a Danish First Division team. He also had the opportunity to play for the Danish Olympic team that failed to qualify for the 1984 games. "I went on a trip to the Canary Islands...and it was the Olympic Team which was playing together. And we were 16 guys going down there and we played two games...It was before we played the qualification games for the Olympics. We won both the games down there and we played very well," said Rasmussen. But there was much more to Erik Rasmussen than just soccer. Before he came to Wichita he attended law school in Denmark. Though he had to give that up, at least temporarily, he was able to bring a little piece of Denmark with him: his girlfriend Heidi and young daughter Sanna.[28]

Rasmussen was a wanderer by nature and a very thoughtful man. When on the road, he sometimes felt he wasn't experiencing everything America had to offer. "It is hard to say my impression of America. I mean, I have been meeting a lot of people, we are travelling a lot. But we are always living in the good hotels. We never see the bad part of America. We only see the luxury all the time. We are only living as first-class tourists. When you get into the big cities, everyone is saying 'Don't go down there, don't walk there,' things like that. So it's hard to say. I've gotten the impression that people are very open here. It's very easy to converse. But I always feel that there are a lot of strange things going on in your society, a lot of bad things...like drugs...alcoholics...The country is so unbelievably big. So it's hard to say. There are good things and bad things going on."[29]

BILL KENTLING: An interesting guy. Very bright and introspective. When we went on the road he would just walk in a city. Got lost more than once. Fearless...would just start walking. He would really try to immerse himself into whatever the culture was in the community we were going to. I do remember him getting lost in Tacoma once...just walking in the fog. It was his way of figuring out America.

DR. TAMARA PRYOR, CLINICAL PSYCHOLOGIST: My all-time favorite was Erik Rasmussen. [Roy and I] went over to Denmark and spent time with Erik and Jorgen. We stayed at Jorgen's. I can remember getting up and they'd be serving Heinekens for breakfast. Jorgen would play on these local soccer teams.

We all rode our bikes to the game. Jorgen is riding down the lane drinking a Heineken on his way to play a soccer game. I really liked the Danish players. Jorgen could be a grumpy guy, but was just brilliant. Erik was all cerebral. He'd be the only one on the road trip who would be sitting and reading some classic book. That was just Erik. He was a deeper thinker, I would say. I really loved to have conversations with him; well-traveled and well-read. But he wasn't easy for Roy because Erik was going to do things his own way and what were you going to say? He was the star player, so you had to let him play by his own rules.

TERRY NICHOLL: Erik was a mystery...such an enigma. He was so different. But brilliant...The wonderful thing about Erik is that he'd say, "I'm going back for a glass of wine." He'd end up going for a four or five hour walk before the game. And then he'd get his three goals, and two assists...He was such an interesting character. He'd talk about stuff, and I had to get ready for the game, and get me body ready. But he'd have a glass of wine and talk about the political situation here and there, run out on the pitch and be fantastic. I'd prepare perfectly, get extra sleep, and be falling all over the ball.

He played for his country and coached at a very high level in Denmark. He was always up for going into a different place just so he could experience a new city. He particularly liked Baltimore. He'd talk to me about the terrible drug epidemic there. He's probably living in a tent somewhere, writing a book about living in a tent. He'd be an interesting guy even if he didn't play soccer.

DAVE PHILLIPS, WINGS RADIO ANNOUNCER, 1986-93: Roy had a curfew. If you weren't in by midnight it was $100. Keep in mind, Erik [Rasmussen] had played for the Danish national team and was one of the greatest talents in the world...He got paid pretty well for coming over to America, but a big part of his motivation was seeing the United States...he wasn't about to come in at midnight. He wanted to experience everything America had to offer. He wanted to see the cities all day and the nightlife. But he didn't want to do it by himself, so he grabbed Terry Nicholl..."You come and I'll just pay your fine."

I can't remember how many conversations between Roy and Erik there were: "Hey listen, we have a 12 o'clock curfew." Erik said, "Right, I'm not coming in at 12. Here's the money, I'm paying up front." Roy says, "I need you in here [by then]." [Erik says] Well, you're not gonna sit me." Roy would have to admit, "No, I'm not going to sit you...go have fun." They didn't abuse it. They didn't come stumbling in...Erik was always ready to play the next day.

ROY TURNER: We'd go to cities and Erik would disappear, looking at buildings and architecture.

Then one day, he wandered a bit too far...

ROY TURNER: One year we went to San Diego for a game. The day before, Erik had gone to Mexico on his own. I get a call in my room that night at about 10:00. Erik says, "I'm stuck in Mexico, I can't get out. My visa's no good." He couldn't get back. Eventually he found an American couple to put him in the trunk of their car. He came to the game like nothing happened.

According to The Wichita Eagle: *"Rasmussen went to Tijuana, Mexico with team-mates Jan Olesen and Keld Bordinggaard...But when the group tried to re-enter the U.S., Rasmussen - and only Rasmussen - was told his paperwork was not in order and that he'd have to remain in Mexico. 'I was thinking I'd have to spend the night down there...' said Rasmussen. [He] then flagged down a motorist. 'He was a very nice man....They asked him questions when we got to the border, but they didn't ask me anything. And I didn't say anything.'"*[30] *However, Terry Nicholl remembers a few more details about Rasmussen's adventure that conflict with the official record...*

TERRY NICHOLL: He nicked over the border. He got caught [coming back] for not having his visa. So he couldn't get back in. So they put him in a holding cell. He got out of an upstairs window. He told me he snuck out through either a back window or lavatory window...he clambered down some kind of drain pipe and got back into the country by stopping an American who had a truck, and he had a tarp in the back. So he said, "Would you get me back into the country? I have a soccer game tomorrow night; I have to get back in." He got underneath the tarp and got back at 4:00 am.

Needless to say, Rasmussen's teammates greeted him with comments like, "Hey Erik, how'd you like Mexico?" and whenever they saw a policemen, "Erik, it's the border patrol." "I think Erik wanted an early start on the World Cup in Mexico," quipped Bill Kentling. "I did tell him when we went to Minnesota...to forget about Canada," joked Turner.[31]

ROY TURNER: One time at the airport, we went through the metal detector, and [Erik] made a comment about a bomb. They took him aside and detained him for a bit while they asked questions. He did it for a laugh. He was an entertainer. Knowing how bright he was, he knew better, but that was just his personality.

TOM SHINE: [*Eagle* reporter] Mal Elliott called me on a Saturday and [said] Erik Rasmussen made a bomb joke at the airport. They snatched him and took him away. Mal was right there. They were taking up a collection to try to spring Erik.

"I said 'I have a bomb in there. Is that OK?' And I was laughing while I was saying it. Then they took me to the police office and they started to read me my rights... and I was sitting there feeling like an unbelievable criminal because of that joke," Rasmussen told The Eagle. *Eventually he was released without charges. "I am pretty sure right now he regrets it...he was trying to cheer everyone up and it all backfired. It was a bit of a surprise for him," said Terry Nicholl.*[32]

ROY TURNER: He was a really funny guy. He was close to Terry Nicholl and would make fun of Terry.

Not to mention, an easygoing kind of guy...

ROY TURNER: Erik was the easiest person to do a contract with. I did the contracts. Erik would say, "I want x dollars." And I would give it to him. It usually took 20 minutes. I knew if I didn't give it to him, he might leave.

TERRY NICHOLL: I'd see Roy when he was heading out to Denmark to get Erik for the next season. We always said he'd have to get the big suitcase out... meaning he'd have to load it with cash to get Erik to come back to play. [laughs]

But what Rasmussen did with his money wasn't what you might expect from a young professional athlete flush with cash. According to The Wichita Eagle's

Fred Mann: "Erik Rasmussen...doesn't do anything after he scores goals except pat his teammates on the head...He is quiet and humble - a true rarity among MISL stars. Last year, the Wings tried to give him a gimmick. They thought it would be neat if Rasmussen took the ball out of the net after a goal and kicked it into the crowd. That would give him some pizzazz, they thought, make him more colorful and marketable - make him a real MISL superstar. Rasmussen hated the idea. He had another one...For each of his goals the rest of this season, including the playoffs, Rasmussen will give $50 from his own paycheck to Jamie Harris, the 6-year-old Wichita girl who needs $100,000 for a liver transplant... Rasmussen hope that individuals and businesses will help out by pledging 10 cents to $50 per goal. So far, such pledges have raised the value of an Erik Rasmussen goal to $110.40." [33]

Mann quotes Rasmussen as saying: "I'm not in it to bring myself into focus. I don't really like the idea of superstars and things like that. I don't like throwing my shirt or my shoes or the ball, or whatever. When I started to be a professional, I always kept in mind that if I was fortunate to make a lot of money, I would like to give some of it to people in need...I think that everybody who is lucky to have some money should keep that in mind." [34]

The long-running connection between the country of Denmark and the Wichita Wings is one of the most rich and fascinating stories of the franchise. That such a small country would send so many of its soccer players to a little city in Kansas is quite remarkable. It was a unique relationship in that no other MISL team had many Danes at all. About a dozen Danes played for the Wings over the years, and they comprised some of the best players the team ever had. Kim Roentved, Erik Rasmussen, and Jorgen Kristensen alone are almost certainly three of the top five players in the history of the team.

ROY TURNER: I spent an awful lot of time recruiting in Denmark.

TOM MARSHALL, GENERAL MANAGER, WICHITA WINGS, 1979:
When Roy started bringing in the Danes, one of the English players said, "I can't believe he's bringing these Danes in to take our jobs."

ROY TURNER: I think we had a great opportunity to get the top players in Denmark at that time. It wasn't that the Danish players were better suited to indoor than everyone else. It was that we were getting the best Danish players, while the English players in our league weren't, for the most part, the top players from England...After 1982 I went to Denmark and scouted for two weeks. Because of the success I had with Jorgen and Kim, they had great connections in Denmark, I was able to get great talent from there and pay them more than they were making in Denmark. Plus, they all spoke English.

The Danish Mafia recommended Frank Rasmussen. Frank was really good, but Erik, Jorgen and Kim were his three friends, so it was difficult for him sometimes because he wasn't quite on their level and they were all buddies he lived with and hung out with. He was a good role-player, and wonderful in power plays and defense. I couldn't buy a team of Erik Rasmussens because I didn't have the money. You needed guys in supporting roles. Players always think they are better than the role they are given. Some of them never accept it. Some will complain to this day that "if Turner had played me more I'd have been a star!" That's just part of coaching. Everybody wants to be on the power play. But that's where you see your best players. Everybody thinks to themselves, "I should be on the power play," but you can only have five guys on it. Because of Frank's friendship with the other Danes, he thought he should be on their level.

BOB BECKER, OWNER, WICHITA WINGS, 1979-80: I remember flying with Roy to Denmark on recruiting trips. Per Roentved was captain of the Danish national team and we were playing the British. Those Hooligans were something else. I say, "We," because I considered myself a Dane at the time and we played them to a tie, which was pretty impressive. Kim [Roentved] and I have been friends over the years. I remember going to parties at his condo. We've remained friends all along.

Kim Roentved took that trip to Denmark with Bob Becker and Roy Turner. As Roentved remembers it, the three of them went out to the hottest nightclub in Copenhagen...it was the early '80s, so imagine Studio 54. Turner had had a big day and took a little nap in the corner. A bouncer said he needed to leave, but Bob

Becker insisted he not be disturbed. Becker kept buying more and more bottles of champagne...about ten of them. Their party kept getting bigger and bigger after each group of bottles. More and more Danes kept joining them. Becker had rented the fanciest Mercedes they had and they spent those days driving him around in style.[35]

TOM SHINE: Jorgen spoke about six or seven languages. They taught us some inappropriate Danish words.

STEVE SHAAD, FRONT OFFICE, WICHITA WINGS: I always got along with the Danes. They were very nice to me. I had a blown knee one year and was waiting for surgery. I was on crutches and Kim and Per, or even Jorgen, would get my luggage off the carousel and carry it to the hotel for me, which I thought was pretty unusual for professional athletes.

The Danes liked to play a game at the airport...Jorgen wasn't the friendliest guy, so he would sit by himself at the airport. The other Danes would be drinking and send me over to Jorgen with a Danish phrase to say to him, and Jorgen would respond with another phrase to bring back to them. Things like "mother f***er" or "you have big breasts." I didn't know [what I saying] at the time, I was just repeating it back to them. When I'd say one of these phrases, Jorgen would bust out laughing and say something in Danish for me to say back to them. Later, we were at a party in downtown Wichita and Kim pointed out a Danish friend from across the room. Without him knowing, I walked over to her and said, "I know some Danish." She said, "Oh you do?" Fortunately, the first phrase I said was "Good day." Kim came over and said, "Steve, you can't share the Danish words we taught you!" And for the first time he told me what they actually meant. I still use my Danish to this day. [laughs]

TOM SHINE: The Danes could come here and play soccer full-time and get paid for it. Back at home they had to have another job. Jorgen ran a bar in Copenhagen. Per ran a hardware or athletic store. They all had other jobs AND played soccer. Kim Roentved bought a white Corvette and shipped it back to Denmark so he could have it for the summer. They loved it here...the team helped find them housing. They could make a little money doing appearances.

MARK WEDDLE, WINGS FAN: One of the lesser known Wings lived down the street from my childhood home in southeast Wichita. One day I was kicking a ball around in the front yard when a beautiful white Corvette rounded the corner. The driver...[Kim] Roentved! He made a face and flashed a peace sign at me as he passed. I nearly lost my mind I was so excited!

TOM SHINE: I remember playing a celebrity basketball game with Frank Rasmussen. He was a very good athlete...not a good basketball player, but a good athlete. We were trying to explain to Frank, "You've got this guy...this is your guy [to guard]. We came down the court and he wasn't guarding his guy. He said, "I'm going to guard the guy with the ball." So he would always guard whoever had the ball...and we had to rotate to his guy [laughs]. He would guard the shit out of him. But he couldn't score.

An interview with Missile Magazine *in December of 1984 allowed Bill Kentling to reflect on the state of the franchise after nearly five years as the general manager of the Wings. "...Our first objective was to keep the Wings alive and functioning in a city that historically has not been classified as major league. That we have done. The next objective was, obviously, to try to make a penny...a dollar-eighty...something...make a profit. I don't know that that is possible...But I still believe - maybe not this season - but I believe it is possible to break even or turn a profit, even in our small city with our small facility, if we can get proper ancillary income from the league." That extra income could theoretically come from television revenue. The Wings could only hope.*[36]

"We set out to provide a vehicle for this community to play up in class: to play Chicago, Los Angeles, New York, St. Louis, Kansas City, and we in fact, are competing successfully with those cities...we're playing up in class. We're not playing Amarillo, we're not playing Evansville," Kentling continued. How long would he stay with the Wings? "I think at some point my growth in this job begins to cease...I'm obviously still growing in this job. But I see that growth becoming limited at the end of this season, perhaps within the next season...I'm not going to

be the General Manager of the Wichita Wings for the rest of my life. But I think there are people on our staff who may well be." That premonition would eventually come true.[37]

As for the future of indoor soccer, nationally, and in Wichita, Kentling was optimistic. "I'd say the chances of the league failing are just as good as the chances it will succeed. But the sport, the product, will be here and I would always want Wichita to be in as part of whatever the power base was that controls and operates the sport... Wichita wouldn't be considered for an entry into the MISL now. We probably got in at the last chance Wichita will have in the foreseeable future to get into major league sports."[38]

(Greg Fox/Missile Magazine) Roy Turner attempting to motivate the lads.

Missile Magazine *interviewed Roy Turner that same month about the franchise from the perspective of its coach. "I would like to be able to plan on a long-term basis for a club, with regard to youth programs and working more with potential* talent. *I'm afraid in professional soccer the way it is today, you don't get paid much for potential, you get paid for results today. That's been very frustrating...We're not in a position to be able to develop talent on the Wichita Wings," said Turner. The injection of talent into the MISL from across the globe had made it that much harder for local boys to make it. However, despite the necessity of the "win now" philosophy, the Wings would finally see inklings of the long anticipated rise of the American player in the latter half of the 1980s.*[39]

For Kevin Kewley, it was his sixth season with the Wings. He was the only player left from Wichita's first game in 1979. The style of play in the MISL had changed since that November day, and his game had changed with it. "I think it used to be a run and gun game. You know: you'd go down to one end, have a shot, the ball would bounce around, maybe miss...go down to the other end and have a shot. Now it seems that teams are waiting, maybe counter-attacking a little bit more. I think you've got to put a lot more thought into the game. In the early days, players would just kind of cheat a little bit, maybe not play so much defense...look to score goals and points...or maybe just use it to keep fit, because the outdoor game was still really important then," Kewley told Missile Magazine.[40]

"When I first started playing...it was just go out there and run as hard as you could...not worry about other players so much...have a shot...make a few tackles...I really didn't have a lot of discipline. I just sort of played however I felt. The players are different now. There's so many situations where you need specialists...like power play offense and defense...the sixth attacker when you pull your goalkeeper...Roy's kind of gone to specialist teams, as have other teams," said Kewley. The game had become more strategic and team-oriented since those early days. "The quality of the players in the league has gone up and up every year. These quality players have now adapted to the indoor game itself and that makes for better play on both sides. I think it's probably a much better game," he continued.[41]

The media landscape for the 1984-85 season was a mixed bag across the MISL. For the Baltimore Evening Sun, *the Blast were considered the number one sports story in the winter. Their reporters perceived that assignment as "ranking second only to the baseball Orioles" in terms of prestige. The Force regularly made page one of the* Cleveland Plain Dealer's *sports page. This made sense considering the Force averaged 13,000 fans; 7,500 more per game that the Cleveland Cavaliers. In the* St. Louis Post-Dispatch, *the Steamers received coverage on par with the NHL's Blues, making page one in their coverage. In Kansas City, the Comets were regarded as one of the four major league sports teams by the* KC Star. *The Las Vegas Americans received "all kinds of ink" from the* Review Journal. *The San Diego Sockers, who were selling out games left and right, received outstanding coverage from the* San Diego Union, *the* San Diego Tribune, *and the* Los Angeles Times *San Diego edition. Reporters from all three papers traveled with the team.*[42]

Coverage in Chicago, Minnesota, Pittsburgh, Dallas, and Tacoma was decent. In Los Angeles, coverage for the Lazers was almost non-existent, despite the fact that Lazers owner Jerry Buss also owned the LA Lakers. For the media in New York, it was as if the Cosmos did not exist. However, in Wichita, the media and the Wichita Wings had an excellent relationship. It started with The Wichita Eagle, *where Randy Brown, Mal Elliott, Tom Shine and others covered every move the Wings had made since 1979. All the local television sports departments from KTVH/KWCH, KAKE, and KARD/KSN produced segments on their broadcasts about the Wings. Both KSN and KAKE would televise games over the years.*[43]

ROY TURNER: Randy Brown went on to be one of my best friends. Dennis Shreefer from Channel 12, [Andrea] Joyce, and Jim O'Donnell. We got to know them and they were very supportive.

KEVIN KEWLEY, DEFENDER, WICHITA WINGS: They'd be at practice most days.

ROY TURNER: I worked my ass off for the media in this town. You have to go to dinner with them and socialize. I'd go to baby showers, I'd go to anything.

STEVE SHAAD: Mike Kennedy was great, and we got him talking about the Wings. Bruce Haertl was on the radio and I did color with him. We had John

Wright on KFDI and he was one who never missed a media game and he got to be a real fan. I'd go deliver a release to him and he'd put me on the air or tape something. Without a doubt, our media coverage was a huge part of our early success. I couldn't recreate it with the [Wichita] Wranglers [baseball team], but we played off the international flavor and the Orange Army.

TOM MARSHALL: Mal Elliott was one of the fairest newspapermen I ever ran across.

BILL KENTLING: One of the many things we had going for us was that from Day One, *The Wichita Eagle* treated the Wichita Wings and the MISL as it if were major league. [KARD/KSN] was the first television carrier of the Wings. Mike Oatman at KFDI was great to us, [as was] Barry Gaston at KFH. The media in Wichita couldn't have been better to us. That really helped because in a lot of communities the MISL was fighting for whatever coverage it could get.

We had beat writers, Gary Dempsey and Tom Shine, that really covered the Wings and the MISL. In most of our communities we really did have good coverage, which was pretty amazing because if you went out for the baseball team in junior high and got cut after the first week, it still sort of qualifies you as a baseball expert. But nobody had played indoor soccer! So for these guys and gals to throw themselves into it and try to cover it, it was really pretty amazing. We all gravitate towards things that are easy. And this wasn't easy. The media was wonderful. In Wichita, we didn't have a bad media partner. They were all terrific. We did [KARD/KSN] for four years and the next two were with [KAKE], because they outbid [KSN] for the rights to it. The TV games...they found they could sell them.

Of course, the media wouldn't have been the media without critical coverage. They were tough, but fair.

BILL KENTLING: I remember several columns that Randy wrote that were not complimentary. I remember Roy was quite frustrated when Randy was addressing that we didn't do well on the road. I remember his column saying the Wings played like drunks and winos on the road.

Even though the Wichita media spent countless hours each month covering the Wings, they didn't quite cover everything.

ROY TURNER: Maybe the media didn't work hard enough to find out about the DUIs and the like. We were living it up in those days and things would happen. But you didn't read about it.

From the perspective of a reporter for The Eagle, *covering the Wings was a pretty good beat.*

TOM SHINE: The first game I actually covered was...in St. Louis at the Checkerdome. There was a crapload of people there. It was hoppin'...We never really had a full-time Wings writer. Whoever was available they'd send to cover a game. I did it, then Gary Dempsey did it, then Mal Elliott did it.

I liked the beat. I got to travel a little bit. The team was easy to work with. Steve Shaad was a great PR guy. Bill Kentling would tell me anything I wanted. Roy Turner was always available. If I couldn't find him, I'd go to Body by Schliebe and interview him there. Even after losses, they were professional about it. Mike Dowler was the only guy that ever got mad at me, but then he apologized. They all were [thoughtful], even though most of them weren't college educated. They had a worldliness to them.

The Chicago Tribune had a full-time guy who covered [the Sting]. Dallas had a young woman who covered [the Sidekicks] full-time. The problem was in those cities, you are low down the list. Baltimore had a woman who is a national columnist, who covered them for a while. We probably had more coverage than almost anybody. Here, they were a big draw. It's kind of like San Antonio right now. They have one major league team. I bet you the Spurs get great play every day that they want it. We were that way.

When it was a big game or the playoffs I could get [the Wings] on the cover. I always thought I got good play. It helped that they won. I preferred that they win because I get better coverage and it's a better story. I never had Bill Kentling complain about the coverage...[The Wings] were always very accommodating. They knew they needed the media. Bill Kentling was a former journalist and was a great source. The league was very accommodating, even at the headquarters level. The locker rooms were always open, the practices were always open. They understood they needed to get the story out to the community.

I always went to Kansas City, because I could drive. I very rarely went east because it was so expensive. When Dallas joined the league I'd drive or ride the team bus. I watched games in Phoenix, LA, and San Diego. I went to a game in Tacoma. We traveled as money was available. I went to a game in Chicago once because we had money in the budget. It was in the old Chicago Stadium. Jim Hawley and Steve Shaad were doing the radio. They had to hire an engineer to do the broadcast because it was a union building. Steve said, "What if I don't hire you?"..."Then your broadcast may go off in the middle of the game." So Steve said, "Then you're hired." We get done, I'm still writing, and the team has left. The engineer says, "Where are you guys going?" I say, "We're going to go out and call a cab and go back to the hotel." He says, "Cabs won't come here because they're gonna get robbed. I wouldn't go outside." So he gave us a ride home. I think we tipped him another $50.

The players had been assembled...the pens and microphones of the Wichita media were at the ready. All the Wings had to do was take the field and win some games. At first, that's what they did. The Wings went 13-8 to start the 1984-85 season. Then, the bottom fell out. After their hot start, Wichita went 8-18 the rest of the season. The 20th Anniversary Wings Yearbook detailed the sad story of the Wings' collapse: "Once again, injuries were one of the biggest reasons for the Wings' strug-gles. Mike Dowler missed a handful of games late in the season, and the Wings only won one game without him in the lineup. Midfielder Omar Gomez and defender Barry Wallace missed the tail end of the season...But the biggest loss was undoubt-edly the loss of Jorgen Kristensen. "The Magic Man" was having a typically stellar season, highlighted by a team record-tying five assist performance against Las Vegas on December 8th. But Kristensen went down in late January, and only played spo-radically the rest of the way. To say the Wings missed him was an understatement: of the 17 games he missed, the Wings won only three."[44]

BILL KENTLING: We never really got in sync. We had some injuries early. We never had that scorer in front that we had hoped to get. We weren't as good at home as we had been. You lose three or four of those and it changes everything. It makes all the difference in the world. We just weren't as good as we thought we were.

It was a frustrating season for the Wings. They seemed to have all the pieces to the puzzle after assembling a collection of excellent players. However, key injuries to three star players doomed the team to their first losing season. The string of semi-final playoff appearances was broken at five. And then, in a blow to the team and to the fans, star forward Andy Chapman was sold to the Cleveland Force. Though he would return several years later, the loss of Chapman stung.

ROY TURNER: Cleveland bought Andy Chapman for cash in 1985. Andy was a fabulous player for us. We got the bid and I talked to him about it...and he decided he wanted to go. It wasn't like we kicked him out. I'm sure they gave him more money than he made here. Erik Rasmussen had become our star and I don't know whether that made Andy want to leave. I don't know. He was one of the most popular players we ever had. When Cleveland came in we realized we really needed the money. We didn't want to stand in his way and the offer was fair.

There are [several possible] reasons why people leave: we think less of them than another team; we need the money; they could become a star on another team when they aren't one here; or, it's just time for a change.

BILL KENTLING: Andy and Roy had a rift. I can't recall the details. One season their relationship deteriorated. One of the nice things about being in college is you only hear the coach for three or four seasons. I think it's a lot harder when you listen to the coach for eight or ten years. By the end of it you've heard everything there is to say. They just got on each other's nerves after a while.

ANDY CHAPMAN, FORWARD, WICHITA WINGS: It wasn't financial at all. Not one bit. I met the girl who became my wife in 1981. I was only 21 and Patti was a little bit older than me. And I wasn't ready for settling down and getting married. There was no way, and I was very honest about it. I came back [to Detroit] in 1982 to play [outdoor] and we lived together and talked about the future, but I still wasn't ready. In '83 and '84 we sorta broke up. She had come to visit in Wichita prior to that. She came in the Christmas of '81 when I was living with Jimmy Ryan.

At the end of the '83-'84 season I decided to fly back to Detroit because I missed her. We decided to get married, and we ended up squeezing it in before the start of the '84-'85 season. We got married Sept 14th, and we go to St. Maarten on our honeymoon. Scary time for me, getting married for the first time. We rented an apartment in Wichita. Patti was used to working all her life and now she's sitting at home in an apartment. She's basically [in Wichita] just because I play football here, away from all her family, her sisters. It was a very hard adjustment for her.

Everyone was in a bit of shock that I got married. It was a big surprise. I called my mom in July and I told her I was getting married in two months and she fell out of her chair. It was a big change for me, understanding it all. It was a whole life-changing thing. By the time I got through that winter it affected how I was playing. I couldn't focus. Patti wasn't happy here. It was a completely different lifestyle for her. The reason we left and went to Cleveland [was for my marriage]. I went to Bill Kentling and said I need to go to another town for the sake of [my marriage]. One place I'd like to go to is Cleveland. Financially they are a great organization and geographically it's only two or three hours from Detroit, for my wife. That was the sole reason. It was one of the first times a contract changed hands. That contract was running out at the end of that summer. They purchased it for about $30,000 from the Wings. Me and Patti ended up buying a condo there. I then negotiated a four year contract with Cleveland.

Incidentally, that condo was purchased with Chapman's winnings from Jim Hershberger's Most Versatile Performer (MVP) competition. Only 14 games remained on the contract that Cleveland purchased for around $30,000-$35,000; a testament to the value of Chapman's talent. "Everyone keeps getting caught up with playing time, but that's only one of many things involved in the issue," Chapman told The Eagle.[45]

Roy Turner was sad to see Chapman leave. "I need [Chapman] to leave like I need a hole in the head. I will really miss him," said Turner. It was a blow for the players as well. "I am surprised they allowed Andy to go, really...I suppose it was up to

Andy in the end. Perhaps he felt he needed to move on to a fresh challenge," said Terry Nicholl.[46]

Fred Mann of The Eagle *put the transaction in perspective: "The outright sale of one of the most popular sports figures in any town is bound to launch a search for villains and heroes, but the sale of Andy Chapman to the Cleveland Force cannot be viewed in such simplistic terms. It seems to have come about for a variety of reasons that reflect the evolution of a young man, as well as the evolution of his team and his sport."*[47]

Mann continued: "He met with Wings General Manager Bill Kentling, not to demand a trade, but to talk about his concerns for the future, as they had done many times before. They decided that now was the time to make the change, for their mutual benefit. And so, over the objections of Wings coach Roy Turner, who wanted to keep all the scoring punch on the team he possibly could, the deal was struck."[48]

ANDY CHAPMAN: It was meant to be in my journey. I arrived in Wichita in 1979 and I left on March 1, 1985. I'd gone from a 19-year-old with dreams to a 25-year-old married man with a wife pregnant with our first daughter. In a short amount of time I experienced a lot. I wouldn't have had it any other way. It was fantastic. It was time for me to go on into a different stage.

TERRY NICHOLL: I was sad because it's hard to replace those kinds of characters...

CHARLIE MINSHULL-FORD: 1985 was kind of a tense year. Jeff Bourne was gone. Andy was sold, and it was strange not seeing him there. The camaraderie wasn't the same. Roy would start taking things out on me and Al [Green] that year. It was the nail in the coffin for me. I didn't want to be around it anymore. I was doing my job and was getting berated for it. I'll never forget my time with the Wings. I'd do it over again if I had the opportunity.

You can only take so much and when a job isn't fun anymore...Roy made you feel like it was all your fault the team was losing. He was so worried about having a losing season, and I think it got to him. One time our practice facility got broken into...they kicked in a door and took all the players' shoes and train-ing gear. We didn't have enough shoes...especially for Kim, who had huge feet. Roy would take out those things on me and others.

The role of equipment manager was one that took place mostly behind the scenes. But it allowed Minshull-Ford a unique view into the daily life of a professional player.

CHARLIE MINSHULL-FORD: I was a jack of all trades. I took care of the equipment, took care of uniforms, set up the referees' and visiting team locker rooms. I liked it because I was able to go to school and have some free time as well. [Team trainer] Al Green taught me how to do some of the trainer kind of stuff. I only traveled on one game.

For home games I'd come in around 4:30 am for morning practice. I'd set their uniforms out. It was hard to know who was suiting up, so I'd put all the uniforms out. It always drove everybody nuts because Roy couldn't decide on a starting lineup until the last minute. I made sure all the game balls were ready in the referees' locker room. I'd set up and ice down the beverages...make sure we had enough towels on the bench...make sure the ball boys knew their duties. After the game I'd make sure the locker room was clean. I was the first to arrive and last to leave.

If they won, it was happy [in the locker room]...players would get their slice of pizza, the Danes would get their special beer, and then the rest of the guys got Michelob and Budweiser because they were sponsors. The locker room was different than high school football or WSU baseball; more sedate, less hyped up. They were professionals. I never saw anybody push or shove, or get nasty. There was some name-calling during practice, but no come-to-blows fights. I don't recall anybody ever getting separated or sent home for fighting.

Each player had his own peculiarities...

CHARLIE MINSHULL-FORD: Kim didn't like the way the towels were washed. Terry Nicholl always wanted a certain style of compression shorts. Mike Dowler wanted his uniform and shoes laid out a certain way. Each player had their own little superstitions. Terry Nicholl would always roll his socks down a certain way because that was lucky. Andy would always need two towels to take a shower with. I think I spent half my time doing laundry.

I remember in 1982 the numbers fell off jerseys and you had to wash them a certain way. The ones with the stitched lettering lasted longer. Shorts would get rips and tears...I'd keep an abundance of shorts and socks. Dowler would go through a jersey a season because he'd tear out the elbows. We didn't go through that many jerseys. For a road game, I'd take all the bags over to air freight at the airport. One time I had to go out to the airport in a 4x4 vehicle because it had snowed that night. It was like 3:00 or 4:00 in the morning.

After the New York Cosmos folded their tent 33 games into the season, the Wings landed three of their players in a late season push to make the playoffs. David Brcic, who had just played on the US Olympic team, appeared in five games. Though he earned a solid 4.69 GAA, the Wings went 1-3 during his stint as replacement starter. Luis Alberto had the biggest impact of the three Cosmos, accumulating eight total points and eight blocks in his 13 appearances. Former Danish national team player Flemming Lund appeared in five games and then retired after his stint with the Wings.[49]

KEVIN KEWLEY: Flemming [Lund] wasn't popular with anybody. I don't even think the Danish players liked him.

One bright spot in an otherwise dreary season was the ESPN-televised All-Star game. On February 24th, in Cleveland, Roy Turner coached the Western Division side to a high-scoring 11-7 victory. Jorgen Kristensen made an assist, Roentved added two more, and Erik Rasmussen scored twice to defeat their Eastern Division rivals. In a controversial decision, Stan Stamenkovic, of the losing team, was named MVP. According to The Eagle's Tom Shine: "It was gratifying to see the look in Roy Turner's eyes after he led the Western All-Stars to...victory. It was not an easy season for Turner, and that victory, for at least one day, made everything right with the world."[50]

TOM SHINE: I covered the All-Star game in Cleveland in 1985 when Roy was the coach. I still hate [ESPN's] Bob Ley because of that. ESPN did the game and we were voting on MVP. ESPN said, "We need your ballots." But it was the middle of the fourth quarter and it was tied. [We said], "The game's not over yet." They said, "Well, we need it now." So we vote for Stamenkovic. Then the game ends and his team lost, and Zungul scores the winning goal [for the other team], and Bob Ley is on the air saying, "They picked the wrong MVP, it's terrible." We were like, "Hey asshole, it's because you needed our ballots before the game was over!" I still hate Bob Ley.

Kim Roentved showed his greatness all season long in 1984-85 by putting in a gutsy performance from the back. "Watching Kim Roentved play made the entire season worthwhile. He played with as much heart as any athlete I've ever seen. He tried to carry the entire team on his shoulders and when he failed, he felt personally responsible. How Kevin Crow was named [MISL] Defender of the Year over Kim is an absolute mystery," said Shine.[51]

Despite their poor 21-26 record, the Wings made the playoffs thanks to a new wildcard series that expanded the playoff field to ten teams. The MISL would immediately discard the wildcard format at the end of the season.

BILL KENTLING: We did something that year in the league that I wish we hadn't. I thought the wildcard was a joke. Fifth place teams shouldn't be rewarded.

The Wings were matched up with the Minnesota Strikers in a best-of-three series. But the playoffs that year would be remembered more for the antics of Minnesota goalkeeper Tino Lettieri, and the stuffed parrot he kept in goal, than anything performance-related. The Wings lost the first game in Minnesota off of a late-game shot by Jan Goossens. The series then moved to Wichita for a crucial game two. The Wings had the game well in hand when the fireworks began...

"Things started to get ugly when Steve Litt and Terry Rowe were ejected with just less than a minute to play for fighting. Trainer Al Green escorted Rowe off the field. When Green tried to re-enter the field so he could get back to the Wings' bench, Minnesota goalkeeper Tino Lettieri - one of the world's seriously goofy people - wouldn't let him. First he slapped at Green's hand when he tried to open the gate. Then Lettieri held the gate shut. That brought a response from Bill Kentling, then

the Wings' general manager. He tried to push the gate open while Lettieri held it closed. Kentling's a big guy and I thought the entire south section of the dasher boards were going to fall over. It was truly an unforgettable moment in MISL history," wrote Tom Shine.[52]

It didn't end there. Shine continued: "...at the final buzzer, Lettieri hip-checked [Terry] Nicholl as Nicholl chased a loose ball. Nicholl got up and started chasing Lettieri. Players from both benches followed. David Brcic and Roentved led the Wings charge and if Roentved had reached Lettieri, he would have hurt him in a serious manner. Order was finally restored and Turner himself escorted Lettieri off the field. 'I didn't talk to him,' Turner said after the game. 'I just didn't want anyone to kill him.'"[53]

ALAN SHEPHERD, MISL REFEREE: I can always remember the Tino Lettieri-Bill Kentling atmosphere. I always remember [San Diego Sockers coach] Ron Newman saying, "It's a show!" Tino always had a parrot in the back of his net.

KIM ROENTVED, DEFENDER, WICHITA WINGS: Tino was making fun of Bill Kentling in goal during a game. Someone stole Tino's good luck parrot he kept in goal with him. Tino starts making fun of Bill Kentling's gut. All hell broke loose. Tino ran away like a chicken in Ethiopia he was so scared. Everyone was chasing him. We were going back to Minnesota the next day. Like five or six guys were suspended from the fight.

BILL KENTLING: Minnesota called a timeout. Chris Davis was behind the goal with me. I asked him to steal the parrot, and it was on from there. [Lettieri] got pissed off. We got everything we wanted from it: Lettieri kicked off for a game.

TERRY NICHOLL: [Lettieri and his parrot] was lunatic, but so much fun. Then putting it under his shirt, imitating Kentling's girth. He had taken it too far. I remember we were on power play defense and it was near the end of the game. Lettieri was up to all kinds of stuff. He said something like, "You'd better not come down here again." Then, I was one-on-one against him, and I put it past him and he kicked me up in the air, and I fell down. I tried to get up to have a fight and he just kicked me down again. All the lads were saying, "It's a two-hit fight. Lettieri hit Nicholl, Nicholl hit floor." [laughs] Everybody chased after him on the field. Then he started running towards Mike Dowler. I think he thought maybe there was a Goalie Union and that Mike would protect him. That was funny! Kentling was always good at promoting. [He would say], "Sometimes you've got to get a two-minute penalty because you don't want someone coming in here thinking they ran the show."

TOM SHINE: Bill Kentling said after the Minnesota game, "You give me a fight and I'll guarantee a sellout."

Kentling himself was fined $350 for his involvement in the altercation with Lettieri. David Brcic was suspended for a single game. But Kentling did indeed get what he wanted. When the Wings flew to Minnesota for the final game in the series, Tino Lettieri couldn't play due to a suspension for violent conduct. He was also fined $1,250.[54] Sadly, it didn't make a difference. Backup Minnesota goalie Craig Scarpelli earned the one and only MISL win of his career against the Wings in that third and final game. An overtime goal by Jan Goossens advanced the Strikers to the quarterfinal round of the playoffs.

There would be one final blow in a year filled with bad news. After the end of the 1984-85 season, longtime Wings goalkeeper Mike Dowler signed a contract with the Tacoma Stars. It was the end of an era. After the Wings folded in 2001, Dowler still held the Wings single-season record for most games, minutes, shots faced, saves, and wins. He is the Wings career leader in shots faced and saves. He had four of the dozen or so shutouts in MISL history as of 1985. He would be missed.[55]

ROY TURNER: Mike Dowler was one of the biggest losses we had. That was all about money. A tremendous loss.

BILL KENTLING: Tacoma was willing to spend more than we thought we had and got him. I was sorry Mike got away.

MIKE DOWLER, GOALKEEPER, WICHITA WINGS: I have obviously had a long time to think about this and I am of the opinion that we get a little wiser and calmer as we get older. To be frank though, the time was right for me to go. In all walks of life, not just sports, I am a great believer in setting yourself new challenges in an attempt to get the best from yourself. It was not a financial decision at all, but I had been with the Wings for five seasons and I believe that I may have been getting a little "stale." It may have affected my attitude towards my fellow players and even some of the staff within the club. If that was the case, I would like to offer my sincere, if somewhat belated, apologies.

An Oral History

Norman Piper, Private Investigator

File #394: "The Case of the Secret Agent"

———

IT WAS THE SUMMER OF 1985, and it was so hot you could have fried an egg on the asphalt of the Coliseum's parking lot. The competition to sign new players was heating up as well. Word had it that Carl Valentine was ripe for signing. Valentine had won a Soccer Bowl for the NASL's Vancouver Whitecaps in 1979. Now, he played the striker position for West Bromwich Albion (West Brom) in the top level of English football. Bill Kentling wanted him in Wichita for the upcoming indoor season...and it was Norman Piper's job to make it happen. It wouldn't be easy task.

NORMAN PIPER, ASSISTANT COACH, WICHITA WINGS: I remember going to England to try to sign a player. Bill Kentling asked me to sign Carl Valentine.

BILL KENTLING, GENERAL MANAGER, WICHITA WINGS: We sent Norman Piper to England with a check. Norman wasn't to produce the check until everything was on the up and up.

NORMAN PIPER: It was a weird situation. I went over [to England] and I met, supposedly, his agent. But I knew a guy that was a manager for Ireland and he knew Valentine. I called [the manager] up and asked him who Carl Valentine's agent was. He called me back the next day and said he'd spoken to Valentine and that his agent lived in Canada. I said, "What?" He goes, "Yeah, he doesn't have an agent over here." I thought to myself, "What do I do now?" This supposed agent was taking me to soccer games in West Brom where Valentine was playing and wouldn't let me speak to him. So I smelled a rat. Bill Kentling had given me a check, but I kept it in my pocket. I wouldn't give it to [the supposed agent]. I said, "No, I want to see Carl Valentine." He said, "Well, we can't do that right now. We better get back to London." We got there and he said, "See ya, bye." I put the check in my bank account and when I left [England] I took it back out again and made a bunch of money in interest! Then I wrote a check back to Bill.

BILL KENTLING: He came home with the check eventually. We could never figure out who Valentine's real agent was....but he ended up signing with Cleveland.

Valentine would sign with the Cleveland Force in November of 1985 and go on to play three seasons there. He continued to play in the MISL until the league folded in 1992. But he never did play for the Wings.

CHAPTER 18

An Oral History

Chico and the Men

———

"It was the best team I ever had."

- ROY TURNER, ON THE 1985-86 WINGS.

NOT ALL THE OFFSEASON NEWS was as dreary as the failed Carl Valentine signing. Wedding bells rang for Coach Roy Turner on June 18th, 1985. His romance with KU Medical School psychologist Tamara Pryor had blossomed into something special. They married in Negril, Jamaica in front of "60 guests, including both sets of parents." According to Turner, "We got married on the rocks, and the ocean was behind us...[It was] as romantic as it sounds." Former teammate Kyle Rote, Jr. was among the many soccer people to attend.[1]

DR. TAMARA PRYOR, CLINICAL PSYCHOLOGIST: I had a nightmare that I showed up at the Coliseum and the entire Orange Army was there. My wedding party was all dressed in orange and blue and everyone dribbled balls out onto the floor before we could get married. That's how we ended up on island in the middle of nowhere.

Kenny Cooper was the best man...Joe Howarth, Ron Loewen, and Billy Kentling were in the wedding. We got married on a cliff overlooking the ocean. Then we had a reception at the beach and we danced in the sand. It was a two week party. It was wonderful.

Being married to a local celebrity was a new experience…

TAMARA PRYOR: I think it was pretty easy to get used to [his celebrity]. You just expected it. People wanted to come up to the table and talk to him. And Roy was very good with it. He couldn't know several thousand people personally, but you would have thought he did because each person felt like they knew him because he was a public person. They'd come up and want to talk about the game or the next game…They'd want to talk soccer and Roy lived and breathed soccer. I loved the game of soccer, even before I met him, so I was comfortable with that. I didn't find it to be an irritation. People were always very nice about it. He was always generous with his attention and time.

The funniest things would happen. Only Roy could go into Piccadilly [Market], buy a bunch of groceries, go to checkout and realize he didn't have his billfold, because Roy never had his billfold. They would say, "Roy, no problem." People just wanted to do things for him. He'd go to the dry cleaners and they'd say, "This is on us."

At the league level, it was a relatively stable year. Unfortunately, for the first time in MISL history there was no franchise in New York City. This was a loss of prestige for a league that prided itself on competing in major cities around the country. The only team to fold was the Las Vegas franchise. The Las Vegas Americans lasted only one year in the league, but their demise would eventually yield great dividends for the Wings.

The departure of key players meant that Turner and Kentling needed new talent to fill in the gaps. Dowler left for Tacoma and Chapman was in Cleveland. And they weren't the only ones who would depart. Gregg Willin would spend most of the 1985-86 season in LA with the Lazers. Karsten Christensen was gone. Ian Anderson, Mark Snell, and Tony Peszneker all left after successful multi-year stints with the Wings. The New York Cosmos signees from the previous year, Alberto, Lund, and Brcic, did not return.

Roy Turner's wedding also led to good news on the player acquisition front…

ROY TURNER, HEAD COACH, WICHITA WINGS: An owner came to me during my wedding in Jamaica in 1985 and said, "We realize you've always been under-budget and we'd like to help you out." He gave us money to be used exclusively for the recruitment of new players. We got four players as part of that: Dave Hoggan, Chico Borja, Michael Fox, and Jorge Espinoza.

Unfortunately, getting Borja, Fox, and Espinoza proved to be quite an ordeal. The Pittsburgh Spirit and the Wings were pursuing the trio in July of 1985. Both teams claimed to have inked a deal with Las Vegas. After neither team would budge from its claim, MISL Commissioner Frank Dale stepped in to try to reach a fair solution. At a September hearing, former Las Vegas team officials declined to testify. Thus, "the Spirit was unable to prove its deal preceded the Wings' agreement with Las Vegas." Dale ruled that the Wings were the rightful contract holders.[2]

ROY TURNER: We faced stiff opposition from getting them. Pittsburgh tried to sign them as well. The commissioner ruled in our favor and we got them.

"The hostages are freed and are coming to Wichita," said Bill Kentling. According to The Eagle, *"the mood at the Wings' office Thursday was jubilant. Staffers broke out champagne upon hearing Dale's decision." Roy Turner's reaction was similar: "Thank goodness. We always felt we made a deal...and complied with everything asked of us. We think it was a fair decision." Not surprisingly, the Spirit felt differently. "To say we're disappointed, that's an understatement. All along, we thought we were the only club that consummated a deal between the two parties," said Pittsburgh General Manager Chris Wright.[3]*

BILL KENTLING, GENERAL MANAGER, WICHITA WINGS, 1980-1986: Our ability to get Borja, Fox, and [Espinoza] from Las Vegas really meant a lot...[Pittsburgh] thought they had a claim that was equal to ours. I had sent in our money and the league cashed the check. That was my legal grounds for saying they were our players. You accepted our money and it constitutes a deal, and the MISL commissioner upheld it.

Jorge Espinoza was a Chilean defender with five years of American professional experience. He began his stateside career with the NASL's Chicago Sting, with whom he won a Soccer Bowl in 1981. He then migrated to the MISL, spending three years in Memphis and then a season in Las Vegas. Prior to his American debut, he had played with a First Division Chilean club as well as the Chilean Olympic National Team.[4] Thanks to his top-notch skills defending the finest scorers in the league, Espinoza had been chosen for the MISL Select Second Team during the previous season.[5] In his 31 games with the 1985-86 Wings he would contribute 58 blocks and 11 assists while hitting the back of the net twice.[6] Though it was his only season with the Wings, it would be a productive one.

ROY TURNER: Jorge Espinosa...I brought him in to be a man-to-man marker. He reminded me of myself, but with a little more skill. They called him the "Magic Marker."

Alongside Espinoza came Mike Fox. A much-heralded midfielder originally drafted by the NASL's New York Cosmos, Fox would become one of the Wings' best American success stories. Fox was a California boy at heart, growing up in the Los Angeles area and playing college soccer at Cal-State Fullerton in nearby Orange County. After being drafted by the Cosmos, he spent most of his time playing for the 1984 US Olympic Team alongside Chico Borja. He would appear in all three of the team's games. "That, for me, was probably my best experience in soccer so far," he told Missile Magazine *in 1986.[7]*

While with the New York Cosmos, he would become the only American starter during the retirement game of the great Italian star Giorgio Chinaglia, appearing alongside legendary players like Carlos Alberto and Franz Beckenbauer in front of 77,000 Italian fans.[8] After a year-long stint in Las Vegas, he would spend five seasons in Wichita. Throughout his time with the Wings, Fox would contribute dozens of points and blocks each year. In the 1985-86 season, Fox would end up with 33 points and 28 blocks while playing in 42 of the team's 48 games.[9]

ROY TURNER: Mike Fox was a national team player and a good role-player on our team.

The third member of the trio from Las Vegas became one of the greatest players the Wings would ever put on the pitch. Chico Borja was born and raised in Quito, the capital of Ecuador. His father Carlos had a modest job at a bank. But with ten children, it was no easy task to make ends meet. The family sent Chico's oldest brother, Carlos Jr., to the United States in hopes he would pave the way for the rest of the family. At age 12, Chico and the rest of the Borjas moved to New Jersey. "I came here and the first thing after the airport my brother said, 'Would you like to go eat chicken?' I said, 'Whose birthday is it?' We went to Kentucky Fried Chicken. They have no place like that in Ecuador," Borja told The Eagle's *Gary Dymski.*[10]

Like Mike Fox, Borja had been drafted by the New York Cosmos of the NASL. He set the Cosmos rookie scoring record with 15 points outdoors in 1981-82. Also playing alongside Fox on the 1984 Olympic team, Borja became a mainstay on the US National Team during the 1980s. Though he only appeared in 28 games with the Las Vegas Americans in 1984-85, he accumulated 54 points on 24 goals and 30 assists.[11] *Borja was the real deal and the Wings knew it. They paid him the princely sum of $60,000 in 1985-86 (roughly $135,000 in 2016 when adjusted for inflation.)*[12]

CHICO BORJA, MIDFIELDER, WICHITA WINGS: To be honest, I was not looking forward to [coming to Wichita]. I was with the Las Vegas Americans and the team folded. From what I remember, they had six players that Wichita and Pittsburgh were fighting for. Jorge Espinosa, Mike Fox, and I got chosen by the commissioner to go to Wichita. I had a brand new wife and brand new kid and I was looking forward to going to Pittsburgh because it was closer to New Jersey. I got picked up by Vernon Riggs at the airport and he told me we were going to stay around here because it was near Soccer West [where the team practiced]. There was a hotel like two blocks away. I was going to stay there and the next day go to practice and meet the team at Soccer West. I remember opening up the shades [at the hotel] and there were a bunch of cows right outside the hotel room. My wife and I looked at each other and went, "Oh my God!" [laughs] That was my first day in Wichita.

Obviously, without any doubt, in my heart, it was the best decision I ever made in my life...though somebody made it for me! We had the most amazing fans and friendships we created and two of my beautiful daughters were born there. The next day, Vernon took me on Kellogg all the way to the east side and saw a lot of golf courses, and that's one of my hobbies. I remember moving to Rockborough Apartments on Rock Road and met a girl who worked there named Maria who became like another mom to my son.

ROY TURNER: Chico loved it in Wichita...he was a big fish in a small bowl.

Though he had played forward for the New York Cosmos, he would make his name as a halfback. At the midfield position, Borja created opportunities for everyone around him. By the end of his career he was the Wings All-Time Career Leader in assists, with 345 in his two stints with the club from 1985 to 1987 and 1988 to 1994. He is third and fourth on the All-Time Season High list with 53 and 52 assists respectively.[13]

"I'm not a goal-scorer, a guy who gets the ball from somebody and scores. I'm an assist man. Name me one midfielder who is on top of the league in scoring. It's harder for me to score goals," Borja told The Eagle.[14]

CHICO BORJA: I was a better midfielder. The best thing I did was create... my intelligence made things happen...created opportunities for other people and myself to score. Coming with the ball, with guys in front of you...trying to create; instead of being at the top and hoping somebody would create for me, so I could score.

Borja's impact on the team was profound. A case could be made for Borja, Rasmussen, or Roentved as the team's franchise player during the latter half of the 1980s; each had their own special talent.

CHICO BORJA: I was one of [the franchise players]. We had Erik [Rasmussen]. Dale Ervine came [in 1986] and I assisted on him as much as I did on Erik. I'd like to think that I was a big part of what Dale became. We'd find each other all the time...in the free kicks we were deadly. I know that between Erik and Kim and I, we were up there...While it lasted, I enjoyed indoor soccer. I had my best years in indoor soccer, without a doubt.

ROY TURNER: Chico's game was explosive. Not everyone knew what he was going to do next, and I don't think he did. He was dynamic, loved to please the crowd and to entertain, and he had the skills capable of doing that. His personality on the field was a little different than that off the field. He had great rhythm and a lot of that South American talent.

The team had to fit around Chico, more than Chico would fit around the team. His talent was explosive and very individual. Opposing teams went after him and after Erik [Rasmussen], but you'd never know they had gone after

Erik. After [Borja] scored a goal he would get very excited. He invented some of those moves that became common.

TERRY NICHOLL, MIDFIELDER, WICHITA WINGS: Chico Borja... what a spark plug he was! I would have paid to watch Chico. You could go to the Kansas Coliseum knowing you'd see sparks and creativity. He played 100%...he was all out.

On defense, it was a different story...

CHICO BORJA: I remember having defensive runners: Somebody would lose the ball and I'd come out. Somebody would come in for me, win the ball back and I'd jump back in and try to create. It was great, I didn't have to defend that much [laughs]...I still don't know how to spell "defense." [laughs]

(Don Marler/Missile Magazine) Kim Roentved and Chico Borja celebrating a goal.

BILL KENTLING: I'm shocked that Chris Christie is the governor of New Jersey. I thought Chico would be the governor by now! That sort of good-looking, flashy guy that all the girls want to date and all the guys want to have a beer with. He was a really good guy who was this typical American immigrant story: large family comes from Ecuador and settles in New Jersey and their kid becomes a star player. I liked him a lot. He's like a lot of people, selfish yeah, but good players have great confidence in themselves. They want the ball at the end. Sometimes it works out and sometimes it doesn't. Chico was demonstrative, probably to a fault. I think that gets on the nerves of people who are better at controlling themselves. Chico was a little like Omar Gomez. They were excitable and at the end [of the game] they wanted the ball. On those nights they scored the winning goal it was pretty superb and on the other nights when they didn't...it was less than superb.

You can be too emotional and worry too much about the officiating. The only thing that Chico did, and I say this as the guy that really liked Chico and worked very hard to acquire him, is that Chico had a habit of doing something that I don't think any athlete should ever do, which is "show-up" his teammates. He would break out for a long pass, the goalie might miss him with the pass, and Chico would put his hands on his hips or raise his hands. There's no point in showing-up your teammate. I wished he hadn't done that. But when he scored I thought he was pretty spectacular. Great players, are they selfish? Well, yeah, you can characterize it that way. But I want a guy with confidence enough to want the ball at the end. Look, I could make the same criticism of Tatu. He held the ball too long...but I want him with the ball with five seconds to go!

Wings fans loved Borja's passion to win. But to some of his opponents, that passion was seen in a negative light. "I don't know what his problem was. Listen, I'm not going to say what I want to say about him," snarled Ralph Black of the Tacoma Stars. "He is a poor excuse for a human being. That's some sort of low-class act when someone spits in my face. Only animals do that..." said Chicago Sting player Neil Roberts. In an ironic twist of fate, Roberts would find himself as Borja's teammate later that season.[15]

But it wasn't all venom. Pittsburgh Spirit Coach Don Popovic sang Borja's praises: "Chico, in my opinion, is one of the most outstanding soccer players in the country. He has the speed, tremendous speed, he's one of the fastest players with the ball. He has a very strong, precise shot, and the dribbling, very good. Everything a soccer player is supposed to have, he has." His own coach knew how valuable he was that first season. "He means a helluva lot to this team. I'll tell you, he's so intense it's incredible. Our team attitude this year has been remarkable, and he's a big reason," said Turner. Jorge Espinoza, Borja's roommate on road trips, agreed: "Chico is a helluva player. He can do things no one will expect." [16]

Borja's temper was much-discussed at the time. Everyone knew it existed, but the explanations for it varied. When an Eagle *reporter asked Borja whether his temper was a weakness, "Mike Fox, sitting next to Borja, nodded his head yes. Jorge Espinoza, eating lunch at the same table, smiled." Borja saw his temper as a possible advantage: "It's not a weakness at all. If you let that be a weakness then you're not a soccer player. What I try to do is intimidate them instead of letting them intimidate me...I'm a Jekyll-and-Hyde player. You have to have it. If you don't have it as a professional, then you shouldn't be playing. Once you get onto the field, you have to change. You have to concentrate. You can be nice to the guy after the game, go out for drinks, dinner, whatever. But you have to remember that it's not only a game, it's your profession."* [17]

CHICO BORJA: For me, I was a soccer player and a lot of defenders and coaches said, "Try to get under Chico's skin." If you got under my skin it was because of how you played me...it was because of trying to hurt me. If you try to hurt me, I'm going to react in a negative way. I know the difference between trying to hurt me and playing me hard. I believe I played as hard even if somebody upset me. I never thought [my temper] hindered my game at all.

Every single team had great players I respected. The ones I hated to play against were the same ones everybody hated to play against: Neil Megson from Tacoma, Gino Schiraldi [from the Comets]. They came at me and tried to hurt me.

KIM ROENTVED, DEFENDER, WICHITA WINGS: I think Chico's personality had some good things and bad things...the good things were hard to find sometimes. He was a hell of a soccer player. He was a Dr. Jekyll and Mr. Hyde. We all would see him at Christmas parties and the like being a nice guy. But he had this egotistical thing about him. It's too bad, but it's part of what makes him a special player. Chico wanted to win more than anybody. If he could take the glory for a win, even better. That's what separated him from being a likeable person to a disliked person. I have seen Chico being the kindest person, great husband, great dad. Sometimes it's hard as a teammate when you play with somebody who has that ego.

It is extremely hard to coach also. You have to be a sort of psychologist and try to figure out how to get the best out of a guy like that. Roy did a fantastic job of managing it. Anybody can go out and buy a team, but how do you get them to play well together? That's where Chico was a dilemma...he went out there and he played some fantastic games and he won a lot of games for us. Unfortunately, there were games he lost for us at critical times because of his temper. His temper got in his way out on the field at times...he couldn't control it. Maybe he wanted to put on a show or maybe it was just an instinct. He wanted to be a star in front of the people. That's where the problem was... sometimes it's better to be a team player. His positives outweighed his negatives because of his pure talent. There were a couple games we could have gone a step further and it could have made a difference if he'd been able to control his temper.

ROY TURNER: Sometimes he went to the box at key points in a game. I'm not saying it cost the game, but it didn't help us. Chico tried to change for the better.

KIM ROENTVED: He was also very intelligent. So sometimes that made you try to play triple-psychologist, because he'd try to defend his actions and it was hard to argue about it.

KEVIN KEWLEY, DEFENDER, WICHITA WINGS: He was a great player, but he was one of those players, like Jorgen, that demanded perfection. He had an unbelievable desire to win. He was kind of like the leader of the American guys. He had been an Olympian and made the most of what he had. He was great in public. There was a clash of personalities there between him and Jorgen and him and Erik. The egos get in the way when they decide who takes the free kicks. He and I never had any problems. If he respects you, there are no problems. Like Jorgen, if he thought you were subpar, he'd let you know! Chico thought other people were there to get him the ball, which was true sometimes. I know Erik and Chico didn't get along very well. It was a clash of personalities. They just didn't like each other. I think Kim got drawn into that. The Danish guys would stick up for each other; the British and American guys would do the same. When I look back, I think this was what happened sometimes. The American players looked up to Chico. The divide between players by country never was public. There was a public perception that Roy favored English guys, which wasn't true. He just wanted guys that would win.

STEVE SHAAD, ASSISTANT GENERAL MANAGER, WICHITA WINGS, 1985-86: Chico was always very nice to me...I got along well with him. He was kind of a brand of his own. He marketed himself extremely well. Not always the player that should have the ball at the end of the game. He didn't come through in the clutch sometimes. Tried too hard, or took the ball on his own, instead of playing team-ball. He was one of the best businessmen as well. He had his academy for kids. After he retired he ran some very successful camps.

Chico Borja and Roy Turner spent eight seasons together as either player and coach or player and team president. That long tenure is probably the best evidence that they developed a good working relationship, despite the inevitable strains that resulted from a hyper-competitive sport like indoor soccer.

CHICO BORJA: I'm a professional and I always have been. I played as hard in practice as I did in the game. [Coach Turner] did his job and I did mine. I was thankful that he and the general manager fought to get me. We grew on each other in a sense. I'm very competitive and so is he. We had our disagreements a few times at the beginning, but I think that the fact that he realized what my work ethic was...there were never any issues with that. Sometimes we would butt heads a little bit on a few things, but it was always for the benefit of the entire team. We developed a relationship where we respected each other. I played hard for my family first, and then for the fans, and for the "shirt"...in that order.

Chico Borja had a huge impact on the Wichita Wings during his long tenure with the club. He stands fifth on the All-Time Career Leader list in games played, at 303. He is fourth in goals with 266, in front of the great Andy Chapman and just behind one-time league MVP Erik Rasmussen. As mentioned earlier, he is number one in all-time assists as well. Borja is sandwiched between Erik Rasmussen and Omar Gomez at third on the list of all-time power play goals. He ranks second only to Rasmussen in game-winning goals, at 30. Additionally, in the 1986-87 season he would score nine game-winning goals, tying Erik Rasmussen for the single-season record.[18]

Al Smith set a different kind of record for the Wings in 1985-86. After graduating from the University of Tampa, "Fast Al" Smith was the fourth overall draft pick in the MISL draft. What made him unique that season was that he was the only black American player in the league. In fact, in the history of the MISL, there had been only four black American players as of the 1985-86 season. In his three seasons with the Wings, Smith would become a solid contributor on defense.[19] *In 1985-86, after playing sparsely in the first half of the season he would eventually get his chance. "That was really a tough time. But I looked at the situation and how the team was playing. After a while, I just figured it was a learning experience, and I'd have to deal with it," said Smith. After several injuries, Smith earned a starting spot in January 1986. "[Speed is] probably the first factor that helped me get into the lineup. Second is I'm a decent defender," Smith told* The Eagle's *Gary Dymski.*[20] *In 24 games that season he would accrue nine points and 29 blocks. That was 23 more appearances than MISL veteran Nick Mangione would make for the Wings that year.*[21]

The Wings also saw a big impact from another American newcomer. Tim Walters had grown up in St. Louis, the mecca of American soccer. After two successful seasons in Denver with the MISL's Avalanche, he came back home to play for the

Steamers. Though he spent three seasons playing at the Checkerdome, there was no love lost when he departed. His relationship with Steamers' coach Dave Clements and team president Thomas Bowers had deteriorated. So when he scored against the Steamers as a member of the Wings, even though Clements had departed, it was sweet revenge. "...I wasn't treated very well there...That's why it was nice to score, sort of putting it in the big guy's face," Walters told The Eagle.[22] *Walters would play in all 48 of the Wings' games in his only season with the club, accumulating 34 blocks and 18 points.*[23]

BILL KENTLING: We got Tim Walters from St. Louis to play in front, but he was a better midfielder. We thought Timmy might be the answer and he was a great teammate, and great distributor, but didn't finish at the rate we wanted him to. I'm not knocking Timmy Walters; he played his butt off. We just didn't get the goal scoring production we had hoped out of Tim.

At this point in Wings history, it might have seemed like Wichita had become Denmark's American colony. Yet another Dane joined the team in 1985-86. This time, Denmark thought they had beaten the American spell-checkers. Keld Bordinggaard was a member of the Danish National Team and his club had played against Liverpool FC in the European Cup. Like many of the Danish players, he had played their version of indoor soccer, which differed in that the field was smaller and the goalkeepers couldn't use their hands.[24] *In his lone season with the Wings, Bordinggaard became known as "The Comet Killer." Starting with the third game of the season, when he scored three goals against Kansas City, about half of Bordinggaard's 24 goals would come against the Comets.*[25]

Bill Kentling and Roy Turner were faced with a difficult situation in 1985-86: how to replace Mike Dowler. The solution turned out to be a two-headed monster, so to speak: One Danish head and one Irish head.

ROY TURNER: Don't forget at that time we had two goalies, [Jan] Olesen and [Seamus] McDonagh. You want to be fair. I rotated them at times...but that was the only time [I ever did that]. You [usually] couldn't afford to have more than one legitimate number one goalkeeper.

BILL KENTLING: I was part of the group that brought Seamus to the United States. He was a very gifted goalkeeper who had been a good English Premier League goalkeeper.

(Howard Eastwood/1987 Wings Calendar) Top-notch
Irish goalkeeper Seamus McDonagh.

KEVIN KEWLEY: He was born in Ireland but grew up in England. When I played with him in England he was known as Jim McDonagh.

Seamus McDonagh, aka "The Pride of Ireland," had spent several years playing First Division football in England for Bolton and Everton before making his way to Wichita. Like most English players he started playing professionally as a teenager, 17 in his case. But a broken leg resulted in blood clots in his lungs, almost killing him before he had a chance to make his mark. "The center-forward came clean through and I came out to meet him. I met him at the penalty spot and I saved it, I pushed it away. But I was layin' on me left side and he was about 14 stone, you know, a big lad, bigger than me; he just jumped on the floor and slid into me and ran into my shin bone. With the weight of him and me layin' on my leg, it just snapped. Both bones cracked. I was up after three days, but you know the veins broke too and the blood started clotting and it washed around me system. Three weeks later I just collapsed. At Christmas I just collapsed, I couldn't breathe...It was 50-50 if I might live...The specialist was askin' me, 'Can you do anythin' else, besides play football?'" said McDonagh.[26]

After a long recovery he went on to success at Bolton, which moved up to First Division while McDonagh was there. They then sold him to Everton for 300,000 pounds, a huge sum. He ended up back in Bolton a year later. McDonagh was born in England, attended school there, and spent most of his playing career in England. But his early years had been spent in Ireland. Both his parents were amongst the many Irish who went to England seeking work. His mom was a nurse from Tipperary and his dad came from County Mayo on the west coast of Ireland. McDonagh would play 25 international games (caps) for Team Ireland prior to coming to Wichita. As an Irish National Team member, he faced teams from Brazil, West Germany, Holland, Spain, Czechoslovakia, Wales, England, Chile, and the Soviet Union, where he played at Lenin Stadium in Moscow.[27] But on March 11, 1986 he would show his American pride by singing the national anthem at a Wings game.[28]

CHICO BORJA: I remember him singing the national anthem and he did a great job.

McDonagh would play 33 games in goal to Olesen's 16 that year. With a 4.94 GAA and a 16-16 record, McDonagh's numbers were respectable. However, Olesen had better numbers, with a 3.72 GAA to go along with his 11-5 record.[29] But there was one category where Olesen couldn't hope to compete with McDonagh: worst temper. More about THAT in the next chapter.

(Greg Fox/Missile Magazine) Danish goalkeeper Jan Olesen after his incredible goal.

Jan Olesen had played for Koge, the same team that produced Erik Rasmussen. Also a veteran of the Danish National Youth Team, Olesen had been spotted several years earlier by Norman Piper on a recruiting trip to Denmark. "He is a fine outdoor goalkeeper. He plays the ball with his feet as well as I've seen anybody play," Roy Turner told The Eagle. At 6'2, he was big for an MISL goalkeeper, but was also known for his agility and quickness.[30] He would prove this on December 3rd, 1985. Taking the ball off a short pass while in his own goal, Olesen dribbled down the left side of the field, flying by one, then two, then a third Steamer, before shooting it between Slobo Ilijevski's legs and into the net. What made it somewhat ironic was that it was Ilijevski who was better known for wandering from his goal. He was the first Wings goalie to score a goal and only the second MISL goalie to do it with his feet. The remainder of the previous goalkeeper goals had been thrown into an empty net during a sixth attacker situation. The official attendance of 6,403, an average midweek crowd, made noise like 64,003.[31]

TERRY NICHOLL: I was on the pitch when Jan Olesen scored. He kind of just took off, didn't he? "Is he gonna give it to me? Is he gonna give it to me? Don't give it to me, shoot! Goal!" I think it went through Slobo's legs. Brilliant. I think Jorgen made a joke after the game like, "Nicholl, thank God he didn't give it to you because you would have missed." [laughs]

KIM ROENTVED: Jan Olesen spoke almost no English...other than "hello" and "thanks."

Financially, the team was in decent shape in 1985-86. Attendance would hover around 8,500 per game, just 1000 shy of a sellout crowd. Revenue was important, especially for a small-market team like the Wings. Losing money was a normal occurrence, but owner Frank Carney and the rest of the front office always sought to find that elusive profitable season. Director of Media Relations Steve Shaad had just been promoted to Assistant General Manager for 1985-86 and hoped he would be the one to achieve it.

STEVE SHAAD: For the Wings to have made a profit, we would have had to increase ticket prices and prices for advertising on the boards. We were always afraid if we raised ticket prices then the crowds would go down. We didn't increase the prices very much. But with us losing money on a consistent basis and getting close to capacity, it would seem it would have been a good time to increase prices.

My first year as assistant GM, Bill [Kentling] says, "Steve, you need to do a presentation on your sales budget for Frank Carney tomorrow." I revered Carney, so I definitely didn't want to give a presentation to him. So I do it and am going through what we will sell in various ads, and I get to the subject of dasherboards. I told him this was our largest source of revenue. We had 65 boards, selling for $1,500 each...And we'd sold out for five years straight. He asked, "What will you sell them for next year?" I told him we had been selling them for $1,500 for a while and had generated a lot of loyalty from the people that buy these and so we'd sell them for $1,500. Carney says, "We had a little saying at Pizza Hut: 'When the restaurant's full, it's time to raise the prices.'" I replied, "Do you want me to raise the prices?" He says, "Oh, that's your decision, do whatever you feel is right." Needless to say, I raised the prices.

After such a disappointing season in 1984-85, with a losing record of 21-26, the Wings' slogan in 1985-86 was "Fighting Back." The marketing campaign included a commercial featuring Kim Roentved running through a banner emblazoned with that very slogan. Indeed, the Wings would fight back with an improved roster and a renewed drive to reach the MISL Championship. The team they had assembled was very impressive on paper.

ROY TURNER: It was the best team I ever had.

BILL KENTLING: We had a really good team, offensively and defensively. We had…Americans playing key roles on the team. In our six years the American kids had really come along. It was a fun, good-looking ball club.

CHICO BORJA: We had an amazing team. I went from an All-Star team in Vegas to an All-Star team in Wichita. I believe every team in the league at that time was an All-Star team. I believe we had the best players anywhere in the world playing indoor soccer. Every team had three, four, five superstars who could play. The amazing wizardry of Erik, Jorgen was an amazing assist player. Kim, with his fighting spirit, he was one of a kind. I've never seen a more competitive guy than him. For me, it was "what can I do." I believe there is an "I" in team. I brought my best. I believe that helped us win a few games. I wish we would have won the whole thing, but it was very physical…we played against some serious, serious teams in that time.

ROY TURNER: Erik was the star on that 1985-86 team and Chico admitted that. The talent level on that team made it somewhat difficult to coach. McDonagh was on that team. It took an awful lot of work to keep them on the same page.

KIM ROENTVED: There's the coaching part of it, then there's the communication part of it. A guy like McDonagh wasn't hard to coach as a goalie. But managing the personalities was harder.

ROY TURNER: I created a lot of the style, but the guys created it as well. Terry Nicholl knew what his role was. The league got better and better. That last year I was coach was a great team and we could have won the championship.

The role for Terry Nicholl that Turner spoke of was as captain of the team. He would be replacing a 30-year-old Kevin Kewley, the only captain the Wings had ever had.

KEVIN KEWLEY: In 1984 or 1985 I stood on the ball and thought I broke my ankle. I was never the same after that. I had to read the game better and didn't get as far forward because I knew I wouldn't be able to get back. I remember playing Chicago and they had this little guy from Chile. He beat me bad and I thought, "He's never done that before." I realized then that I had to change my game. I knew he had either had gotten faster or I'd gotten slower. He wasn't faster.

I talked to Roy and we both understood my influence on the game wasn't the same. I'd had a bad ankle injury. I couldn't get forward like I used to. Roy asked if it would help if I gave the captain's band to someone else. I said, "Yeah" because I didn't want to be captain just because they felt sorry for me. We signed a bunch of new players and I wasn't assured of being in the starting lineup. It made sense. Terry Nicholl got it.

TERRY NICHOLL: Kevin Kewley was a brilliant captain. I loved Kevin Kewley.

The Eagle *reported that Turner surveyed the team's veterans: "...They all indicated Terry Nicholl was their choice. He will represent the players of the club fairly and I believe he will represent management fairly...He has leadership qualities," said Turner. Nicholl added, "I hope to follow where Kevin left off and set a good example and forge team spirit. If a player has a problem that he doesn't think he can go to management with, he can come to me."*[32] *In an interview with* Missile Magazine, *Nicholl expounded further on the job of captain: "...I think it is essentially being a good listener. It is being a go-between as far as coach and management and players. It's being able to listen to players, understand their problems and be able to sort them out quickly. Being captain on the field in indoor soccer you don't really do the job that maybe you do outdoors. You've certainly got to be sort of a cheerleader and get the guys going as best you can."*[33]

The first couple months of the season seemed to herald a breakout year. On November 15th, 1985, the Wings played their home opener against the Minnesota

Strikers. It was a rematch of the playoff loss just a few months before; something that was almost certainly on the minds of the players as they took the pitch that day. Thankfully, the result was different. Though it didn't reduce the sting from their last meeting, it was a sweet 8-5 win in front of 9,343.[34]

Then, on November 23rd, the Wings did what they had never done before: beat the San Diego Sockers. Steve Zungul's team had been the Wings' "Great White Whale." But after starting the game down by four goals, the Wings roared back to outgun the Sockers 11-9. Erik Rasmussen scored five goals, tying a Wings record. He added two assists, for a total of seven points, which broke the previous team mark of six. Rasmussen's third goal was an impressive one. As Gary Dymski of The Eagle wrote: "Wings goalkeeper Seamus McDonagh said the goal - scored at such a sharp angle that it drew gasps and ahhs from the press box - seemed to signal the end for the Sockers. 'It looked like an impossible angle,' said McDonagh, shaking his head."[35]

A week-and-a-half later, Jan Olesen made his presence felt when he scored a goal from the keeper position. To top that off, on December 14th, 1985, Olesen recorded a shutout against none other than Mike Dowler and the Tacoma Stars. Dowler, who had four shutouts as a Wichita Wing, had now played in all three 1-0 games in MISL history. Scoring a goal and recording a shutout...not a bad month.[36]

1986 would begin with a thud. The Wings started off the New Year with maybe the worst loss in team history to that point, a 9-0 drubbing in San Diego. As book co-author Mike Romalis recalls: "I remember being so frustrated that I kept turning the radio off...turning it back on...AND THEN TURNING IT OFF AGAIN! I was on the verge of tears. It was so bad. I remember a 'highlight' of Kim Roentved trying to pass the ball back to Jan Olesen...only for the ball to go OVER Jan's head and into the goal."

The Wings' poor performance was partly due to a ridiculously bad sickness/injury situation. Prior to the January 31st game against Tacoma, six Wings were doubtful or questionable due to the flu. Steve Wegerle was out due to a knee injury. Tommy O'Neill had strep throat and Jan Olesen had a fractured thumb, making them both doubtful to play. Two players had colds bad enough to make them questionable, Jorge Espinoza had a groin injury, Frank Rasmussen had bruised calves, Terry Rowe's hamstring was hurting, and Al Smith had a bad foot. Only Tim Walters, Barry Wallace, Erik Rasmussen, and Kim Roentved were healthy.[37]

Erik Rasmussen, Chico Borja, and Kim Roentved were all named to the All-Star team that year. Rasmussen upheld his reputation as a Good Samaritan when the Western Division players elected to donate the All-Star game MVP's first prize, a new car, to charity. "I initiated the discussion today to give the money to charity. I think it says a lot for our team to make that kind of commitment, but any time we as professional athletes can give something to the less fortunate we are glad to make our contribution." Actual MVP, Branko Segota of the Sockers quipped, "I already have a BMW."[38]

Erik Rasmussen put in an All-Star-level performance against the Chicago Sting on February 21st, scoring a record seven goals in one game. Only three other players in MISL history, none of them Wings, had achieved this single game goal total. The normally sedate Rasmussen uncharacteristically kicked the game ball into the stands after the game. "The reason for that was that Wichita has the best crowd in the league. They deserved it," said Rasmussen.[39]

Rasmussen's game, already top-notch, improved in 1985-86. As he became more comfortable with the indoor game, his assist total began to increase markedly. Already a prolific goal-scorer, this made him even more deadly on the pitch. "I'm reading the game better right now. I'm playing with more confidence, and I knew when to pass the ball," he told The Eagle.[40] *Rasmussen's assist total would rise from 11 in 1984-85 to 41 in 1985-86.*[41]

Despite excellent performances from Rasmussen and Borja, the Wings sought another consistent goal-scorer. After spending a couple months pursuing him, Wichita signed Dave Hoggan in early February 1986. The Scottish midfielder/forward had played with Seamus McDonagh for the English First Division Bolton Wanderers before coming to the MISL. The Wings bought him from the Pittsburgh Spirit, where he had clashed with Coach Don Popovic. "I had problems with Pop, and Pop had problems with me. The two of us never saw eye-to-eye," said Hoggan.[42] *Earlier in the season, Popovic had kicked Hoggan out of the locker room after a game and "then told him he could walk the few blocks back to the hotel." Needless to say, their relationship never recovered.*[43]

ROY TURNER: Dave Hoggan was a great player who took the role we gave him. A total team player. He had a temper too, and he'd be the first to admit it. All in their own way, they had tempers.

Less than a month later, and just in time for the playoffs, the Wings added an All-Star defender from the Chicago Sting. Neill "Big Bird" Roberts hailed from South Africa, but had spent a number of years playing in the United States. He started in the ASL and then moved to the NASL, with stints with the Atlanta Chiefs, Tampa Bay Rowdies, and Toronto Blizzard.[44] *Roberts was a standout on defense in Chicago, which is why the Wings were reportedly willing to pay $30,000 for the remainder of his contract for that season. "Roberts is the perfect guy for this time of year. He's played forward, midfield, and defender. Obviously, that he's played all those positions, shows that he has some skill," Bill Kentling told* The Eagle.[45]

Dave Hoggan had just left Pittsburgh and Don Popovic, only to return there on February 28th for a rematch against the Spirit. The Wings dominated in a 10-2 victory. Hoggan had two goals and an assist, Erik Rasmussen scored three times, and Chico Borja had five points on three assists and two goals. Despite the Wings' dominating performance, Popovic gave them little credit: "I really didn't think it was them. It was us. It was our worst game. We were absolutely flat." Spirit star Stan Terlecki let his foot do the talking. As The Eagle *reported: "...[Terlecki] took out Hoggan along the backboards with a well-placed kick to the knee. As Hoggan was being helped off the field, he repeatedly yelled at Terlecki. Hoggan had never gotten along with Terlecki in the two years he played with the Spirit...Terlecki did not deny he deliberately tried to trip Hoggan."*[46] *All this occurred during a Friday night game televised by KSN. The Orange Army was watching, and would not forgive Terlecki when the Spirit traveled to Wichita days later.*

Hoggan would continue to prove his value to the Wings on March 9th, scoring two goals in the franchise's second victory against the San Diego Sockers. Rasmussen added three goals to combine with Hoggan to account for the team's entire scoring effort. Though the Sockers had traded Steve Zungul to Tacoma, they still had Branko Segota and Juli Veee, making them the most dangerous team in the league.[47]

When the Pittsburgh Spirit came to the Coliseum for a rematch on March 11th, the Wings and their fans were ready. Bill Kentling had aired TV ads promoting the game as "Stan Terlecki Appreciation Night." One fan responded with a banner that read: "We have a rope, we have a tree, let's hang Terlecki." The game itself was relatively free of drama as the game headed into the last minute of the fourth quarter tied 4-4. However, when Keld Bordinggaard tipped in an Erik Rasmussen shot in the last second at the game's end, all hell broke loose.[48]

Pittsburgh coach Don Popovic charged toward the referees, loudly proclaiming that the goal had been scored after the buzzer had sounded. On his way to the locker room he encountered Bill Kentling. Words and shoves were exchanged. "He put his hands on me...I spun him around and took him up against the railing," said Kentling. The mob scene behind the goal also included Spirit players, fans, and police. "I saw a mountain of people with Bill Kentling as the central character. Several punches were traded. Kentling [landed the best shots], but Popovic and (Spirit player) Paul Child had a good tag team going, though." said Terry Nicholl.[49]

STEVE SHAAD: Bill had him in a chokehold up against the railing.

TERRY NICHOLL, MIDFIELDER, WICHITA WINGS: I think Bill Kentling got it. He used to say, "If there's nothing happening, make it happen." One game I had to separate him and the Pittsburgh team's head coach. I was right there...coming off. Popovic and me were going through the gate at the same time, and he didn't like that, so I let him go in front of me. I don't know what Bill Kentling said, but [Popovic] started windmilling Kentling. I had to jump between them. Bill always said, "Don't be afraid of all that." We didn't want it to be hockey, but we wanted passion...people prepared to go and fight for Wichita.

BILL KENTLING: It was a long-simmering situation going back to our acquisition of the three players from Las Vegas. The team we beat out for those players was Pittsburgh...That whole thing went back to Pittsburgh feeling like we had snookered them, which we had...Popovic had been frustrated since that. He came when the game was over and saw me, and suggested I do a physical act which I'm not sure how I would accomplish, and I'm sure I made a smart-ass remark. It was "on" from there. The rest of it is on videotape. I'll say this, there were a whole lot more of them than there were of me, but those guys should get back in the gym because they weren't much.

Happily for the Wings, this victory clinched a berth in the MISL playoffs. Pittsburgh would go on to finish fifth in the Eastern Division and narrowly miss the post-season. They would fold after the end of the season, having never beaten the Wings in Wichita. One reason for the Wings regular season success had been the team's improvement on the road. Opponents had always struggled to beat the Wings at the Kansas Coliseum. But it was the road that had traditionally tripped up Roy Turner's lads. In 1985-86, the Wings managed a 10-14 road record. They had bettered that record only once, in 1981-82, and would never improve on it through the end of the MISL in 1992.[50]

Individual achievements abounded in 1985-86 as well. Kim Roentved would win MISL Defender of the Year for the second time. "I think it should have been three. He didn't get it last year, and I thought he deserved it," said Roy Turner. "I think it's very hard to tell everybody just what he means to us...If there's anybody who ever doubts Kim Roentved's desire to win, they haven't seen him in action... He's become a leader. When he came here, he was a young man who didn't know what he really was. He had to learn how to deal with his own success in that time - coping with what people make you. Now he's OK with it," Turner commented. "He's developed into a real leader here," said Bill Kentling. Roentved would set a career high in assists and points, at 38 and 64, respectively. Also, he led the team with 80 blocks.[51]

Erik Rasmussen had a standout year as well. On March 28th, 1986, in a 9-2 victory over the Kansas City Comets, he became the first Wing to break the 100-point barrier. "It's nice to get it (100th point) at home," said Rasmussen. The Eagle reported that Rasmussen "received a standing ovation from the fans after his achievement was announced on the public address system."[52] *He would end the season with a total of 108 points. He also set the team record with 67 goals, a mark which would never be broken.*[53]

The Wings knew they would eventually have to face San Diego in the playoffs if they wanted to win the MISL Championship. It was a daunting task, considering the Wings had never beaten them in San Diego and had accumulated a 2-4 record against them during the regular season.[54]

KIM ROENTVED: We had more fantastic games against San Diego over the years than anyone other than St. Louis. That was purely because we were a good matchup with them. We won some and lost some heartbreakers.

ROY TURNER: We were the one team that could really challenge them.

But first, the Wings had to face the Tacoma Stars in the first round. It would not go well. There was evidence the Wings were looking past the Stars to their likely second round opponents, the Sockers. The Eagle quoted Kim Roentved as saying, "I don't care who we play in the first round. I'm worried about the second round."[55] *It was only human nature. After all, the Wings had gone 4-2 against the Stars during the regular season. However, Tacoma had gone 2-1 against the Wings since they added "The Lord of All Indoors," Steve Zungul.*[56]

ROY TURNER: That particular season was one when Tacoma basically broke the bank. Taking Zungul from San Diego...wow...and they had Preki and Dowler. They were on the same path as we were as far as challenging San Diego.

KIM ROENTVED: They built around that core of Dowler, Zungul, and Preki.

CHICO BORJA: Oh my gosh, the talent they had? Tacoma had Preki, Zungul, Ralph Black, and Dowler. It was very difficult to win at all. They had a complete team. They had two-and-a-half maybe three lines. They could go that deep. Most teams only had two. It was never a lack of effort.

ROY TURNER: It was a bit more of a rivalry [with Tacoma coach Alan Hinton] than with Cooper. He had quite a career in England. He wasn't lacking in confidence...he would always try to play mind games whenever he would coach. I tried to not let it affect us. The type of thing he would do is say before the game that "we're the complete underdog" even though everyone knew they were just as good. He'd make little comments that were meant to stir the thoughts of the other coach.

It was almost the year of the Wichita Wings on the cover of Sports Illustrated...

ROY TURNER: *Sports Illustrated* was in Tacoma when we were up there for the playoffs in 1986. They interviewed me each day, with the idea that if we won, we'd end up in the final and they'd put it on the front page about a little town like Wichita making it to a major league final. Obviously, Tacoma won and it was never printed.

The Wings lone win in the best-of-five series would come at home in game one. Kim Roentved would score four of the Wings' six goals to lead the team to a 6-5 victory in a game where they foiled four Tacoma power plays.[57] *The Wings would fall 5-4 in both games two and three: first at the Kansas Coliseum and then in overtime at the Tacoma Dome. The loss at home smarted. The Wings were notoriously bad on the road in the playoffs. They needed every home win they could get.*

The 5-4 loss in Tacoma hurt for a different reason. The Wings were up by a goal in the fourth quarter when Chico Borja earned a two minute penalty for elbowing. "Borja's penalty - which came at the stoppage of play and when both teams were changing - was an emotional crusher for the Wings and uplifting event for the Stars," wrote Gary Dymski in The Eagle. *The Stars forced overtime when Gary Heale scored the tying goal just as Borja left the penalty box. Dymski reported Turner and Norman Piper's reactions: "Wings coach Roy Turner said of the penalty: 'You play a whole season and get into the playoffs and that action with two minutes to go I especially...I've got to choose my words carefully.' Assistant coach Norman Piper interjected: 'Unnecessary, really.' Countered Turner, 'Oh God, that's an understatement. Words can't describe it.'"*[58]

With the Wings down 2-1, the fourth game also took place in Tacoma. A Wings win would have brought the series to a conclusion in Wichita. But it was not to be. The Wings would lose the game 3-2, ending their playoff run.[59] *In his book,* Hot Winter Nights, *Rich Paschette wrote: "The hero of the series might have been [Tacoma's] Neil Megson, who all but erased Erik Rasmussen in the series, limiting The Wizard to just one goal and four assists [in four games]."*[60]

"I can only blame myself. I wasn't effective in the playoffs," said Rasmussen. "It's been very frustrating for him. All the tactics were designed to stop Erik, for obvious reasons. He can't put this on his shoulders," replied Roy Turner.[61] *"Wings forwards Keld Bordinggaard, Steve Wegerle, and Tim Walters did not score a point in the series," wrote Gary Dymski. "The Stars didn't rely solely on Steve Zungul, the MISL's career scoring leader. Zungul was limited to two goals in the playoffs because of superb defense by Jorge Espinoza."*[62]

San Diego would go on to defeat Tacoma and then Minnesota to win the championship. The Wings would reflect on a season that could have been so much more. But, as always, though Wings fans were disappointed they wouldn't be celebrating a championship, they treasured the experience of watching their Wings play. They didn't need a championship to love their Wings.

ERIC SCRIVEN, WINGS FAN: My dad Ben and my younger sister Katie and I would play soccer with an orange and white Wings mini-ball (which I still have) in our front room. The doorway between our living room and our kitchen was the goal. Dad was always Wings goalie Seamus McDonagh. Katie was Chico Borja. Since my name is Eric, I was always The Wizard, Erik Rasmussen. We spent hours kicking that ball around until one day an errant shot knocked my mother's porcelain Virgin Mary figurine off our mantle. That was the end of our indoor soccer sessions.

Part of the team's end-of-season reflection included roster changes. Two longtime Wings would be released within weeks of the playoff loss. Terry Nicholl had joined the Wings in 1981 and spent five years working hard on the pitch. He wasn't a flashy athlete or a big-time goal scorer. But he worked hard to get the ball to the goal scorers on the team. That hard work earned him the captaincy during his final season with the Wings. He would accumulate 112 points and 88 blocks during those years.[63][64] *Just as importantly, the "General" became one of the most popular Wings in town. He spent countless hours building bonds in Wichita as the director of community relations for the Wings. He would be missed. But it wouldn't be the last Wings fans would see of Terry Nicholl. After a stint with the Memphis Storm in another indoor league, he would eventually return to the Wings in a different role.*

TERRY NICHOLL: I was finding it a bit harder to play as many games. My injuries were such that I would miss more. They took me off the defensive power play unit. Age is a miserable thing...it's nasty. The clock starts ticking at 33 or 34. Age caught up with me. It was just time. My body said, "Enough." I needed to play at a slightly less competitive standard. The coach in Memphis offered me a good deal. It was time for me to be an assistant coach. We had a rough start to the season, and they made me head coach.

The seemingly ageless Jorgen Kristensen, the MISL's oldest player at 39, would not be offered a contract for the 1986-87 season. He had joined the Wings in 1980, already a seasoned international player. "In his six-year career with the Wings, Kristensen - known as the 'Magic Man' for his superb ball-handling skills - had 74 goals and 261 assists in 224 games. He [ranked] third in the MISL in career assists and 11th in career scoring...Kristensen was a four-time All-Star for the Wings and earned All-Select honors three times. He was captain of the West squad in the 1983 All-Star game and assisted on Kim Roentved's game-winning goal in overtime." According to Roy Turner, "The talents of Jorgen Kristensen have done more in developing the style and success of the Wichita Wings than any other single factor."[65]

An Oral History

On the Road...

———

A TRIP TO THE KANSAS Coliseum would bode ill luck to most MISL teams. It was a rough place to play, especially when filled to the rim with orange-colored fans. On the other hand, the road was never kind to the Wichita Wings. The 1980-81 season provides the perfect contrast: 18-2 at home...5-15 on the road. But for the players, road trips were not just about work. It was a chance to bond with their mates, have some drinks, and stay in some pretty nice digs. Good times were had...even better times if they managed to steal a win...

KIM ROENTVED, DEFENDER, WICHITA WINGS: Life on the road with the Wings...you could write a Bible-sized book. It was easy...the nicest hotels, the bus and plane waiting for you. I would usually room with either Jorgen, or my brother Per, or Mike Powers.

Living on a tight budget was not exactly priority number one...

ROY TURNER, HEAD COACH, WICHITA WINGS: We went first-class everywhere...We always stayed at the finest hotels. We'd go to this hotel in Kansas City and in the lobby there was a huge waterfall. [Wings forward] Mickey Thomas went to the bellhop and said, "Until you get that leak fixed I'm not staying at your house."

KIM ROENTVED: We'd fly into the downtown KC airport because it was closer to the arena and the hotel.

ROY TURNER: Every trip we went on, those card games were always going on. There were times I got a little scared because guys lost way too much money. Erik Rasmussen was the best card-player.

TOM SHINE, REPORTER/EDITOR, THE WICHITA EAGLE: On the bus, the guys all played cards, Roy Turner among them. Hearts or spades, one of the two.

The team flew everywhere, especially in the early years. Whether the flight was to Kansas City or to San Diego, it meant lots of time spent in airports. And the lads had to do SOMETHING...

ROY TURNER: The team's favorite pastime was to bet on whose bag would come up first on the baggage claim.

KIM ROENTVED: Steve Shaad would put a string on a dollar bill and yank it whenever someone would try to pick it up. He'd have 20 guys laughing.

STEVE SHAAD, ASSISTANT GM, WICHITA WINGS: I was in Las Vegas...a guy lunged for it, lunged for it, lunged for it again, and then he popped me in the back of the head.

ANDY CHAPMAN, FORWARD, WICHITA WINGS: I remember Omar Gomez and Miguel Filardo and I were in St. Louis and for whatever reason, they attached themselves to me. Miguel couldn't speak a word of English. I had a watch and the second-hand was easy to confuse with the other hand. We were hanging out with them at some sort of store in the airport. We always had fun in the airport...played lots of crazy games, put dollar bills on the ground and when people walked by we'd pull it away. So I looked down at my watch and realized we were late for the gate. The plane was pulling out and Kevin Kewley was waving to me through the window. Roy's face was like...really pissed looking. I said,

"Miguel, why didn't you tell me the time?" He didn't know a word of English, but we had to wait there for an hour. We got in big trouble when we finally arrived on another plane. There was always something going on when you were on the road.

When traveling, it was important to maintain a professional demeanor in the public eye...

ROY TURNER: Coaches enforce a dress code. I didn't allow jeans and wanted them to dress up. Some players had different ideas about what "dressing up" meant. McDonagh came to the airport one day with an overcoat over a track suit.

KIM ROENTVED: Roy told me to "take that f****** hat off!" one time. I doubt I had taken a shower that day.

ROY TURNER: It was always amazing seeing how many people would wait for us back in Wichita at the airport.

KIM ROENTVED: Any time we lost we'd have curfew. We weren't just there on a vacation. There were rules.

KEVIN KEWLEY, DEFENDER, WICHITA WINGS: Winning on the road was hard because of referees, change of diet, change of habits, not being comfortable. It was a combo of everything. The home team was expected to win. The first couple years the Wings were particularly good at home and bad on the road. I remember going to Baltimore on a long road trip and thinking, "We have no chance." The atmosphere in Baltimore was very difficult. We only won there a few times.

We were in Buffalo on a road trip stuck in a snowstorm in the hotel and Burt Reynolds and Goldie Hawn were there making a movie [called *Best Friends*]. Goldie was jogging around the indoor track and a couple of the guys were trying to chat her up. She told them to "f*** off" and called security.

KIM ROENTVED: That same game Roy didn't show up till halftime because he'd been at a funeral. We HAD been winning. Then we lost the game [laughs].

KEVIN KEWLEY: I remember seeing Burt Reynolds in the lobby and he was so cool. The boys all said, "Hey," and he said, "Hi guys, how are ya doing?"

STEVE SHAAD: Norman Piper, Roentved, and Kristensen and I would always go watch horse racing on road trips. In Buffalo, we went to see harness racing. It snowed seven inches and we stayed for the whole race. There were about 16 inches by the time we got out. At the end of the night it had been a record snowfall for Buffalo...something like 26 inches. Roy had to come in on a snowplow to get to the game. They used refs out of the stands for the game because the real refs couldn't get there. There were only about 500 people at the game.

NORMAN PIPER, FORWARD, WICHITA WINGS: It snowed so much we could hardly get back. It was snowing like crazy.

BRUCE HAERTL, WINGS PLAY-BY-PLAY ANNOUNCER, KFH RADIO: [Kim Roentved] was the guy that I always gravitated to on the road, he and Steve Shaad. The three of us spent a lot of time on the road together. I'll never forget the night we were in Buffalo. It snowed 24 inches in 24 hours. Even for Buffalo, that set a record. It was the night that David Letterman first did "Fun with Velcro" where Letterman jumped onto a wall of Velcro. I'll never forget Kim's uproarious laughter, to the point where he could barely control his bodily fluid. Every time I see Rocket, we laugh about that that.

Steve [Shaad] has taught me everything I know about horse racing [laughs]. As a young kid, you have a nice little per diem. I didn't care about food, but whenever we went into a city where the ponies were running, Shaad and Haertl were there. We didn't miss many races. There were many times we went to Hollywood Park. I learned to read a daily racing form from Steve Shaad. In all seriousness, we formed a tight bond as broadcasters. When we were on the road, Steve was my color guy. He and I worked very seamlessly, right from the get-go. We got along well and understood each other's role.

He never sweated anything. Like one time I was in LA and I was out with my younger brother and a couple young ladies, and it occurred to me I needed to get back to the Fabulous Forum, and the concept of traffic in LA was lost on me. I walked in five minutes before air, wearing beach togs...Shaad, not even remotely sweating, chuckled and said, "Never a doubt." We had each other's back that way. He was always damn good at what he did. He was a damn good media relations guy. He had a lot of PT Barnum in him and was willing to suggest some things that were outside the box. What a jewel of a guy.

STEVE SHAAD: I remember going to Hollywood Park racetrack in LA. After a while it was just Kim and I. Eventually he gave me money to bet and left for the hotel. "If I win any money, just slip it under the door." So, I came back after curfew and he had won $300 on the 11th race. So I knocked on the door and said "We won, we won!"

KIM ROENTVED: There were times when the dance team would go on the road, and things would happen. There were official rules on fraternization, but they weren't always followed. Some of them were very good looking.

ANDY CHAPMAN: I loved it. Absolutely loved going on the road. Most of the players, except me and Kim, were married. It wasn't ALL glamorous, because it depended on where you were in the stage of your life. But I friggin' loved it! From [age] 16 to 38 I used to take a nap in the afternoon every day. You went to the hotel, got up in the morning, did some training, took a nap in the afternoon, played that evening.

It could be in the middle of the winter in Wichita and you'd go on a road trip to San Diego or LA or San Jose or Phoenix. It was brilliant...like going on holiday! I loved it. The more experience I got the better I understood the layout of the hotel. If you were looking to break curfew you'd know how to get in through different doors, to get in without being seen [laughs]. I remember one time we were hanging out on the hotel roof in Kansas City and Roy went absolutely crazy because the security guard saw us.

When we used to go to San Diego, the [hot tub] was right outside the sliding glass door of this room that was bigger than every other room. By the time I got to Baltimore, I'd done it before. We'd land in San Diego, and Kenny Cooper was the coach. I would call up the hotel immediately upon landing in San Diego and I would tell them I was the trainer, Steve. "I just need to have you make sure that Chapman gets into room 303. He has to use the [hot tub] because he has a hamstring problem." They'd hand out the keys at the hotel and sure enough they'd hand me that key. The other guys would say, "How'd you get that room?! How'd you get that room?!" I'd say, "It's just luck." [laughs] You learn lots of little tricks along the way.

TERRY NICHOLL: Roy's parties were famous. If we went on the road and didn't have a game the next day, Roy's after-game speech would be, "Great win lads...party in my room!" Everyone would cheer. His parties would have all the cheerleaders, referees, opponents...he'd fill the bathtub with beer. It was a brilliant time. Roy would be happy and the characters you'd meet...you'd be there with the player who had just elbowed you in the nose and the refs who had just given you a yellow card.

TOM SHINE: I remember a game in [Dallas] Ft. Worth and they were still building the field...the carpeting didn't fit so there was a foot of concrete around the edges. The goals were the wrong size and Mike Dowler kept touching them and saying, "The paint's still wet." There were big patches of concrete in the goal box. It was an exhibition game against the Sidekicks when they first started. That was when the NBA was getting involved, I'm pretty sure it was owned by the Mavericks people at the time.

Road trips to Los Angeles to play the Lazers inevitably involved a celebrity sighting or two...

TOM SHINE: Jimmy Buss ran the [LA] Lazers and it was horrible. And now he's running the [LA] Lakers, and guess what? The LAKERS are horrible. He used to hang out at the games with [actor] James Caan. He was always on the bench with Jimmy. The best part of going to LA was the Laker Girls became the Lazer Girls. We used to go up to the Forum Club to hang out with them. Then the game would start and there were like 900 people there. You could have shot a cannon off in there. It didn't draw at all. They were another one of the NBA teams who were interested in filling dates when the NBA wasn't there.

Every [team] had an after-game bar. That was one of the draws of the league is that they'd have parties afterwards. It was a big single woman's league.

They had a lot of women fans. The Wings games and the Comets games, in St. Louis...a lot of single women there...a big pickup place. The Comets had a bar inside of Kemper Arena you could go to. The Forum had a bar you could go to. I think I saw [NBA player] Vlade Divacs there once. We used to go to Fuzzy's in Westport [after a Comets game]. We must have won because Roy was in a good mood. He led a sing-along on the bus all the way back to the hotel. He enjoyed life...he had fun.

I went to Minnesota and covered a game. [The Minnesota Strikers] were owned by the Robbie family [who also owned the Miami Dolphins]. We were up there and Roy set a curfew of midnight. So we were in the hotel bar and had maybe an hour. So Ian Andersen lined up seven shots and said, "I only got an hour," and started throwing down shots. I was surprised by how good of athletes they were. Frank Rasmussen smoked all the time. They all smoked. Jorgen did a little bit. Jeff Bourne did...he drank "a little bit" too. Frank was an unbelievable athlete. I asked Frank, "How the hell can you smoke?" It was always right after a game. And he said, "Oh, I don't have too many. I just have a couple. But it's the beer that kills your legs, not the smoking." All the Europeans smoked. It was part of their culture. And they drank Michelob.

LARRY INLOW, DEFENDER, WICHITA WINGS: I can remember watching Frank Rasmussen smoke at halftime. Erik too.

CHAPTER 19

An Oral History

Cooking Up Change

———

"It's kind of hard to think that with the talent we
had we didn't go further. But it was because other
teams had talent and great coaches too."

- CHICO BORJA, ON THE 1986-87 WINGS.

*IN APRIL OF 1986, AS the 1985-86 season was winding down, it was announced
that the commissioner of the MISL, Frank Dale, would be stepping down to take a
lesser executive position with the league. Dale had served as the US Ambassador to
the United Nations, president of the Cincinnati Reds, and director of the Cincinnati
Bengals prior to his one year stint with the soccer league...an impressive resume. But
Dale's leadership was questioned by some of the team owners. The* Eagle *reported:
"He came under fire from several owners at a league meeting in January for his handling in several areas, including the league's national cable contract with ESPN...
Sources close to the league have said Dale would have been relieved of the remaining
two years of his contract had he not taken the position of senior executive."*[1]

*Dale's move would end up profoundly affecting the Wichita Wings. It would set
into motion a series of events that would shake up the Wings' organization from
top to bottom. The first domino to fall was Dale. The next...was Wings' General
Manager Bill Kentling.*

346

BILL KENTLING, MISL COMMISSIONER, 1986-1989: Sometime in the 1985-86 season we realized that Commissioner Dale, who was a very nice human being, was not gonna be as proactive for us as we had hoped. There was in those days, an executive committee of the league, of which I sat on. We unilaterally decided we needed to make a change. So, the fellas that had come in from the NASL and the original MISL people asked if I would become commissioner. I gave it some real thought. I had to weigh moving from Wichita, and decided I would do it. I asked every other member if they wanted to [be commissioner] and the decision was "No." Our thinking was, we kind of invented this and we needed someone on the inside to do it. There really wasn't a search.

The "search committee," which included four executives from across the league, seemed likely to choose Kentling from the start. St. Louis Steamers' President Thomas Bowers stated that Kentling's familiarity with the league and influence on it "put him in a favorable position...No. 1, he knows soccer; No. 2, he knows the soccer business; and No. 3, he has an extensive marketing background and he's also helped the league on a variety of committees." Kansas City Comets owner David Schoenstadt added that "...the Wichita franchise is an absolute model of a team being well run, financially as well as on the field...He's got my vote." Lazers' owner Jim Buss, son of Jerry, agreed: "Bill's a very sharp man. I think Bill will be it, he'll have my vote."[2] But prior to the official decision, league issues occupied a great deal of Bill Kentling's time during the latter part of the 1985-86 season.

BILL KENTLING: The last few weeks of the season I was doing as much on the league front as I was with the Wings. Steve Shaad, Roy Turner, and the staff really finished out that season.

On May 20th, 1986, it was announced that Kentling would sign a three-year contract to be the new commissioner of the MISL. Kentling stated that his priorities were to bring additional income to the smaller franchises, acquire a regional or national TV contract, improve the officiating, and enhance the league's image nationally. ESPN held the TV contract during the 1985-86 season, but not only did the deal fail to generate revenue for the MISL, it cost them $40,000. To improve the MISL's national standing, Kentling would soon move the league offices from Chicago to New York City.[3]

The move to the Big Apple was calculated to give the MISL a bigger media footprint. It coincided with a new franchise called the New York Express, partly owned by American soccer star, Shep Messing. Kentling and the rest of the league saw the New York media market as a vital component of growing the league's national presence. To get that coverage, he needed the Express to succeed on the field. "They have to be in the chase for a playoff spot the first year. They were allowed to bring in a full complement of seven foreigners in one year (this year) but I don't know how competitive they will be because they're all new to the indoor game," Kentling told The Eagle. "We need some national attention. If [Kentling] can't do it, nobody can," added Turner.[4]

With the negotiation of a better deal with ESPN, Kentling hoped to get more media coverage. When it came to team finances, he quickly negotiated a salary cap, or "player cost cap" as he preferred to call it. Teams that violated the cap would be fined $100,000. On the field, he instituted a series of fines for diving and faking injuries. "A number of players are slowly but surely ruining the presentation of our game and adding to the already difficult job of officiating by continuing to dive and fake injuries," said Kentling.[5]

BILL KENTLING: I thought I could do it with a purpose. I knew there was one real battle that had to be fought and I knew I was strong enough to fight it...and that was I knew we were gonna need a salary cap in the league. You were gonna have to protect owners from themselves.

ALAN SHEPHERD, MISL REFEREE: Kentling became more friendly to the referees when he became commissioner [laughs]. He did it well. He did both jobs well.

Reaction to Kentling's move was uniformly positive. The Eagle's editorial staff wrote that Kentling's move was "good for the league and the game of indoor soccer...For the last couple or three seasons, he has been something of a de facto league commissioner...And if ever there was a promoter of excitement and enthusiasm for this game, his name's the same as what will be emblazoned on that first ball: Bill Kentling."[6] *Both Roy Turner and Steve Shaad were sad to see him go. "We've done pretty well together," said Turner.*[7] *Turner and Kentling had become very close, especially considering the innate difficulties of a relationship between a coach and general manager in the cutthroat world of professional sports.*

ROY TURNER, HEAD COACH, WICHITA WINGS, 1979-1986: Bill was a great friend. When we negotiated contracts, we'd do it on a napkin. I usually didn't even have a written contract with him. Just a handshake agreement.

Kentling's tenure had been impressive. He ushered the Wings into their second season after Bob Becker's departure as owner. Over his six year tenure as GM he'd increased attendance from 5,145 to a peak of 9,391. Though the team lost $750,000 his first year, he led a Save the Wings effort in the summer of 1981 that raised $605,000 and kept the team alive. His philosophy, as The Eagle's *Fred Mann put it, "was a belief that the Wings should be a part of the community, and that the players should be considered next-door neighbors rather than remote professionals." At the league level, Kentling had negotiated the MISL's national television contracts with both Sports Time and ESPN in 1983 and 1984.*[8] *His accomplishments were many. There would never be another like him.*

But who would replace Kentling?

ROY TURNER: Bill Kentling went to run the league and we mutually decided that the only person who could replace him as [Wings' chief executive] was me. Bill Kentling, the owners, and I all thought it was what was best for the future. I couldn't have done both jobs. Bill thought [becoming commissioner] was for the benefit of the league. He had been very involved in the league and very close to [longtime MISL commissioner Earl] Foreman. The league was going through change at that time, and it was a very tough job indeed. It would have been difficult for anybody to make it work. He did a great job but things were already on a downswing.

Roy Turner was named President of the Wichita Wings, a position created for him. Steve Shaad would move up from assistant general manager to GM. "This is a key time. My decision [to become president] was made because I didn't trust anybody else to take over this franchise. It sounds vain. I'm afraid it means too much to me," Turner told The Eagle's *Mal Elliott. Turner knew the MISL was entering a difficult era. Even the*

St. Louis Steamers, one of the league's historically strong franchises, were beginning to struggle. Turner recommended a cautious approach: "Wichita deserves a winner, but we have to be patient. We want to win as much as anybody but we still want to be here next year. So many teams have come and gone and we have been around so long."[9]

BILL KENTLING: By this time Frank Carney had stepped down as the managing general partner and Bill and Mary Lynn Oliver became the managing general partner.

The changes just kept coming. William "Bill" Oliver Jr. was an attorney by trade. His wife Mary Lynn was a noted philanthropist and the youngest daughter of Walter Beech, founder of Beech Aircraft Company. In addition to being a senior partner at Martin, Pringle, Oliver, Wallace, and Swartz, Bill Oliver would take over the role as representative of the 80 shareholders, and leader of the nine general partners. Oliver had been an investor since 1980 and had represented the Wings on the MISL's Board of Directors for two years. Though Frank Carney would no longer be the managing partner, he continued as one of the nine general partners of the club.[10]

BILL OLIVER, MANAGING GENERAL PARTNER, WICHITA WINGS, 1986-92: Frank Carney got me involved. In the beginning, I had more contact with him than anybody else. Frank kind of moved away...he went to Montana. They were looking for somebody...and I was drafted. I loved the game. We went to EVERY game...I was pretty involved by '84. We became good friends with Roy and his family...He's a great guy and still a good friend. I love to be around him. I think he was one of the reasons that I got interested. When I finally got around to meeting him and working with him, I realized he was a great guy and really enjoyed him.

Oliver ran into many of the same problems encountered by previous owners. Foremost among those challenges: making a profit was next to impossible. Despite the lack of financial reward, Oliver worked hard to maintain the special place the Wings held in the hearts of Wichitans.

BILL OLIVER: I was more interested in getting more fans [than more investors]. That's the beginning and the end: the number of seats you fill. We did a lot of talking about how we could get more fans interested...[Even after selling out the Coliseum] we still couldn't make ends meet. I sat down one time, and figured if we sold out every game, we'd break even. That was discouraging. But we had such great fans. I probably let it go on longer than I should have.

I never told anybody that we'd make any money. I never told that to ANYBODY [laughs]. We sold it on [the idea of] "the good of the city"...Your product is better than your [financial] basis. The Wings were that way. We had a good product.

New commissioner, new president, new general manager...and a new coach. It must have seemed strange for the players to look down the bench and not see Roy Turner there. He'd been the only coach the Wings had ever had. But the team needed him in the front office, and the head coach position needed to be filled.

(Howard Eastwood/1987 Wings Calendar) Scottish soccer legend Charlie Cooke takes over as coach from Roy Turner.

Charlie Cooke. Sometimes known as "The Bonnie Prince," after the similarly-named historical figure, he was a boy from Greenock, Scotland who grew up to become an international soccer star... and eventually, the second head coach of the Wichita Wings. He was a true world-class player, earning 16 caps for Scotland and leading Chelsea FC to glory in his 289 appearances with the top-level English club.[11] He came to the Wings from Dallas, where he was the assistant coach on a successful Sidekicks squad. Prior to that, he had been a representative for Nike. "People don't realize what a great player Charlie Cooke was. Great is a term that I feel is overused, but anybody who pretends to know anything about soccer places the word 'great' beside Charlie's name," said Roy Turner.[12]

ROY TURNER: [Charlie Cooke] had been an assistant in Dallas, and had done a great job there. He was an all-world player. They called him the Bonnie Prince...A board, including me, hired [him] to be the new coach. It was a very attractive job for many people...I was bound and determined to stay out of the coach's business the next year because I didn't think it would be fair to anybody. We all had to do things differently.

TERRY NICHOLL: Charlie Cooke is a god in England and Scotland.

STEVE SHAAD, GENERAL MANAGER, WICHITA WINGS, 1986-87: Brilliant player by reputation. His relationship with the Wings players was much different than Roy's. Charlie was much more a taskmaster. Much sterner than Roy. I got along well with him, but didn't have the same kind of relationship with him that I had with Roy. He would make fun of my lack of soccer knowledge, versus Roy explaining things to me. "Shaddy, you are hopeless, you know nothin'!" [he'd say] in a humorous way.

DAVE PHILLIPS, RADIO ANNOUNCER, WICHITA WINGS, 1986-93: Charlie Cooke was a man's man and was one of the best 11 players in the world when he played for Chelsea. He had an aura about him...commanded respect when he walked in a room. He took so much of his time to teach me the game...

CHARLIE MINSHULL-FORD, EQUIPMENT MANAGER, WICHITA WINGS, 1982-85: Charlie Cook was the Nike Rep I had to deal with all the time. He was a typical Scottish personality. Very quiet, very reserved.

Cooke had big plans for the Wings. He sought to break them down and build them up again as better players. "The only way to find out how good players are is to test them. Do something to make them uncomfortable. See how good they are. It's more than pressure, or technique. It's an attitude. You look at performance, not just results. There are some wonderful players who are already effective, but they can do so much more, and they don't even know it themselves. There are some wonderfully skilled forwards, and a lot of coaches are afraid to ask them to grunt and strain. You're not doing your job as a coach when you don't ask them to do this. You are doing them a disservice. You can't ever let up, even when you're winning. In this game, things can turn around quickly," said Cooke. "Pressure" was key to Cooke's strategy. And things WOULD turn, as Cooke predicted, but not in the direction everyone expected.[13]

CHICO BORJA, MIDFIELDER, WICHITA WINGS: Even Roy, I think, decided there was some need for a change, and hoping that would make the difference. For me it worked, obviously. But everybody else was getting stronger and better also. It's kind of hard to think that with the talent we had we didn't go further. But it was because other teams had talent and great coaches too.

As usual, the Wings said goodbye to familiar faces in 1986. Jan Olesen experienced a difficult knee injury in the off-season back in Denmark, forcing him to retire from soccer. Olesen, who had split time with Seamus McDonagh in 1985-86, had been 11-5, with a 3.72 GAA.[14] *This left McDonagh as "The Man" in goal. Olesen's fellow Dane, Keld Bordinggaard, also stayed home in Denmark, ending his one year stint with the Wings. Another departure was "The Magic Marker," Jorge Espinoza, who was stolen away by the Kansas City Comets prior to the beginning of the 1986-87 season. "Kansas City was very persistent and made an offer we couldn't refuse," said Roy Turner. Espinoza joined the oldest player in the MISL and longtime Wing, Jorgen Kristensen, who was also signed by the Comets.*[15]

Scottish defender and two-year Wings veteran Tommy O'Neill was put on waivers after visa problems delayed his arrival in America by five weeks. The delay caused him to lose his spot on a roster already filled with defenders.[16] After two productive years, Steve Wegerle would leave the Wings for the Tampa Bay Rowdies, now a member of the American Indoor Soccer Association (AISA). He would be joined there by Tim Walters. Steve McLean would leave for the newest MISL franchise, the New York Express.

Wichita East High product Dat Ly almost had his soccer dreams come true that year. Ly was the first Kansan drafted by the Wings, or any professional soccer team, for that matter. He had trained with the team for a week the previous year and even scored a goal in the scrimmage at tryouts. Unfortunately, the three-time All-City soccer star was cut before the season began. However, he went on to become the starting kicker for New Mexico State's football team.[17]

In 1986-87, the average Wings player was 5 foot-10 ½ inches tall, weighed 172.4 pounds, was 28.9 years old, and wore size 7 ½ shoes. Legend has it that the best soccer players have small feet, something that Dave Hoggan (size 6) would surely have agreed with. New draftee Dale Ervine (size 9 ½), the team's "Bigfoot," likely disagreed.[18][19] What everyone could agree on was that eight new pairs of shoes were found in the locker room that year.

32 year old English midfielder Gary Stanley joined the Wings after many years of First Division English football. He was a member of England's All-Select Team and a two-time Welsh Cup winner.[20] He would appear in 29 games for the Wings that year, the more productive of his two seasons with the team, accumulating five points on two goals and making 28 blocks.[21]

Backing up Seamus McDonagh in goal was Bill Irwin, a late addition to the squad. The 35-year-old keeper had previously been the fill-in for Tino Lettieri in Minnesota.[22] Irwin would play nine games for the Wings in what would be his only year with the club. He finished the year with a 2-6 record and 6.17 GAA.[23]

The Wings added a new forward in Diego Castro, formerly of the Dallas Sidekicks, where Cooke became familiar with the Chilean. "Charlie already knows me, and I know him. I am looking forward to playing for him. I think the stage is set for me to give my best effort," said Castro.[24] *The 24-year-old would appear in 27 games, make five assists, accumulate 23 blocks, and score eight goals, two of which were game-winners.*[25]

A second new forward arrived in the form of a quick-witted Englishman named Laurie Abrahams. Previously a Comet, Abrahams would end his career in Wichita, where he made a reputation as a player would make up for his lack of speed and power shots with a very high level of creativity on the ball. "Laurie's running? We've got people who can walk faster than that," joked Roy Turner. The Eagle's *Mal Elliott reported that Abrahams was well aware he could "come off as a smart-aleck, or someone who's not serious enough about the game."*[26] *However, Abraham's creative goal-scoring and passing were no joke. He would contribute 22 points in his 23 appearances, as well as scoring six power play goals.*[27]

The Wings added one of Cosmopolitan Magazine's *Pro Sports Hunks of the Year in forward Mark Kerlin.*[28] *His blonde locks drove the ladies crazy and he wasn't bad on the pitch either. The Phoenix, Arizona native would play two seasons with the Wings. "Speed is my main attribute. My game is to take people on and go to the goal and shoot. I'll be playing the game that got me where I was...This is the best career move I could have made," Kerlin told* The Eagle. *When he played with the MISL's Phoenix Inferno, Kerlin juked Ian Anderson so effectively that Anderson's fellow Wings left a jockstrap at the hotel front desk with Anderson's name on it. The attached note read: "I found this on the carpet near where I scored last night. I figured it must belong to you. Signed Mark Kerlin."*[29] *He would appear in 49 games in 1986-87, scoring 38 points on 18 goals.*[30]

LARRY INLOW, DEFENDER, WICHITA WINGS: Tommy O'Neil and Mark Kerlin were running a camp out at Soccer West. The shoe of the time was the Nike Dasher. It was a blue suede shoe...it was what Erik [Rasmussen] wore. I was begging my mom for these shoes. Mark Kerlin walks by, with his long curly mullet. So I had to go because the camp was about to start. He sits down and is talking to us kids. He takes his sweats off and has the most purple soccer socks; they almost look like leg warmers that women would wear in the '80s. I couldn't understand why he'd wear purple legwarmers to the camp! [laughs]

1986-87 would see the Wings sign a big-time star from across the pond. Mickey Thomas was "one of only 10 players in the world to appear in more than 50 World Cup-quality matches."[31] *The Welshman had previously played for Chelsea FC, Manchester United, Everton, Stoke City, and West Brom, among others. His wealth of experience playing First Division English soccer would prove to be an asset for the Wings. "Charlie [Cooke], a fantastic player in his own right, wanted to come over and assess my physical condition. He didn't have any problems over my skills. He took one look at me and knew I was in good shape and so Wichita bought me and I immediately became one of the first costly transfers for the indoor league in the USA," said Thomas in his autobiography.*[32] *How good was Thomas? Manchester United had sold him to Everton in 1978 for 450,000 pounds. "We're not saying he's Jorgen Kristensen, but he's as close as we can come," said Wings president Roy Turner. "He is also leftsided and is very skillful on the left side like Jorgen," added Coach Charlie Cooke.*[33]

BILL OLIVER: We had some of the best players who ever played soccer...like Mickey Thomas. He's a famous guy in England. Mickey Thomas is something else. He never slows down.

"Strangely, as soon as I got off the plane at Kansas I felt quite at home. It was also nice being in America because no one knew who I was. It was a completely fresh start. I took my kids over with me. We were all starting a new life...and I loved that period in my life...Playing, though, was full of frustrations. Part of my game was being aggressive, but in indoor soccer you weren't allowed to touch anyone. Physical contact was kept to a minimum. I quickly found this out to my cost as I was constantly sin-binned or even sent off," said Thomas.[34] *Despite his frustrations, Thomas managed to score 11 goals from the midfield position in his 34 games in the first of his two years with the Wings.*[35]

LOUIS MCCLUER, WINGS FAN: As the years went by, my family grew; my parents had grandkids that started attending the games, including mine and my wife's. Our first child was a boy we named Jonathan Michael. His nickname growing up was Mickey, named after Mickey Thomas, who was his favorite player. We always called him Tricky Mickey.

"You've got to be colorful, so I've been told. They call me Mental Mickey, anyway. So don't be surprised if I do something different," said Thomas. In Wichita, he became Tricky Mickey. "I've got a couple of tricks. They had me on the opening of a lot of TV shows a whole year in England, doing football tricks. Of course, playing for the biggest team in England, you get a lot of publicity," stated Thomas.[36]

But the biggest addition to the Wings in 1986-87 was a young draft pick from UCLA. They called him "The Bruin." He had won a NCAA title and spent time on the qualifying squad for the 1984 US Olympic Team. Now, he would take his talent indoors. His eight year career in Wichita would be special. He would play 338 games for the Wings, with only Kim Roentved and Kevin Kewley playing more. He would trail only Kim Roentved for most goals scored, with 305. He would be fifth on the all-time list in assists, game-winning goals, and power play goals, with 162, 25, and 23, respectively. And he twice scored 62 goals in a season...only Erik Rasmussen would exceed that total.[37]

ROY TURNER: Looking back, Dale Ervine was the first American genuine goal-scoring threat that we had. We were the only league in town, so the MISL did have the best American players. We had a combine and a draft that year.

DAVE PHILLIPS: Dale is one of my all-time favorite Wings.

TERRY NICHOLL, MIDFIELDER, WICHITA WINGS: Dale was a lovely lad. Just so genuine and upfront. I got to play with him AND got to coach him, so I got the best of both sides of him. He would keep going on EVERY play.

Over the course of his time with the Wings he would prove that an American player could be a goal-scoring star for the team. And the people of Wichita were excited to have an American star.

STEVE RADEMACHER, WINGS FAN: One game that we were at, Dale Ervine had scored a goal and threw a ball into the stands. I was sitting down and it landed in my lap. He had signed it. To this day I still have that ball.

LARRY INLOW: I enjoyed knowing Dale Ervine. He was a true professional.

DALE ERVINE, MIDFIELDER, WICHITA WINGS: Must have been June of '86 there was the indoor draft and I was playing some outdoor with the [Western Soccer Alliance's] LA Heat. I had just played four years at UCLA and the Heat was paying me. It wasn't a whole lot. The [MISL] held a combine so all the MISL coaches could be there and then they'd hold their draft the same weekend. But the Heat didn't want me to go because I was signed with them...so I couldn't go. The rumor I heard was the LA Lazers had the number one pick that year and it upset Peter Wall, who was coaching them, that I couldn't go.

Long story short, I knew Mike Fox very well and he was playing in Wichita. He may have been playing on that Heat team. So when the draft came around he obviously put in a word with Roy [Turner] and I think they had the seventh or eleventh pick. So anyway, I get this phone call that I had gotten drafted by Wichita. And I had gone to a lot of the Lazers games and had seen Wichita play and they ran very much a possession game...a lot of Europeans and Danes who liked to play with the ball, which was nice to see; instead of just hitting it up and have one guy doing the work. So I got drafted by them and I was excited. [I was] 22 years old and there was really no other way to make a decent living in the sport of soccer unless you went indoor. I was excited for the opportunity and went to Wichita and I trained.

I actually stayed with Mike Fox for the first month and a half. I was basically trying to find out if they wanted me. Soccer's a little different... just because they draft you doesn't mean they want to sign you. You have to go prove yourself. It worked out and little did I know eight years later I'd still be there. I really, really enjoyed it. Initially it was a big adjustment for two reasons: 1) Going from outdoor to playing indoor and 2) Going from a college atmosphere, where we had won the national championship my senior year, to a professional atmosphere. It was a big difference. These guys have wives and kids and this is how they make a living. They're not just playing and going to school. This was their livelihood. There were a lot of adjustments and on top of that it was a whole new city.

Brian Begley knew all the players and he used to work for Scholfield Honda at the time and would come to all of our practices. I finally signed after I was there for a month and Begley said, "Ervine, on your first day of practice Turner said, 'We're going to sign him right away.'" I didn't know those things. I was trying to prove myself and get a spot.

I do remember though when I scored my first goal at the Kansas Coliseum. I was a young kid, I was pretty excited. I guess that stayed with me my whole career. I kind of went on this long run and at halftime we got in [the locker room] and Charlie [Cooke] was pissed off about something. I don't know what happened, but again, he's so passionate...his mind starts going and he starts thinking of stuff. Then he said, "Ervine, what the hell are you running around the field for? You scored one f****** goal and now you're running around the field." I said I didn't mean anything by it. He says, "Don't tell me you didn't mean anything by it!" Laurie Abrahams is sitting nearby and he says, "Dale! Dale! Don't say shit. Just leave him alone! If you say something you're just going to throw fuel on there..." Looking back it was one of the funny times. I mean, what am I even saying anything for? Just let him rant. He's already yelled at five guys before he comes to me. "Who the hell do you think you are, scoring a goal and running around the field?" I didn't know anything other than if you said anything he'd just go longer. You learn.

(Don Marler/Missile Magazine) Dale "The Bruin" Ervine
would become an American goal-scoring sensation.

This would not be the last time Charlie Cooke's temper would rear its head. But Cooke had nothing to yell about after the team's pre-season exhibition game against the Kansas City Comets. The "Kansas Cup" was played outdoors on July 19th, 1986 at Lawrence-Dumont Stadium in downtown Wichita. Though many of the new players were not there yet, it was an opportunity for Cooke to get to know some of the returning players. The Wings won 3-1 in front of 6,800. It provided a hopeful start for the new season.[38]

New managing general partner, new commissioner, new GM, new coach...and with the departure of Terry Nicholl, the Wings needed a new captain. The Eagle reported that Charlie Cooke approached Kim Roentved about taking on the role. He accepted. "You not only have to be captain off the field but also on the field...I'll be the middle hand between the players and the coach. The coach can't see everything at once. Charlie and I seem to have good communication," said Roentved. Roentved believed the team was the best Wings squad ever. "We have a great blend of running players and working class players, and our draft choices have great potential..." he added.[39]

Coach Charlie Cooke had big plans....and big changes in store. The team would now play a high-intensity pressure game. "We're in a transition period. It's hard to apply pressure if only one player does it. The whole team has to do it. Coach Cooke and the players know it will take some time to blend," said Chico Borja. In the new offense everyone was expected to go forward and attack, even defenders.[40] *During practice, you would find Cooke mixing it up with the players, only a few years distant from his playing days. He would share tips on world-class moves he learned in England, throw them into wind-sprints, and put them through drills. "He's an intense man," said Kim Roentved.*[41]

Each practice included foot drills. "It's fundamentals, like the five-finger exercise in piano. Anybody can do these things, but the key is to do them under pressure. And they've got to be done quickly..." said Cooke.[42] *The Charlie Cooke style of coaching would be controversial amongst many players during his two seasons with the Wings. Some players adapted...others did not.*

Cooke's strategy paid off right away in the season opener. Steve Zungul and the Tacoma Stars came to Wichita in a rematch of the last season's playoffs. The Wings, led by the defense of Seamus McDonagh and a hat trick by Erik Rasmussen, triumphed 6-4, revenging their playoff series loss. Steve Zungul was shut out by McDonagh, who stopped him on a breakaway, a power play, and an attempted assist off a restart. "I knew what he was trying to do. I was not going to get beat on any lucky shots," said McDonagh.[43]

The Wings would be able to boast a 4-2 record against their rival during the 1986 87 regular season. St. Louis had been supplanted as "chief rival" by the Stars in the minds of many fans and players, mostly thanks to the previous year's playoff series and the presence of the MISL's "Lord of All Indoors." Both team's front offices were more than happy to stoke the flames. Wings' GM Steve Shaad asked the league to fine the Stars for insulting comments made in a game program: "After their fluke victory over the Tacoma Stars in the opening game of the season, the hated Wichita Wings - only team in the MISL named for a defunct brand of cigarettes - has the gall to come to town this weekend..." the program stated.[44]

Two weeks later, on January 23rd, 1987, The Eagle *reported that Tacoma was under investigation by Commissioner Bill Kentling and the MISL for tampering with other teams' players and violating the salary cap, adding fuel to the anti-Stars fire amongst Wings fans.[45] The Wings would down the Stars in February, with another hat trick, this time from Dave Hoggan. In April, it was Chico Borja's turn to subdue the Stars with a two goal and one assist performance. The Wings' success came despite the fact that Tacoma was the MISL's winningest team, ending the regular season 35-17.*

Wings fans were able to watch victories like these on both local and national television in 1986-87. ESPN televised the Wings' February 1st, 1987 win against the Steamers in St. Louis, putting an end to a four-year losing streak against St. Louis on the road. It wouldn't be a Wings-Steamers matchup without controversy, which was provided by an elbow to Steve Pecher's head from keeper Seamus McDonagh. "I'm just glad to win here no matter how it happens. It's been so long," said Kim Roentved.[46] On March 22nd, ESPN would again televise the Wings, this time in a loss against the Kansas City Comets. On local television, the Wings contract had switched from KSN to KAKE-TV, channel 10. KAKE would air six games during the 1986-87 season. Talented sports anchor Mark Allan would do the play-by-play coverage for the next three seasons.[47]

ROY TURNER: Mark Allan was the best sportscaster around and he did the games.

It wouldn't have been the MISL without "smack talk" between rivals. In the 1986-87 season, there was plenty to be found. San Diego Sockers star Juli Veee was fined $500 for criticizing some of the Steamers players as old and slow.[48] Back in the Midwest, the Steamers made a press release as follows: "RUBE: (roob), n. An unsophisticated countryman, hick. RUBE NIGHT: (roob nit), n. February 25 vs. Wichita." Not to be outdone, Steve Shaad and the Wings produced an All-Ugly team in Missile Magazine that featured Steve Zungul, old foe Tino Lettieri, former Wing Drago Dumbovic, the Steamers Angel DiBernardo, and Benny Dargle of Cleveland. After being fined $300 by Bill Kentling, Steve Shaad said: "...it probably wasn't in good taste."[49]

There were a lot of "characters" around the league. But few could rival Wings goalkeeper Seamus McDonagh.

ROY TURNER: Seamus McDonagh was a handful. An Irish temper...probably the biggest handful I ever had as a coach or GM. We had concerns about Charlie Cooke's health with Seamus [laughs].

BILL KENTLING: He was just wound a little different than the other 19 guys on the team. There were some things he did well. On many teams there's always one guy that scares everyone else. Seamus would have been that guy. You go to the K-State football locker room today and ask them, "Who's the guy on this team that everybody's afraid of?" and they'll all point at one guy. You aren't quite sure what they're gonna do. If four of you go out, you don't want to be the last guy in the car with that guy. Seamus and I never had a crossed word, but I wasn't a teammate. Nobody was ever quite sure what he was thinking or was gonna do.

In December of 1986, McDonagh and Coach Charlie Cooke became involved in a dispute over playing time. Cooke benched McDonagh in favor of backup keeper Bill Irwin during a December 14th game against the Minnesota Strikers. McDonagh, having shared time with Jan Olesen the previous year, was angry because he believed this time-sharing would continue throughout the rest of the season. This led to Cooke banning McDonagh from practice and Roy Turner unsuccessfully attempting to trade McDonagh to another MISL team. Within days the dispute was resolved and McDonagh returned to practice. "Yes, we've resolved it. I'm the goalkeeper and that's what I wanted all along. I'm going to *put all this behind me. I can't wait to get started," McDonagh told* The Eagle's *Mal Elliott.*[50]

And then there was his post-game tirade in Baltimore on April 3rd, 1987. After losing 7-4, McDonagh let a reporter know how he felt. As described by The Eagle: *"Seamus McDonagh was in no mood to talk...He took a greasy chicken drumstick in his hand and cut loose at a reporter who asked what had happened to the Wings' defense. 'What do you know about [expletive] football,' McDonagh screamed, waving the drumstick toward the Wings' locker room door. 'Get the hell out of here.'"*[51]

KIM ROENTVED, DEFENDER, WICHITA WINGS: One time, we played a playoff game in Tacoma and Seamus had said he didn't feel appreciated and refused to play. Kevin and I begged him to play, which he eventually did. Another time, we lost a game and Seamus felt like it was Barry Wallace's fault. There was a bunch of drinking [happening] on the bus. Seamus kept throwing beer cans at Barry and calling him a wanker. They get back to Wichita and players go back to their apartments. Barry and Seamus lived in the same apartment complex. Barry went up to his apartment to get his baseball bat. And he went to Seamus' [apartment] and started hammering on the door. Seamus' wife opened up and Barry went in looking for him. Seamus ran out the back door to get away from Barry.

KEVIN KEWLEY, DEFENDER, WICHITA WINGS: Seamus was having a bad game on the road...so Charlie [Cooke] was going to pull him. Charlie told the backup Bill Irwin to get ready and warm up. So, Seamus just sat down by the post and wouldn't get up. Coach said, "Kevin, go get Seamus." I told him Charlie was going to suspend him if he didn't come up. He cussed up a storm and eventually came out.

ROY TURNER: Charlie said we should look into getting a restraining order on Seamus.

KIM ROENTVED: He should have hired Barry Wallace to protect him.

ROY TURNER: He was a very aggressive human being.

CHICO BORJA: He was a Jekyll and Hyde person. He was a very family-oriented guy. We lived together at Rockborough Apartments...In the goal, he was tough. He DEMANDED respect in the back. He demanded Kim come back and cover. He was a great player, great goalkeeper and he demanded respect, and I always appreciated that.

But behind the feisty exterior was a man who appreciated the loyal fans of the Orange Army.

ERIC SCRIVEN, WINGS FAN: I can still remember my first time meeting a Wings player. I was seven-years-old. Like a lot of kids my age I played indoor soccer at Soccer West, which also happened to be where the Wings trained. My dad and I had gone into the locker room there so I could change for my game. Sitting there was none other than Seamus McDonagh. He was getting changed after training and listening to a soccer match on a small radio. My dad asked him who he was listening to and they began conversing. Seamus then turned his attention to me and asked if I enjoyed playing soccer and told me what mattered was having fun. We then told him our story about breaking my mother's Mary figurine, which he got a good laugh out of. After he left, my dad still couldn't believe we had just sat and talked with Seamus McDonagh.

McDonagh would have a couple particularly good moments that season, both against the LA Lazers. One featured his nimble mind, and the other his overall skill as a keeper. In a March 1st, 1987 win in Los Angeles, McDonagh was trying to retrieve a pass from Kim Roentved when a Lazers player rushed him. The quick-thinking Irishman called a timeout, knowing that the referees would ignore his signal because he was out of the box. The Lazers, however, bit on his trick and eased up. McDonagh took advantage of their relaxed state and kicked the ball downfield to Mike Fox, who fed it to Dale Ervine for an easy goal.[52] In April, McDonagh would get his first shutout as a Wichita Wing against the Lazers. It was an 8-0 victory at the Kansas Coliseum. McDonagh accumulated 17 saves on 25 shots on goal. "The big story was their goalkeeper. He played the best I've seen in eight or nine years of indoor soccer. He stood up and took everything we threw at him," said Lazers coach Keith Tozer.[53]

On January 27th, 1987, a little piece of the Cold War came to the Kansas Coliseum. The Wings played an exhibition match against the Soviet team Dynamo Moscow. 8,305 fans watched the Wings narrowly win 7-6. The Soviet coach was quoted as saying his top two forwards, who had three goals between them, "...only played 50 percent of the level they should have played." A number of Wings ticketholders protested the Soviet Union's human rights record by placing posters of Soviet dissidents and prisoners of conscience in their seats.[54]

For the Wings, the 1986-87 season would be ruined by an extraordinary number of serious injuries. The longest season in MISL history, at 52 games, it would seem particularly long for the Wings. It started with Kim Roentved hurting his knee and missing all of November and December. Dave Hoggan missed 10 weeks with an ankle injury. Both players would play only 35 games. Frank Rasmussen would play only eight games due to a stress fracture in his foot. Mickey Thomas suffered what at first appeared to be a potential career-ending knee injury. He would miss 18 games. Barry Wallace would miss 10 games to a dislocated shoulder. Norman Piper, called back to duty to fill in, would break his arm. Worst of all was the loss of Erik Rasmussen, who missed 17 games after hurting his ankle.[55]

CHICO BORJA: We could have had a great year but a lot of us got hurt.

Former Dallas Sidekick Mark Evans was signed to shore up the Wings on account of their injury woes. He would eventually start over a dozen games in a row that season, contributing 34 blocks on defense.[56] *The Wings would struggle guarding their goal throughout the year. They were only saved by their potent offense. Despite leading the league in penalty minutes for part of the season, Chico Borja was having a banner year, flourishing under Charlie Cooke's system. He would lead the team in goals AND assists, with 51 and 36, respectively.*

Another bright spot was Dale Ervine, the 1986-87 "Iron Man." The rookie would be the only Wing to play all 52 games. He contributed on both offense and defense, accumulating 21 total points and 27 blocks.[57] *Ervine battled John Stollmeyer of the Cleveland Force for the MISL's Rookie of the Year award. Though he would lose out, Ervine still made his mark and was clearly going to be a force to be reckoned with for years to come. "He's a physically big fella with fairly good quickness. Overall, he's a robust type of athlete...He's doing a strong-running, hard-working job for us," said Charlie Cooke.*[58]

Another rookie had a great year during the 1986-87 season. For Wings fans that preferred to listen on the radio, the Dave Phillips-era had begun. He anchored the radio broadcast, which moved from KFH 1330 AM to KRZ 1240 AM. Phillips had a wealth of broadcasting experience in college football and basketball. He would do play-by-play for the Wings for eight years, eventually setting the record for most Wings games broadcast by any radio announcer.[59]

Up I-35, at Kemper Arena, the Comets schemed to add more Wings to their club. They hoped that Jorgen Kristensen would soon be coached by Roy Turner. But they would be disappointed when Turner declined their offer. "I told them there was still too much work to do in Wichita," said Turner.[60] *The Comets also added Norman Piper to the list of candidates for the head coaching job.*[61] *Luckily for Wichita, they would end up hiring Dave Clements, formerly of the Steamers. However, Turner and Piper wouldn't be the last Wings they'd attempt to lure to Kansas City...and the next time, they'd succeed.*

When February of 1987 rolled around, it was time for the annual MISL All-Star game. The Wings would contribute Kim Roentved, Chico Borja, and trainer Wayne Fuller to the West squad. Erik Rasmussen had been voted on the team but would not play due to injury.[62] *What made that year's game most exciting was the announcement it would take place at the fabulous LA Forum, the home of Magic Johnson and company. LA Lakers and Lazers owner Jerry Buss pulled out all the stops. The teams stayed at the exclusive, and expensive, Stouffer Concourse Hotel, and attended a pre-game party in Beverly Hills at Buss' Pickfair Estates. The cost of all this? Between $125,000 and $200,000. The Forum would sell out all 15,893 seats for the game.*[63]

Meanwhile, across the country, Bill Kentling and the MISL's New York HQ had to deal with a New York Express disaster. The league's newest team was crashing and burning. On February 3rd, 1987 they came on a road trip to Wichita with a woeful 2-19 record. Wings' GM Steve Shaad referred to the Express as a black mark on the league. "I just think that what New York proves is how tough this league is...You just can't come into this league and take on the Clevelands, Baltimores, Minnesotas, and Dallases in the first year..." said Kentling. Regarding the team's aging stars, including Shep Messing and Ricky Davis: "The team they put together would be a good team in 1980, 1981, but this is 1987," he continued.[64]

On February 17th, in a move that surprised and infuriated the league, the Express announced they were folding. The MISL would be forced to change the season schedule with games to replace those the Express would now miss. But even worse, it was terrible publicity. The MISL HQ had moved to New York City in order to help promote both the new team and the league as a whole.[65]

BILL KENTLING: The league offices had been in Chicago. We collectively made a decision that we needed to be in New York City. We had a powerful team there. It turned out to be a wretched and expensive mistake because the New York team folded during my first season as commissioner and we were stuck there for no good reason.

Throughout the 1986-87 season the Wings would hover around the .500 mark. By season's end, they stood at 27-25, 18-8 at home and 9-17 on the road. The Wings tied San Diego for 3rd, but lost the tiebreaker, putting them in the fourth and final playoff spot in the Western Division. This meant that the Wings would again play the Tacoma Stars in the first round of the playoffs. With a 4-2 record against Tacoma that season, it seemed that the Wings might have a good chance to advance. But Tacoma had the better overall record, and thus would host three of the theoretical five games. And, in fact, it would take all five games for the Stars to win...with three wins in Tacoma.[66]

The first two games in Tacoma went to the Stars, 9-7 and 9-1. Game three in Wichita was an emotional affair. The Wings were on the edge of elimination and the team responded. With a commanding lead, the Wings soared into the fourth quarter assured of a win. In frustration, Tacoma's Gerry Gray gave Erik Rasmussen a swift kick as he lay on the carpet. The Eagle's Fred Mann described what happened next: "[Mark] Kerlin rushed to Rasmussen's defense and shoved Gray away, whereupon [Neil] Megson tackled Kerlin and wrestled him to the ground. Both benches emptied, and you could almost hear the phones in the Wings' ticket office start to jingle with fans ring up to buy a ringside seat for Wednesday's match." The Wings won 10-3 in a game that, ironically, was on Mother's Day.[67] *At the post-game press conference, aired on KAKE, Erik Rasmussen said, "How can human beings kick a guy on the floor? If I was standing up, they can kick me all day, but it's a disgrace to themselves to show behavior like that?" Game four would also go to the Wings, sending the series to a final game in Tacoma. Sadly, with the help of a Steve Zungul hat trick, the Stars would prevail 4-2.*[68]

DALE ERVINE: It wasn't a horrible year, but if you look at the home record to the road record it would have been drastically different. It was a good first year and we had a lot of talent but, again, every team did. Zungul in Tacoma and Preki, there were a lot of good teams.

Though the Wings would make a few more playoff runs over the rest of the MISL's existence, they would never again achieve a regular season winning record until they joined the National Professional Soccer League (NPSL) in 1992-93. The glory years of the club had now passed by. However, there was still life left in the Wings. More importantly, there was still love for the team. The Wings averaged over 8,000 fans per game in 1986-87 and even more would come the next year. They'd need them.

On April 25th, the Wings announced that the team would fold unless it came up with 1,800 season tickets and $150,000. It was estimated that they would lose between $560,000 to $600,000 by the end of the season. The drop-off in the oil business resulted in losing some investors. "I don't think anybody understands the seriousness of this. But in my eight years here, this town hasn't done anything but surprise me, and I hope there is one surprise left for me," said team president Roy Turner.[69]

The number of partners had gone from over 50 to only 28. The team needed corporate support and it needed it badly. "It would be a disastrous blow to the future of sports in this city if the Wings went under. It is difficult to imagine another major-league team of any sort wanting to come to Wichita if the city loses the only major-league franchise it has ever had," wrote Fred Mann.[70] *In order to give the funding effort a little publicity, Wichita mayor Bob Knight declared May of 1987 "Wings Appreciation Month." "I don't think you can overstate the contribution of the Wings to the city," he said.*[71]

After a great deal of suspense, on May 23rd, 1987, Bill Oliver read off the results from the Wings' fund drive, and announced, "...the general partners have decided to fund the budget for the next season, and the Wings will..." The rest was drowned out by "hoots and cheers and applause." The Wings would be back thanks to $140,000 in investments, including $40,000 from Buck Alley, $30,000 from the Sedgwick County Commission (rent reduction), $71,000 from new investors, and "an amazing 5,810 tickets...sold in three weeks."[72]

BILL OLIVER: We'd get saved and just squeak it out. I loved those Save the Wings campaigns. They were kinda fun.

The love and devotion of the Orange Army toward their Wings was undeniable. They had saved the team yet again. That passion was also noticed by a fan up I-35. Kansas City Comets fan Brian Holland's first trip to the Kansas Coliseum, despite his Comets losing, left a good impression: "[December 19th, 1986] was my first-ever visit to the cacophony known as the Kansas Coliseum. Disappointing game result, to be sure, but I was most impressed with the home of the Orange Army/Wing-A-Lings; in spite of its location way out in the boonies. I especially liked its intimate sightlines, the sheer noise when the crowd got into the game, the extra-wide comfortable seats and my favorite feature of all, the FREE parking! My friend and I sure didn't feel cheated and had a great time--well-worth the road trip; and we would make three more pilgrimages to the Coliseum for Comets-Wings tilts..."[73]

An Oral History

Summer Vacation...and a $5,000 Beer

———

Every summer, in the MISL's offseason, kids from around Wichita would flock to the Wichita Wings' summer camps. Various players worked as camp counselors, including some of the most famous Wings. These camps were one of the ways the Wings were able to cement their bond with the community. Because the players were so approachable and friendly, kids and parents alike felt like the Wings were part of their family. It was a great time to be a kid in Wichita, Kansas.

KEVIN HIMES, RUGRAT AND WINGS EMPLOYEE: All those years when I was 12, 13, and 14, I went to those Wings camps. I remember one when George Ley was the head guy. It was at Coleman Junior High and real hot. We were standing around having a water break. Some of the guys started kicking the ball around. [This kid] kicked it and it hit [George Ley's] cup and splashed him in the face. He made us run for 15-20 minutes. It was hilarious. He was a good guy.

As Himes got older he became a trusted apprentice for various players. It was a pretty sweet deal to be 18 years old and hanging out with the Wichita Wings.

KEVIN HIMES: My summer job my junior and senior year was doing the Wings camps. I was a counselor. By this time a couple of the guys would call me their apprentice. It felt like I was good enough to play pro soccer someday because all these guys around me were approving me. And they were great players!

Norman Piper was taking me to Emporia for a camp for a week. Terry Nicholl would drive me to El Dorado in his Lotus. I was on top of the world, as you could imagine. By senior year, 18 years old, I had a little moustache and a long, curly mullet and I could get into the bars with them. No one ever carded me because I was with Terry Rowe, Steve McLean, and Andy Chapman. We'd go to [a club called] Streetlights. The boys liked to go out…a lot. I got so schnockered that Norman had to go put me in his car…I sat in the parking lot for two hours and then he took me home. I snuck in the house…still lived with my parents…I was out partying with the Wings.

I had a camp team, Terry Rowe had a camp team, Steve McLean had one. We'd play each other on Friday to see how the kids had developed and what they'd learned. I had always been fascinated with English soccer. Some of the players had tapes and we'd go watch it. There was one on during the evening. So we watched that game and you listen to those English crowds and you can hear them all doing this chant. So I asked Terry, "What are they saying?" He told me they were saying, "John Barnes is a wanker, is a wanker." Weeks later we're at another camp and my team was on the bench and we started this chant, "Terry Rowe…is a wanker, is a wanker." And Terry comes running over there and says, "What are you doing? Do you know what that means?" And we said, "No, not really. We know it means you suck." Then he explained what it meant. There were parents there, but they had no idea what a wanker was either. He just sprinted off the field to tell us that.

The Wings wouldn't just stay in Wichita. There were kids all across Kansas that wanted to be just like Andy Chapman or Kevin Kewley. So they took the show on the road…

KEVIN HIMES: We go to Ulysses, KS. "Bring the Wings to Ulysses," they said. There were players that went out in a van on Monday and they did the camp. Then there were two or three that went on Friday. So I got to fly to Ulysses with a couple of the players in a private jet. We had one game against the police chief, the fire chief, the mayor, and all the townspeople, and just annihilated them. They had a good crowd of people there, maybe 200-300 people. After the game they set up this table to sign autographs, and the players said, sit down Kev. So I sat there and signed autographs for 15-20 minutes [laughs]. The next week I come back to the office and am emptying the trash and getting Virginia some coffee. Somebody calls from Ulysses and says, "We've got buttons from Kim Roentved and Terry Nicholl, but we want one from that other Kevin." The office says, "We only have Kevin Kewley." They said, "No, his [last] name starts with an 'H'." They wanted a button for me! [laughs] I was like, "Wow, that's cool!"

VIRGINIA CREAMER, DIRECTOR OF OPERATIONS, WICHITA WINGS: We'd travel around on a big ol' House of Schwan RV going from town to town. One of my jobs was making sure they always had a golf course to play on. We couldn't use the bathroom in the RV because it was stuffed with their golf clubs. Every country club in every little town, we'd play golf.

STEVE SHAAD, PR DIRECTOR, WICHITA WINGS: I think it was about 1984 that Budweiser sponsored a goodwill caravan across western Kansas. We went to Garden City, Dodge City, Hays, and Russell. We took Roy, an Angel, Jeff Bourne, Ian Anderson, and myself. I was the front man and set up clinics and media interviews in each town. I had communication with the soccer people in each town. It was a phenomenal success. Because of our TV coverage we had a lot of fans there. Our driver was Ed Speicher, the sales manager for House of Schwan. We are on our last stop in Russell. Ed buys us all dinner at the country club. They ask us what we all want to drink and everyone asks for a Budweiser or Bud Light, and then they get to Jeff Bourne. He says, "Coors Light." Everybody looks up and we all look at Ed. Next round of drinks, same thing happens. I thought it probably doesn't matter much to Ed. After the trip, I called Barry Schwan to tell him how much of a success it was and thank him for it. He says, "That's good, because it will be the last time we sponsor it. If Jeff Bourne doesn't know enough to order a Budweiser drink on a Budweiser caravan then we don't want to be a part of it." That was $10,000 we lost for the next year...$5,000 per each Coors Light.

CHAPTER 20

An Oral History

From One to Another

―――――

"In pro sports, if you don't win you're in trouble...
it doesn't matter what style of soccer you play."

- NORMAN PIPER

IT WAS HARD TO IMAGINE the Wings without Kim Roentved. But during the offseason prior to the 1987-88 season, Wings fans began to realize "The Rocket" might not return. Up to five teams expressed interest in the Danish free agent. Two of them, Los Angeles and Kansas City, were considered front-runners. The previous year, Roentved had earned $70,000, or just over $150,000 in 2016 dollars. However, The Eagle's sources indicated that Roentved "could now command a six-figure salary." The Wings made what Turner called a "very high" offer, but it was rejected. Before long, it was announced that Kim Roentved would become a Kansas City Comet.[1]

ROY TURNER, PRESIDENT, WICHITA WINGS: In the summer of 1987 Kim signed with KC. You'd need to talk to Kim to find out why he did it. But he was very well-rewarded, around $200,000, when he went to KC. I definitely think it had something to do with me not coaching anymore. I was in Europe when he left the team. I found out when I was on vacation there. It was a surprise. Would I have tried to stop it if I'd had the chance? Certainly.

374

KIM ROENTVED, DEFENDER, WICHITA WINGS: Under the circumstances it wasn't hard to leave the Wings. It was time for me to leave because of where I was at with Charlie Cooke. I respected him very much as a coach because he did it his way, without compromise, whether I liked it or not. But there was an opportunity for me. It wasn't about the money difference. I was looking forward to a new challenge. Moving to a bigger city also was exciting.

ROY TURNER: KC offered me the coaching position as well...the year before [Roentved] left. They asked me what it would take to get me to coach. I told my ownership here about it, but my passion was here. I couldn't leave. Jorgen went to KC too. He finished his career there. Frank Rasmussen went as well. They apparently thought an awful lot of our team...and our coach!

Kim Roentved's time in Wichita was only temporarily at an end. He would return in a few short years, and spend most of the 1990s as a Wing. However, it was a huge loss in 1987. Roentved did so many things for the team that it was hard to see how he could be replaced. The Wings would struggle without him. There would be no doubt about his legacy as a Wing. By the end of his career, he suited up as a Wing in 534 games. He led the Wings all-time list in scoring with 309 goals. He assisted on 344 goals, second only to Chico Borja in Wings history. He was the all-time leader in blocked shots with 678, fourth all-time in game-winning goals, and second all-time in power play goals.[2]

And then it got worse. Chico Borja, the Wings' scoring leader the previous season, found himself the recipient of a very generous offer from Dr. Jerry Buss, owner of the LA Lazers. Though Borja made $90,000 (almost $200,000 in 2016 dollars) with the Wings in 1986-87, the Lazers were able to offer even more.[3] Borja would take what ended up being a one-year California vacation before returning to the Wings in late 1988. His first appearance back in Wichita in a Lazers uniform saw Borja make the game-winning goal...and for the first time in a while, Wings fans couldn't celebrate along with Chico.[4]

CHICO BORJA, MIDFIELDER, WICHITA WINGS: That was about a contract...[The Lazers] were looking to improve their team and thought I was one of the players to make that happen. I had a 200% raise in my salary, and I play for my family, which was going to set us up really nice. With all the bonuses and everything there was no way the Wings were going to be able to match it. It wasn't an easy decision. It became something for my way of life, so I could start saving. With the salaries we were making, it wasn't enough [prior to the move]. We were making kind of good money. But can you imagine if we were making the money that hockey was making? I'd be retired by now. [That decision] was all salary-based...Kim and I left at the same time and it must have been tough for the Wings. They didn't make the playoffs obviously.

DALE ERVINE, MIDFIELDER, WICHITA WINGS: After my first year, Chico went to LA and Kim went to Kansas City. You lose two guys like that, it's hard to replace them.

Barry Wallace would follow Roentved to Kansas City, ending a productive three-year stint with the Wings. Neil Roberts would head off to Minnesota to play for the Strikers, while Laurie Abrahams would end his ten year professional soccer career. Chilean midfielder Diego Castro would also depart. Significantly, both of the previous season's goalies would not return. Both Bill Irwin and Seamus McDonagh would move on to successful coaching careers. McDonagh's time with the Wings had likely been too tumultuous for it to continue for the long term. However, his performance on the pitch did deserve respect, at 25-18 with a 4.67 GAA the previous year.[5]

It wasn't possible to replace Kim Roentved, but the Wings hoped that a new addition named Mike Stankovic might be able to come close. The defender came to Wichita from the Baltimore Blast, where he had helped win the 1984 MISL Championship. Stankovic would be one of three Yugoslavs to join the Wings that season, becoming the first players from that country to play in Wichita. Though he was on the downslope of his career, Stankovic would have a standout season in 1987-88. In 48 games he would score 22 goals and make 32 assists while accumulating 41 blocks. His point total would be third highest on the team behind Dave Hoggan and Erik Rasmussen.[6]

ROY TURNER: Stankovic was not the player when he came here that he was in Baltimore.

The Wings also needed to replace two goalies. Matt Kennedy, the backup Minnesota keeper, was half of the equation. The other half was a 27-year-old Yugoslav named Nenad "Ziggy" Zigante. In broken English, Zigante told The Eagle *why he came to the Wings: "I heard here (in Wichita) is people, coach and everything, who is like family, and I like to try for these reasons in Wichita. And is no mistake. I came here. I believe in me. I know I must work and learn because this kind of soccer for me is new, different from Europe. Rules here are different. People here is quicker than in Yugoslavia."* [7]

Indeed, it was no mistake. Zigante would be forced to carry most of the goalkeeping responsibilities on his shoulders during the season due to a terrible eye injury to Matt Kennedy. "And he did it with nothing but his lightning-quick reflexes because when the season ended he was still learning some of the basics of the game," said The Eagle's *Mal Elliott.* [8] *Kennedy would end the year with an abysmal 4-17 record in goal, while Zigante ended the season 19-14. His performance would so impress the league that he would be named the MISL's Newcomer of the Year. There would be a third keeper that year: David Vanole. He only appeared in one quarter, but the young US National Team member would make a mark in the 1988 Olympics and three years later when he helped America advance to the 1990 World Cup Finals.* [9]

The Wings also signed a trio of midfielders and forwards in Pedro DeBrito, Juan Carlos Molina, and Mirsad "Mickey" Kahrovic. [11] *DeBrito was fresh off a championship with the Dallas Sidekicks. Another great addition to the Wings was former Olympian Jean Willrich. The German-American forward would add some offensive spark in his 50 games with the Wings that season, accumulating 39 points, roughly equally divided between goals and assists. He would also make 26 blocks and score three game-winning goals.* [10]

ERIC SCRIVEN, WINGS FAN: ...We waited in line for a half-hour to meet Wings midfielder/forward Jean Willrich. Willrich had just come to Wichita from the San Diego Sockers, where he had been MVP of the NASL Finals. He had also played with the US Olympic team in 1984. Dad and I looked through all my MISL cards until we found a Jean Willrich card. I was so nervous waiting to get it signed, but I can remember how kind Jean was when we finally got to the front of the line. He gladly signed my card and told me how happy he was to meet me. I still have the card and try to remember the impact his kindness had on me when dealing with impressionable kids like myself.

There was one more addition to the Wings' family that season…this one much smaller than the rest. On October 8th, 1987 Wings president Roy Turner and his wife Tamara welcomed Kamden Turner into the world. He would be the apple of his father's eye.

ROY TURNER: The hospital room had more cards and orange than you have ever seen.

DR. TAMARA PRYOR: Kamden had a list of his favorite players. He was always around…I don't think he ever missed a game.

Hopes were high that these men and their fellow Wings would make Charlie Cooke's second year a big improvement over his first. Though it was a record-high 56 game season, every single game counted, and the first game of the year brought good news. A sellout crowd of 9,674 watched Erik and Frank Rasmussen, Jean Willrich, and Dave Hoggan score goals in a 5-3 win over the San Diego Sockers in the November 7th, 1987 home opener. "I'm a lucky person to score the winning goal…I was holding my hands up to Jesus and saying, 'Let me go out and do something for them,'" said Willrich.[12]

There were bright spots early in the season, but they were few-and-far-between given the team's inconsistent start. Terry Rowe had a great start to the season, and though only 23-years-old, he provided veteran leadership. His patented off-the-wall passes to himself gave him four goals by Christmas and both Charlie Cooke and Roy Turner noticed his top-notch play. Turner saw his skilled use of the boards as "a tremendous gift…" and Cooke admired his energy and said that "you can depend on him for good defense."[13]

Dale Ervine also started to come into his own. It was only his second year, but he was adding to his stable of skills. "…What he's added now is the ability to get by people and get off shots and crosses. He's not a passive defender, which is what I like," said Charlie Cooke. "I think he's probably the best new American player in the league," said Roy Turner.[14]

DALE ERVINE: I was just trying to make sure I could keep getting better as a player. Growing up, my dad always said, "You're only as good as your last game." His point was: no one remembers what you did last game. Be consistent, not just in scoring, but in your effort.

Despite their best effort, the Wings couldn't quite put it together through the first few months of the season. By the end of December the Wings were 6-12 and at the very bottom of the MISL cellar. No Wings team had had a worse start. "When you're ahead 4-2 and you let the lead slip away before halftime..." said forward Erik Rasmussen, his voice trailing off. 'It's difficult to say how frustrating it is.'"[15] *Even more frustrating was the team's performance on the road. The Wings would lose an astounding 13 straight road games through the end of January. In the end, it was too much for the ownership to take. On January 30th, 1988, they pulled the plug on the Charlie Cooke era.*

ROY TURNER: The owners fired Cooke after a year-and-a-half. In a board meeting they decided the results weren't good enough.

KEVIN KEWLEY, DEFENDER, WICHITA WINGS: I remember we lost in KC and were coming back on the bus and Roy sat next to me and he asked me if I would coach. "You need to keep quiet, but we are getting rid of Charlie." I said I would do it if he needed me to. In a few days Terry Nicholl was hired and I was made his assistant. The team had stopped responding to Cooke. I liked him because was as honest as the day. If he thought you were shit, he'd tell you. That was the way he motivated you. Erik [Rasmussen] hated it. I remember one time in Minnesota, basically he was screaming at Erik and got a few of the guys to join in. I stood up and basically said, "Leave Erik alone, he's the best player we've got. If he was playing against us we'd be panicking." Here we are giving Erik stick when we should be praising him. Erik didn't let the goals in. He was there to score goals. We should be thanking our lucky stars we have a player like him. He thought Erik wasn't playing hard enough. It wasn't true. Charlie was a great one-on-one coach, but struggled with tactics. He was so brash, which some guys didn't like. I remember I said to him one time "Why do you never get on me?" He said, "I know you always give 100%, I don't have to worry about you."

Charlie Cooke's philosophy was play high-pressure no matter what. I'd go round and round with him about that on a long road-trip. We didn't always have the legs to do that. He said, "No, this is the way we do it." Eventually he did change though...Cooke's style was totally different than Roy's. Dallas had won the crown the year before [he came to Wichita] and Charlie was the assistant. The rumor was that he did all the coaching for them. He came in and completely changed everything. Practices were harder. There was no taking it easy. He told everyone that they were fighting for a spot on the team, whether you had been here forever or had just walked in the door. He rubbed some people the wrong way, Erik especially. Charlie hated how he strolled around. Some of the older guys didn't like it. You can't play 100% pressure all the time. It doesn't work. It would wear on us. I didn't get a regular spot on the rotation until December [of 1986]. We won, and he never doubted me after that. He wanted defenders to fly forward like maniacs. I thought Charlie was the best... coach I'd ever seen at improving guys' skills. He'd shout at Erik. He'd make all the players do these series of drills. I do it with my players now. It worked, it did make people better. But for the team, he didn't have a Plan B. It was just Plan A: fly at them.

KIM ROENTVED: Charlie Cooke was coaching the wrong team. He had come from Dallas. They didn't have the same technical talent we had. He made their team successful because of Tatu. Half the time they'd just kick it down to Tatu in the corner. But that wasn't Rasmussen's style. If it was my last option I might have done that, but we wanted to play soccer. Charlie wanted us to do something different. You are better off trying to adapt to the players you have. I respected him, though I didn't get along too well with him.

You live and die with your decisions, and Charlie did that more than anyone I've ever met. Charlie wouldn't listen to players. When I play around with the guys today as a coach, I always try to listen. I didn't leave because of that though. I left because of money. I thought that Charlie had already made the decision to get Mike Stankovic and I knew they couldn't pay both of us. I think he wanted him because of their relationship, not necessarily because of his abilities...Some of the drills Cooke came up with; the players just didn't buy into. You had guys on the team like Rasmussen that would just laugh at the drills.

DALE ERVINE: Charlie Cooke was very intense. He was such a good player when he played that I think there were parts of him that wanted to play again. He trained with us, he did the drills with us, he did the running with us. His passion for the game was amazing. He just loved it. The main difference [between Roy and Charlie] was they had different personalities. Charlie was still living and breathing the game...wanting to play...that was the impression he gave because he knew he could still play. The guy was a phenomenal player. It was different in that Charlie would feel every mistake...he was just living the game every minute. To a certain degree that's good but the drawback is if there was one simple mistake you made, there would be something said from him because he expected so much from himself and he then expected so much from us. We were fine with that. Whereas Roy was more of "this is what we need to do guys, let's go out there." It was more of a relaxed nature, a calmer nature, even though you know inside he was burning with competition. It was just a difference in how they came across to the players.

Charlie liked to do [the drills] because he was the best one at them. We would do dribbling drills, step overs...quick little feeds. It's good for the indoor game to have that. But these guys would look around and say, "Really?" I was 22, these guys are 30. If we don't know how to do this by now we're never going to be able to do it in a game. Just accept us for what we have. My first year I couldn't say a word. I was like, whatever. It was strange to be doing drills like that at that level because you normally don't at that level...You train, you go over tactics. But trying to build up somebody's skills so they can do a step-over when they're 31 years old, that's a little late in their career. And it was almost every day, these drills. But at the end of the day...it wasn't a horrible thing. But I think it was something that was so different than what they were used to before that no one really loved it.

The thing with Charlie was that he was so passionate and so intense that it was always: "Get out there guys and give them pressure. Everywhere on the field we want pressure." There was no real change from a tactical standpoint and when you look back, playing a home game in the front of 9,600 at the Kansas Coliseum, it was difficult for teams to come in there: it was a smaller venue, the fans are right on top of the field, and we were thriving off the atmosphere. To go on the road and play the same way, well, the team we're playing against is a little sharper because they're at home with their home fans. From a coaching standpoint I just think you have to have a different sort of tactical plan. There are things you can get away with at home that you can't always get away with on the road. It's okay because you're switching every one-and-a-half or two minutes, but if one person of the five on the field isn't completely engaged with everybody else when they're pressuring, then you get broken down and it's suddenly a two-on-one going the other way.

…You're not going to sit back at the halfway line and let them bring the ball up and slow it and try to counter. You're pressuring all the time. And at home, it's okay because the fans are in the game. If we got a goal early, we would pretty much run away from teams. If you got one goal, you're going to get two or three because of the momentum. But on the road it doesn't work that way. You've also got to adapt to the talent you have in your locker room. You can't just say, "We're going to play this way." If it doesn't suit us, you can't do that all the time.

But look, Charlie loved the game. He was very passionate about the game and he gave me my first opportunity. There was some butting of heads of how we were playing and how the trainings went. It wasn't done in a bad way; it was just about how passionate this man was about playing. Back then Charlie was about 46, if I remember right. I'm telling you, he was still very fit and if we put him on the field he would be one of the top two or three players on the team. That's how good he was as a player. So I think it was a little difficult for him to separate that playing and coaching because he just loved it so much. He still wanted to play.

BILL OLIVER, MANAGING GENERAL PARTNER, WICHITA WINGS, 1986-92: …I would go down to the locker room after the game. One time I was there after we lost a game…and I wasn't supposed to be there. Charlie was so livid, it was scary. I said to myself, "I wouldn't play for him if I was a soccer player." That was no way to coach a team. Charlie was kind of hard to understand anyway, but Jesus Christ, I've never heard anything like that before...

NORMAN PIPER, ASSISTANT COACH, WICHITA WINGS: Charlie was a very demanding coach. At that time he used to like to play high pressure, and we didn't have players who could do that. I think some of the players couldn't adapt to it. In pro sports, if you don't win you're in trouble...it doesn't matter what style of soccer you play.

CHICO BORJA: The reason why I started scoring goals and not making assists was because of Coach Charlie Cooke. He turned me into a forward. I remember after practice he'd have me turning and shooting, turning and shooting, dribbling and shooting. He said he needed me to play forward. I wasn't used to that. He made me a goal-scorer...I scored a lot of goals when he put me up there. And also, I had the ability to do assists. You know how I was in terms of not taking any crap.

Charlie Cooke had the same mentality of a Seamus McDonagh and I did not mind that at all. He demanded that you play hard, that you play your heart out every single game. He would remind you if you didn't. I remember scoring three or four goals one game and he said, "You should have done this better." I was like, "Damn." I never minded that. Different strokes for different folks. He was a great coach for me. I was surprised when they let him go. I wish he would have stayed. I think he could have taken us to the next level.

In his autobiography, The Bonnie Prince, *Charlie Cooke addressed his time in Wichita: "Wichita wasn't a particularly successful or satisfying experience for me as a head coach, although I think it taught me several hard but enlightening lessons. While being almost unbeaten at home, we had problems getting results away from home, which pissed me off [sic] no end and led me to say some things I'm not so proud of today. I was sacked midway through my second season, and I took that dismissal hard, for although I knew I had plenty to answer for, I felt hugely let down and perhaps by nobody more so than myself for not seeing things as they were, rather than as I would have liked them to be..."* [16]

Cooke wasn't the only one who was fired. His assistant coach, Norman Piper, the "First Wing," was let go as well.

NORMAN PIPER: It was difficult because you look back at what you did for the franchise...it was a little bit disappointing.

The Memphis Storm would lose their coach when the Wings quickly hired Terry Nicholl to take the reins of the leaderless Wings. The Storm played in the American Indoor Soccer Association, widely considered an inferior league to the MISL. Nicholl had been named "Coach of the Year" the previous season. "I always loved the Wichita Wings, and that's why I'm back here," Nicholl told The Eagle.[17] On February 12th, he would be welcomed back to Wichita by a sellout crowd of 9,674 old friends. He would thank them with a 5-2 victory over Dallas.[18]

TERRY NICHOLL, HEAD COACH, WICHITA WINGS: When I came back to coach that [first home] game...That was the most nervous I ever felt about a game, and I've played in front of 40,000 in Liverpool, Everton, Manchester United, and against the Algerian national team. That's what it meant to me, coming back.

DALE ERVINE: Terry [Nicholl] had this love affair with Wichita, having played there, and he was so pleased to get the opportunity to come back to coach us. Terry and Charlie [Cooke] were similar in that they [basically] said, "Okay boys, roll up your sleeves guys and get to work, skin your knees, do whatever the hell you have to do, we have to get ready to play here tonight." So they were similar in ways, Charlie and Terry. Terry did bring a little more sense of, tactically, dropping [the pressure] off a bit. But he was very passionate, very demanding. He wanted to make sure when you were out there that you performed.

Terry wasn't that far removed from playing. He was only three or four years from when he last played. He still had that understanding as a player. He would also get frustrated with certain mistakes but you can't blame him. His livelihood is riding on what we do on the field. He had a lot of similar qualities with Charlie in that they wanted to win so badly. He did his best. Before games he would prepare us with stuff on the board. I think Terry took it up an extra step tactically trying to help us a little more. They were both a big part of my success.

Nicholl would name as his assistant coach none other than the last original Wing left from season one: Kevin Kewley. Nicholl would continue Roy Turner's old tradition of having his assistant coach also be a player. Kewley would continue to provide solid play from the back.

TERRY NICHOLL: Kevin was the best assistant I ever had. Absolutely brilliant.

KEVIN KEWLEY: Being a player-coach could be taxing. I sliced my Achilles one summer and came back and played. Terry was coaching at the time. I practiced for four weeks and I played and Terry told me I was the best player on the field.

The hire was a good one for Dale Ervine. It marked the beginning of his transformation into an offensive threat.

DALE ERVINE: I was always an offensive-type player. However, when you're breaking in to a squad with a lot of veterans it was easier to break in at the back. All the game is in front of you and it was easier to become acclimated to the indoor game. Terry Nicholl asked me if I wanted to move up front when he became coach.

Nicholl would quickly end the Wings road losing streak with a 4-3 overtime win in Los Angeles. This was followed up by an impressive 7-4 win against the Sockers, only the second win in San Diego in Wings history. After the team's 0-13 start on the road under Cooke, Nicholl would earn a 5-10 away record by the end of the season. Though the Wings would make a late-season run at the final playoff spot in the Western division, an April 12th overtime loss to Tacoma would end their playoff hopes. This would give the Wings a 3-9 OT record on the year. It would mark the third year in a row the Wings' season would be ended by Tacoma and the first time in Wings history they would not make the playoffs.[19]

After two straight playoff series losses in 1985-86 and 1986-87 (and a fight on Mother's Day 1987 no less), the Wings' current big rivalry was clearly Steve Zungul's Tacoma Stars. That did not mean the St. Louis Steamers, in what would be that franchise's last season in the MISL, were not out to defeat their former chief rival. Wichita played its last game in St. Louis against the Steamers in a televised game on March 18, 1988. KAKE's Mark Allan and Roy Turner did the commentary before a desolate crowd of 4,746 at the 18,000-seat former Checkerdome, now renamed "St. Louis Arena." [20]

The Steamers built a seemingly insurmountable 6-2 lead against a sluggish Wings side going into the fourth quarter. Whether because of pride, tenacity, or a combination of both, the Wings staged a comeback and with 22 seconds left in regulation Kevin Kewley scored. Mark Allan and Roy Turner shouted in unison "THE WINGS HAVE TIED IT!" Roy Turner then referred to Kewley as "the Steve Zungul of Wichita." He then added, "If I sound happy it's because I am." All Steamer goalkeeper Slobo Ilijevski could do was wipe his brow in shame. [21]

At that 22 second mark the Wings almost managed to do to the Steamers what had occurred nearly seven years prior when the Steamers came back on the Wings during the infamous March 27, 1981 semifinal match. It didn't even matter that the Wings' playoff chances were nearly nil by that point of the season. And, very coincidentally, KAKE happened to show a highlight clip of that very '81 match during the halftime break, a game in which Mark Allen also happened to do play-by-play. "That is still one of the most memorable evenings I've ever spent in my life," he recalled during the break. "I was down on the St. Louis bench, we televised that game and I was wired down on their bench and I'll never forget the pressure and the emotion I felt that particular night right back in this building." [22]

The Wings almost won it. Ken Fogarty of the Steamers scored 11 seconds into overtime on a shot that flew over Matt Kennedy. Nearly two weeks later, on April Fool's Day 1988, the Steamers dragged into the Kansas Coliseum for what would be the final Wings-Steamers matchup. The Steamers won 2-1 on a game-winner by Daryl Doran. In overtime. The bullet-ridden Steamers lost a few battles with the Wings between 1979 and 1988. They did not, however, lose the Nine Year War.

Events at the league level had been a distraction throughout the season. "On February 26, Commissioner Bill Kentling announced the MISL would cease operations in June unless its players' union agreed to a reduction of the salary cap for the following season." After a series of confrontations between the league and the union, the league imposed an April 16th deadline. Five minutes before the deadline, the players union agreed to a new salary cap, saving the league for at least one more year.[23]

Despite the many lowlights, Erik Rasmussen brought many smiles to the faces of Wings fans during the 1987-88 season. His inspired play earned him the MISL's scoring title and its MVP award, both of which were firsts for a Wing. His Wings' record 112 points came from 55 goals and 57 assists.[24] *Just after the early February naming of Terry Nicholl as head coach, Rasmussen scored 13 goals and five assists in one four-game stretch. The scoring race went down to the wire as "The Wizard" bested Preki by two points. He would earn the scoring title with just 4:27 left in the season in San Diego.*[25]

Rasmussen's MVP award was the first for a non-playoff team member in MISL history. "It's a nice feeling. I am a little surprised. They don't usually consider anybody from Wichita," said Rasmussen. "I remember saying at a press conference when we signed him that it was just a matter of time before he would be the MVP. I'm glad it came through so soon. In a year that was so frustrating, it's kind of nice for our fans to know we can take something out of this season," said Turner.[26] *But that wouldn't be the ONLY thing that Wings fans would take with them. On April 8th, 1988, a post-game auction saw Erik Rasmussen's jersey sell for $2,075, which beat the old record of $2,025 from a Kim Roentved kit.*[27]

DALE ERVINE: Erik was not only a great teammate in the locker room, but an unbelievably talented player. I think it was my second year, he was joking around...Erik at one practice bet [Mark Kerlin, Mark Evans, and I that] he'd score more goals than all of us. This must have been 1987-88. Well, it's not a tough bet. My first year I only had 10 goals, playing at the back. The guy was so good on the ball. Some of the goals he scored...he was phenomenal. Guys like him and

Chico...how the heck did we not ever win it all? It's amazing to me. The pieces were there, but it was more individual as opposed to team. We'd get so close but we'd have a breakdown.

The 1987-88 season also provided at least one moment of levity...

TERRY NICHOLL: I got a call one day: "There's a Wings car at the airport." Mickey Thomas left his car there that he'd been loaned. He was flying home that day. I went there, and saw this Honda or Subaru...it was parked in the middle of the lot, not between the lines...close to the entry. All four doors were open, the trunk was open, and the car was still running. He had left the car running....with the doors open.

What was less funny was that the Wings were seriously bleeding cash. Wingathon '88, televised by KWCH Channel 12, helped alleviate some of the pressure. 450 season tickets were sold and $10,000 was raised to help the Wings.[28] Tim Witsman, president of the Wichita Area Chamber of Commerce, devised a plan for the "Sedgwick County Commission, Wichita City Council, and the Wichita/ Sedgwick County Partnership for Growth to underwrite excessive monetary losses by the franchise" for the next season. Additionally, these entities would provide an advisory board to help monitor the team's finances going forward. After losing nearly $700,000 during the 1987-88 season, the Wings could breathe a sigh of relief. They had been saved again.[29]

An Oral History

The Art of Coaching

———

THROUGHOUT THE WINGS' HISTORY IN the MISL, there were only three head coaches: Roy Turner, Charlie Cooke, and Terry Nicholl. Those men only had four assistant coaches: George Ley, Norman Piper, Kevin Kewley, and Kim Roentved. Charlie Cooke aside, five of those men learned much of their craft from Roy Turner.

KEVIN HIMES, RUGRAT, WINGS EMPLOYEE: Roy was very serious. He was definitely what a coach should be. He wasn't there to play around.

AL MILLER, HEAD COACH, DALLAS TORNADO: I watched him blossom as a coach [in Wichita]…There was never any doubt in my mind he had all the tools to be a good coach. Back in those days, professional indoor soccer was "the game." It was a great spectator sport. It avoided all the elements that the Americans didn't like about the outdoor game…as in lots of goals. It was hockey and soccer combined. It was terrific.

NORM HITZGES, RADIO ANNOUNCER, DALLAS TORNADO: I recall Roy coming back with the Wings and his teams reflected him. Soccer is a working sport…and his teams had a very high work rate.

BILL KENTLING, GENERAL MANAGER, WICHITA WINGS, 1980-86:
Roy understood if you had the ball it was hard for the other team to score, so we
played a possession game. A lot of people would refer to as pretty soccer...a lot of
passing, a lot of, in basketball terms, high weaves. He taught a very pretty game, a
precision game. When you get the Jorgen Kristensens of the world who can really
pass the ball, it's very entertaining soccer; as opposed to knock it to the other end
and crash the boards. Roy was like a lot of coaches early in their career...most
good coaches are control freaks, and I don't say that in a pejorative way, but most
coaches like control. They are very comfortable that their approach is the correct
approach. I don't care if you are talking about John Wooden, Gregg Marshall,
or Roy Turner, there is a similarity of all good coaches...it's not a democracy.
Coaching high school kids and grown professionals is a little different. You are
always going to have somebody thinking they can do it a better way, particularly
when we brought in English players, Danish players, Latin American players...
we were a lot like the United Nations and in some cases language was a barrier.
In broad general terms Roy was seen as a very good coach. To achieve what he
achieved on a limited budget is pretty astounding stuff to look back on.

ROY TURNER, HEAD COACH, WICHITA WINGS: One of the keys to
being a successful coach is being involved in every part of the business...Don't
let the fans run the franchise. They have an important role, and the coach has an
important role as well. The fans have to be patient for a little bit. Fans have to
leave it to the coach to determine who plays. There were guys I kept around too
long because the fans were in love with them...

TERRY NICHOLL, HEAD COACH, WICHITA WINGS: Roy went to the
more experienced players and corralled us. He was smart...and then brought in
the young American talent with it...plus the older Euros. I thought the blend
worked really well. I thought we were one of the more handsome teams in the
way we played.

I felt that Roy was always supportive of me. When I first came over it
was a huge adjustment. I was a working up-and-down midfielder in England.
Suddenly you are put into the indoor game and one second you have to crack
a ball into the back of the net, and two seconds later you have to be able to

make a crisp pass on the edge of the box. You had to be an all-around player. I always felt that Roy was great at keeping people confident. That was his best asset.

Roy was very rarely critical in training. He encouraged all the time...that positivity helped...I would room with Erik. Roy would room line members together...so you got even closer. That was another reason why Roy was smart. Sign mature players, keep them confident, and let them express themselves. That's what I got from Roy. Roy was very clever as a coach. The American players had the attitude, the Brits had the finishing talent, Roentved's defense, Jorgen's passing, Erik's goals.

One of the most difficult jobs a coach is charged with is letting players go. The longer they play with the team, the harder it is...

ROY TURNER: It's hard for a coach to tell a guy you don't need him anymore. The time was right. It wasn't fun to tell Jorgen we couldn't use him anymore because his game wasn't what it was at his peak. It's standard procedure...it's what you have to do as a coach. If they didn't accept it, then they'd go try to play somewhere else. Let's be honest, not many players plan for life after soccer. It's never gonna end...and all of a sudden they are out of work. "Shit, what am I gonna do?" But you know in the back of your mind that it's time.

It's even harder when the player or coach has become a good friend...

ROY TURNER: All had to be let go, [but] Kevin, Terry, and Norman still are my good friends. But it wasn't easy to let a guy go. What I was able to do was to bring these guys all together and we had a fantastic team spirit. We all went to battle together. You don't think it will end at that point. It was hard because I was very close to those guys and wanted them to be happy.

The daily and weekly grind of coaching a professional team wasn't easy for coaches or players. Personalities, skill sets, attitudes...these things would differ from man to man. A coach couldn't necessarily have the exact same standard for every player at all times.

ROY TURNER: We all believe in fitness, but with some players, you almost have to have two training sessions: one for the regular guys and one for the "thoroughbreds." A sprinter is more likely to pull a muscle in practice. If you have shooting exercises before the game you leave out some of those guys. Guys knew and understood that you don't push a Jorgen Kristensen on a Friday morning.

A typical week for the team: It depended on what time of year it was. In the preseason you'd do two-a-days. First, you get it all out of their system from the game before. Sometimes you bring them back the next day to do that, and then give them the next day off to recuperate. You'd work on conditioning. You work on power plays and set-pieces. I'd disguise a lot of the stuff I did with games because I wanted to be sure they'd laugh. Sometimes we'd have several little teams and they'd have a great time fighting it out to win. Practices would be one-and-a-half to two hours. It would depend on the time of the week, and what people needed. I had Erik stay after sometimes and practice shooting with his left foot because everyone knew he'd eventually go to this right every time. They gave him the left foot...Tatu would stay behind for 40 minutes after practice hitting balls...

BRUCE HAERTL, WINGS PLAY-BY-PLAY ANNOUNCER, KFH RADIO: One thing Roy was really good at: the fact that we would go on the road, they would practice, and Roy was good at changing things up. Instead of having a soccer practice, we'd play American football. The rule was that none of the Americans could play quarterback. To sit and watch these wonderful athletes, who were so remarkably gifted and talented, try to throw a football, was always something I'll chuckle at. None of them could do it. It was amazing to me that these guys could be so talented...it just goes to show about skill sets. I thought Roy was good at shaking things up like that. I think that guys really appreciated it. I know I did, as a guy on the fringes of the club, reporting on the team.

ROY TURNER: We'd always watch game tapes. We'd share those with the other teams and vice-versa. The hardest part was coming home and still watching game tapes. I always had to be careful what I'd say after the games. If we lost I wouldn't want to let my emotions get the best of me. I'd watch game tape first and then make sure what you are saying is what happened, because your memory isn't always accurate. That's the hard part....watching the bloody game tape after you just lost.

CHARLIE MINSHULL-FORD, EQUIPMENT MANAGER, WICHITA WINGS, 1982-85: He'd take every loss very hard.

ROY TURNER: The prep time didn't really decrease over time. I spent an awful lot of time preparing for the other team, an awful lot of time on what I would say to the guys before the game. I would use some of the veterans to help with speeches during the playoffs.

I remember when we were getting beat by San Diego at home I brought them into a huddle and asked, "Do you all want to get some autograph books and have them sign them? Are you that in awe of them?" Then we went out and beat them. I remember tying St. Louis once with a shorthander...because I wanted to beat them so bad. It was the last game of the '84 semifinals. I had to do something totally different to turn this thing around. All the players were totally with it too. I wasn't scared to take a gamble.

All of Turner's assistant coaches would go on to successful coaching careers in soccer, at various levels of play. And all of them would come up through the Wings organization as players first.

ROY TURNER: I like an assistant coach with a close relationship with the players. I can only get so close as the coach. A player-coach can do that. Norman was very well-respected by the guys.

Kim Roentved was another one of those well-respected player-coaches...

KIM ROENTVED, DEFENDER, WICHITA WINGS: Roy and I have very similar coaching styles: Whatever wins a game, that's what we believed in. Roy's teams always were good at passing and moving...[Player] ego came into play at times when I was coach. Other coaches might jump in the middle of disputes. I only do that if I have to. I let the players sort it out because they will learn more from that usually...Every day I go to practice I learn. I learn every day.

Choice of captain is very important. You have to find the guy that has relationships with all the players and [whom] everyone respects...someone that players will share problems with. And you as the coach have to have a relationship with the captain so he'll share things with you. And he has to be a damn good player so he can lead by example. Roy will tell you this, and it's true, that I was pissed off when I didn't get chosen as captain [in 1985-86]. It's pride. I was then chosen as captain under Charlie Cooke...It can be difficult to decide when is the right time for a new captain to take over. Sometimes it becomes overwhelming for a guy.

It couldn't have been easy to be the coach of the Wichita Wings, and NOT be named "Roy Turner." Following a legendary coach can be a difficult task. And without a doubt, Turner would leave behind a winning legacy and a towering reputation. But Turner's successors would go on to accomplish something just as important: His "coaching tree" of George Ley, Norman Piper, Kevin Kewley, and Kim Roentved (not to mention the many Wings who coached after retirement) would teach and inspire countless players at the youth, collegiate, and professional levels for many years to come. THAT might be Roy Turner's most important legacy.

CHAPTER 21

An Oral History

Old Friends and Old Enemies

———

"That asbestos suit gets really heavy. You get tired getting
up every morning knowing there is a fire to put out."

- BILL KENTLING

TERRY NICHOLL AND THE WINGS *knew that something needed to change in 1988-
89. And so it did. Matt Kennedy, Mark Evans, Gary Stanley, Juan Carlos Molina,
Mickey Thomas, Mickey Kahrovic, Al Smith, Mark Kerlin, David Vanole, and
Dave Hoggan did not return. Longtime Wing Frank Rasmussen would make his
way to the Comets in what would be his final season in the MISL. His long tenure
with the Wings, from 1981 to 1988, produced 135 total points and eight years of
solid play. The Wings would miss his veteran presence.*[1]

*But there was a wrinkle when it came to signing new players. The MISL and their
players' union had agreed to a salary cap over the summer. It saved an overspending
league from collapse, but it also meant that many players would see reduced salaries.
Each team had a $850,000 salary cap and a $750,000 minimum and no player
could make more than $90,000. If average revenues reached $4 million per club,
"the league agreed to raise the salary cap to…$1.12 million." The new salary cap
had real world consequences for every team.*[2]

TERRY NICHOLL, HEAD COACH, WICHITA WINGS: ...One of my first jobs when I went back to Wichita was to cut the salaries. The league had brought back the salary cap. I had to go to them and say, "Oh by the way, I need to reduce your salary." It wasn't a pleasant thing for me to do. When I talked to Roy initially, I said, "I've got to establish myself as the coach...why wouldn't I be the one to tell them?" It would make it clear I was coming back as the manager, and not a player. It was a tough thing to do...Some of the cuts we had to make made a fairly comfortable life into more of a struggle. I was all about morale.

Despite the tightening of the purse strings, there were player additions that brought great joy to the members of the Orange Army...

ANDY CHAPMAN, FORWARD, WICHITA WINGS: Each year there were new salary caps coming into play. The money we were getting was starting to dwindle. Terry Nicholl called me during the summer of 1988. He [had come] back to Wichita. I was going to move [my wife] Patti, who was pregnant with [our son] Dillon, back to Detroit and purchased a house for Patti to move into. And [Jimmy Ryan's wife] Janie Ryan came over and lived with Patti to help her out with [our daughter] Lily and Dillon. I went back to Wichita in September of 1988 and ended up playing there for two seasons.

"When I left here, I never thought it would be the last time I played here...I loved playing in Baltimore. I had a wonderful time there. But it's not the same as putting on a Wichita jersey..." Chapman told The Eagle. *"Andy is excellent at making himself available. Target men are much sought after in our league and Andy is one of the best at it. Since he left us, the league has improved dramatically and Andy has become an all-around player," said Wings' president Roy Turner. Terry Nicholl was excited to have him back: "Andy will give us a little bit different picture. Erik likes to get the ball after a buildup. Andy likes to be involved in the buildup."*[3]

TERRY NICHOLL: Andy Chapman didn't look like Andy Chapman in a different uniform.

DALE ERVINE, MIDFIELDER, WICHITA WINGS: Andy [Chapman] was obviously a very good player. I remember watching him in college (like I said, I used to go to all the Lazer games.) As a player, Andy was always moving, always knew what spot to get into. If shots were coming he was always…at the far post. Andy loved the game, he really enjoyed playing. I learned a lot from watching him. I think there a few years where he and I always rotated. He was very positive, he was good in the locker room with his joking around and his camaraderie…As you go through a career like that, you end up spending a lot of time with these guys. Back then we played 48 games or 52 games. Andy would always keep the locker room loose, always a good laugh. He loved Wichita; he had a passion for the game as well.

But Chapman wasn't the only fan favorite to return. Chico Borja would return to Wichita from his adventure in Los Angeles. His deal with the Lazers, $500,000 over three years, had been a fantastic one.[4] Ironically, the new salary cap made his return possible.

TERRY NICHOLL: It enabled us to get Chico back. He'd kept his house here and made fantastic money in LA. He would have earned an absolute fortune in LA. But then the salary cap was $90,000 for one player, so he decided to come back. But for Chico, he was going to earn the top salary anyway, but the salary meant more here than it would have in LA.

CHICO BORJA, MIDFIELDER, WICHITA WINGS: Terry Nicholl brought me back. LA promised me a three-year contract and when they couldn't do it, they had to trade me…When Terry called I came home.

"The final piece of the offensive puzzle is put together. I think it gives us on paper one of the most potent offenses in the league," said Wings coach Terry Nicholl. "I never thought I would be able to get Chico back. I think Andy Chapman with Chico is the best combination possible. We'll see if it works on the field as well as we think it works on paper. Chico is great at picking the ball up deeper and running at the defense. I don't think we ever counterattacked last year. It's really exciting for the fans," Nicholl continued.[5]

More veteran leadership came in the form of defender Victor Moreland. The 31-year-old former Northern Ireland national team member came to the Wings

*by way of the Dallas Sidekicks, whom he captained to the 1987 MISL champion-
ship. "Whether we give him the captain's band or not, he will be a leader for us,"
said Coach Terry Nicholl. "I like to express an opinion on the field. I like to help
younger players. When I came into the game, the older players helped me. I'm not
always right, but I do my best for my team and the players," Moreland told* The
Eagle.[6] *Moreland would be stalwart on defense that season. His 82 blocks led the
team...not that he was a slouch on offense. He would score eight goals and make
nine assists as well. His three years with the Wings would be productive ones, as
he continued his excellent defensive effort in 1989-90, blocking 86 shots.*[7]

LARRY INLOW, DEFENDER, WICHITA WINGS: Victor Moreland was
one of the meanest defenders, but nicest guys.

TERRY NICHOLL: Victor Moreland would light a cigarette in the showers. He
didn't think I would be able to smell it if he ran the showers. He'd have a light
before the game. Then, he'd go out and win every tackle. These were old school
habits.

[One time] we won in Dallas, where Victor used to play. I told the lads I
wasn't setting a curfew. "The only curfew is the bus is leaving at 9:00 am for
the airport in the morning...does everybody hear that?" Three players, Victor
and Erik and someone else missed the bus and the plane. "You left me and Erik
behind!" [Victor] said.

*Joining Moreland from that Dallas championship team was Perry Van der Beck.
With 23 caps for the US National Team, Van der Beck's ability couldn't be denied.
He started playing professionally at the age of 19, and thus, even with 10 years of
experience, Van der Beck was only 29-years-old.*[8] *He would play all 48 games that
year, contributing on both offense and defense. His value was such that he continued with the Wings for another three seasons after 1988-89, ending up fifth on the
Wings' all-time blocks list.*[9]

TERRY NICHOLL: Perry Van der Beck...PVDB...he was one of the fittest lads
I ever played with. One time, they tested our lads for oxygen efficiency. They
couldn't get [Perry's] heart up to a place where he would go into deficiency. He

was too fit to get where he would almost pass out. He was one of the fittest people they ever tested.

I told Victor Moreland we were gonna run up and down a hill I found. We put a heart monitor on Perry. Victor's heart was going to 225, and we couldn't get Perry's [heart] past 170. He was that fit...or Victor wasn't that fit....one of the two. He used to complain about Victor's smoking..."I'm gonna get second-hand smoke in that shower!" [he'd say]. Erik liked to go in there [to smoke] sometimes too.

One of the Wings' best pickups in 1988-89 was a 30-year-old Uruguayan named Chico Moreira. According to The Eagle's *Mal Elliott, the defender was a "strong and deadly tackler. Like an animal stalking his prey, Moreira draws a bead on streaking players, stands his ground and at the last moment plucks the ball away." Terry Nicholl agreed: "When a player takes his eyes off the ball to see where he's going, Chico moves in and takes the ball. There's an art to it. It's a gift." Nicholl also saw Moreira's value going forward on offense. "He's hard to play high pressure against. The faster you go into him, the faster he'll dance around you."[10]*

Moreira would prove that there wasn't just one top-notch Chico in town. He would be named the Wings' MVP at the end of the year, and would also be chosen for the All-MISL Second Team.[11] His 77 blocks were second only behind Victor Moreland. Like Van der Beck, he would spend three years with the Wings. He would set the Wings all-time record for most blocks in a season, with 92 in 1990-91.[12]

ROY TURNER, PRESIDENT AND GM, WICHITA WINGS: As part of Chico Moreira's contract negotiations, his wife went on a hunger strike because the contract offers weren't good enough. It was in the paper and everything... The wives always think their husbands are a lot better than they are. So they sometimes tell people in the community that they are the best and deserve more playing time, etc. In a community this size, this can cause difficulties. Because their husbands were a big deal in the community; when they spoke, people listened. But it wasn't always a very educated speech. It's natural...they were sticking up for their husbands. And if their husbands weren't playing, "Roy Turner doesn't know what he's doing." But that's normal for any sport.

To avoid uncomfortable situations, Turner's wife, Tamara Pryor, usually didn't socialize with the players' wives.

DR. TAMARA PRYOR, CLINICAL PSYCHOLOGIST: I learned early on that if Roy wasn't playing one of the players as much as [the player] or wife thought he should play, they'd be inclined to try to get to Roy through me.

Tom "Tommy" Soehn was one of several rookies to join the Wings that season. Other than one season in Denver, Soehn would play for the Wings through 1996. His 47 games were productive, earning him talk of MISL Rookie of the Year honors. Though he didn't win the award, he did make 32 blocks, the sixth highest total on the team. His career would take off the next season, when he reached 80 blocks. By the end of his career, he would have the third highest block total in Wings history, behind only Kim Roentved and Terry Rowe.[13] After his playing days were over, Soehn would go on to a very successful coaching career in Major League Soccer (MLS).

The Wing's number one draft choice that year, Roger Chavez, would be replaced in November by Yugoslavian sensation Goran Hunjak. A friend of Ziggy Zigante, the midfielder had starred in the second division Yugoslavian league until coming to America. "Goran Hunjak is very good one-on-one and he can get a lot of shots off. He is creative and a good passer," said Terry Nicholl.[14] Hunjak would spend four seasons with the Wings and later play for two different teams in MLS, including the Kansas City Wizards.

LARRY INLOW: Hunjak was such a silky player. He was so good.

Joey Kirk and Daryl Green were the other two rookies on the squad, playing 30 and 26 games respectively. The only other new player was a second goalkeeper with eight years of MISL experience named Cris Vaccaro. An MISL All-Star the previous year with the Chicago Sting, Vaccaro earned the seldom-given praise of team owner Lee J. Stern, "...He was one of our outstanding players and I don't give that out too lightly. There isn't anybody else I could say that about..."[14]

Vaccaro would be tested early. Zigante would miss the first 14 games of the season, forcing Vaccaro to take the leading role. He would thrive in goal that year, accumulating a 22-14 record and 4.02 GAA. Zigante would never recover his leading role that season, spending less than a quarter of the time in goal that Vaccaro did. Ziggy's 1-9 record was a major disappointment. Vaccaro's 61.1% winning percentage in 1988-89 would be the best in Wings' history.[15]

Almost as important as his play on the field was Vaccaro's sense of style. "His uniforms are a dazzling array of brilliant stripes, zig-zags and geometric designs resembling patterns in a kaleidoscope," wrote Mal Elliott. "He and his wife Maureen do the designing and a local seamstress puts it all together," Elliott continued. Vaccaro was proud of his fashion sense: "I have different color shoes. I haven't popped those out yet. I may come out with a pair of red shoes that match a shirt. You gotta match colors. You can't go out there unfashionable. I was just bored with the styles that were out. I wanted to start something new. I'm not trying to be a showoff...Looking good is half the battle. That's my motto."[16]

The MISL that these players encountered in 1988-89 was a far cry from the heady days of the early '80s. The league seemed to be teetering on the edge of collapse. During the summer of 1988, four teams folded: the Chicago Sting, the Minnesota Strikers, Cleveland Force, and shockingly, the Wings' old nemesis, the St. Louis Steamers. Only seven teams remained in the league. If it hadn't been for the salary cap, that number might have been zero.[17]

TERRY NICHOLL: The league started to deteriorate. The storied franchises started to waver. Some of the teams that had been there all along started to wobble. I think we were ahead of hockey [at one point]. Then hockey became more popular. But I think the league lost its way.

In many ways, the 1988-89 Wings had finally fulfilled the promise that Roy Turner and the MISL had made during the early years of the Wings: that American players would eventually rise to prominence. Chico Borja, Dale Ervine, Mike Fox, Cris Vaccaro, Perry Van der Beck, Jean Willrich, and Tommy Soehn all played vital roles that season. Borja was a star, and Ervine was on his way to becoming one.

DALE ERVINE: I moved into midfield my third year, which was a lot more natural for me...as opposed to being at the back. When Terry put me at midfield it was more natural because I knew I had two guys behind me, [as opposed] to playing defensively and knowing I only had one guy [my defensive partner] behind me. And that year went very well...I had 26 goals and that was pretty much the start of knowing that I can be consistent. That's the one thing I always wanted to be. I wanted them to know what you were going to get with Dale. He may not play his best game all of the time but effort should never be questioned and you know the passion is going to be there. And as the scoring came, you start realizing that you can do this consistently. The last game is over; the next game's the most important you're going to play. It just started evolving.

The 9,686 home-opening sellout saw the Wings face the Comets, and their old friends, Kim Roentved and Frank Rasmussen. It was a very physical game, with Roentved and Chico Borja battling throughout. Both Frank Rasmussen and Roentved did two minutes in the penalty box, for pushing and tripping, respectively. "I know how dangerous Chico is and he knows I'm an aggressive player. I know he understands. But the refs never understand," said Roentved. "We go at each other. It's great. We kick each other and we both go all out," replied Borja. Roentved had two goals while Borja had one goal and an assist in a Wings' victory.[18]

But in a weird turn of events, the Wings, forever hard to beat at home, suddenly found themselves struggling at the Kansas Coliseum. January saw a four-game home losing streak. That month ended with two straight overtime losses, with a third to follow a few days later.[19] These OT losses were sandwiched between an exhibition game win against Lokomotiv Moscow; the Wings' second game against a Soviet team in two years. This visit reflected the lessening tension brought on by Glasnost, especially compared to the last visit. "We had to watch everything we said to them. It's not that way this time. And there are no KGB around. If they are, they're in disguise," said team president and GM Roy Turner.[20]

The Wings struggled to escape mediocrity throughout the season, and stood on the threshold of "not very good" when they hit 16-22 on March 17th. But various individuals kept pulling the Wings back on track. Mike Stankovic became the hottest power-play shooter in the league. The MISL had moved the kick further back, and everyone but Stankovic was struggling. As of January 5th, 1989, he was shooting 60% while the rest of the league sat at 35%.[21]

The team's penalty killing unit was saving the day as well. Terry Rowe, Kevin Kewley, Chico Moreira, Dale Ervine, Perry Van der Beck, Mike Fox, and Tom Soehn, in various combinations, broke a Wings record with 16 straight penalty-killings as of January 11th. Terry Rowe used his quickness to neutralize opposing players, while Kewley was the brains of the unit. Together with the Wings' power-play squad and penalty-shots, the Wings' earned a 25-7 advantage in special situations up to that point in the season.[22]

For Terry Nicholl, learning on-the-job was the only thing he could do. "I'm still maybe watching the game too much as a player. I get caught up in it more emotionally..." said Nicholl. The Eagle's Fred Mann opined on the Wings' struggles: "When a team doesn't play up to the level expected of it, the head coach is the first place you look. It's also the first place Nicholl looks. He is intensely introspective, perhaps to a fault. But this team should not be five games under .500 right now, fighting to make the playoffs, and he knows it...This was a team that had everything, all the ingredients, a team that not only should survive in the MISL, but prosper. Instead, the Wings have been frustrating and erratic, often terrific and terrible in the same game..."[23] *But Nicholl was learning. In particular, he was figuring out what players played well together...*

TERRY NICHOLL: When I was coaching I'd like to get linkups. Dale Ervine and Chico Borja really, really played together well. Dale was the working forward, and Chico was the spark plug. They were brilliant....Chico and Erik didn't play as well together. There was only one ball. If you could have devised a game with two balls, it would have been fantastic.

It wasn't a great year for all the Wings. Andy Chapman's return was marred by an ankle injury that required surgery. It would sideline him for the second half of the season, although he would return for part of the playoffs.

ANDY CHAPMAN: I had a bad injury in January of that season. I had started off well and then I popped a tendon in Dallas. Basically, they found two guys who could perform the surgery [in the whole country] and one was in Detroit. I did the rehab, and they told me I wouldn't play for six months. But I ended up playing three months to the day after I had surgery...I came back too soon.

For MISL commissioner and former Wings' general manager Bill Kentling, 1988-89 would be his last season involved with indoor soccer. On March 14th, 1989, Kentling announced that after his contract expired on May 31st, he would no longer continue as MISL commissioner. Mal Elliott of The Eagle *reported that "Kentling and Bill Oliver, Wichita lawyer and the Wings' managing general partner, agreed that the commissioner's biggest problem is being the disciplinarian over people who are his employers." Kentling said it best: "It's hard to fine an owner on Monday and then on Tuesday ask him to help with a project."* [24]

"...I think the first unhappiness for Bill was the result of the fines he had to levy against Los Angeles and Tacoma," said Oliver. In prior seasons, Kentling had fined the Lazers for player tampering and the Stars for violating the salary cap. "I don't think we would have a league if it weren't for Bill and the work he did last summer," commented Oliver. Roy Turner, who worked with Kentling for six seasons, summed up his feelings: "I'm sad. I'm proud of all he's accomplished in nine years. And whatever he does, I'm sure he's going to call me after every Wings game to find out the score and who scored...I think this league has taken its toll on people in the last three of four years. I think it's taken its toll on Bill, but he has fulfilled his contract. He hasn't said it to me, but if he is in any way burned out, I can understand why. He made some decisions for the benefit of the league that were not popular decisions. He established that he wasn't in a popularity poll." [25]

BILL KENTLING, MISL COMMISSIONER, 1986-89: I was commissioner for three seasons. I had signed a three-year contract. About six months before the contract expired, I announced to the Board of Directors that I wouldn't be available for any more. After nine years I'd had enough and wanted out. What you learn is that this is a very long relay marathon and I carried the baton nine years, which is enough...That asbestos suit gets really heavy. You get tired getting up every morning knowing there is a fire to put out.

The Wings season had been disappointing. They hadn't had a winning re-cord since January. And it didn't help that they struggled to win close games: they would finish the season 3-7 in overtime games. When midnight struck on March 25th, 1989, the Wings were six games under .500 and below the playoff threshold. With only three weeks to go in the season, the Wings needed to make a move. They would do just that, starting their winning streak against the Comets and going on to beat Baltimore, Tacoma, San Diego, Los Angeles, and the Comets again to win six of their final eight games. It was enough to secure the fifth and final playoff spot.[26]

The Wings would face Tacoma in the playoffs for the third straight time, not count-ing the previous year's playoff absence. The first two games were in Tacoma, which didn't bode well for the Wings. But out of the blue, the Wings became road war-riors. Mike Stankovic helped shut out Preki, Tacoma's star midfielder, on his way to two goals in a 4-1 game one victory.[27] *The next day the Wings earned their second straight road playoff victory 7-4. Mike Stankovic, Erik Rasmussen, Victor Moreland, Terry Rowe, and Perry Van der Beck all scored. Chico Borja added two goals of his own and made one assist. But he wasn't happy yet. "I'm not smiling. And I'm not going to smile until it's all over. We thought we had won it two years ago and we didn't," he told* The Eagle.[28]

Though the Wings would uncharacteristically lose game three at home, they would win the series 3-1 with a 6-2 victory in game four. Erik Rasmussen scored four goals in their triumph. "When Erik is finishing like that, there's not much you can do. They have a good chance of winning it. I predict them and San Diego in the final," said Tacoma defender Neil Megson. "They are the toughest team I ever played against. I have to outsmart them, sneak around them and use a toe instead of an elbow. I was able to do that a couple of times and find Erik. My hat is off to Erik. All I have to do is get it to him and he'll finish. He can finish a tennis ball," said Chico Borja. Mal Elliott described the scene in the locker room afterwards: "... [Borja] sat in the dressing room ignoring a bottle of champagne, his head drooping to his chest. He did not appear elated. 'I don't feel anything right now,' said Borja. 'I'm so exhausted.'" [29]

It was the first time the Wings had beat Tacoma in a playoff series, and the first time since 1983-84 that the Wings had advanced to the semifinals. Since 1985, Tacoma had become the new "Steamers": the team that the Wings couldn't quite ever beat in the playoffs. But just like in 1983, the Wings had finally thrown that monkey off their back. Good riddance.

The Wings would play Kenny Cooper's Baltimore Blast squad in the semifinal series. On May 13th, the Wings took the pitch in Baltimore for game one. It was a rough-and-tumble match that ended with the Wings "losing their cool," as The Eagle's *Fred Mann put it. In the fourth quarter, with the Wings up by one goal, David Byrne shoved Perry Van der Beck into the boards, drawing a foul. He then shoved Van der Beck to the ground. It seemed that the game might be over at that point. However, several Wings players, including backup keeper Ziggy Zigante, left the bench and joined the fray. Shockingly, no two minute penalty against Byrne was called. Instead, the Wings would lose a man due to leaving the bench, get scored on, and end up losing 5-4 in overtime. The game-winner? Courtesy of David Byrne.* [30]

The other takeaway from that first game of the series was that Chico Borja was enemy number one in Baltimore, Maryland. Borja tripped Tim Wittman, causing him to fly into the turf and hurt his ankle bad enough that he was done for the entire series. Nobody in Baltimore would forget. "It was painted in the media as the biggest affront to Baltimore since the attack of Fort McHenry," said Fred Mann. In game two, Borja was "booed every time he touched the ball..." [31] *The Wings lost that game as well, this time 6-4. After a third straight loss, this time in Wichita, the Wings were on the ropes. They were down 3-0 in a best-of-seven series.*

But Borja would not be deterred by the angry Baltimore media, players, and fans. In game four, again in Wichita, he went out and scored a hat trick, staving off defeat for at least one more game. [32] *Down 3-1 in the series, game five would be the last in Wichita. The Wings would have to win at home and then twice in*

Baltimore to advance to the MISL finals. Thanks to Erik Rasmussen and Terry Rowe, they would accomplish that first task. Erik Rasmussen scored two goals in the Wings 7-5 victory. "One name. Erik. What else can you ask him to do and how many times can you ask him to do it?" said Chico Borja. Terry Rowe assisted on one of Rasmussen's goals, and scored one of his own. "Can you remember a game when Terry Rowe didn't do a job? I can't. He's always in there, playing a super game, giving me everything he's got," said Terry Nicholl.[33]

As described in the Wings 20th Anniversary Yearbook, *the Rasmussen goal assisted on by Terry Rowe was particularly impressive: "...Erik took a pass from Terry Rowe, and once again proceeded to dribble through the entire opposing team. Every Baltimore player had at least one chance at taking the ball away from him, but they all failed. Finally, after he faked out Ken Fogarty so bad that he could do nothing but fall straight down, Rasmussen shot it into the corner past Scott Manning for an easy goal..."*[34]

And then it was all over. Game six in Baltimore was an 11-1 blowout. The Wings were simply too exhausted to continue. "You can have all the heart you want, but you only have two lungs. We needed an extra lung. Two are not enough. We came from so far down the last month...I've never given so much of my life to anything - except maybe my marriage. I think our bodies were saying, when we got down, 'Hey, you're too tired for this,'" explained Chico Borja. "They just outplayed us. We were never really in this game. They deserved to win," said Erik Rasmussen.[35]

But what a year it had been for Chico Borja. He led the Wings in scoring during the Baltimore series. His 53 assists tied with Preki for first in the league, resulting in them sharing the MISL's Pass Master award. He came in second in total points, with 87.[36] *It was good to have him back in Wichita. Soon, the Orange Army would have to re-learn the lesson that it was important to treasure great players...because they wouldn't be around forever.*

On September 11th, 1989, Erik Rasmussen announced that he would depart Wichita to return to Denmark to play outdoors for Brondby in the top Danish league. His move was also calculated to make it possible for him to join the

Danish national team. "It has a little bit to do with the salary cap but that's not the main thing. I am 28 years old and this is my last chance to make a career outdoors," said Rasmussen. According to The Eagle, *Rasmussen signed a three-year deal that would pay him more than the MISL maximum of $90,000 per year.*[37]

Rasmussen was positively stellar in his five years as a Wing: 246 goals, 423 total points, 57 power-play goals, 28 hat tricks, and 29 game-winners. Mal Elliott described his play as so good that it "mesmerized his own teammates." "Unfortunately, sometimes they just stood and admired," added Terry Nicholl. "I love [indoor] soccer. I like the players on the team and I was happy with Terry as coach. It will be hard to give up. But at the same time, I have to go on with my career," said Rasmussen. Though "The Wizard" would eventually return to play in Wichita during the late 1990s, it would be the end of his MISL career. He was a special player, and no Wing before or since had his kind of skill with the ball.[38]

ROY TURNER: Eventually after the 1988-89 season [Erik Rasmussen] told me that he wanted to go back and play in Denmark. I sold him for an awful lot of money. He was our highest sale ever. I used that money to pay bills.

DALE ERVINE: Chico was a lot more north/south, whereas Erik would go north/south, then east/west, turn your ankle on ya, and walk it into the net. He scored some goals that were phenomenal. There were very few players that got a ball and guys were afraid to come near them...Erik was one of them. People were afraid to go near him. It's like Messi now. "If I get too close, I'm done." But that didn't always work either, because he still beat them. He deserved that [1988 MVP award]. Every game you could count on him.

An Oral History

Healers, Helpers, and Haulers

———

You can't run a major *league professional soccer team without a staff. Owners, front office staff, equipment managers, trainers, announcers, doctors...plus all the Coliseum employees. It was a team effort. And those folks were part of the team as well. Al Green, Wayne Fuller, and Karl Glick all served the role of trainer over the course of the MISL years; helping Wings prepare their bodies for the rigorous training and game performances. Danny Bunker, Chris Knapp, Charlie Minshull-Ford, Kelly Little, Wayne Fuller, and Mike Budnowski all served as equipment manager at various times from 1979 to 1992; lugging uniforms and soccer balls this way and that...and preparing the Coliseum for game play.*

ROY TURNER, HEAD COACH, PRESIDENT AND GM, WICHITA WINGS: Our trainer Al Green was a real character. They called him "Stoplight" because he was so red.

CHARLIE MINSHULL-FORD, EQUIPMENT MANAGER, WICHITA WINGS, 1982-85: Jorgen would use that nickname...[Al] had a lot of wit and humor.

ANDY CHAPMAN, FORWARD, WICHITA WINGS: There was Al Green...
.I used to call him Green Al. Al was friggin' brilliant. I can picture his face in my brain. He was like a brother to every player...he had a different relationship with

[each of us]. As in all families, there were times when [the players] didn't get along...because of what happened on the field or someone is not working hard enough...and then you'd go and bitch to Al Green about it...because you saw him every morning. He was stretching somebody...he was taking care of them. He knew all the players intimately.

When soccer players, some of them in their thirties, played as many as 56 games in a season, there were bound to be physical challenges. Dr. Alan Bonebrake served as team chiropractor over much of Wings history. He was succeeded by Dr. Ron Cody. When Wings broke, the team doctors were there to fix them. Dr. Art Fromm and Dr. Charles Henning filled the role during the first two seasons. Henning would continue on throughout the entire MISL era, save the final season. In the third season Fromm would be replaced by Dr. George Tiller. Though Tiller would become well-known for other reasons, to the Wings, he was their general practitioner. Henning filled the role of orthopedic surgeon and sports medicine specialist. During the 1991-92 season, Dr. Ken Jansson and Dr. Joseph Sack took over as team doctors.

KEVIN KEWLEY, DEFENDER, WICHITA WINGS: Dr. Henning was a fantastic guy. He always would push you away from surgery. He was more about stretching and stuff like that. He'd see us tackling and tell us to stop because of the wear and tear on our Achilles...which we couldn't do. He was all about preventing injuries, not curing them. The trainer at the time said Henning was the best in the country when it came to knee surgery...he said he'd stand in line to have him do the surgery.

BILL KENTLING, GENERAL MANAGER, WICHITA WINGS, 1980-86: Henning, the orthopedic guy, and Tiller, the family practitioner, and their staffs... we couldn't have kept our team on the field without those two. They donated their time. One of them was at every game and sometimes both were there. Our team was not 22 years old...we had some veterans. Between those two they kept them healthy for the entire season. They were part of our success. If Henning saw you walk to your car, he'd stop you and have you stretch [laughs]. The thing I remember with the most pride: we weren't like a lot of leagues...we didn't do the things "necessary" to keep a player on the field, which is pretty rare now.

ANDY CHAPMAN: The older you get, it becomes even more [clear] how special that time was, and how special that group was, and how special it was being there. That includes everyone...not just the players, but the Virginia Creamers, the Bill Kentlings, the Frank Carneys, the [team] doctors...I remember George Tiller, who got shot...the other doctor, Chuck Henning. I had a great relationship with him. I used to keep the locker room light and breezy. [Henning] was so reserved... he used to walk in [the locker room], and my standard line was, instead of HIM asking everybody else how they felt, I used to say, "Hey doc, are you feeling better?" [laughs] He would always say, "Yes." He had not been sick, but I'd always ask, "Are you feeling better?" He never once said, "What are you talking about, Andy?" He just went along with it. When I heard he passed away [Chapman pauses]...he's a piece of your family.

CHARLIE MINSHULL-FORD: Dr. Tiller would always have us over to his pool in the summer.

The Wings family was huge. The players weren't just accessible to the fans, but to the Coliseum employees.

TERRY NICHOLL, PLAYER AND COACH, WICHITA WINGS: I remember the workers who used to clean up the Kansas Coliseum. They'd yell down during practice and say, "When are you gonna score, Nicholls?!?" [laughs]

ANDY CHAPMAN: Then you had Steve Shaad, Virginia Creamer, the security guards at the Coliseum, you got to see them all the time...J.B. Johnson...just incredible.

CHAPTER 22

An Oral History

Stayin' Alive

___

"In September of '89 I drove back [from Detroit]
knowing it was my last season in Wichita. I entered the
'80s in Wichita and exited the '80s in Wichita."

— ANDY CHAPMAN

THE 1989-90 SEASON WAS HERE...and "The Wizard" was gone. In order to help account for the loss of scoring, the Wings would move Dale Ervine up to the forward position. He would deliver up front, almost doubling his scoring output from the previous year. In fact, he would score twice as many goals as any other Wing. The San Diego Sockers tried to steal Ervine away, but the Wings matched their offer. They knew that he would be a key component to a winning team. "We're delighted to have Dale back. He had a great season last year and we feel that Dale linking up with Chico Borja can once more be a threat in the league," said Coach Terry Nicholl.[1]

DALE ERVINE, FORWARD, WICHITA WINGS: In my fourth year [Terry] moved me up [to forward] and I went from 26 goals to 48 goals...My relationship with Chico [Borja] was obviously very good. I was fortunate...Terry came up to me [during the] preseason and said, "Dale, why don't you try playing up front."

And obviously that was so much more natural for me than playing at the back and then having Chico playing behind me. And Chico's vision and his skill and his understanding of the game...You know, his mind is thinking way ahead of other players. So after a few trainings I'm like: if I get Chico the ball he gets it back to me. And he didn't mind getting [the ball] back to me because I was putting them in. So it was making him feel good because even though Chico could create his own goals, don't get me wrong, he enjoyed setting people up. He really enjoyed that part of the game. For me it was really a blessing to be able to play with somebody like Chico. When he would get the ball I would know what he was going to do as [soon as] he knew what he was going to do. We had a very good connection and it just evolved. I was finishing for him and that gave me confidence. We just had a really good relationship for several years. Even off the field Chico was just a good guy...

Dale Ervine would show his worth immediately, scoring two hat tricks in pre-season games. "I'm playing somewhere that's instinctive. The offensive midfielder and forward are similar. It's just that you're getting more offensive opportunities," said Ervine.[2]

On the defensive end, the Wings would yet again see a revolving door at the goalkeeper position. Cris Vaccaro would file a contract grievance against the Wings when they matched Tacoma's $65,000 salary offer, but, according to Vaccaro, didn't agree to the camp and endorsement deals he wanted. Essentially, it was a disagreement over the details of the contract paperwork. The MISL ruled against the Wings and Vaccaro left for Tacoma in September of 1989. The dispute left bad blood between the Wings and Alan Hinton's Stars. Everyone was looking forward to the October 28th opening game between the two squads. "Oh goodness. That's going to be fun," Vaccaro told The Eagle.[3]

The Wings took a look at a quartet of new goalies that year: Winston Dubose and Manny Sanchez made a handful of appearance, but it was Ron Fearon and Kris Peat who would be the top two men in goal, in that order. "Fearless" Fearon, an Englishman, had no indoor experience, but would be the MISL's number one keeper by December. "I think his instincts must be above almost anybody who has come into the league. We could have an all-star in February that has just come into this league. Has it ever been done before?" asked Wings president Roy Turner. "I think some keepers would have trouble indoors because of the style. Every good goalkeeper can make saves. But you've got to be that much more alert and good at distributing the ball and good with your feet. And I think you've got to have good vision," said Fearon.[4] Fearon would get the Wings their opening day "revenge victory" over Cris Vaccaro and the Tacoma Stars in front of 8,262 Wings fans.[5] Fearon would play in 33 of the Wings 52 games that year, going 18-14 with an impressive 3.86 GAA.[6]

TERRY NICHOLL, HEAD COACH, WICHITA WINGS: I got Ron Fearon over to play when I was coach. I remember the Friday before his debut, I was teaching him the boards, and how our opponent would use them. He was gonna play in front of 9,500 people later that night. "Bloody hell, this will be interesting," [I thought]. But he went out and played very well.

Behind Ron Fearon was a young goalkeeper named Kris Peat. Peat would come to prominence in the years to come, but in the 1989-90 season he took a backseat to Fearon. Peat would accumulate an 8-9 record in 17 games that year.[7]

The MISL landscape would change as the LA Lazers ceased to exist and the St. Louis Storm and Cleveland Crunch took their place. Now at eight teams, the league returned to a two-division structure; with the Wings in the East alongside Baltimore, Kansas City, and Cleveland. In order to make a playoff run against this lineup of teams, the Wings would recruit new talent. After a four year absence, defender Gregg Willin returned to the Wings. This time, he would be a bigger offensive contributor, adding 14 goals and 14 assists to his 54 blocks. His value would skyrocket when ace defender Chico Moreira suffered a knee injury in December. Moreira wouldn't return till March, making his season a frustratingly short 28 games.[8]

A pair of Englishmen named Ian Fairbrother and Peter Ward came to the Wings that season. Ward was a highly heralded forward who had starred for both the

Cleveland Force and the Tacoma Stars. The previous year, he had led the MISL in power play goals with 12, and accumulated 60 total points. But in Wichita, he would struggle to find the goal.[9]

A healthy Andy Chapman played in all 52 games that year. With 21 goals and 24 assists, he would be the third highest point scorer behind Ervine and Borja.[10] Chapman celebrated his 400th MISL appearance in November with a bicycle kick goal against the San Diego Sockers in a winning 4-2 effort.[11] At the beginning of the season, Chapman would be selected to join the Wings' All-Decade Team. Chapman would make the second team, joining Cris Vaccaro, Mike Stankovic, Kevin Kewley, Mickey Thomas and Dale Ervine. The first team squad included Mike Dowler in goal, alongside Terry Rowe, Kim Roentved, Chico Borja, Jorgen Kristensen, and Erik Rasmussen.[12] Not a bad lot. Sadly, it would be Chapman's swan song.

ANDY CHAPMAN, FORWARD, WICHITA WINGS: In September of '89 I drove back [from Detroit] knowing it was my last season in Wichita. I entered the '80s in Wichita and exited the '80s in Wichita.

In general, offensive success eluded the 1989-90 Wings. Rasmussen was gone, and Mike Stankovic and Peter Ward combined for a total of only six goals. The team was averaging less than four goals per game.[13] In January of 1990, in an attempt to solve their scoring woes, the Wings traded Stankovic and Ward to Baltimore for noted Wings' nemesis, midfielder David Byrne, and the one-named Yugoslavian forward Keder. The famously red-shoed Byrne was taken by surprise by the trade, but would adjust. Keder looked forward to playing with one Wing in particular: "Is beautiful for me [that] I will play with Chico Borja and David Byrne, probably the best players in this league..."[14]

As the Wings 20th Anniversary Yearbook *noted, "the move paid huge dividends for Wichita. Keder would score nine goals late in the year, and was a constant nuisance to the opposition. Byrne, who had been known as a Wing-killer during his years in Minnesota and Baltimore, produced 19 goals and 16 assists in 28 games... Both players ranked among the team's top playoff scorers."[15]*

As Roy Turner told The Eagle, *it was likely the biggest trade in Wings history. "You could call it a blockbuster trade," said Baltimore coach Kenny Cooper, longtime pal of Turner. The deal involved salaries totaling over $300,000, evenly distributed between the two teams. "I know for sure David Byrne will help Wichita," Cooper added. Turner told* The Eagle *that the deal took shape after Stankovic asked to be traded following a loss of playing time.*[16]

Byrne would score one of the more unusual goals of the season. On February 18th, against the Cleveland Crunch, in the second of his three goals that evening, Byrne would take a page from the Old Testament. "Standing on either side of the ball were Cleveland goalkeeper P.J. Johns and defender Bernie James. Each thought the other would control the ball and they parted for Byrne much the same way that the Red Sea parted for Moses," wrote Mal Elliott. It was a sight to behold. "In my 12 years in this league, I've never seen a goal scored like that," said Crunch coach Kai Haaskivi.[17]

Chico Borja, Dale Ervine, Chico Moreira, and Ron Fearon would be rewarded with a trip to the All-Star game in 1989-90. But with the Wings hovering around .500 all year long, the individual talent wasn't translating to group success...that is, unless you counted the San Diego Sockers. The Wings would rack up a seven game win streak against their longtime foe. It finally ended in April after starting the previous season.[18]

DALE ERVINE: I look back on my fourth year and we were always right around .500. It always seemed we had more talent than what our record actually showed. We were never an easy team to play against. I don't think teams would say, "Oh great, we get to play Wichita tonight!"

The Eagle's Fred Mann believed that the Wings might just be too talented for their own good: "The Wings this year have as fine a collection of soccer players as has ever worn the orange. It is a team full of flashy stars. With star-like personalities...This is fun, having all these talented, creative soccer stars around...But when things go wrong, they can lose patience, lose cohesiveness and lose games...Especially on the road...On the road, MISL teams generally succeed by playing conservative, keep-it-close soccer so that they are in a position to win the game at the end. But the Wings are not a conservative team. So their own nature often works against them on the road; they are subverted by their strengths."[19]

Those road woes led the Wings to a 26-26 finish, despite going 18-8 at home. The Wings would be matched up with the Kansas City Comets in the playoffs. The Comets home-field advantage became even tougher to overcome after they beat the Wings 5-4 at the Coliseum in game one. A 4-3 loss in game two left the Wings on the brink.[20] But Chico Borja saved the day on the road in game three when "he stripped the ball from Kansas City's Dale Mitchell and slid a crossing pass to Perry Van der Beck. With 46 seconds left, Van der Beck shot from 18 feet to beat goalkeeper Jim Forsek at the far post and win the game 4-3." Dale Ervine remarked that "Chico proved tonight why he's one of the best players in this league."[21]

Unfortunately, the Comets would triumph in the fourth straight game with a one-point differential. The 5-4 loss in Wichita brought the season to an end. The loss brought introspection on the part of Roy Turner: "There are defeats I remember as a player and defeats I remember as a coach, and I don't think the hurt of Saturday night will ever go away from me...Saturday night brought a lot of things home to us that maybe we thought in the first place...It is not as much abilities as it is personalities, character, and attitudes...We've got far too many players who don't accept roles. It's a must that we go for a more youthful team, not just in ability, but because of their attitude towards the game and their acceptance of the roles..."[22]

In the offseason, the last of the original Wings, Kevin Kewley, would retire. Without any doubt, Kewley was the quintessential Wing. From 1979 to 1990 he provided veteran leadership, tough defense, and a goal or assist just when the Wings needed it. At 407 games played, he appeared in more MISL games than any other Wing. He scored 119 goals, the seventh highest for any Wing in the MISL era. He made 133 assists (sixth highest all-time through 1991) and 275 blocked shots (third on the all-time MISL list).[23] Kewley's number eight jersey would be retired the following season.[24] He would continue as Terry Nicholl's assistant coach into the 1990-91 season.

KEVIN KEWLEY, DEFENDER, WICHITA WINGS: It was a mutual decision. I knew I needed to move on from being a player and they knew it too. I thought about coaching elsewhere. I got offered a deal to coach in Harrisburg, Pennsylvania in the 1990-91 season. A week before I was supposed to start I called up there and knew something was wrong. They had told me they would pay for the moving expenses, and when I called back they reneged on that. I knew it was just a cop-out because a week later they announced another guy got the job.

———

The 1990-91 season began with the Wings facing the same teams, in the same league. But now, with the MISL hoping to take advantage of the arrival of the World Cup in 1994, the league dropped "indoor" from its name and became the Major Soccer League (MSL). To promote the league, the MSL sent teams to play in Europe. The Baltimore Blast defeated Oldham Athletic, a second division English league team, by the impressive score of 6-1. Meanwhile, over on the continent, the St. Louis Storm won a FIFA indoor tournament in Zurich, Switzerland.[25] Back in the New World, a MSL select outdoor team played the US National Team to a draw and a loss in two exhibitions.[26]

In order to ramp up scoring, the MSL enlarged the goals by a third. But no matter how big the goals were, the Wings couldn't quite get their offense going in 1990-91. They would post the second-lowest goal total in the league that year. Their poor performance was reflected in the stands. Average attendance would dip to 6,251, the lowest since the beginning of the 1980s.[27]

Team president Roy Turner's season was a special one from the very beginning. On November 3rd, 1990, his wife Tamara gave birth to daughter Brogan. She and Turner's son Kamden now mirrored Turner's own childhood: one boy and one girl, just like Roy and his sister Maureen.

ROY TURNER: My family was a great part of my success…My wife and kids were my biggest supporters…Tamara, Brogan, and Kamden were such a major part of those great years. Watching game tapes in the middle of the night is very hard on all coaches' families.

DR. TAMARA PRYOR, CLINICAL PSYCHOLOGIST: Brogan has a memory of dressing up as a chicken when the San Diego Chicken came to a game...she was one of the peeps. She would dress up like one of the cheerleaders when she was really little.

ROY TURNER: I left the locker room early to watch my son Kamden dressed as a chicken at half-time.

Turner would coach both his kids' soccer teams throughout their childhood, including a six-year stint at the middle school and high school levels at the Independent School.

In 1990-91, team president Roy Turner would make good on his promise to find younger players who were willing to accept their roles. Two players from California, Danny Pena (age 22) and Brad Smith (age 25), brought youth and excitement to the Wings. Pena, a defender, would make 44 blocks and 37 points that season. Smith, a forward, added 23 goals and 12 assists. Both had played outdoors with Dale Ervine. Scottish-American defender Steve Pittman (age 23), renowned for his left-footed blasts on goal, would make 54 blocks and 32 points. Scotsman Vincent Beck (age 27), who had played for Terry Nicholl in Memphis, would make 65 blocks in his 42 games. Englishman Jason Hasford (age 19) and Jimmy McGeough (age 25), of Northern Ireland, rounded out the youth movement.[28] [29]

Several familiar faces would return for the Wings. The great Omar Gomez, El Indio, returned for one year. Though in his mid-30s, Gomez would score 21 goals and make 27 assists in his 43 games. Cliff Brown, coaching locally at Newman University, would fill-in for injured goalkeepers Kris Peat and Ron Fearon during a four game stretch. Longtime MISL veteran Cha Cha Namdar, former Wing Diego Castro, and Roberto Benigno, would also make a few appearances for the squad due to a series of injuries to Wings regulars.[30]

Those injuries would doom the 1990-91 team. Fearon and Peat reversed roles this year, with Peat the starter for most of the season. But both went down, forcing the Wings to bring in the aforementioned Cliff Brown. Nine Wings would have significant injuries, with a total of 230 man games missed.[31]

ROY TURNER, PRESIDENT AND GM, WICHITA WINGS: We were decimated so much by injuries. We lost four players in one game...The injuries were a major factor in the early '90s, but the team spirit wasn't the best we ever had.

On February 4th, 1990, after losing to the Comets, the Wings ownership decided that the team's 13-20 record wasn't good enough. Terry Nicholl would pay the price. Along with assistant coach Kevin Kewley, Nicholl was let go. Roy Turner was named as Nicholl's replacement.[32]

ROY TURNER: The ownership brought me back in 1990 after Terry Nicholl was fired. I enjoyed being back on the sideline.

BILL OLIVER, MANAGING GENERAL PARTNER, WICHITA WINGS: ...I remember talking to [Roy Turner] and said, "Why don't you come back and coach?" I was running the team then, and it was my idea to bring Roy back. He was reluctant, but did agree to it. I had to talk him into it.

TERRY NICHOLL: The only thing that sticks out in my mind is that I was at my house...I had no ill feelings towards anybody because I was disappointed in myself. I had a knock on the door and it was Bruce Haertl that interviewed me. I remember saying to Bruce, "This is all good stuff, because the Wings have been a big part of Wichita, but I think a much more newsworthy thing is American lads going to war [in Kuwait]."

I was happier as a player for Wichita, than a coach for Wichita. When you're a coach, you're relying on other people to do what needs to be done. I didn't have a winning record. Roy had a great winning record. Charlie didn't have a winning record...Overall, [my system] didn't work because I didn't get the winning record that Roy had...There were less people watching. The league was starting to show some signs of decline. If I was a part of the decline, I'd like to apologize to everyone. I should have won more...I was more disappointed in myself than anyone else. I thought I'd let the city down...I loved Wichita. I only wanted to make the Coliseum [have that] warm glow...the furnace it had been when I was a player.

DALE ERVINE: I think at that level it's very difficult for a coach to have long-term success with the passion and personalities that Charlie and Terry had. What I mean by that is, when things are going well, it's okay because of their passion and they get on you all the time and they're pushing you. But when things don't go well, players don't respond well to that sort of style. These aren't kids in college. These are guys making a living and some of them making darn good money, so they don't want that sort of communication at that level. It's just who they are. When you're winning it's okay, but...when things don't go well it's almost as if you're fighting one another as opposed to...[being] in this together.

Although Turner couldn't turn the season around, several Wings did see a measure of success. Dale Ervine would set a new record for an American player, with 62 goals. In addition to being a career-high, it marked the ascendancy of Ervine as the Wings best scorer. Chico Borja also had a special year, with 29 goals and 41 assists.[33] What made it even more special was his performance at the 1991 All-Star Game on February 13th in Kansas City. The East squad won in overtime, thanks to a fabulous performance by Borja. His three points and two assists set a league record and resulted in him being named MVP of the game.[34] As a bonus, the winning players won prizes. Sadly, those prizes had diminished in value over the years...

CHICO BORJA, MIDFIELDER, WICHITA WINGS: I remember the All-Star game in KC...that was a high [moment]. When you play with the best players against the best talent...For me to be the MVP was crazy. I won a little refrigerator...I was hoping to win a car [laughs].

But it was a tragedy in Andover, Kansas that impacted Chico Borja the most that year. An F5 tornado tore through a trailer park, killing 13 people.

CHICO BORJA: We were playing a golf tournament with Dale Ervine for the Cancer Society. We were at Terradyne [Country Club] and we were at the furthest part of the course. A guy said a tornado hit at McConnell but we kept playing. Then, all of a sudden it starts to hail. We got on our carts and by the time we got to the 18th hole it was like snow. We drove the cart into the basement there. They said there was a tornado coming. We went up to the lobby and saw this huge mile-wide [tornado] coming right at us. Then it made a right towards Andover. Within 20 or 30 seconds you could see roofs flying off. It was crazy....almost like a movie. Dale and I took the car and started driving and knew that somebody would need help of some kind. Another friend of mine's mom lived in a trailer part up there in Andover. It went right through it. I knew his mom lived there, so Dale and I and couple other guys went there. There were tears coming down my eyes. It was like a bomb dropped. We were trying to listen [in the rubble]. There were only three trailers left standing and one of them belonged to my friend's mom. The Salvation Army came in with 18-wheelers and trucks. We hooked up with them, and we delivered stuff. We were there till 2:00 or 3:00 am. We just reacted. We all become human when something like that happens.

The Wings would sneak into the playoffs with a 21-31 record in 1990-91. It was a minor miracle, considering they were 4-22 on the road. A 6-0 loss in Kansas City against their division semifinal opponents was followed by a 9-8 defeat in Wichita.[35] It was a terrible season for the Wings. But at least it was over.

The summer of 1991 produced a great deal of news for the Wichita Wings. Dr. Charles Henning, the Wings' orthopedic specialist, died in June after his sailplane crashed in Colorado near Durango. Henning had served the Wings loyally since the team's first season in 1979. His loss would be felt throughout the Wings community, past and present. Meanwhile, the team found itself in financial trouble again. The team had lost $500,000 during the 1990-91 season. Senior partner and longtime investor Robert Beren announced that unless the people of south central Kansas *could purchase 5,000 season tickets, the Wings would fold. "'Unless someone rides up on a great white horse, this is it," said Wings general partner Darrel Rolph.*[36]

Things were so bad that two separate groups were wrangling for the rights to start a new Wings franchise in the rival National Professional Soccer League (NPSL). The NPSL, formerly called the American Indoor Soccer Association, with its lower labor costs, hoped to take over indoor soccer in Wichita if the Wings folded. However, the NPSL would have to wait. Between May 28th and June 28th 1990, the Wings went from 2,500 to 5,035 season tickets sold. Pizza Hut put the team over the top with a purchase of 100 tickets. However, most of the sales were regular folks from around Wichita. "If it had all been corporate, it would have been a little bit false. Now we know this city loves us," said head coach Roy Turner. Incredibly, 1,200 of the tickets were sold in the last two days of the ticket drive. ''My brother [Darrel] and I could find not one glimmer of hope. We hadn't even gotten to the point of discussing what we would do if there were 5,000. It seemed that impossible," said general partner David Rolph. By reaching the 5,000 ticket mark the Wings qualified for funds from the Wichita-Sedgwick County Partnership for Growth.[37] *The Wings were back in action for another season.*

With Roy Turner returning to the bench, the general manager duties were passed on to Hugh Nicks, the Director of Marketing for the Sasnak Corporation, which managed a number of Pizza Hut and Carlos O'Kelly's restaurants. Turner would concentrate on making the Wings better on the field and dealing with the league, while Nicks would take care of the business of running a soccer team.[38] *But dealing with the league meant dealing with an organization that seemed to be collapsing. Indeed, the Kansas City Comets would fold before the 1991-92 season began. In July the MSL set a deadline of August 1st for a new collective bargaining agreement with the players union. Costs had to be cut, or the league might not survive. At the last minute, a deal was struck and the MSL played a 40-game schedule in what would become its final season.*[39]

Roy Turner's style as coach was new for Wings star Dale Ervine, who had only played for Charlie Cooke and Terry Nicholl.

DALE ERVINE: Roy Turner brought this stability, calm, and confidence with him that we hadn't had in my four years. [It was] just a different approach. The other [coaches] were on our side, don't get me wrong. But the way Roy would approach it [was that] he was passionate but it didn't come across that he was above you; he was with you and that's where I think the differences were. But there were probably some qualities that Charlie and Terry had that we wish Roy would have had…

Roy pretty much let us play. He'd talk to us between shifts, but Roy was very positive behind the bench, always encouraging, but in a voice that didn't seem like he was panicking. "Come on Dale, we need a goal!"

Turner brought longtime fan-favorite Kim Roentved back to the fold as a player-coach. He would serve the Wings well in both capacities.

KIM ROENTVED, DEFENDER/ASSISTANT COACH, WICHITA WINGS: In 1991, I almost signed a three-year deal with the Colorado Foxes, an outdoor team. My wife was literally out there looking at a house. But Roy asked me to come play indoor in Wichita. Ron Newman asked me to come to San Diego, which sounded nice as well…Going from player to coach for Roy was the easiest transition because we were very close.

ROY TURNER: It was hardly any different at all. I always had respected his opinion, no matter how young he was.

In 1991-92, the Wings were without the services of Chico Moreira, Victor Moreland, Omar Gomez, Jason Hasford, Vincent Beck, Ian Fairbrother, and Ron Fearon. Forward Dan Donigan was acquired from St. Louis and would score 30 points in his 39 appearances. Canadian midfielder Steve Morris would play in all but two games, accumulating 13 points and 11 blocks. The Wings would also add Scottish defender Doug McLagan, Theo Kulsdom, and Dave Reichart.[40]

The Wings got off a hot start in 1991, starting the season 8-3. Much of their success was due to consistency in goal. Kris Peat earned the starting keeper spot after the departure of Ron Fearon. He would make the most of his opportunity, compiling a 17-15 record and 5.43 GAA. The Wings chose not to carry a backup keeper for the first half of the season; a choice they would soon regret. After a great start, Peat was selected for the MSL All-Star game thanks to his "cat-like quickness and great ball control skills." He would lead the Wings to a 13-10 record and went into the February 8th, 1992 game against Baltimore at the top of his game. But Peat injured his elbow after falling to the turf, forcing forward David Byrne to fill-in for the rest of the game. Desperate for a replacement, the Wings turned to former Blast keeper Scott Manning. By the time Peat returned, 13-10 had turned into 14-16.[41]

The Wings would lose 16 of their last 22 games, causing them to finish behind Baltimore for the last MSL playoff spot. So, in the MSL's last season, the Wings would not make the playoffs. It would be only the second time in the team's history that the Orange Army couldn't march into the Coliseum for a playoff game. However, the previous summer's season ticket drive proved that the community continued to love their Wings. Attendance averaged 8,569, an increase of 37% from 1990-91. They even sold out two overtime losses to San Diego.[42]

DAVE PHILLIPS, WINGS RADIO ANNOUNCER, 1986-93: In the 1991-92 season we missed the playoffs, which as unbelievable because that would have been the one year the team would have made money, if we'd made the playoffs... [instead] we lost $140,000...All we had to do was beat Dallas. Tatu didn't even suit up. Their goalie banged his hand early in the game...so they took him out. They put in their other big scorer in the net for the rest of the game. How we lost, I don't know.

The last year of the MISL, it wasn't the Wings popularity that was waning. It wasn't Wichita that collapsed. It was the league...We were down to six teams. If one was out we were done. At the end of the year, there was no hope of resurrecting it. The whole season had a pall cast over it...We were selling out every game and then the rest of the league abandons us.

In the months that followed, the MSL began to crumble. The Tacoma Stars and St. Louis Storm ceased operations, leaving just five teams in the league. On Friday, July 10th, 1992, league Commissioner Earl Foreman, one of the men responsible for founding the MISL, was forced to announce that the league had ceased operations.[43] *"My emotions right now are somewhat confusing. I'm still not sure I believe it myself. We've been close to this several times. I should be pretty good at it and have my speech prepared, but I'm not. I feel very sad indeed because so many people brought so much enjoyment, and now we're going to miss it,"* Roy Turner *told* The Eagle.[44]

BILL OLIVER: ...When the league broke up and we didn't have any New York's or LA's, that's when I lost interest. Who's going to come out to see Des Moines, as opposed to New York? I thought it was doomed at that point. And I was right... There was less money and we didn't have the players...It was a highlight for me, in my life. I regret that we couldn't make it.

Oliver had been incredibly generous with his financial contributions to the Wings, losing money on a yearly basis. Once the MISL folded, he decided to make a clean break.

BILL OLIVER: Totally out. I'm not going to give you any numbers, but we lost a lot of money. We put a lot of money in that team.

Thankfully for Wings fans, the NPSL represented a glimmer of hope that indoor soccer would continue in Wichita. Roy Turner negotiated with former team owner Frank Carney for the Wings name and logo, allowing the team to continue as the same entity. Meanwhile, the people of Wichita began to invest their own money in a team that would be owned by the community. NPSL teams operated on budgets roughly one-third to one-half the size of those of MSL franchises. This made it possible for the Wings to continue on a smaller scale, with smaller dollar figures from local investors.[45] *The investors, led by Mike Relihan, would form an executive board to manage the operations of the team.*[46] *The Wings would go on to thrill local fans for another nine seasons.*

As for the legacy of the MISL, the Wings 20th Anniversary Yearbook *said it best: "It had been quite a 14-year run for the league. In all, 32 franchises representing 26 cities had come and gone. Nearly 30 million fans had attended league games, and were entertained by some of the greatest stars in the history of U.S. soccer...Steve Zungul,*

Branko Segota, Juli Veee, Stan Stamenkovic, Tatu, Kai Haaskivi, Dale Mitchell, Preki, Brian Quinn, Kevin Crow, Andy Chapman, Chico Borja, Erik Rasmussen, Kim Roentved, Mike Dowler, Slobo Ilijevski, Zoltan Toth...the list went on and on..."[47]* *That the NPSL years could not equal the glory days of the MISL was not a knock on the new league, it was praise for the excellence of the old one. The death of the MISL was mourned by many...and deservedly so. The MISL had been a big deal.*

AL MILLER, HEAD COACH, DALLAS TORNADO: At its height, the talent level of the MISL was outstanding. It was a high quality game. Stan Stamenkovic from Yugoslavia, who played for Baltimore, was an All-World type player. There were just a lot of good players. In soccer, you want some piano players and some piano-carriers. There were a lot of young guys brought over like [Kevin] Kewley and [Omar] Gomez. That league was strong. It was a high-quality spectator game. I'm shocked that the indoor league didn't stay big.

BILL OLIVER: Compared to what professional players make today it wasn't much, but we were competitive world-wide at the time.

STEVE SHAAD, FRONT OFFICE, WICHITA WINGS: Kentling promoted this as major league. We outdrew WSU basketball, and the Steamers outdrew every NBA team. We promoted it as "Wichita against the big boys"...St. Louis, KC...all the places that looked down their noses at Wichita as too small. We've got a team that can compete favorably against them and beat them. David vs. Goliath. It gave people something to cheer for and we had these great international players, and we gave them all nicknames. They were very friendly and got along with the public.

For one of our playoff games, we had higher Nielsen TV ratings than any other local network for that night...We didn't anticipate we'd be drawing 9,800 per game in a few years. We eventually were sold out on the weekends and big crowds on the weekdays. It was a culmination of a lot of hard work and momentum built up over the years.

BILL KENTLING: There were teams, particularly ones in really major markets...[for them] money was something to light your cigarettes with...Kim was our highest paid player, in the $70,000s. But there were people making more than that [on other teams]. That wouldn't have been in the top five in the league... [The MISL] had a lot of ABA [American Basketball Association] to it in the old days.

ANDY CHAPMAN: Even when I talk to people nowadays... there seems to be a renewed interest in the '80s. I always said someone should do a documentary on the whole of the '80s with [the MISL]. It would be fascinating because [MLS fans] now still don't realize that in the '80s we were going into stadiums and there were 18,000 people rockin' in St. Louis. The Kansas Coliseum was rockin', and sold out. We would go to Chicago and it was just packed. Cleveland...average attendance in '85 and '86 was 13,500. The Cavaliers were drawing 7,000...The league was just booming.

TOM SHINE, REPORTER/EDITOR, WICHITA EAGLE: We were playing Baltimore, LA, New York, San Diego. It was a nice thing that we got to play against those teams. It was a thing to do in town during the winter. If we didn't outdraw WSU basketball, it was close. I remember one game, Bill [Kentling] was excited because people were scalping tickets out front. It made the city feel pretty good. We were always in the playoffs.

DALE ERVINE: With no outdoor league going at the time all the best players in the country had to be driven to the indoor game. The talent level was very high. We were able to pay players decent money back then...the Zunguls, the Roentveds. There were a lot of veteran players who were in their thirties but were still very, very good. The level of play was very high.

The question becomes: What killed the MISL?

AL MILLER: There was some suspect management. But at the end of the day, if you don't own the arena and don't get the concessions, parking, and TV revenue, it's hard to be in the pro sports business when you have to pay salaries. The rent cost us and you can't live on ticket sales alone. The US Soccer Federation didn't help much either. The outdoor soccer guy thought of the indoor game as inferior and stupid. Our federation, if they admitted the truth, would have to have admitted that's how they felt about it, even though they took a lot of players that we had developed who later became national team members. There was always a craving amongst these people for the outdoor game to flourish without the indoor game to compete with it. No matter what you do, indoor will never replace the outdoor game.

TERRY NICHOLL: The league started to deteriorate. The storied franchises started to waver. Some of the teams that had been there all along started to wobble…I think the league lost its way.

KENNY COOPER, HEAD COACH, BALTIMORE BLAST: The MLS came in and helped cause the end of the MISL. The outdoor game got a second chance. They had a blueprint for it, and it proved to be successful.

BILL KENTLING, WINGS GENERAL MANAGER/MISL COMMISSIONER: If you look at the people who were involved when it was really relevant, a lot of those people went to do other things. There is no gracious way to say that.

DOUG VERB, MISL EXECUTIVE, DIRECTOR OF PRESS AND PR: There were two things that happened that really stymied the league in the third or fourth year: [no salary cap and going with FNN-Score instead of ESPN]. [League Commissioner] Earl Foreman was right on that fine line between a genius and maniac. He knew that it was important to go out and form a union. I thought, "Why?" His thought: it's going to happen anyway if we're successful…he was out in front of it. One of the big negotiations was gonna be we're gonna form this union, and from our standpoint, we want to have a salary cap. At that time, only the NBA had it. So we went to Ed Garvey, who was the head of the NFL Players Association, and they had a connection with Johnny Kerr, who was trying to form the NASL union, and that's what they were trying to do…It was Earl presenting it as, "We have to have a salary cap." The owners would not vote on the union, therefore not voting on the salary cap because some guys, particularly the guy in New York, Luciani, he took a Donald Trump approach…"If you don't have deep enough pockets to be in the league with me, you shouldn't be in the league." We desperately needed the salary cap. I was out of it when they finally got a salary cap. They kept lowering it to keep people in business. It should have been in 1980 or '81...it would have given us stability and not having turnover of owners. It doesn't look good if you are always losing owners. It would have given [teams] a chance to really grow.

ESPN...but they didn't have the NFL yet...Sportscenter had become entrenched and they were something important. We went to them and told them we literally built the game for TV. Down to taking different colored balls and rolling them on the turf to see what looked best...the time outs...putting microphones in the locker room, on the coach, and the bench...well ESPN loved all that stuff. So they gave us a Friday night window of a game of the week... like 8:00 to 10:00 every Friday night throughout our season. The three of us on the marketing committee thought this was great. It would cost no money. The exposure! We worked very hard with the local teams on the arena deals and television deals. We produced a lot of the games for them.

The three of us went into the league meeting and said, "This is great!" [Wichita] stood up at the meeting and said, "You're telling me you are going to put this on TV at 8:00 on Friday night? That's when I play my home games!" We were all dumbfounded. Earl Foreman said, "Bill [Kentling], if you think that somebody in Wichita is going to stay home and watch Philly and New York instead of seeing your game in person, then you've got a bigger problem than we think." I think we would have defeated that provincial attitude but FNN-Score came along and it was going to battle ESPN. Nothing would beat ESPN. FNN-Score came in and offered us a nickel and the owners went for it. I don't see this as hindsight. Even if ESPN stopped growing right there and then it would have been an incredible piece for us. We would have taken corporate money to promote the game and start doing things that would help us grow in the future. It would have given us stability. I'm not laying this all on the feet of Bill Kentling. Because someone came in and offered us a little bit of money the majority of owners [went for it]. Every year we'd come to the end of the season, you'd have the excitement of the playoffs... meanwhile, everybody who wasn't in the championship was wondering if they'd fold. Was the league going to fold? So many of the people, good solid people, were cut. A lot of them went on to a lot of big things.

CHICO BORJA: I remember that ESPN would show us a lot of times. We were on there every week. Hockey just took over and they didn't show us every week anymore. The rest is history.

ANDY CHAPMAN: Unfortunately, as we got to the end of the decade it started to fade. A number of factors...we got a little too big for our boots....we had the union and salary caps were starting to get implemented. The quality of the players started to [decrease]. By the time we got into the early '90s, each franchise had less of a budget to work with. There weren't great, great players playing. The standard of the players just wasn't there.

DALE ERVINE: Even the last few years of the MISL or MSL there was uncertainty. From a player's standpoint, it's disheartening. You put in your efforts and it seems that the financial part of the league is going in a different direction than your personal career. There was nothing else. It's amazing how far the sport has come in 20-25 years. There was nothing else back then. The level of play was a little bit lower which leads to a more physical game.

Roy Turner would take on the roles of both team president and head coach until 1994-95, when he handed the coaching reins to his trusted friend and assistant, Kim Roentved. But financial pressures again threatened to derail indoor soccer in Wichita in 1996. On February 22, 1996 Turner announced he would step down as team president at the end of his contract. "Change has to happen to keep the Wings in Wichita. I'm proud of the 17 years. It has been wonderful...For 17 years I've lived in a fantasy, but we're dealing with reality now. Someone else needs to try to take this thing to the next level," said Turner. "It's obviously a sad day. He gave me the chance of a lifetime...I thank him from the bottom of my heart," remarked Kim Roentved.[48]

According to The Eagle's *Fred Mann: "Turner should be applauded for making the ultimate sacrifice to try to save what he holds most dear. Turner ran the Wings as best he could, and that was better than any soccer executive in America because the Wings have been the country's longest playing soccer act."*[49] The Eagle's *editorial board weighed in on Roy Turner's legacy in Wichita: "For the last 17 years, Mr. Turner has been an overwhelmingly positive asset to the Wichita community. In fact, his longevity as a Wichita sports figure puts him right up there with such local legends as Hap Dumont, who founded the National Baseball Congress, and Ralph Miller, the revered former coach of the Wichita State University men's basketball team...Roy Turner should be recognized for what he is: a man who has successfully devoted countless hours of professional and public service to Wichita and to the Wings, and to making this a more exciting community in which to live."*[50]

ROY TURNER: ...There were many angles on what happened. But I believe my wages were higher than they wanted to pay. I retired because I did not see me having a future with that ownership. It was very hard for me when the previous ownership group left. The new one had different policies and philosophies. Maybe they said, "We can save money if Roy leaves." I was never asked to leave. I got up one morning and completely decided I'd had enough. I thought me moving on was the best idea for the franchise. I didn't want to see the franchise go anywhere. We'll never know if it was the right decision.

CHAPTER 23

An Oral History

A Legacy of Orange

———

"No matter where I go, someone will talk about how big it was in their lives. We didn't realize until later on in life how big it was."

- ROY TURNER

THE SHEER VOLUME OF TALENT that the Wings put on the pitch is nothing short of astounding. The top level of English football, now known as the Premier League, was previously called "First Division." Thirteen Wings played, or would play First Division football. Forty-five Wings played on national or Olympic teams across the world. It begs the question: who were the best players to ever play for the Wichita Wings?

DAVE PHILLIPS, WINGS RADIO ANNOUNCER, 1986-93: The most important thing...was....that I knew I was watching world-class athletes. For those incredible winters from 1979 till 1991-92 you had some of the best soccer players in the world playing in that old barn. Chico Borja easily could have played First Division soccer overseas. These guys were as good as the guys in Europe. I hope people appreciate that.

KEVIN KEWLEY, DEFENDER, WICHITA WINGS: If I was starting a team, I would pick Kim [Roentved] first. He'd be the franchise player. That's easy for me to say now because I saw what he did, even at an older age, at such a high level. My admiration for him went through the roof. Then, I'd pick a forward like Erik [Rasmussen] or Zungul.

ROY TURNER, HEAD COACH, WICHITA WINGS: I think Kim has been our best player over the years. He was so strong. His legs were huge. For the indoor game he had everything. A great all-around player...No one ever really equaled Mike Dowler as a goalkeeper.

STEVE SHAAD, FRONT OFFICE, WICHITA WINGS: Kim, in terms of impact on the team, as defender and sixth attacker and never-say-quit-player.... Jorgen as a playmaker. He could put the ball right where it needed to be. If people finished every pass he laid out for them, we'd have had 50 more goals in a season....Erik Rasmussen in terms of score-making ability. One of the more colorful and exciting players was Andy Chapman. His kind of flamboyance made people pay to come watch him play. He was one of the best businessmen on the team.

BILL KENTLING, GENERAL MANAGER, WICHITA WINGS: There was a fella who was on power play offense, power play defense, never missed a game, was the Captain, could play one-touch if you wanted to play one-touch, could go bump-in-the-night and knock the crap out of Pecher if he wanted...and that was Kim Roentved. It slights several guys when you pick one because Mike Dowler was magnificent in goal. There were certain things a Barry Wallace could do from the left side. You look at Borja...we could talk about eight or 10 guys. But if I had to pick one guy, it would be Roentved, slightly over Erik Rasmussen.

CHICO BORJA, MIDFIELDER, WICHITA WINGS: You start with either Kim [Roentved] or Erik Rasmussen. Kim is a solid defender, player, and leader. Erik [Rasmussen] was an amazing goal-scorer. Either one of those two.

ANDY CHAPMAN, FORWARD, WICHITA WINGS: I could look at it a couple of ways. I remember having a conversation with [Director of Sales and Marketing] Dave Bennett in a bar one night. If he was gonna start a franchise, it would be me. Steve [Shaad] said it should be Kim. I think Kim might have even been there. For me, Jorgen [Kristensen] was a fantastic player, but he was in his thirties. It's a hard one to answer. It would have to be Kim for me. Kevin Kewley was instrumental with all his experience. But from raw dynamic strength, defense, his shot, his power, and youth, I'd have to say Kim.

NORMAN PIPER, MIDFIELDER, WICHITA WINGS: Jorgen [Kristensen] would be one of them. Andy Chapman. I never played with Erik Rasmussen. The late Jeff Bourne was a good player. I think I would have built a team around Jorgen. I would get the ball and just give it to him...The Magic Man!

TOM SHINE, REPORTER/EDITOR, WICHITA EAGLE: I still think Roentved was their best player ever. You could argue Erik Rasmussen was pretty good too. Roentved could do more stuff; though Rasmussen was unguardable, as they'd say in basketball. Roentved was the heart and soul of that team. If someone needed to get knocked on their ass, Roentved could do that too.

DAVE PHILLIPS: I was blessed to see the greatest complete soccer player ever in Kim Roentved. He was the anchor of the team's defense. When they went on a power play, he directed that. The anchor of the penalty killers... if there was a sixth attacker he'd play goalie...if there was a fight he'd play enforcer. In addition to being the best player on the field, he was the toughest as well.

TERRY NICHOLL, MIDFIELDER, WICHITA WINGS: Kevin Kewley and Kim Roentved were two of the best fullbacks to ever play indoor...Kim Roentved made tackles no one else could. He was brilliant by the boards, had a great shot, was fearless and so confident. You couldn't find a replacement for Kim. He made defending look easy. He'd tackle well. He did everything well. Brilliant...Kim [was the best] overall. Scoring goals it was Erik. Chico was close. Jorgen was the best passer. Andy with his bicycle kicks. Goalkeeping, I would say Mike Dowler. Omar Gomez was a good creator; Jeff Bourne was a great finisher.

Though the Wings would make the playoffs almost every year, and field some of the best teams the MISL ever saw, a championship eluded them. It had to be frustrating. However, Wichita's love for the Wings was not correlated to their success in the playoffs.

BRUCE HAERTL, RADIO ANNOUNCER, WICHITA WINGS: Those players that were a part of that...my guess is that every single one of them would be very proud of the contribution they made to the Wichita Wings and to the growth of soccer in the community, coming from all points of the world. But I'll bet you, dollars to donuts, not winning a championship, at least at the time, was something that irritated them greatly. I was on that bus and plane a few times coming back from playoff losses, and there weren't many words spoken.

TERRY NICHOLL: When you go out and you are giving everything and it's obvious you are giving everything, I think fans are okay. We were always in-and-around...we qualified just about every year. Being part of the playoff picture at least. It was a healthy relationship that the players had with the fans, as good as anything I've seen in pro soccer.

ANTHONY VILLEGAS, WINGS FAN: The Wings won and the Wings lost. In my 16 years (1985-2001), the Wings went to the playoffs all but three times. No championship. The Wings taught me you can have something special without having it all. The journey, the players, the fans: that's what made the Wichita Wings' legacy. That's why Wichita soccer can be great. And it will be great again.

After conducting dozens of interviews, it became clear to us just how important the Wings were to the people who played for them...who rooted for them...who coached them...who owned them...who worked behind the scenes to make them a success. The Wings truly did make this town big...bigger than our 400,000 people...bigger than life.

ROY TURNER: There's no history when you start. All of a sudden you are a part of something in those first five years that is special. Everybody loves us. There was no leaving in those days, amongst the core group. We were building something together. The crowd made a big difference to this team...It doesn't matter where

I go, people know me as "Coach of the Wings." When Kim comes down [to Wichita] he points it out.

We were all so into it, and it still amazes me how important we were to so many people, even up to today. I was at a reception the other day and there was an introduction by the Chamber of Commerce, and I said, "Roy Turner, Wichita Open Tournament Director." And he said, "No, tell them WHO YOU ARE." i.e. from the Wichita Wings. No matter where I go, someone will talk about how big it was in their lives. We didn't realize until later on in life how big it was.

KEVIN KEWLEY: Anywhere I go, western Kansas, or anywhere, there's always someone who will talk to me about the Wings.

DAVE PHILLIPS: What a legacy [Roy Turner has]. He changed the face of sports in Wichita. How many people can say that? Without Roy, soccer would never have taken off like that.

ROY TURNER: They all sat in the same seats every year. It became their family. Every year they'd renew their tickets and see each other's kids growing up...For the most part I had a great playing career, but the '80s and the Wings were the highlight of my life. It just happened.

We always felt we were the underdog...little Wichita playing Chicago and New York who were spending more money. When we brought this group together the players had no idea it would become so big. Did it affect them? I don't know. Kim Roentved was driving his white Corvette around town. [laughs]

KENNY COOPER, HEAD COACH, BALTIMORE BLAST: I told someone the other day: who would have believed Roy Turner would have settled in Wichita, Kansas! It's a great place...small city, big town. Great people. He's been an icon in Wichita. He introduced people to the game and helped keep the franchise alive. It wasn't easy. Soccer was not making money. At the end of the day it's all about performance and generating revenue...season tickets, corporate sponsors.

Roy's entire coaching career was in Wichita, and mine was entirely in Baltimore. It's amazing, between the two of us we played for Dallas nine years together and then coached for 16-17 years together in the MISL. It wouldn't happen today. Players don't spend that amount of time with one club anymore. Coaches don't either. In those days you could only keep the game alive for so long. It was hemorrhaging, as most young sports do. It was a matter of keeping owners interested and then finding other investors, partners, season tickets holders, and sponsors. It's a 24/7 kind of job. He's done the same with golf. Great assistant in Debbie [Burch]. She's been a great foot soldier. You can't do it by yourself. You have to surround yourself with good people.

STEVE SHAAD: We made an impression on people. People still know me from the Wings, even though I spent 17 years with the [Wichita] Wranglers [baseball team]...What I learned from the Wings is to be honest and be consistent. People are going to have fun, so don't do things that cause them to not have fun.

TOM MARSHALL, GENERAL MANAGER, WICHITA WINGS, 1979: That sense of Wichita pride we had was special...I don't know if I gave enough credit to Wichita. I don't believe that my efforts would have been rewarded elsewhere. Wichita was a special place, especially at this time. Old money created a base for the community pride and "new money" took chances. I believe the amount of money and overnight success stories in Wichita at this time period could not be matched anywhere else in the country. Koch Industries, fast food endeavors like Pizza Hut and Spangles, oil successes - matched with aviation and its entrepreneurs. This created a climate of financial optimism, as well as a strong competitive spirit. I doubt if some carpetbagger from New York, living in a double-wide with an older car and a sordid past, could have got to first base anywhere else with his dream but in Wichita...

BILL KENTLING: Do I look back on it? I do. I look back on my six years more fondly than my three as commissioner. When you are competitive you like having your own team. When you are commissioner all you can cheer for are the umps! So yeah, from a competitive standpoint it was really fun. I think we achieved a lot. We are talking about kids who can play now because of what guys from Denmark, Argentina, Wales, and England did 30 years ago. That's pretty cool stuff...We were very good at recognizing controversy and taking advantage of it. I'm sure we were pissing off some people, but we were inventing a sport. We were making up stuff.

MIKE DOWLER, GOALKEEPER, WICHITA WINGS: As a professional sportsman, success is all about winning. Unfortunately, the majority of players can only look on with envy at those select few who win the "Big One," whatever that big one may be. So, from that point of view, I was disappointed that we weren't able to enjoy more success on the pitch. However, I was able to be part of a team that played some of the best football I had ever seen. I had the opportunity to play alongside some well-known, talented players who had tasted success and fame in their respective countries. We were extremely well-supported by our fans in the Orange Army, and to be young and "world famous" (well, within Wichita at least) was an enjoyable novelty that both I and my little family look back on with pleasure. To us, Wichita was a big, fast, vibrant city, and one that, for five years, a city we thought of as home.

LOUIS MCCLUER, WINGS FAN: It wasn't just the team; it was the players, the coaches, the fans, the sellouts...the Kansas Coliseum being packed and so loud you couldn't hear what someone next to you was saying...the rivalries with Kansas City, St Louis and despising players like Slobo, Steve Pecher, and Tatu. Not sure whether it was because you hated them as a person, although Pecher came close, but they were so good, you knew they would cause problems against the Wings. There were so, so many great memories of the Wings, they can't all be written. Both my parents are gone now, but even today I can still see them dressed in Wings attire, sitting in the Coliseum, rooting for the boys. And nothing can take those memories away from me.

CHICO BORJA: Wichita was the best time of my career...The biggest thing in Wichita was that the fans loved us. We as players played our hardest every single game for those people. They realized that...I will always cherish those years.

JOHN MORRISON, WINGS FAN: I have tons of memories. The Wings weren't just a team; they were a way of life. On our block there were five houses. Four of the five families had season tickets. The fifth family was a retired couple who often traveled, but when they were in town they would go to games too. My family would travel to KC to games. We traveled lots of places though. The first time I was even in California was to see the Wings and Sockers play. First time I was in Memphis was to see the Wings play the [MISL's] Americans. Christmas and Thanksgiving were holidays spent at home so we wouldn't miss games. For the life of the franchise, there were very few games we missed. It wasn't just something to do, it was something we loved doing. We had season tickets, were active members in the Orange Army, bought all kinds of merchandise and went to many team functions. It was a fantastic time.

ANTHONY VILLEGAS: The cold, the wind, the snow. Marching slowly up "the hill" to the doors of the Kansas Coliseum, ready to witness battle yet again. Misery melts away as the doors open to reveal a punch of sounds, smells, and pure electricity. The crowd of 9,000 fans buzzed. We're "Gonna Fly Now." The air raid sirens screamed. I watched countless players transform from "crazy dumbasses" to "glorious bastards" whilst we all loved to hate Slobo.

ANDY CHAPMAN: A lot of those guys were there year-round. Kevin, Roy, Norman, Jimmy Ryan...they lived there in the community and they made it their homes. Some have been there 35-36 years. It says a lot about that town. A few of the players married local girls and raised families there. It's obviously a very special place...There is a need in me to go to Wichita again. It's important to me. It seems like the right thing for me to do...I still have dreams occasionally at night where I'm playing and Wichita is in it. Roy is part of the dream and Kevin [Kewley].

DR. TAMARA PRYOR, CLINICAL PSYCHOLOGIST: I met Roy during those glory days of the Wings, before he stepped into the front office. We would go every summer over to Europe and he'd go to these combines and recruit players and I got to see a lot of England and travel around and spend time with his family. They were just the hottest ticket in town. It was a great, fun time...[Roy] is the life of the party.

VIRGINIA CREAMER, ASSISTANT DIRECTOR OF OPERATIONS/ ANGELS COORDINATOR, WICHITA WINGS: Bill [Kentling], Steve

[Shaad], Dave [Bennett] and I, and Roy, of course, were so passionate about making it work. We did work and work and work to keep that team alive. It was a labor of love for all of us.

TOM SHINE: [The Wings] started going to two-for-one tickets. We had a lot of people here [at *The Wichita Eagle*] who started going. They enjoyed it. There were a lot of women who were going out there. It was an hour and 50 minutes, two hours tops. The ball was easy to see. The rules were pretty simple...don't use your hands. You can get beer and mixed drinks, even on a Sunday, which was hard to do in Wichita at the time. And if you wanted to, you could go and meet the players afterwards at the Hatch...All the teams did sponsored parties afterwards. The idea was that it was so social that you could see Andy Chapman and he would talk to you, sign autographs for you. They were all sort of your size too...Everyone had a sense of shared purpose: the players, the managers, the front office. [They] wanted this to succeed.

ALAN SHEPHERD, MISL REFEREE: For the city as a whole, it was a great 20 years. It did a lot for the economy and gave a lot of people opportunities: players, refs, coaches. It was a fun time. Those were top-level players who played the game right and did a lot of things for the community.

DALE ERVINE, FORWARD, WICHITA WINGS: I think that those of us who were in Wichita for a long period of time, well, when I'd go home to California for the summer people would say, "Ervine, how can you live in Kansas?" And I'd say, "You don't understand. The place is great. They take care of the players, our games are filled every night, 80% capacity if not more." It was great and I think the people that stayed there really appreciated that. The ones that would leave didn't really have that same appreciation.

BRUCE HAERTL: I thought [the Wings were] absolutely huge...or finding a word that is north of huge. The impact of the Wings is still being felt to this day when you look at youth soccer in the way it has exploded. The genesis was the Wings. The amount of work they did in the community...Bill Kentling, Roy Turner, those guys got it. They understood you had to be accessible to the people.

They did a great job with post-game parties, making the players available to the fans...to the point where fans and players socialized. It was the early '80s and they were wild times...fun times. Always fun, and with the purpose of building this team's identity with the community.

People I talk to now about the Wings can't believe it that was the hottest ticket in town. Now, that's saying something since Wichita State in 1981 went to the Elite Eight. There were plenty of times I remember trying to get tickets for people and not being able to do it, because it was sold out. It was a hot ticket. There were games you couldn't get near. Randy Smithson and Jay Jackson and a lot of my friends at WSU playing basketball were guys I'd bring out to the Kansas Coliseum. They would go as a curiosity and end up going again because they enjoyed it and became fans in their own right. A lot of that had to do with the fact that all of those guys, to a man, understood selling the game, the product and themselves, and giving back to the community. I don't think I've ever been around a team that gave back to the community better than the Wings did. They really understood the importance of that. I commend Bill Kentling and Roy Turner for that.

It was a pretty remarkable three years [of broadcasting] and they were some of the best years to do what I did. I had the game in St. Louis at the old Checker Dome that they played in the semifinals that the Wings just missed going to play Zungul and the Arrows. I interviewed [baseball legend] Stan Musial at halftime, who was part-owner of the Steamers. I'm a 20-year-old kid, getting paid, traveling with this team, interviewing Stan Musial at halftime... how could life get any better for me? By that second and third year it was absolutely crazy. This town was in love with the newness and the European flavor and that they were a pretty damn good team.

You've got to know about the age in which we were living, and socially, the types of things that were going on. A lot of people close to the program were very good reflectors of what was going on at that particular time. There were a lot of things going on that guys partake in and have fun. This was a merry band. These were a group of guys who loved hanging with each other. Rarely did they go their own ways on the road. That was the real magic of that group... By and large, it was a great group of guys that played very good soccer...winning soccer...and had winning lives. They had fun, made the most of their experiences in this country, learning about it and gave back to it. Nothing impressed me more than their willingness to give back to the community. That's why so many people are warm and nostalgic about the Wings. They may remember the team was about to fold two or three times, but they also remember what it was like to be packed in the Coliseum. It is amazing to me how often people will say "I used to listen to you do the Wings." I'm very thankful for that...The Wings made a difference in people's lives.

TERRY NICHOLL: I was as proud to be a Wing as I was to be a Sheffield United player...or any team that I played for. It was fun to be a Wing. It had such a standing in the city that if you were a Wing, usually people knew you. You didn't have to say, "I play for the Wings."

NATHAN MOORE, WINGS FAN: In 1980 I was eight. A kid growing up during a time when Ronald Reagan was elected president, John Lennon was murdered outside his home, and Japan surpassed the United States in auto manufacturing. My friends and I wouldn't care about any of these events until much later in life. In 1980, when we were eight, we only cared about the Wichita Wings.

During school, specifically during recess, since recess was important to us, my friends and I would not play football or baseball...we would play soccer. And while we played soccer we would get dirty, and we would get sweaty, but we did not care because we were playing for the Wings. During those 45 minutes of uninterrupted freedom from the classroom, if a teacher happened to look out a window, we knew that she would not have seen 11 dirty and sweaty boys kicking a partially deflated ball around on a dirt field. She would have seen Dowler, Piper, Chapman, Borja, and the rest of the Wings playing and fighting for the city of Wichita.

When I was eight, my weekly winter highlight was waiting in the mile-long line to exit highway I-135 to enter the parking lot of the Kansas Coliseum. As a kid, climbing up the hill past the two metallic bumper bulls, and getting in line to enter the arena to watch the Wings play was akin to attending a Pentecostal service, eating two corner pieces of birthday cake, and staying up all night watching Elvira, Mistress of the Dark. High up in the shadowy confines of our seats, my brother and I would laugh nervously at the boisterous drunks, scramble passionately toward the entrances as the Wings Angels threw out miniature plastic soccer balls, scream and holler when the Wings scored a goal, and pray to Jesus for a miracle when the Wings were behind with time running out (because Jesus also loved the Wings).

Now I am 42, and at times when I am disheartened and confused about how busy and complicated the world has become, I ask myself where in time I would go, if I could...and I always come back with the same answer. I would go back to 1980, when I was eight, when the world was still mysterious, and the Wings were all I cared about.

An Oral History

The Boy Who Became a Wing

———

"Chico Borja went above and beyond for me, and
in a lot of ways made me the player I was. The
opportunities I was given came through him."

- LARRY INLOW

THE WINGS WOULD PRODUCE MANY *young fans during the MISL era. A few of
the boys who crowded the field seeking autographs after home games would themselves become Wings. One of them was named Larry Inlow. A 1993 graduate of
Wichita Southeast High School, Inlow would enjoy a very successful soccer career at
Newman University under former Wing Cliff Brown before turning pro. He would
be drafted by the NPSL-era Wings and play from 1997 until the club's dissolution
in 2001. Still coaching both adults and youth through recent years, Inlow's story
illustrates the continuing impact of the Wings on the soccer community in Wichita.*

LARRY INLOW, DEFENDER, WICHITA WINGS: My very first Wings
game ever was due to my godfather Gary Roushkolb, who was a season ticket
holder. I really didn't know much about it, and to be honest, when the flyer
came from kindergarten to say, "Do you want to play soccer?" I went home and
told mom and dad that I thought I wanted to play. They said, "Ok, great." They

tried to find teams, and at the time it was called WUSA (Wichita United Soccer Association). That's where my career started. My dad was my coach because there just weren't that many teams then. One day my godfather had two extra tickets so he brought my dad and I, and his son came. I could tell you we sat just to the right of the south tunnel on the glass. I remember it just like it was yesterday. That would have been in 1980. I just got bit, right then and there. I didn't get to go back much.

My dad was never a soccer player, so I remember him reading a book on how to coach just so we could have practice. As time went by, and I got a little bit older, he started to realize his capacity as coach had been met; even though he did a great job and we had lots of fun. I moved on to a traveling team, the Wichita Bandits, with Keith O'Donnell. Once you start to get into that realm you start going to the Wings camps. My friend Darren Snyder and the Snyder family owned Soccer West. He came to play for the Bandits. Darren would call and ask me to spend the night, but he didn't mean at his house, he meant at Soccer West. They'd lock us in the building and we'd spend the night playing soccer all night long. Then Pat would come and wake us up in the morning as teams were showing up to play.

With the Bandits traveling a lot, I started to come to these Wings camps and clinics. Back then that WAS the elite. There were no academies and developmental programs. You'd go there and learn. It was a fantastic experience. I can remember being on the field with my group and Chico Borja was teaching us how to shoot like he does: how to follow through and land on your shooting foot. I'll never forget it. Years later he and I were good friends. I went to live with him when I was with the Kansas City Wizards Developmental Team in my summers in between college seasons, back when Ron Newman was the coach...Learning from the Wings in the early days was a real privilege.

One of the first times I ever met Kim Roentved outside of the Coliseum was when [future Wichita Wing] Braeden Cloutier's father owned Soccer Kick up by Northwest High School. I was walking in to buy some indoor shoes because I had gone to play at Soccer West for the first time and I had outdoor cleats on. I didn't know. They told me I couldn't play and I was devastated. So me and another boy, every single shift, would switch shoes real quick on the bench. Who was walking out? Kim Roentved. I couldn't believe it. He signed everything I could find. Years later, he drafted me out of college and I ended up playing for him for a long time.

There were so many different guys that I liked for so many different reasons. Erik Rasmussen was always one of my favorites because he was so fantastic on the ball. I knew then that would never be my game. I was a banger...I'd get in there and mess things up and then give it to those guys who could do stuff like Erik. Terry Rowe was another big one for me because he worked so hard on defense and was so smart. Even watching Kris Peat and Ziggy Zigante...he gave me one of his gloves after a camp and I wore them to school.

Chico Borja went above and beyond for me, and in a lot of ways made me the player I was. The opportunities I was given came through him. In my younger years he and I became friends and he started training me one-on-one. My mom reached out to the Wings office and he started training me. The biggest turning point for me [was when] I went down to the Roy Rees Soccer Camp and [Rees] was a coach for the U-16 US national team. We lived on a college campus. That was the biggest turning point for me. I was really trim and fit. It changed everything for me. My confidence went up. Having that kind of top level training was fantastic.

I came back from that and I'm looking for something more and am really hungry for it. Then we found an avenue to Chico and we'd meet at the field and bring a bag of balls and cones and we'd get after it. Pretty soon I'm over at his house. He used to live off 21st and Woodlawn in a house that had a pool. I'd go over there and swim and BBQ and then go train. He'd go do the Chico Borja Camps and I'd help him do them, along with [Wichita Wing] Eddie Henderson. As things progressed, he said, "I think you should start training with the Wings." It became a great personal relationship. He talks to Roy and he approves me training with them. I show up as the nobody high school kid.

Larry Inlow would soon discover that playing with a bunch of experienced professional athletes was no joke...

LARRY INLOW: We split into two teams and it's two-touch with other restrictions...Then you have your training session and drills in the middle, and at the end of the day you play All-In again. But this time the winning team gets to vote for the worst player on the losing team. And that person is the "Wanker of the Day" and gets to wear a special shirt that's not a nice shirt. So the end of the All-In Game is very "game on." Nobody wants to be voted wanker. We're playing and it's me, Dale Ervine, Chico, and some others. I'm like 16 or 17-years-old. I had posted up inside the box and get the pass. Tommy Soehn is up against me. Dale Ervine is trailing me at the top of the box. The ball comes in to me and I don't know how or why I did this, but it worked great: I trap it, shimmy to the right, and then I pass it back to Ervine and he crushes a goal and we win. So the next practice I get the ball and I'm running back towards my own goal, and I'm gonna collect it nice and easy and pass it to Kris Peat and he's gonna give it to Chico. I barely get my foot on that ball and I swear a Mack truck hits me from behind. There's Tommy Soehn. Chico comes up beside me and says, "You might play a little quicker." Out there, considering my rank, it was a lesson to be learned. Keep your head up, look around, and play the ball quick. Those guys can travel so fast and they are thinking...they already know what's gonna happen two plays later. Learning how to read the game like those guys was the challenge.

[Wings forward] Eddie Henderson was my very good friend. [During the "Wanker of the Day" process] it was really easy to pick on people you knew, and vote for them. Eddie looked straight at me because he knew I was gonna vote for him just so I didn't make anybody else mad. He's my friend so it doesn't matter if I make him mad; but I'm not gonna make Terry Rowe or these other people mad. So it comes around to me and right as I'm about to say, "Eddie is my choice," Kim Roentved is on Eddie's team...right when I point, Eddie says, "Kim, Larry is voting for you!" Kim says, "Larry, did you vote for me!"... "Kim, no, I would never do that!" [laughs]

I earned a scholarship at Northeastern University in Boston. I get an NCAA packet and have to get some booster shots. A week-and-a-half later I got home from a jog and didn't feel right. My hands and feet felt weird. I blew it off. It never quite came back around. I told my mom, "Something's not right." She thought I was nervous about moving to Boston. Pretty soon, my hands and feet would be asleep all the time. I went to the doctor and they said, "We'll keep an eye on it." Then I started to lose strength...then I had to lean on things when I walked...then I started walking with a cane. Then I'm in a wheelchair, and they start doing all these tests. They think maybe I have MS. But it's not that. Then I'm immobile. I'm exhausted all the time.

One day we go out to St. Francis. Dr. Olmstead was there. He checked my reflexes, and they were all gone. He asked for the nurse, and said, "I need you to get a room ready in ICU." He looks at me and says, "You have Guillain-Barre Syndrome." Essentially, your plasma is attacking your body and shutting your immune system down. They think it was because I had a tainted flu booster that I took because of the NCAA requirement. They admitted me to the ICU and put a catheter into my chest and would give me an oil change of plasma and shock me to keep the nerve endings alive. The day they admitted me was the day I was supposed to fly out for preseason training at Northeastern. I was in the ICU for three weeks. By then I had atrophied so bad that I was learning to walk again. For the next full year I was in rehab and had to start from scratch. Chico would come up to sit with me. One day, he brought his LA Lazer All-Star jersey and asked me to hold onto it. He was real with me. He said, "I know you believe in God, and I do too, but I need you to do me a favor and not ask him to do something for you. I need YOU to get up and do it yourself." I always remember that. He was right, I could ask for all the help in the world, but until I do it myself I'm just gonna lay here.

Near the end of that year off, I'm watching a Newman University game, leaning against the fence. Cliff Brown had asked me to come to Newman before I had signed with Northeastern. I turned him down because I was going to Boston. So at his game, I said, "Hi," and he didn't really look over. I thought he must be mad at me. Brian Cushing, my best friend, played there. After the game, I said, "Tell Cliff I'm sorry if I made him mad." He didn't even recognize me because I had lost so much weight. Long story short, through the rehab, my goal was to get back on the field. What better chance do I have than to build core strength from the bottom up. I asked Cliff if I could come train with the team. Things rebounded quickly and Northeastern called and asked if I was ready to come. But the doctors were nervous about me leaving, so I stuck around here. I asked Cliff to give me a scholarship and he did. I was there for four years and became captain.

While at Newman University, Inlow had an opportunity to train with another group of professionals during his summer vacations.

LARRY INLOW: Chico and I became very close personal friends. He got me into the Wings. When he decided to leave and become part of the [Kansas City] Wizards coaching staff, he said, "Why don't you come up to KC and train with the Wizards?" I thought, "Yes!" In college I was three-time All-Conference, two-time All-American, so I had always thought it would be outdoor or nothing. So every summer in college I would drive to KC and live with him and his family and train with the Wizards at Arrowhead Stadium. I would train during the week and watch the game at Arrowhead if it was at home. Then I'd leave Arrowhead, come back to Wichita, hang out with the family for a day-and-a-half, get some clothes and come back and do it over again. [MISL star] Preki was there, and he was unbelievable. So good. We were at practice one day. Coach Ron Newman says we're gonna play one-on-one. I was matched against Preki. His knee hit my knee and I was mortified I had hurt him. I can remember Ron walking over and asking if I was alright, and that was it. Eventually, they asked me to be part of the "B team" for the Wizards and play against the other MLS teams. When they asked me that, I asked them if it would wreck my college eligibility. I wanted to do it more than anything, but I still had to go to school, and they couldn't guarantee that it wouldn't. Then Ron Newman was fired, and my "in" was gone. The new coaching staff came in and that was it for my MLS opportunity.

In 1997, after college graduation, Larry Inlow would find his road to a professional soccer career would begin with the Wichita Wings. He wouldn't be the only Wichita boy to grow up to become a Wing. Shon Padilla, Brian Cushing, Jamie Harding, Kevin Law, LeBaron and Mike Hollimon, Braeden Cloutier, among others, all grew up watching the Wings play. As adults, they would become Wings just like the players they so admired.

LARRY INLOW: In the NPSL you could sign a developmental contract. It was their way to develop young guys who could eventually step into a full contract. You could be a developmental player and suit up for a game. Shon Padilla was there before Jamie Harding, Brian Cushing, Kevin Law, or I came on board. Jamie and "Cush" signed before me, and then I signed a year later. They were local talent that got their shot. They are still highly involved in youth soccer today. In the beginning, when I first signed my contract, it was a learn-as-you-go kind of thing. They would give you subtle hints: "Next time, try it down the wall." No craziness or yelling. But the next time you didn't do it, they'd let you know. Roentved and Kewley, they were very good teachers. They let you play, they didn't handcuff you. They didn't put restraints on you like some coaches, who have their systems and don't let you deviate.

[The first home game as a Wing was] an amazing thing. It's an amazing amount of pressure. That's why Kim took me on the road first because there is no pressure. I don't have anyone to impress out there. But at home you have your parents, your wife, and all your friends. As a player, you are thinking, "I don't want to disappoint them." But the reward is phenomenal.

Inlow had the great fortune to play with several of the great players from the MISL-era Wings, including Erik Rasmussen, Terry Rowe, Kim Roentved, and Kris Peat.

LARRY INLOW: Playing with Erik [Rasmussen] was unbelievable. He was older but it didn't matter. He was timeless. Every morning I'd pick up Terry Rowe for practice and we'd stop and get his coffee and when we pulled up, Erik would be outside the building in his tracksuit. We'd sit there getting taped up and he would walk straight in, get onto the field and start jogging laps. I don't mean getting after it and stopping to stretch...I just mean light jogging. As soon as Terry and I came onto the field, he'd say, "Alright boys, see ya." Then he'd show up for the game on Friday and score six goals. He was just unbelievable. He was limiting the wear-and-tear on the old body and that was perfectly okay with every single one of us. All you had to do was give him the ball and get out of his way. He never really crushed the ball. He'd find the corners. His spin move...I loved it.

[He was] super nice off the pitch. The night of my home debut, three days after the end of my college career, we came back from a road trip to Edmonton. Erik took me out on the town and we had a great time...There was a lot of explorer in Erik. A brilliant man on AND off the field, and a great friend to boot. I have nothing but appreciation and gratitude for everything he taught me...If there was anything to be done to help people, or youth of any country excel, it doesn't surprise me that Erik would be a part of it.

The first time I met Terry Rowe I didn't understand a word he said. He stuttered on top of a serious accent. The first couple weeks I just shook my head, or said, "What?" Then, it started to click and I was on the same page as him. I went over and met his wife and had tea with him. Everyday we'd go to practice together. I considered him a very good friend.

Tommy O'Neill was very nice and approachable. All those guys were so approachable. Those guys made such an impression on the youth that they wanted to support them. Those guys built a dynasty that was long and true. The impact spread far and wide. It's important to keep it alive...I got to play against Andy Chapman when he played for the Detroit Rockers. We were out playing in the Palace. I looked at Jamie [Harding] and said, "Look! That's Andy Chapman!" So we started talking to him.

Kevin Kewley was a big influence on me. He was one of those players, and even into his coaching career, that still coached youth soccer. Jamie Harding played for him. He always had a vested interest in youth soccer. He believed so much in the youth that he signed us to contracts. I can't thank him enough for his contribution to the city of Wichita...Lebaron [Hollimon] was the real deal. He had a storied history with Wichita.

Roy Turner was my general manager in Mississippi [with the Beach Kings]. I didn't get his Wichita wisdom, but I got all his wisdom when he came down to Mississippi in the Eastern Indoor Soccer League. He was a fantastic general manager. I really enjoyed playing for him. Between him and the head coach, Gary Henley, there wasn't anything that wasn't taken care of. Anything that was promised was taken care of.

Without [the Wings] it would be so vastly different. I couldn't imagine soccer here without the Wings setting the tone. They were so big...bigger than life in the beginning. Real superstars. How many people can say they made hundreds of thousands of dollars playing indoor soccer? The money I made I thought was fantastic, but it was nothing compared to what they made in the early days. It was real... NFL, NBA, NHL real. There was unbelievable talent from around the world. Just to have that in a place like Wichita, it's still impacting people to this day. How many players have come through here that had world class talent? Those guys blazed a trail for us coming up, and that's what I want to do for the youth today. You've got to pass it on. [Wings goalkeeper] Sammy [Lane] was talking about the old days, and said, "Boys, I'll tell you this, you don't know what you have until it's gone." And Kevin Kewley once told us, "One day you will stop playing soccer and it will be for one of two reasons: You'll say you're done or someone will tell you you're done. So make the most of this."

In 1978, Tom Marshall held an exhibition game at the Kansas Coliseum featuring Roy Turner and the Dallas Tornado. The proceeds from that exhibition would pay for new youth soccer fields near 13th and Greenwich. The ultimate irony is that Larry Inlow would play on those very fields as a boy. The legacy of the Wichita Wings continued through the 1990s with Larry Inlow and other boys who would be Wings. It would continue further with a new generation in the last few years. That legacy continues...and will never die.

Wings on National and Olympic Teams

———

Name	Country	Notes
Ayre, Garry	Canada	1973-77 Nat. team: 9 caps/1976 Olympics
Bordinggaard, Keld	Denmark	1983-90 Nat. team: 4 caps
Borja, Chico	USA	1982-88 Nat. team: 11 caps-3 goals/1984 Olympics
Brcic, David	USA	1979-85 Nat. team: 4 caps/1980 and 1984 Olympics
Cooke, Charlie	Scotland	1966 and 1970 World Cup qualifiers: 16 caps
DeBose, Winston	USA	1979-85 Nat. team: 14 caps
DeBrito, Pedro	USA	1983 Nat. team: 1 cap
Diffey, John	USA	1988 Nat. team: 7 caps
Donigan, Dan	USA	1990 Nat. team: 1 cap
Dunn, Jason	USA	1994 Nat. team friendlies: 3 caps
Eck, Ted	USA	1989-96 Nat. team: 13 caps-1 goal
Eichmann, Eric	USA	1986-93 Nat. team: 29 caps-4 goals/'88 Olympics. 4 games
Ervine, Dale	USA	1985-93 Nat. team: 5 caps
Fox, Mike	USA	16 caps/1984 Olympics: 3 games

Garcia, Freddie	USA	1974 Nat. team
Haynes, Brian	Trinidad	1987-96 Nat. team: 21 caps-8 goals
Holness, Kevin	Canada	1995-96 Nat. team: 9 caps-2 goals
Hooker, Jeff	USA	1984-87 Nat. team: 12 caps-1 goal/1984 Olympics: 2 games
Ivanow, Mike	USA	1973-75 Nat. team: 10 caps/1976 Olympic: 5 games
Kirk, Joey	USA	1987-88 Nat. team: 7 caps
Kouzmanis, Tom	Canada	1995-97 Nat. team: 5 caps-4 goals
Kristensen, Jorgen	Denmark	1971-78 Nat. team: 19 caps-3 goals
Kusch, Garrett	Canada	1997-2001 Nat. team: 21 caps-1 goal
Liotart, Hank	USA	1975 Nat. team: 4 caps
Lund, Flemming	Denmark	1972-79 Nat. team: 20 caps-2 goals
McDonagh, Seamus	Ireland	1981-85 Nat. team: 25 caps
Moreira, Chico	Uruguay	1976-81 Nat. team: 24 caps
Moreland, Victor	N. Ireland	1978-79 Nat. team: 6 caps-1 goal
Myernick, Glenn	USA	1977-78 Nat. team: 10 caps/1976 Olympic qualif.: 4 games
Ortiz, Oscar	Argentina	1978 World Cup winner: 23 caps-3 goals
Pittman, Steve	USA	1990-97 Nat. team: 3 caps
Radwanski, Ed	USA	1985 Nat. team: 5 caps
Rasmussen, Erik	Denmark	1990-91 Nat. team: 2 caps/1984 Olympic qualifiers

Roentved, Per	Denmark	1970-82 Nat. team: 75 caps-11 goals-Captain
Thomas, Mickey	Wales	1976-86 Nat. team: 51 caps-4 goals
Turner, Roy	USA	1973 Nat. team: 2 caps
Vaccaro, Cris	Puerto Rico	1992 Olympic qualifying
Van Der Beck, Perry	USA	1982 and 1986 World Cup qualifiers: 23 caps-2 goals
Vanole, David	USA	1986-90 Nat. team: 18 caps/1988 Olympics: 9 games
Velazco, Arturo	USA	1988 Nat. team: 2 caps
Ward, Peter	England	1980 Nat. team: 1 cap
Watson, Clyde	Guyana	1982 World Cup qualif.: 3 caps-4 goals
Wegerle, Steve	S. Africa	1974 Unofficial S. African Nat. team
Welch, Art	Jamaica	1966 & 1970 World Cup qualif.: 4 caps-1 goal
Willrich, Jean	USA	1984 Olympics: 2 games-1 goal

Wings in English First Division (Premier League)

———

Name	Team	Notes
Anderson, Willie	Manchester United	1967-73: 9 games
Bourne, Jeff	Derby County	1971-77: 73 games-14 goals
Earle, Steve	Leicester City	1973-78: 90 games-20 goals
Hoggan, Dave	Bolton	1979-80: 3 games
Kewley, Kevin	Liverpool	1977-78: 1 game
McDonagh, Seamus	Bolton/Everton	1978-81: 124 games
Moreland, Victor	Derby County	1978-80: 42 games-1 goal
Nicholl, Terry	Sheffield United	1973-75: 22 games-1 goal
Ryan, Jimmy	Man U/Luton Twn	1963-74: 24 games-4 goals (Man U stats only)
Stanley, Gary	Chelsea/Everton	1977-81: 99 games-7 goals
Thomas, Mickey	Man U/Evrtn/Chelsea/Stk	1978-91: 240 games-41 goals
Wallace, Barry	Queens Park Rangers	1977-79: 18 games
Ward, Peter	Nottingham/Brighton	1979-83: 31 games-7 goals

NOTES

Chapter 1 - Humble Beginnings
Includes information from author interviews with Roy Turner and Kevin Kewley.

1. Simon Jones, "Liverpool in the Blitz," *History Today,* July 7, 2003, accessed June 19, 2015, http://www.historytoday.com/simon-jones/liverpool-blitz.
2. David Kynaston, *Austerity Britain: 1945-1951,* [New York: Walker and Company, 2008], pg. 105.
3. Ibid., p. 19.
4. Ibid., p. 107.
5. Ibid., p. 246-7.
6. Ibid., p. 190.
7. Ibid., p. 192.
8. Ibid., p. 249.
9. Dave Kratzer, "Roy Turner," *The Wichitan,* November 1983, 20.
10. "Toronto Falcons Rosters," accessed June 25, 2015, http://www.nasljerseys.com/Rosters/Falcons_Rosters.htm.
11. Steve Holroyd and David Litterer, "The Year in American Soccer - 1967," accessed June 25, 2015, http://homepages.sover.net/~spectrum/year/1967.html.
12. "North American Soccer League Statistics," accessed June 25, 2015, http://www.nasljerseys.com/Stats/Standings.htm.
13. "North American Soccer League Players," accessed June 25, 2015, http://www.nasljerseys.com/Players/T/Turner.Roy.htm.
14. "North American Soccer League Statistics."
15. "North American Soccer League Players."
16. "The Year in American Soccer - 1967."
17. Ibid.
18. "Cleveland Stokers Rosters," accessed June 25, 2015, http://www.nasljerseys.com/Rosters/Stokers_Rosters.htm#1968.
19. "North American Soccer League Statistics."
20. Steve Holroyd and David Litterer, "The Year in American Soccer - 1968," accessed June 25, 2015, http://homepages.sover.net/~spectrum/year/1968.html.

21. Steve Pate, "Turner the Wild Beast," *The Dallas Morning News*, June 14, 1974.
22. "The Year in American Soccer - 1968."

Chapter 2 - Digger the Destroyer

Includes information from author interviews with Roy Turner, Al Miller, Steve Pecher, Norm Hitzges, and Kenny Cooper.

1. "North American Soccer League Statistics," accessed July 6, 2015, http://www. nasljerseys.com/Stats/Standings.htm.
2. Staff, "Tornado Loses Turner...", *The Dallas Morning News*, August 7, 1969.
3. "North American Soccer League Statistics."
4. Steve Pate, "Turner the Wild Beast," *The Dallas Morning News*, June 14, 1974.
5. Temple Pouncey, "Mad Dogs and Englishmen," *The Dallas Morning News*, July 9, 1978.
6. Roy Edwards, "A Stronger Tornado," *The Dallas Morning News*, March 29, 1970.
7. "North American Soccer League Statistics."
8. Staff, "Best Again an All-Star," *The Dallas Morning News*, October 11, 1970.
9. Pouncey, "Mad Dogs and Englishmen."
10. Steve Holroyd and David Litterer, "The Year in American Soccer - 1971," accessed July 8, 2015, http://homepages.sover.net/~spectrum/year/1971.html.
11. Michael Lewis, "Back In The Day: The NASL's Longest Game," accessed July 8, 2015, http://www.ussoccerplayers.com/2011/09/back-in-the-day-the-nasls-longest-game.html.
12. "The Year in American Soccer - 1971."
13. Colin Jose, *North American Soccer League Encyclopedia*, [Haworth, NJ: St. Johann Press, 2003], 300.
14. Steve Holroyd and David Litterer, "The Year in American Soccer - 1972," accessed July 8, 2015, http://homepages.sover.net/~spectrum/year/1972.html.
15. Jose, *NASL Encyclopedia*, 300.
16. Steve Holroyd and David Litterer, "The Year in American Soccer - 1973," accessed July 9, 2015, http://homepages.sover.net/~spectrum/year/1973.html.
17. "USA - Details of International Matches 1970-1979," accessed July 9, 2015, http:// www.rsssf.com/tablesu/usa-intres-det70.html.

18. Staff, "Hall, Turner Sworn In," *The Dallas Morning News*, April 13, 1976.

19. Pate, "Turner the Wild Beast."

20. Temple Pouncey, "Horton, Diplomats Invade," *The Dallas Morning News*, May 4, 1975.

21. Jose, *NASL Encyclopedia*, 300.

Chapter 3 - Texas Twister
Includes information from author interviews with Kevin Kewley, Al Miller, Dave Phillips, Steve Pecher, Kenny Cooper, Norm Hitzges, and Roy Turner.

1. "North American Soccer League Players," accessed July 9, 2015, http://www.nasljerseys.com/Players/K/Kewley.Kevin.htm.

2. "North American Soccer League Statistics," accessed July 11, 2015, http://www.nasljerseys.com/Stats/Standings.htm.

3. Temple Pouncey, "Zany Promotions Enliven '77 Season For Tornado," *The Dallas Morning News*, April 3, 1977.

4. Temple Pouncey, "Turner Fights To Keep Spot on Tornado Roster," *The Dallas Morning News*, March 22, 1977.

5. Colin Jose, *North American Soccer League Encyclopedia*, [Haworth, NJ: St. Johann Press, 2003], 300.

6. Temple Pouncey, "Pele, Coop Eye-to-Eye," *The Dallas Morning News*, April 24, 1977.

7. "Pele 1977 - Game by Game," accessed July 13, 2015, http://www.nasljerseys.com/Players/P/PeleGameByGame1977.htm

8. Staff, "Turner Out For Year," *The Dallas Morning News*, June 15, 1977.

9. Jose, *NASL Encyclopedia*, 300.

10. Temple Pouncey, "Dallas' Win Ryan's Hope," *The Dallas Morning News*, May 20, 1978.

11. Temple Pouncey, "Best of Tornado," *The Dallas Morning News*, July 16, 1976.

12. Temple Pouncey, "Mad Dogs and Englishmen," *The Dallas Morning News*, July 9, 1978.

13. Temple Pouncey, "It's Turner Night - Or Hinton's," *The Dallas Morning News*, July 8, 1978.

Chapter 4 - Hockey, Hold the Ice...
Includes information from author interviews with Al Miller, Doug Verb, Alan Shepherd, Kevin Himes, Tom Marshall, Jackie Knapp, and Roy Turner.

1. "What A Long Strange Trip It's Been!" accessed July 14, 2015, http://homepages. sover.net/~spectrum/strangetrip.html, [Originally appeared in *Goal Indoor Magazine*, 2004]
2. Temple Pouncey, "Mad Dogs and Englishmen," *The Dallas Morning News*, July 9, 1978.
3. "Dallas Tornado Rosters," accessed July 14, 2015, http://www.nasljerseys.com/Rosters/Tornado_Rosters.htm.
4. "NASL 1970-74 Friendlies," accessed July 14, 2015, http://www.nasljerseys.com/Friendlies/Friendlies%201970-74.htm.
5. "Virginia Squires Timeline History," accessed July 14, 2015, http://virginiasquires.homestead.com/History.html.
6. "MISL Rosters," accessed July 15, 2015, http://www.nasljerseys.com/MISL/Rosters/MISL_Rosters.htm.
7. Staff, "Enthusiasts Propose Soccer Complex," *The Wichitan Magazine*, July 1978.
8. Ibid.
9. Mal Elliott, "Soccer Match To Feature Nation's Best," *The Wichita Eagle and Beacon*, November 28, 1978.
10. Mal Elliott, "Dallas-Houston Soccer Draws 5,800 To Coliseum," *The Wichita Eagle and Beacon*, December 2, 1978.
11. Staff, "Chicago, Tulsa To Square Off In Indoor Soccer Here Tonight," *The Wichita Eagle and Beacon*, February 2, 1979, 5D.

Chapter 5 - Chasing Down the Dream
Includes information from author interviews with Jackie Knapp, Tom Marshall, Bob Becker, Roy Turner, Al Miller, Kenny Cooper, Alan Shepherd, Doug Verb, Norman Piper, and Kevin Kewley.

1. Mal Elliott, "Drive To Bring Pro Soccer To Wichita Is Under Way," *The Wichita Eagle and Beacon*, April 8, 1979, 1D.

2. Mal Elliott, "Wichita Gets Franchise In Pro Soccer League," *The Wichita Eagle and Beacon*, June 29, 1979, 14A.

3. Mal Elliott, "Marshall's Soccer Dream Is Near Reality," *The Wichita Eagle and Beacon*, July 8, 1979.

4. Mal Elliott, "Wings Expected To Join MISL As Expansion Team," *The Wichita Eagle and Beacon*, August 18, 1979.

5. Mal Elliott, "Wichita Awarded Indoor Soccer League Franchise," *The Wichita Eagle*, August 23, 1979, 1C.

6. Mal Elliott, "Soccer Team State's First Major League Pro Franchise," *The Wichita Beacon*, August 23, 1979.

7. Mal Elliott, "Indoor Soccer," *The Wichita Eagle and Beacon*, August 26, 1979.

8. Mike Limon, "Wings Hope To Become 'Green Bay Packers of MISL'," *The Wichita Eagle and Beacon*, September 15, 1979, 5D.

9. Mal Elliott, "Turner Named Coach Of Wichita Wings," *The Wichita Eagle and Beacon*, September 26, 1979.

10. Elliott, "Indoor Soccer."

11. Steve Love, "Wings' Coach Can Bang The Drum With The Best," *The Wichita Beacon*, September 26, 1979, 1C.

12. Mal Elliott, "Piper Becomes First Wing By Default," *The Wichita Eagle and Beacon*, October 10, 1979, 5C.

13. Ibid.

14. Steve Love, "If You Aren't Crazy, You Had Better Be Good," *The Wichita Beacon*, October 10, 1979, 1C.

15. Steve Love, "Children Give A Hand To The Fancy-Feet Men," *The Wichita Beacon*, October 25, 1979.

16. "North American Soccer League Players," accessed July 21, 2015, http://www.nasljerseys.com/Players/B/Barton.Frank.htm.

17. Mal Elliott, "Wings Add Yank, Englishman To Team," *The Wichita Beacon*, October 31, 1979.

18. Staff, "Wings Sign Myernick," *The Wichita Beacon*, November 2, 1979.

19. Steve Love, "This Custer Had To Make Stand," *The Wichita Beacon*, November 21, 1979.

20. Mike Limon, "The Came To Play For Wings," *The Wichita Beacon*, November 5, 1979, 1C.

Chapter 6 - Behind the Orange Curtain

Includes information from author interviews with Doug Verb, Jackie Knapp, Tom Marshall, Bob Becker, Roy Turner, Ray Denton, Virginia Creamer, and Kevin Kewley.

1. Randy Brown, "Marshall Quits Wings," *The Wichita Beacon*, November 23, 1979.
2. Randy Brown, "Marshall Denies Resigning, Won't Stay," *The Wichita Eagle and Beacon*, November 24, 1979. 1D.
3. Ibid.
4. Randy Brown, "Wings-Marshall Conflict Deepens," *The Wichita Eagle and Beacon*, November 25, 1979.
5. Steve Love, "A Wing Dingy Of A Way To Start A Soccer Season," *The Wichita Beacon*, November 27, 1979, 1B.
6. Mike Limon, "Has Internal Turmoil Turned Wings' Dreams Sour?" *The Wichita Eagle*, November 29, 1979, 4E.
7. Love, "A Wing Dingy Of A Way…"
8. Mike Limon, "Wings Take Arrows To Wire in 6-4 Loss," *The Wichita Eagle and Beacon*, December 1, 1979.

Chapter 7 - Sex, George, and Soccer Balls

Includes information from author interviews with Ray Denton, Virginia Creamer, Jackie Knapp, Doug Verb, and Roy Turner.

1. Staff, "Angel Tryouts Draw 28," *The Wichita Beacon*, December 11, 1979.
2. Virginia Creamer, "The Angel Years," *Orange and Blue Review*, 1988.
3. Ibid.
4. Mike Limon, "Wings To Get To Show Off Flashy Uniforms On TV," *The Wichita Eagle and Beacon*, December 5, 1979.
5. Mike Limon, "How Many Really Watch Wings?" *The Wichita Eagle and Beacon*, January 17, 1980, 1C.
6. Alan Schroeder, "Soccer Becomes Part Of Wichita Culture," *The Wichita Eagle*, January 18, 1980, 1B.
7. Steve Love, "He Is A Mouth For Hire," *The Wichita Beacon*, January 16, 1980, 1C.

Chapter 8 - The Lads

Includes information from author interviews with Roy Turner, Kevin Kewley, Tom Marshall, Ray Denton, Andy Chapman, Terry Nicholl, Tom Shine, Mike Dowler, Jackie Knapp, Norman Piper, Virginia Creamer, Al Miller, Doug Verb, and Kenny Cooper.

1. Staff, "Jimmy Ryan: The Look Of Eagles," *Missile Magazine*, Volume III, Issue 5, 1980-81, pg. N-25.
2. Ibid.
3. Randy Brown, "Ley's Future Is Uncertain, So He's Working on Wings'," *The Wichita Eagle and Beacon*, February 24, 1980, 7G.
4. Mike Limon, "Waiting In Wings," *The Wichita Beacon*, December 19, 1979.
5. Ibid.
6. Mike Limon, "Goodbye Ivanow," *The Wichita Beacon*, February 1, 1980.
7. Rob Barzegar, Wichita Wings 1998-99 Souvenir Yearbook.
8. Ibid.
9. Randy Brown, "Indoor Soccer A Game To Stormin' Norman," *The Wichita Eagle and Beacon*, February 16, 1980.
10. Barzegar, 1998-99 Yearbook.
11. Mike Limon, "Gehling's Soccer Career 'Like A Dream'," *The Wichita Beacon*, January 15, 1980, 1B.
12. Steve Love, "Anderson Answers Higher Call," *The Wichita Beacon*, February 7, 1980, 1C.
13. Barzegar, 1998-99 Yearbook.
14. Ibid.
15. Mike Limon, "Mod Sod," *The Wichita Beacon*, December 14, 1979, 1C.
16. Ibid.

Chapter 9 - Disaster, Triumph...and a Savior

Includes information from author interviews with Bob Becker, Ray Denton, Virginia Creamer, Doug Verb, Roy Turner, Kevin Kewley, and Bill Kentling.

1. Mike Limon, "Wings Bury Detroit, Move Into 2nd," *The Wichita Eagle and Beacon*, February 13, 1980.
2. Mike Limon, "Injury Sidelines Wings' Ayre For Season," *The Wichita Eagle and Beacon*, February 22, 1980.

3. Mike Limon, "Wings Owner Withdraws Backing," *The Wichita Eagle and Beacon*, February 26, 1980.

4. Ibid.

5. Steve Love, "Money: It's Why The Wings May Leave," *The Wichita Beacon*, February 26, 1980, 1B.

6. Mike Limon, "Wings Trouble Shocks MISL Official," *The Wichita Eagle and Beacon*, February 27, 1980, 5C.

7. Ibid.

8. Mike Limon, "MISL Sets April Deadline For Wings," *The Wichita Eagle and Beacon*, February 28, 1980.

9. Mike Limon, "Wings To Face Buffalo," *The Wichita Eagle and Beacon*, March 4, 1980.

10. Staff, "Rally 'Round The Wings Wichita," *The Wichita Beacon*, March 6, 1980, 4A.

11. Steve Love, "If These Folks Can't Save Wings, No One Can," *The Wichita Beacon*, March 10, 1980, 1C.

12. Ibid.

13. Steve Love, "Pluto And Mickey Were On Wings' Side - Again," *The Wichita Beacon*, March 12, 1980.

14. Ibid.

15. Randy Brown, "Play It Again Sam; Let's See That Goal," *The Wichita Eagle and Beacon*, March 15, 1980, 1D.

16. Ibid.

17. Randy Brown, "Season Tickets Key To Wings' Drive," *The Wichita Eagle and Beacon*, March 15, 1980, 1D.

18. Mike Limon, "Search Continues For Major Investor In Wings," *The Wichita Eagle*, March 27, 1980, 1D.

19. Mal Elliott, "$760,000 More Needed In Drive To Save Wings," *The Wichita Eagle and Beacon*, March 29, 1980, 1D.

20. Mike Limon, "Carney Buys Wichita Wings," *The Wichita Eagle*, April 16, 1980, 11A.

21. Staff, "Wings Select Hardage As Managing Partner," *The Wichita Eagle and Beacon*, May 20, 1980.

22. Mike Limon, "Ex-Pizza Exec Named Wings GM," *The Wichita Eagle and Beacon*, May 23, 1980.

Chapter 10 - Curve It Like Chapman

Includes information from author interviews with Roy Turner, Kevin Kewley, Virginia Creamer, Charlie Minshull-Ford, Terry Nicholl, Bruce Haertl, Andy Chapman, Bill Kentling, and Christy Roberts.

1. Rob Barzegar, Wichita Wings 1998-99 Souvenir Yearbook.

Chapter 11 - Wings...Version 2.0

Includes information from author interviews with Kevin Kewley, Bill Kentling, Roy Turner, Dr. Jay Price, Tom Shine, Steve Shaad, Virginia Creamer, Kevin Himes, and Andy Chapman.

1. Staff, "Piper 1st Player Signed By Wings," *The Wichita Eagle and Beacon*, June 24, 1980.
2. Staff, "Wings Sign Kewley For 1980-81," *The Wichita Eagle and Beacon*, June 28, 1980.
3. Staff, "Howarth And Chapman To Be Back With Wings," *The Wichita Eagle and Beacon*, July 4, 1980.
4. "North American Soccer League Players," accessed August 22, 2015, http://www.nasljerseys.com/Players/Players_Roster.htm.
5. Lonnie Crider, "Wings Evolve As Local Club," *The Wichita Eagle and Beacon*, October 20, 1980, 3D.
6. Lonnie Crider, "Carney Replaces Hardage As Chairman Of Wings," *The Wichita Eagle and Beacon*, November 21, 1980.
7. Randy Brown, "Wings Soar By 1,000 Season Ticket Mark," *The Wichita Eagle and Beacon*, June 24, 1980.
8. Connie Pickett, "Cheerleading Is More Than Kicks, Smiles," *The Wichita Eagle-Beacon*, October 5, 1980, 1D.
9. Frank Deford, "Show, Sex and Suburbs," *Sports Illustrated*, February 28, 1983
10. Ibid.
11. Ibid.
12. Staff, "Wonder Wing," *The Wichita Eagle and Beacon*, September 21, 1980.
13. Bob Getz, "Lack Of Gratitude Bad For Ex-Mascot's Attitude," *The Wichita Eagle and Beacon*, March 29, 1981.

14. Rob Barzegar, Wichita Wings 1998-99 Souvenir Yearbook.

15. Ibid.

16. Staff, "Wings Sign German Standout," *The Wichita Eagle and Beacon*, September 11, 1980.

17. Staff, "Former Hartford Coach Liotart Signed By Wings," *The Wichita Eagle and Beacon*, October 1, 1980.

18. Barzegar, 1998-99 Yearbook.

19. Ibid.

20. Staff, "Wings Sign Tulsa's Earle," *The Wichita Eagle-Beacon*, October 8, 1980, 19A.

21. Barzegar, 1998-99 Yearbook.

22. Lonnie Crider, "Mancini Appeal Withdrawn," *The Wichita Eagle and Beacon*, January 1, 1981, 8C.

23. Barzegar, 1998-99 Yearbook.

24. Steve Holroyd and David Litterer, "The Year in American Soccer - 1981," accessed September 5, 2015, http://homepages.sover.net/~spectrum/year/1981.html.

25. Mal Elliott, "Three-Time ASL All-Star Signs Contract With Wings," *The Wichita Eagle and Beacon*, August 26, 1980.

26. Barzegar, 1998-99 Yearbook.

27. Lonnie Crider, "Wings' Chapman Stays On Target," *The Wichita Eagle-Beacon*, November 27, 1980, 4E.

Chapter 12 - Two Danes and a Welshman Walk Into The Hatch Cover...

Includes information from author interviews with Roy Turner, Tom Shine, Terry Nicholl, Kevin Kewley, Charlie Minshull-Ford, Bill Kentling, Kim Roentved, Virginia Creamer, Bruce Haertl, Kevin Himes, David Weber, Eric Scriven, Norman Piper, Mark Weddle and Mike Dowler.

1. Staff, "Wings Sign Danish Star Kristensen," *The Wichita Eagle and Beacon*, October 6, 1980.

2. Lonnie Crider, "Wings' Man Of Many Assists Finally Makes It Into Town," *The Wichita Eagle and Beacon*, November 5, 1980, 5C.

3. Ibid.

4. Ibid.

5. Carol DeWoskin, "Kristensen The Master Magician," *Missile Magazine*, January 19, 1984, L-5.

6. Randy Brown, "Great Deal, Great Danes," *The Wichita Eagle-Beacon*, December 11, 1980.

7. Carol DeWoskin, "Kim Roentved: A Rising Star," *Missile Magazine*, December 23, 1983, L-5.

8. Ibid.

9. Ibid.

10. Randy Brown, "Great Deal, Great Danes."

11. Ibid.

12. Staff, "Wings Sign Higgs, Hobgood," *The Wichita Eagle and Beacon*, September 22, 1980.

13. Lonnie Crider, "Goaltending Has Been Good To Van Eron," *The Wichita Eagle and Beacon*, October 23, 1980, 6C.

14. Lonnie Crider, "Wings Goalkeepers: Another Episode," *The Wichita Eagle and Beacon*, October 30, 1980.

15. Lonnie Crider, "Wings Add Another Goalie To The Flock," *The Wichita Eagle and Beacon*, November 13, 1980.

16. Carol DeWoskin, "Dowler's A Dandy In The Nets," *Missile Magazine*, January 21, 1984, L-5.

17. Ibid.

18. Randy Brown, "Next Chapter: Van Eron And His Amazing Knee," *The Wichita Eagle and Beacon*, November 30, 1980, 13G.

19. Wire Service, "Fever's Goalie Wins Honor," *The Wichita Eagle and Beacon*, December 16, 1980.

20. Wire Service, "Wings' Dowler Top MISL Goalkeeper," *The Wichita Eagle and Beacon*, December 30, 1980.

21. Lonnie Crider, "Wings Notch 2nd Shutout," *The Wichita Eagle and Beacon*, January 3, 1981, 1D.

22. Steve Love, "Wings Run Past Stallions 6-2," *The Wichita Eagle and Beacon*, January 13, 1981, 1C.

23. Steve Love, "Wings Sell Van Eron To Philadelphia," *The Wichita Eagle and Beacon*, January 20, 1981, 1C.

24. Ibid.

25. Ibid.

26. Wire Service, "Dowler Wins MISL Title," *The Wichita Eagle and Beacon*, March 10, 1981.

Chapter 13 - The Fog of War, The Agony of Defeat
Includes information from author interviews with Kenny Cooper, Roy Turner, Steve Shaad, Bill Kentling, Steve Pecher, Chris Johnson, Mike Dowler, Kevin Kewley, Kim Roentved, Andy Chapman, Norman Piper, Tom Shine, Mark Weddle, Bruce Haertl, and Louis McCluer.

1. Randy Brown, "The Prophet Turner Takes Look At MISL," *The Wichita Eagle and Beacon*, November 20, 1980.

2. Ibid.

3. Ibid.

4. Rob Barzegar, Wichita Wings 1998-99 Souvenir Yearbook.

5. Randy Brown, "Wings Love (To Beat) New York," *The Wichita Eagle-Beacon*, December 4, 1980.

6. Editorial Staff, "Where Are Fans?" *The Wichita Eagle-Beacon*, December 4, 1980.

7. Al Villegas, "Get Out And Support The Wings Wichita Saved," *The Wichita Eagle-Beacon*, December 7, 1980.

8. Editorial Staff, "Whither The Wind And The Wings?" *The Wichita Eagle-Beacon*, December 11, 1980.

9. Staff, "Chamber Offers Discount Tickets To Wings Game," *The Wichita Eagle-Beacon*, December 20, 1980.

10. Randy Brown, "TV Cameras To Peer Through The Fog At Wings," *The Wichita Eagle-Beacon*, December 28, 1980, 2G.

11. Ibid.

12. Randy Brown, "Ryan Scores Hat Trick As Wings Whip Fog 8-0," *The Wichita Eagle-Beacon*, December 29, 1980, 1C.

13. Randy Brown, "Wings: Ban Fog Forward Mancini From MISL For Life," *The Wichita Eagle-Beacon*, December 29, 1980, 1C.

14. Lonnie Crider, "Fog's Mancini Out For 1 Week," *The Wichita Eagle-Beacon*, December 30, 1980, 1C.

15. Ibid.

16. Lonnie Crider, "Mancini Appeal Withdrawn," *The Wichita Eagle-Beacon*, January 1, 1981, 8C.

17. Lonnie Crider, "Wings Notch 2nd Shutout," *The Wichita Eagle-Beacon*, January 3, 1981, 1D.

18. Lonnie Crider, "Wings Powder Baltimore 10-3," *The Wichita Eagle-Beacon*, January 10, 1981, 1D.

19. Steve Love, "Wings Don't Have It All - Or Want It," *The Wichita Eagle-Beacon*, January 12, 1981.

20. Ibid.

21. Steve Love, "Podunk Of The Plains Meets City By The Bay," *The Wichita Eagle-Beacon*, January 23, 1981, 10A.

22. Rob Barzegar, Wichita Wings 1998-99 Souvenir Yearbook.

23. Dianna Sinovic, "Here Comes Soccer Nut - Er, Principal," *The Wichita Eagle-Beacon*, February 10, 1981.

24. Ibid.

25. Randy Brown, "MISL Misfired On All-Stars," *The Wichita Eagle-Beacon*, February 7, 1981.

26. Ibid.

27. Staff, "Wings' Shutout String Ends With A Thud," *The Wichita Eagle-Beacon*, January 5, 1981, 1C.

28. Staff, "Steamers Whip Wings," *The Wichita Eagle-Beacon*, January 19, 1981.

29. Lonnie Crider, "St. Louis Deflates Wings 8-6," *The Wichita Eagle-Beacon*, January 19, 1981.

30. Barzegar, 1998-99 Yearbook.

31. Lonnie Crider, "There's Still Life In The Wings," *The Wichita Eagle-Beacon*, March 19, 1981.

32. Lonnie Crider, "Wings Capture MISL Quarterfinal Series," *The Wichita Eagle-Beacon*, March 23, 1981, 1C.

33. Lonnie Crider, "Wings GM: Playoffs Ludicrous," *The Wichita Eagle-Beacon*, March 11, 1981, 13A.

34. Randy Brown, "Wings Backs To Wall," *The Wichita Eagle-Beacon*, March 17, 1981.

35. Dave Lange, "The Greatest Indoor Soccer Game," *Missile Magazine*, April 19, 1985, pg. 11-14.

36. Randy Brown, "Wings' Minds Are The Key," *The Wichita Eagle-Beacon*, March 23, 1981.

37. Staff, "Wings Will Face Steamers In Semis," *The Wichita Eagle-Beacon*, March 25, 1981.

38. Lonnie Crider, "The Fun's Over," *The Wichita Eagle-Beacon*, March 27, 1981, 5C.

39. Lange, "The Greatest Game," 11-14.

40. Ibid.

41. Ibid.

42. Ibid.

43. Ibid.

44. Ibid.

45. Ibid.

46. Ibid.

47. Bob Getz, "On MISL Sexiness Scale of 1 to 10, He's 'No. 1'," *The Wichita Eagle-Beacon*, March 27, 1981.

Chapter 14 - Save the Wings

Includes information from author interviews with Roy Turner, Bill Kentling, Dr. Jay Price, Kevin Kewley, Doug Verb, Bill Oliver, Steve Shaad, Terry Nicholl, Bruce Haertl, Tom Shine, Alan Shepherd, Kevin Himes, Andy Chapman, Kim Roentved, Charlie Minshull-Ford, and Kenny Cooper.

1. Steve Love, "Wings Set '81-'82 Ticket Prices," *The Wichita Eagle-Beacon*, April 3, 1981, 5C.

2. "Historic State Unemployment Rates Since 1976," accessed October 30, 2015, http://www.davemanuel.com/historical-state-unemployment-rates.php.

3. Randy Brown, "Financial Woes May Force Wings To Fold," *The Wichita Eagle-Beacon*, June 17, 1981, 5C.

4. Ibid.

5. Staff, "Wings' Support Rally To Be Held Sunday," *The Wichita Eagle-Beacon*, June 20, 1981.

6. Randy Brown, "Wings Fans - One Of A Kind," *The Wichita Eagle-Beacon*, June 22, 1981.

7. Randy Brown, "Wings Are Not Dead, But Time Running Out," *The Wichita Eagle-Beacon*, June 24, 1981, 5C.

8. Randy Brown, "With Extension In Hand, Wings Are Out Begging," *The Wichita Eagle-Beacon*, June 27, 1981, 1D.

9. Staff, "Wings Take Stride Toward Goal With New Pledges," *The Wichita Eagle-Beacon*, July 11, 1981, 1D.

10. Casey Scott, "Wings Are Saved For One More Year," *The Wichita Eagle-Beacon*, July 14, 1981, 1C.

11. Staff, "Wings Net $103,000 From Block Party," *The Wichita Eagle-Beacon*, July 27, 1981.

12. Love, "Wings Set Ticket Prices."

13. Staff, "Rain, Rodeo Delay Wings' Training," *The Wichita Eagle-Beacon*, November 4, 1981, 9C.

14. Ibid.

15. Rob Barzegar, Wichita Wings 1998-99 Souvenir Yearbook.

16. Randy Brown, "Wings Will Be 2 Weeks Behind Other MISL Teams," *The Wichita Eagle-Beacon*, November 1, 1981.

17. Ibid.

18. Staff, "Wings Profiles," *The Wichita Eagle-Beacon*, November 23, 1981, 6C.

19. Carol DeWoskin, "Rasmussen A Versatile Player," *Missile Magazine*, January 15, 1984, L-5.

20. Ibid.

21. Randy Brown, "Thanks, But No Thanks," *The Wichita Eagle-Beacon*, November 5, 1981.

22. Brown, "Wings 2 Weeks Behind."

23. Carol DeWoskin, "Pro Soccer A Nicholl Tradition," *Missile Magazine*, March 4, 1984, L-5.

24. Ibid.

25. Staff, "Wings Sign Goalkeeper Two Days Before Opener," *The Wichita Eagle-Beacon*, November 26, 1981.

26. Randy Brown, "Wings Shorthanded But Not Short Of Optimism," *The Wichita Eagle-Beacon*, November 15, 1981.

27. Randy Brown, "Wings Debut Against Steamers Shapes Up As A Real Wingdinger," *The Wichita Eagle-Beacon*, November 27, 1981, 1D.

28. Randy Brown, "Different Year, Same Story," *The Wichita Eagle-Beacon*, November 28, 1981, 1D.

29. Randy Brown, "Wings Grab Record, Win," *The Wichita Eagle-Beacon*, December 14, 1981, 1C.

30. Staff, "Wings Sign NASL Star," *The Wichita Eagle-Beacon*, December 27, 1981.

31. Mal Elliott, "Bourne Leads Wings To 6-5 Win," *The Wichita Eagle-Beacon*, January 15, 1982.

32. Randy Brown, "Wings' Bourne Finds Right Places At Right Times," *The Wichita Eagle-Beacon*, February 3, 1982.

33. Carol DeWoskin, "Jeff Bourne," *Missile Magazine*, December 10, 1983, L-5.

34. Ibid.

35. Randy Brown, "Smooth-Sailing Wings Are Peaking At Right Time," *The Wichita Eagle-Beacon*, February 14, 1982, 3F.

36. Staff, "Van Eron Stifles Wings," *The Wichita Eagle-Beacon*, February 15, 1982, 1B.

37. Randy Brown, "Wings Eager To Take Another Shot At Van Eron," *The Wichita Eagle-Beacon*, February 21, 1982, 3E.

38. Randy Brown, "Wings Even Score With Baltimore, 6-5," *The Wichita Eagle-Beacon*, February 22, 1982.

39. Casey Scott, "Holding To Principles Is Nice, But A Steady Paycheck Is Nicer," *The Wichita Eagle-Beacon*, April 10, 1982.

40. Barzegar, 1998-99 Yearbook.

41. Casey Scott, "Resisting Suspension, Kristensen Requested Release," *The Wichita Eagle-Beacon*, May 6, 1982, 1E.

42. Ibid.

43. Ibid.

44. Randy Brown, "Wings Give St. Louis A Dose Of Own Medicine," *The Wichita Eagle-Beacon*, May 10, 1982, 1B.

45. Randy Brown, "Wings Will Stay In Wichita, Offer To Sell Rejected," *The Wichita Eagle-Beacon*, May 13, 1982, 1D.

46. "Wichita Wings," accessed November 7, 2015, http://www.oursportscentral.com/misl/wings.php.

47. Casey Scott, "George Ley To Retire," *The Wichita Eagle-Beacon*, April 3, 1982.

48. Casey Scott, "Ley Hopes To Close Successful Career As Winner," *The Wichita Eagle-Beacon*, April 29, 1982, 7D.

49. Barzegar, 1998-99 Yearbook.

Interlude: The View from the Press Box

Includes information from author interview with Bruce Haertl.

Chapter 15 - A Head of Steam

Includes information from author interviews with Charlie Minshull-Ford, Tom Shine, Kevin Kewley, Bill Kentling, Andy Chapman, Ray Denton, Tom Marshall, Roy Turner, Alan Shepherd, Terry Nicholl, Mike Dowler, Kim Roentved, Bruce Haertl, Steve Pecher, and Steve Shaad.

1. Rob Barzegar, Wichita Wings 1998-99 Souvenir Yearbook.
2. Randy Brown, "Merging With NASL Could Damage MISL," *The Wichita Eagle-Beacon*, June 15, 1982.
3. Ibid.
4. Tom Shine, "Ryan Ends Soccer Career, Returns To Scotland Home," *The Wichita Eagle-Beacon*, August 17, 1982.
5. Randy Brown, "Get Your Tickets Early For The CHL Oldtimers Game," *The Wichita Eagle-Beacon*, September 16, 1982.
6. Tom Shine, "He Gave Up Hockey For Soccer Job," *The Wichita Eagle-Beacon*, December 17, 1982.
7. Tom Shine, "Job As Salesman Pays Bills For Wings' Defender O'Neill," *The Wichita Eagle-Beacon*, November 18, 1982.
8. Tom Shine, "Defender Is Earning His Wings," *The Wichita Eagle-Beacon*, January 8, 1983.
9. Barzegar, 1998-99 Yearbook.
10. Tom Shine, "Wings Sign Danish National Star Per Roentved," *The Wichita Eagle-Beacon*, October 27, 1982, 14A.
11. Carol DeWoskin, "Per Roentved: Seeing The World," *Missile Magazine*, January 7, 1984, L-5.
12. Tom Shine, "Per Roentved Is Having Holiday With The Wings," *The Wichita Eagle-Beacon*, November 28, 1982.
13. Barzegar, 1998-99 Yearbook.
14. Randy Brown, "Falklands Crisis Fails to Stop Wings-Gomez Reunion," *The Wichita Eagle-Beacon*, August 25, 1982.
15. Carol DeWoskin, "Omar Gomez: Mr. Excitement," *Missile Magazine*, November 26, 1983, L-5.

16. Tom Shine, "Wings, Gomez Are Happy That 'El Indio' Is Back," *The Wichita Eagle-Beacon*, August 24, 1982.

17. Tom Shine, "Wings' Odd Couple A Hit On Field," *The Wichita Eagle-Beacon*, March 10, 1983, 5C.

18. Brown, "Falklands Crisis."

19. Barzegar, 1998-99 Yearbook.

20. Tom Shine, "Gomez Is Newest MISL Bad boy," *The Wichita Eagle-Beacon*, March 17, 1983, 5E.

21. Tom Shine, "Wings Win Opener, 9-8," *The Wichita Eagle-Beacon*, November 14, 1982.

22. Tom Shine, "Wings Struggle To Win At Home," *The Wichita Eagle-Beacon*, December 23, 1982.

23. Tom Shine, "Consistent Is The Best Way To Describe Wings' Dowler," *The Wichita Eagle-Beacon*, January 2, 1983, 3E.

24. Letter to the Editor, "Wings Coach Should Give Americans More Playing Time," *The Wichita Eagle-Beacon*, March 13, 1983.

25. Mike Limon, "To Americanize, Or Not? MISL Officials Disagree," *The Wichita Eagle-Beacon*, January 13, 1980.

26. Staff, "Wichita Bows In Slugfest," *The Wichita Eagle-Beacon*, January 16, 1983.

27. Ibid.

28. Tom Shine, "Turner Says Scuffle Was Refs' Fault," *The Wichita Eagle-Beacon*, January 18, 1983.

29. Tom Shine, "Roentved Lifts West Over East," *The Wichita Eagle-Beacon*, February 23, 1983, 6C.

30. Tom Shine, "New York's Tactics Fail; Wings Take 4-2 Victory," *The Wichita Eagle-Beacon*, March 28, 1983.

31. Tom Shine, "Wings To Play Steamers Today," *The Wichita Eagle-Beacon*, November 21, 1982.

32. Arnold Irish, "Wings End Checkerdome Hex, Nip Steamers, 4-2," *The Wichita Eagle-Beacon*, December 28, 1982, 1C.

33. Tom Shine, "Wings Protest Cast Used By Steamers' Defender," *The Wichita Eagle-Beacon*, March 17, 1983.

34. Barzegar, 1998-99 Yearbook.

35. Tom Shine, "Once Again, The Steamers Are Standing In The Way," *The Wichita Eagle-Beacon*, April 19, 1983, 1C.

36. Tom Shine, "Wings Find Home Is Sweet In Playoff Victory," *The Wichita Eagle-Beacon*, April 21, 1983.

37. Tom Shine, "Weary Wings Head Into Showdown With Steamers," *The Wichita Eagle-Beacon*, April 26, 1983, 13A.

38. Brian Settle, "Orange Army Winged Victory Over St. Louis," *The Wichita Eagle-Beacon*, April 27, 1983, 1A.

39. Ibid.

40. Barzegar, 1998-99 Yearbook.

Chapter 16 - A Year to Remember

Includes information from author interviews with Roy Turner, Kenny Cooper, Tom Shine, Kevin Kewley, Steve Shaad, David Weber, Chico Borja, Andy Chapman, Virginia Creamer, Dr. Tamara Pryor, Bill Kentling, Tom Marshall, Terry Nicholl, Alan Shepherd, Charlie Minshull-Ford, Bob Becker, Kevin Himes, Bruce Haertl, and Kim Roentved.

1. PJ Rader, "Orange Army Marches With Love, "*The Wichita Eagle-Beacon*, January 16, 1983, 1A.

2. Ibid.

3. Ibid.

4. Ibid.

5. Wichita Wings Promotional Video, courtesy Virginia Creamer.

6. Ibid.

7. Rob Barzegar, Wichita Wings 1998-99 Souvenir Yearbook.

8. Dave Kratzer, "Roy Turner," *The Wichitan*, November 1983, 20.

9. Carol DeWoskin, "Soccer Replaced Skiing For Pierce," *Missile Magazine*, April 3, 1984, L-5.

10. Carol DeWoskin, "Filardo's Humor Scales Barrier," *Missile Magazine*, January 26, 1984, L-6.

11. Barzegar, 1998-99 Yearbook.

12. Ibid.

13. Carol DeWoskin, "Dutchy Has Seen It All," *Missile Magazine*, February 17, 1984.

14. Ibid.

15. Barzegar, 1998-99 Yearbook.

16. Steve Shaad, Editor, Wichita Wings 1983-84 Yearbook.

17. Carol DeWoskin, "Flying Scot Started Game Early," *Missile Magazine*, March 11, 1984.

18. Bill Kentling, "Best Season Ever?" *Orange and Blue Review*, 1988.

19. Carol DeWoskin, "Snell On His Way To First Million," *Missile Magazine*, March 24, 1984.

20. Carol DeWoskin, "Jan Madsen: From Forward to 'Keeper," *Missile Magazine*, February 7, 1984.

21. Barzegar, 1998-99 Yearbook.

22. Ibid.

23. Staff, "Wings Sign Ortiz," *Missile Magazine*, February 7, 1984.

24. Kentling, "Best Season Ever?"

25. Kratzer, "Roy Turner."

26. Steve Shaad, "What's In A Name? Plenty!" *Missile Magazine*, March 16, 1984.

27. Blake Schreck, "Kentling Comments On 'State Of The League'," *Missile Magazine*, February 24, 1984.

28. Steve Shaad, "Wings Back In Division Race," *Missile Magazine*, March 16, 1984.

29. Carol DeWoskin, "Piper A Man Of Many Hats," *Missile Magazine*, April 1, 1984.

30. Barzegar, 1998-99 Yearbook.

31. Ibid.

32. Steve Shaad, "Steamers Are Hot - Wings Cool," *Missile Magazine*, January 26, 1984.

33. Staff, "What Makes This Rivalry So Special?" *Missile Magazine*, December 10, 1983.

34. Ibid.

35. Barzegar, 1998-99 Yearbook.

36. Ibid.

37. Tom Shine, "Wings' Reaction Still Leaves Bourne Bitter," *The Wichita Eagle-Beacon*, January 27, 1985, 1E.

38. Kentling, "Best Season Ever?"

Chapter 17 - A Wizard's Spell

Includes information from author interviews with Dale Ervine, Chico Borja, Roy Turner, Kevin Himes, Tom Shine, Bill Kentling, Terry Nicholl, Charlie Minshull-Ford, Bill Oliver, Dr. Tamara Pryor, Dave Phillips, Tom Marshall, Bob Becker, Steve

Shaad, Mark Weddle, Kevin Kewley, Andy Chapman, Alan Shepherd, Kim Roentved, and Mike Dowler.

1. Frank M. Lindsay, *Missile Magazine*, December 21, 1984, 13.
2. "Olympic Football Tournament Los Angeles 1984," accessed December 2, 2015, http://www.fifa.com/tournaments/archive/mensolympic/losangeles1984/matches/index.html.
3. Rob Barzegar, Wichita Wings 1998-99 Souvenir Yearbook.
4. Staff, "Piper Bittersweet on Retiring #7," *Missile Magazine*, November 24, 1984.
5. Ibid.
6. Staff, "Letters," *Missile Magazine*, December 2, 1984.
7. Barzegar, 1998-99 Yearbook.
8. Staff, "Steve McLean - The Kid," *Missile Magazine*, March 8, 1985, L-4.
9. Barzegar, 1998-99 Yearbook.
10. Ibid.
11. Staff, "Steve Wegerle - The Duffer," *Missile Magazine*, March 30, 1985, L-4.
12. Brian Landman, "Historic 1974 Game...Catalyst For Change," *Tampa Bay Times*, June 7, 2010, accessed December 8, 2015, http://www.tampabay.com/sports/soccer/worldcup/historic-1974-game-between-all-white-and-all-black-soccer-teams-in-south/1100605.
13. Staff, "Barry Boomer Wallace," *Missile Magazine*, April 5, 1985.
14. Ibid.
15. Barzegar, 1998-99 Yearbook.
16. Editor, Wichita Wings 1984-85 Information Guide, 9.
17. Leon Goner, Wichita Wings Guidebook 1999-2000, 52 and 54.
18. Kevin Ray and Pam Sherer, "Rambo Fights For Playoffs," *Missile Magazine*, March 28, 1986, 7.
19. Barzegar, 1998-99 Yearbook.
20. Ibid.
21. Staff, "Karsen Christensen - The Viking," *Missile Magazine*, January 29, 1985.
22. Tom Shine, "Debut Of The Great Dane," *Orange and Blue Review*, 1988.
23. Goner, Wings Guidebook
24. Ibid.

25. Steve Holroyd and David Litterer, "The Year in American Soccer..." accessed December 11, 2015, http://homepages.sover.net/~spectrum/year/1986.html and http://homepages.sover.net/~spectrum/year/1988.html.

26. Shine, *Orange and Blue Review.*

27. Staff, "Erik Rasmussen - The Wizard," *Missile Magazine*, March 1, 1985.

28. Ibid.

29. Ibid.

30. Gary Dymski, "Rasmussen Slips By Border Patrol," *The Wichita Eagle-Beacon*, February [Day Unknown], 1986.

31. Ibid.

32. Mal Elliott, "Rasmussen Detained After Bomb Remark," *The Wichita Eagle-Beacon*, January 4, 1989.

33. Fred Mann, "Rasmussen Gets His Kicks From Humility, Charity," *The Wichita Eagle-Beacon*, March 19, 1987.

34. Ibid.

35. Kim Roentved, Interview by Tim O'Bryhim, The Monarch, Wichita, KS, May 6, 2015.

36. Staff, "Kentling Keeps Wings Kicking," *Missile Magazine*, December 2, 1984.

37. Ibid.

38. Ibid.

39. Staff, "Path To Wichita Colorful," *Missile Magazine*, December 16, 1984.

40. Staff, "Kevin Kewley - The Original Wing," *Missile Magazine*, February 1, 1985.

41. Ibid.

42. Tim Sheldon, "MISL Making Gains In Battle For Ink," *Missile Magazine*, February 1, 1985.

43. Ibid.

44. Barzegar, 1998-99 Yearbook.

45. Tom Shine, "Wings Sell Chapman To Cleveland," *The Wichita Eagle-Beacon*, March 1, 1985, 1D.

46. Ibid.

47. Fred Mann, "Chapman, Wings Both Should Benefit From Cash Deal," *The Wichita Eagle-Beacon*, March 2, 1985.

48. Ibid.

49. Barzegar, 1998-99 Yearbook.

50. Shine, *Orange and Blue Review.*

51. Ibid.

52. Ibid.

53. Ibid.

54. Tom Shine, "Brawling Wings, Strikers Fined $2,500 By MISL," *The Wichita Eagle-Beacon*, April 23, 1985, 1D.

55. Barzegar, 1998-99 Yearbook.

Interlude: Norman Piper, Private Investigator
Includes information from author interviews with Norman Piper and Bill Kentling.

Chapter 18 - Chico and the Men
Includes information from author interviews with Roy Turner, Bill Kentling, Chico Borja, Terry Nicholl, Kim Roentved, Kevin Kewley, Dr. Tamara Pryor, Steve Shaad, and Eric Scriven.

1. Clark Spencer, "Wings Coach Weds on Jamaican Coast," *The Wichita Eagle-Beacon*, [Date Unknown].

2. Tom Shine, "MISL Commissioner Rules In Wings' Favor," *The Wichita Eagle-Beacon*, September 27, 1985.

3. Ibid.

4. Pam Sherer, "Meet Your Newest Wings," *Missile Magazine*, November 15, 1985, 8.

5. Staff, "Wings Profiles," *The Wichita Eagle-Beacon*, October 27, 1985.

6. Rob Barzegar, Wichita Wings 1998-99 Souvenir Yearbook.

7. Pam Sherer, "Fitting In With The Wings," *Missile Magazine*, January 10, 1986.

8. Ibid.

9. Barzegar, 1998-99 Yearbook, 35.

10. Gary Dymski, "Love And Hate," *The Wichita Eagle-Beacon*, February 2, 1986, 1D.

11. Staff, "The Team," *Wichita Wings 1985-86 Information Guide*, 1985, 13.

12. Dymski, "Love And Hate."

13. Barzegar, 1998-99 Yearbook, 106 and 108.

14. Dymski, "Love And Hate."

15. Ibid.

16. Ibid.

17. Ibid.

18. Barzegar, 1998-99 Yearbook, 106 and 108.

19. Pam Sherer, "Rookie Makes Pro Debut," *Missile Magazine*, February 21, 1986.

20. Gary Dymski, "Wings' Smith Making The Most Of His Opportunity," *The Wichita Eagle-Beacon*, February 11, 1986, 5D.

21. Barzegar, 1998-99 Yearbook, 35.

22. Staff, "Walters Was Worth Shot For Wichita," *The Wichita Eagle-Beacon*, April 8, 1986.

23. Barzegar, 1998-99 Yearbook, 35.

24. Kevin Ray and Pam Sherer, "Wings Strike Danish Oil Again," *Missile Magazine*, March 21, 1986.

25. Barzegar, 1998-99 Yearbook, 36.

26. Steve Shaad and Pam Sherer, "The Pride Of Ireland," *Missile Magazine*, February 23, 1986.

27. Ibid.

28. Gary Dymski, "New Wings Relish Big Win," *The Wichita Eagle-Beacon*, March 13, 1986.

29. Barzegar, 1998-99 Yearbook, 35.

30. Fred Mann, "Danish Goalie To Join Wings," *The Wichita Eagle-Beacon*, September 4, 1985, 3D.

31. Rich Paschette, *Hot Winter Nights*, [Parma, Ohio: 2008]

32. Tom Shine, "Nicholl Named Captain," *The Wichita Eagle-Beacon*, October 8, 1985.

33. Pam Sherer, "The General Is Wings Captain," *Missile Magazine*, January 19, 1986, 6.

34. Paschette, *Hot Winter Nights*.

35. Gary Dymski, "Wings End Jinx, Outgun Sockers 11-9," *The Wichita Eagle-Beacon*, November 24, 1985, 1E.

36. Staff, "Wings Blank Stars 1-0 In Overtime," *The Wichita Eagle-Beacon*, December 15, 1985.

37. Gary Dymski, "Injuries Cause Wings To Skid," *The Wichita Eagle-Beacon*, January 30, 1986.

38. Gary Dymski, "MISL Notebook," *The Wichita Eagle-Beacon*, February 20, 1986, 3D.

39. Unknown, "Great Dane," *The Wichita Eagle-Beacon*, February 22, 1986.

40. Gary Dymski, "Wichita's Erik Rasmussen Chipping In More Assists," *The Wichita Eagle-Beacon*, February 9, 1986, 3E.

41. Barzegar, 1998-99 Yearbook, 35.

42. Gary Dymski, "Wings Purchase Hoggan From Pittsburgh," *The Wichita Eagle-Beacon*, February 5, 1986.

43. Pam Sherer, "Hoagie At Home In Wichita," *Missile Magazine*, April 4, 1986, 5.

44. Pam Sherer and Kevin Ray, "Big Bird Sparks Playoff Drive," *Missile Magazine*, Playoff Edition, 1986.

45. Gary Dymski, "Wings Buy Defensive Standout," *The Wichita Eagle-Beacon*, March 2, 1986, 1E.

46. Gerry Dulac, "Chico And The Men Propel Wings Past Pittsburgh 10-2," *The Wichita Eagle-Beacon*, February 29, 1986, 1D.

47. Gary Dymski, "Confident Wings Rally To Defeat Sockers 5-4," *The Wichita Eagle-Beacon*, March 10, 1986, 1B.

48. Gary Dymski, "Wings Win At Buzzer, Earn Berth," *The Wichita Eagle-Beacon*, March 12, 1986, 1B.

49. Ibid.

50. Barzegar, 1998-99 Yearbook.

51. Steve Greenberg, "Wings' Roentved Makes MISL History," *The Wichita Eagle-Beacon*, May 21, 1986.

52. Unknown, "Rasmussen Breaks 100-Point Barrier," *The Wichita Eagle-Beacon*, March 29, 1986, 1B.

53. Barzegar, 1998-99 Yearbook.

54. Ibid.

55. Staff, "Walters..."

56. Barzegar, 1998-99 Yearbook.

57. Gary Dymski, "Roentved's 4 Lead Wings," *The Wichita Eagle-Beacon*, April 10, 1986, 1B.

58. Gary Dymski, "Wings Fall In OT 5-4," *The Wichita Eagle-Beacon*, April 17, 1986, 1B.

59. Barzegar, 1998-99 Yearbook, 35.

60. Paschette, *Hot Winter Nights*.

61. Gary Dymski, "Tacoma Devours Wings," *The Wichita Eagle-Beacon*, April 19, 1986, 1B.

62. Gary Dymski, "Wings' Rasmussen Takes The Blame," *The Wichita Eagle-Beacon*, April 20, 1986, 1E.

63. Barzegar, 1998-99 Yearbook.

64. Does not include blocks from the 1981-82 season due to missing data.

65. Tom Shine, "Wings Release Veteran," *The Wichita Eagle-Beacon*, May 3, 1986.

Interlude: On the Road...

Includes information from author interviews with Kim Roentved, Roy Turner, Tom Shine, Steve Shaad, Andy Chapman, Kevin Kewley, Larry Inlow, Bruce Haertl, and Norman Piper.

Chapter 19 - Cooking Up Change

Includes information from author interviews with Bill Kentling, Alan Shepherd, Roy Turner, Bill Oliver, Steve Shaad, Charlie Minshull-Ford, Chico Borja, Dave Phillips, Terry Nicholl, Larry Inlow, Louis McCluer, Steve Rademacher, Dale Ervine, Kim Roentved, Kevin Kewley, and Eric Scriven.

1. Staff, "MISL's Dale To Step Down," *The Wichita Eagle-Beacon*, April 21, 1986.

2. Gary Dymski, "Committee Supports Kentling," *The Wichita Eagle-Beacon*, April 24, 1986, 1B.

3. Gary Dymski, "Wings Boss Kentling Picked As New MISL Commissioner," *The Wichita Eagle-Beacon*, May 20, 1986, 1A.

4. Mal Elliott, "The Boss," *The Wichita Eagle-Beacon*, November 9, 1986.

5. Ibid.

6. Editorial Staff, "Bill Kentling: MISL Chose Well," *The Wichita Eagle-Beacon*, May 20, 1986.

7. Dymski, "Kentling Picked."

8. Fred Mann, "Colorful, Abrasive, In Charge," *The Wichita Eagle-Beacon*, May 20, 1986, 12A.

9. Mal Elliott, "Turner Hopes To Become The Stabilizing Force," *The Wichita Eagle-Beacon*, November 9, 1986.

10. Staff, 1986-87 Wichita Wings Information Guide, 2.

11. Charlie Cooke and Martin Knight, *The Bonnie Prince*, [Edinburgh: Mainstream Publishing, 2006]

12. Mal Elliott, "Tough Act For Wings To Follow," *The Wichita Eagle-Beacon*, November 9, 1986, 11G.

13. Ibid.

14. Mal Elliott, "Wings' Olesen Calls It Quits," *The Wichita Eagle-Beacon*, September 30, 1986.

15. Mal Elliott, "Comets Pick Up Espinoza," *The Wichita Eagle-Beacon*, September 18, 1986.

16. Mal Elliott, "Wings Put Late-Arriving O'Neill On Waivers," *The Wichita Eagle-Beacon*, November 7, 1986.

17. Mal Elliott, "Wings Cut Loose Ly To Protect Wichitan's College Eligibility," *The Wichita Eagle-Beacon*, October 14, 1986, 1B.

18. Chuck Groth (Staff Artist), "The Average Wings Players Is:" *The Wichita Eagle-Beacon*, Unknown date, 1986.

19. Mal Elliott, "Soccer Feet: Good Things In Small Packages," *The Wichita Eagle-Beacon*, October 26, 1986, 13G.

20. Staff, "Wings Sign English Midfielder," *The Wichita Eagle-Beacon*, August 22, 1986.

21. Rob Barzegar, Wichita Wings 1998-99 Souvenir Yearbook, 39.

22. Mal Elliott, "Wings Offer Ervine Contract, Cut Borer, Sign New Keeper," *The Wichita Eagle-Beacon*, October 21, 1986.

23. Barzegar, 1998-99 Yearbook, 39.

24. Mal Elliott, "Wings Keep On Cookin'," *The Wichita Eagle-Beacon*, September 3, 1986, 1B.

25. Barzegar, 1998-99 Yearbook, 39.

26. Mal Elliott, "Wing Is Quick When It Comes To Wit," *The Wichita Eagle-Beacon*, January 12, 1987.

27. Barzegar, 1998-99 Yearbook, 39.

28. Pam Sherer, "MISL All-Star Hunks," *Missile Magazine*, December 19, 1986, 5.

29. Mal Elliott, "Wings Sign Forward Kerlin," *The Wichita Eagle-Beacon*, October 23, 1986, 1B.

30. Barzegar, 1998-99 Yearbook, 39.

31. Mal Elliott, "Like Magic, Wings Sign World Cup Veteran," *The Wichita Eagle-Beacon*, August 15, 1986, 1D.

32. Mickey Thomas, *Kick-Ups, Hiccups, Lock-Ups*, [Random House: London, 2008], 111.

33. Elliott, "Like Magic…"

34. Thomas, *Kick-ups*, 112-113.

35. Barzegar, 1998-99 Yearbook, 39.

36. Mal Elliott, "Tricky: Thomas Has A Bag Of Treats," *The Wichita Eagle-Beacon*, October 2, 1986, 1B.

37. Barzegar, 1998-99 Yearbook.

38. Gary Dymski, "Wings Celebrate 3-1 Outdoor Victory Over Comets," *The Wichita Eagle-Beacon*, July 20, 1986, 1D.

39. Mal Elliott, "Roentved Will Add Captain To His Job List," *The Wichita Eagle-Beacon*, October 8, 1986, 1B.

40. Unknown, "Intensity Key To Wings' Pressure Game," *The Wichita Eagle-Beacon*, October 9, 1986, 1G.

41. Elliott, "Tough Act."

42. Ibid.

43. Mal Elliott, "Wings Topple Tacoma," *The Wichita Eagle-Beacon*, November 15, 1986, 1C.

44. Mal Elliott, "Wings Want MISL To Fine Tacoma," *The Wichita Eagle-Beacon*, January 9, 1987.

45. Mal Elliott, "MISL Launches Investigation Against Tacoma," *The Wichita Eagle-Beacon*, January 23, 1987.

46. Dan Caesar, "Wings Do The Impossible, Win In St. Louis," *The Wichita Eagle-Beacon*, February 1, 1987.

47. Mal Elliott, "Wings Games Roll On Over To KAKE," *The Wichita Eagle-Beacon*, [Date Unknown].

48. Mal Elliott, "Veee Stands For Vigorous," *The Wichita Eagle-Beacon*, January 16, 1987, 1B.

49. Mal Elliott, "Sockers Have Wings' Respect," *The Wichita Eagle-Beacon*, January 16, 1987.

50. Mal Elliott, "Dispute Resolved; Wings Reinstate Keeper McDonagh," *The Wichita Eagle-Beacon*, December 23, 1986, 1D.

51. Pete Kerzel, "Baltimore Subdues Wichita," *The Wichita Eagle-Beacon*, April 4, 1987, 1D.

52. Mal Elliott, "Soccer Sucker Play Nets LA As Victim," *The Wichita Eagle-Beacon*, March 6, 1987.

53. Mal Elliott, "McDonagh Dazzles Lazers 8-0," *The Wichita Eagle-Beacon*, April 11, 1987, 1D.

54. Mal Elliott, "Wings Hold Off Dynamo Moscow," *The Wichita Eagle-Beacon*, January 28, 1987, 1B.

55. Mal Elliott, "Wings' Piper Breaks Arm," *The Wichita Eagle-Beacon*, January 15, 1987, 1B.

56. Barzegar, 1998-99 Yearbook, 39.

57. Ibid.

58. Mal Elliott, "Rookie On The Way Up," *The Wichita Eagle-Beacon*, March 17, 1987, 1B.

59. Barzegar, 1998-99 Yearbook, 40.

60. Staff, "Wings Notes," *The Wichita Eagle-Beacon*, January 26, 1987.

61. Mal Elliott, "Piper KC Candidate," *The Wichita Eagle-Beacon*, January 24, 1987.

62. Mal Elliott, "Two Wings, Trainer Named MISL West All-Stars," *The Wichita Eagle-Beacon*, January 29, 1987, 1B.

63. Mal Elliott, "L.A.'s Buss Happy To Host MISL's All-Stars," *The Wichita Eagle-Beacon*, February 11, 1987, 1B.

64. Gary Dymski, "Sputtering New York Express Chugs Into Wichita Tonight," *The Wichita Eagle-Beacon*, February 3, 1987, 3B.

65. Mal Elliott, "Express Won't Finish Season," *The Wichita Eagle-Beacon*, February 18, 1987.

66. Barzegar, 1998-99 Yearbook.

67. Fred Mann, "As Fights Go, This One Won't Rate High On Wings' Hit List," *The Wichita Eagle-Beacon*, May 12, 1987.

68. Barzegar, 1998-99 Yearbook, 40.

69. Mal Elliott, "Wings May Fold," *The Wichita Eagle-Beacon*, April 26, 1987, 1B.

70. Fred Mann, "Keep The Wings Afloat Until Smoother Waters Arrive," *The Wichita Eagle-Beacon*, April 28, 1987.

71. Alissa Rubin, "Wings To Tell Commission Of Plight 'With Cap In Hand'," *The Wichita Eagle-Beacon*, May 20, 1987.

72. Fred Mann, "Orange Army And Friends Save Wings From Dunkirk," *The Wichita Eagle-Beacon*, May 24, 1987, 1B.

73. Brian Holland, "Hot Winter Nights: Kansas City Comets 1981-91," https://www.facebook.com/groups/232672316887579/permalink/535061549981986/. Accessed March 20, 2016.

Interlude: Summer Vacation...and a $5,000 Beer

Includes information from author interviews with Kevin Himes, Virginia Creamer, and Steve Shaad.

Chapter 20 - From One to Another

Includes information from author interviews with Roy Turner, Kim Roentved, Chico Borja, Dale Ervine, Eric Scriven, Kevin Kewley, Bill Oliver, Norman Piper, and Terry Nicholl.

1. Gary Dymski, "Five Teams Interested in Roentved," *The Wichita Eagle-Beacon*, June 17, 1987, 1B.
2. Rob Barzegar, Wichita Wings 1998-99 Souvenir Yearbook, 106.
3. Dymski, "Five Teams Interested."
4. Gary Dymski, "Lazers Edge Wings," *The Wichita Eagle-Beacon*, November 20, 1987, 1D.
5. Barzegar, 1998-99 Yearbook.
6. Ibid.
7. Mal Elliott, "...With Zigi The Rookie Goalkeeper," *The Wichita Eagle-Beacon*, November 18, 1987, 1B.
8. Mal Elliott, "Wings...The Nightmare Finally Ended," *Orange and Blue Review*, 1988.
9. Barzegar, 1998-99 Yearbook.
10. Ibid.
11. Ibid.
12. Mal Elliott, "Willrich Scores Winner In Wings' Opener," *The Wichita Eagle-Beacon*, November 8, 1987, 1G.
13. Mal Elliott, "Rowe Rolling Despite Slow Start By Wings," *The Wichita Eagle-Beacon*, December 22, 1987, 1B.
14. Mal Elliott, "Wings' Ervine Quickly Growing In Skills And Confidence," *The Wichita Eagle-Beacon*, January 15, 1988.
15. Kirk Seminoff, "Wings Bow To Sockers," *The Wichita Eagle-Beacon*, December 30, 1987, 1B.
16. Charlie Cooke, *The Bonnie Prince*, [Mainstream Publishing Company: Edinburgh, 2007], 303-304.

17. Mal Elliott, "Wings Put Nicholl In Charge," *The Wichita Eagle-Beacon*, February 2, 1988, 1D.

18. Rich Paschette, *Hot Winter Nights*, [Parma, Ohio: 2008]

19. Barzegar, 1998-99 Yearbook.

20. Paschette, *Hot Winter Nights.*

21. KAKE-TV Broadcast, March 18, 1988.

22. Ibid.

23. Elliott, *Orange and Blue Review*, 49.

24. Barzegar, 1998-99 Yearbook, 44.

25. Mal Elliott, "Rasmussen Wins Scoring Crown," *The Wichita Eagle-Beacon*, April 18, 1988, 1B.

26. Mal Elliott, "MISL Names Wings' Rasmussen MVP," *The Wichita Eagle-Beacon*, June 5, 1988, 1G.

27. Mal Elliott, "Wings Stay Alive With 6-3 Win," *The Wichita Eagle-Beacon*, April 9, 1988, 1B.

28. Clark Spencer, "Staying Late For Wingathon '88," *The Wichita Eagle-Beacon*, June 16, 1988.

29. Clark Spencer, "Plan Devised To Prevent Team's Money Woes," *The Wichita Eagle-Beacon*, June 16, 1988, 1A.

Interlude: The Art of Coaching
Includes information from author interviews with Kevin Himes, Al Miller, Norm Hitzges, Bill Kentling, Roy Turner, Terry Nicholl, Bruce Haertl, Charlie Minshull-Ford, and Kim Roentved.

Chapter 21 - Old Friends and Old Enemies
Includes information from author interviews with Terry Nicholl, Andy Chapman, Dale Ervine, Chico Borja, Larry Inlow, Roy Turner, Dr. Tamara Pryor, and Bill Kentling.

1. Rob Barzegar, Wichita Wings 1998-99 Souvenir Yearbook.

2. Mal Elliott, "MISL Players, Owners OK Changes," *The Wichita Eagle-Beacon*, July 19, 1988, 8A.

3. Mal Elliott, "Original Wing Chapman Returns; Borja Could Be Next," *The Wichita Eagle-Beacon*, September 7, 1988, 1D.

4. Ibid.

5. Mal Elliott, "Borja Says He's Come To Terms, Will Sign With Wings," *The Wichita Eagle-Beacon*, September 12, 1988.

6. Mal Elliott, "Wings' Moreland Gets His Kicks By Leading," *The Wichita Eagle-Beacon*, October 22, 1988, 5B.

7. Barzegar, 1998-99 Yearbook.

8. Mal Elliott, "Van der Beck Intends To Wing-It In Wichita," *The Wichita Eagle-Beacon*, October 24, 1988.

9. Barzegar, 1998-99 Yearbook.

10. Mal Elliott, "Moreira's Advice For Wings: Concentration," *The Wichita Eagle-Beacon*, March 7, 1989, 8A.

11. Staff, "Wings' Borja Named All-MISL," *The Wichita Eagle-Beacon*, June 22, 1989.

12. Barzegar, 1998-99 Yearbook.

13. Ibid.

14. Mal Elliott, "Wings Snare All-Star Goalkeeper Vaccaro," *The Wichita Eagle-Beacon*, August 2, 1988.

15. Barzegar, 1998-99 Yearbook.

16. Mal Elliott, "Vaccaro's Goal Is Dress For Success," *The Wichita Eagle-Beacon*, January 14, 1989.

17. Barzegar, 1998-99 Yearbook, 45.

18. Mal Elliott, "Wings Capture Opener," *The Wichita Eagle-Beacon*, November 6, 1988, 1G.

19. Barzegar, 1998-99 Yearbook.

20. Mal Elliott, "Soviets Call On Wings," *The Wichita Eagle-Beacon*, February 1, 1989.

21. Mal Elliott, "Wings' Stankovic Makes 'Em Pay The Penalty," *The Wichita Eagle-Beacon*, January 5, 1989.

22. Mal Elliott, "When Shorthanded, Wings Possess Killer Instinct," *The Wichita Eagle-Beacon*, January 11, 1989, 1B.

23. Fred Mann, "On-The-Job Training Becoming Rough For Wings' Nicholl," *The Wichita Eagle-Beacon*, March 28, 1989.

24. Mal Elliott, "Kentling Decides To Quit As MISL Commissioner," *The Wichita Eagle-Beacon*, March 15, 1989, 1B.

25. Ibid.

26. Barzegar, 1998-99 Yearbook.

27. Mal Elliott, "Wings Take 1-0 Series Lead Over Stars," *The Wichita Eagle-Beacon*, April 29, 1989, 1D.

28. Mal Elliott, "Wings Rout Stars, Lead 2-0," *The Wichita Eagle-Beacon*, April 30, 1989, 1G.

29. Mal Elliott, "Wings Move On To Semifinals," *The Wichita Eagle-Beacon*, May 9, 1989, 1D.

30. Fred Mann, "Wings Blow Cool, Let Blast Recover," *The Wichita Eagle-Beacon*, May 13, 1989, 1G.

31. Fred Mann, "Wings Depart Baltimore Blue," *The Wichita Eagle-Beacon*, May 17, 1989, 1B.

32. Mal Elliott, "Win Keeps Wings In The Picture," *The Wichita Eagle-Beacon*, May 20, 1989, 1D.

33. Mal Elliott, "Wings Refuse To Die From Blast," *The Wichita Eagle-Beacon*, May 23, 1989, 1D.

34. Barzegar, 1998-99 Yearbook.

35. Fred Mann, "Comeback? Not On This Night," *The Wichita Eagle-Beacon*, May 25, 1989, 1B.

36. Barzegar, 1998-99 Yearbook.

37. Mal Elliott, "Rasmussen Leaves Wings For Team In His Homeland," *The Wichita Eagle*, September 12, 1989, 1B.

38. Ibid.

Interlude: Healers, Helpers, and Haulers
Includes information from author interviews with Roy Turner, Charlie Minshull-Ford, Andy Chapman, Kevin Kewley, Bill Kentling, and Terry Nicholl.

Chapter 22 - Stayin' Alive
Includes information from author interviews with Dale Ervine, Terry Nicholl, Andy Chapman, Kevin Kewley, Roy Turner, Bill Oliver, Chico Borja, Bill Kentling, Dave

Phillips, Tamara Pryor, Kim Roentved, Al Miller, Steve Shaad, Tom Shine, Kenny Cooper, and Doug Verb.

1. Mal Elliott, "Ervine To Stay In Wings' Stable," *The Wichita Eagle*, Date Unknown, 1989.
2. Mal Elliott, "Wings Boot Sidekicks 6-4," *The Wichita Eagle*, October 22, 1989, 11G.
3. Mal Elliott, "Tacoma Triumphs In First-Refusal Battle For Vaccaro," *The Wichita Eagle*, September 19, 1989, 1B.
4. Mal Elliott, "He's Fearless," *The Wichita Eagle*, December 10, 1989, 1G.
5. Mal Elliott, "Fearon Shines In Wing Win," *The Wichita Eagle*, October 29, 1989, 1G.
6. Rob Barzegar, Wichita Wings 1998-99 Souvenir Yearbook.
7. Ibid.
8. Ibid.
9. Mal Elliott, "The Wings In 1989-90," *The Wichita Eagle*, October 22, 1989, 10G.
10. Barzegar, 1998-99 Yearbook.
11. Mal Elliott, "Wings' Defense Smothers Sockers 4-2," *The Wichita Eagle*, November 23, 1989, 1C.
12. Barzegar, 1998-99 Yearbook.
13. Ibid.
14. Mal Elliott, "Byrne Enraged At Way He Heard News," *The Wichita Eagle*, January 22, 1990, 1B.
15. Barzegar, 1998-99 Yearbook.
16. Mal Elliott, "Wings, Blast Cut Deal," *The Wichita Eagle*, January 21, 1990, 1G.
17. Mal Elliott, "Byrne's Three Goals Do The Trick For Wings," *The Wichita Eagle*, February 19, 1990, 1G.
18. Barzegar, 1998-99 Yearbook.
19. Fred Mann, "Wings Can Be Too Talented For Own Good," *The Wichita Eagle*, February 6, 1990, 1B.
20. Barzegar, 1998-99 Yearbook.
21. Mal Elliott, "Wings Revive Playoff Hopes With 4-3 Win," *The Wichita Eagle*, May 5, 1990, 1B.

22. Mal Elliott, "Soured Season Has Wings Thinking Change," *The Wichita Eagle*, May 9, 1990, 1B.

23. Wichita Wings 1991-92 Media Guide, 28.

24. Barzegar, 1998-99 Yearbook.

25. David Litterer, "The Year in American Soccer - 1991," accessed March 12, 2016, http://homepages.sover.net/~spectrum/year/1991.html.

26. Barzegar, 1998-99 Yearbook.

27. Ibid.

28. Ibid.

29. Wichita Wings 1990-91 Media Guide.

30. Barzegar, 1998-99 Yearbook.

31. Ibid.

32. Ibid.

33. Ibid.

34. Litterer, "The Year in American Soccer - 1991."

35. Barzegar, 1998-99 Yearbook.

36. Mal Elliott, "Critical Condition Wings' Owners Say Deadline Will Stand," *The Wichita Eagle*, June 26, 1991, 1B.

37. Mal Elliott, "Their Biggest Win," *The Wichita Eagle*, June 29, 1991, 1A.

38. Wichita Wings 1991-92 Media Guide, 6.

39. Barzegar, 1998-99 Yearbook, 61.

40. Barzegar, 1998-99 Yearbook.

41. Ibid.

42. Ibid.

43. Ibid.

44. Mal Elliott, "Buzzer Sounds For MSL, But Soccer Isn't Dead," *The Wichita Eagle*, July 11, 1992, 1A.

45. Mal Elliott, "Wichitans Kick In For Indoor Soccer," *The Wichita Eagle*, August 1, 1992, 1A.

46. Barzegar, 1998-99 Yearbook, 67.

47. Barzegar, 1998-99 Yearbook, 65.

48. Bob Stratton, "Wings' Turner Resigns," *The Wichita Eagle*, February 23, 1996, 1C.

49. Fred Mann, "Alas, Poor Turner: A Tragic Victim," *The Wichita Eagle*, February 23, 1996, 1C.
50. Editorial Board, "Thanks, Roy," *The Wichita Eagle*, February 27, 1996.

Chapter 23 - A Legacy of Orange
Includes information from author interviews with Kevin Kewley, Roy Turner, Steve Shaad, Bill Kentling, Chico Borja, Andy Chapman, Norman Piper, Tom Shine, Dave Phillips, Terry Nicholl, Bruce Haertl, Anthony Villegas, Kenny Cooper, Tom Marshall, Mike Dowler, Dr. Tamara Pryor, Louis McCluer, John Morrison, Virginia Creamer, Alan Shepherd, Dale Ervine, and Nathan Moore.

Epilogue: The Boy Who Became a Wing
Includes information from an author interview with Larry Inlow.

Appendix A: Wings on National and Olympic Teams
Sources for Appendix A include:

* http://www.tampabay.com/sports/soccer/worldcup/historic-1974-game-between-all-white-and-all-black-soccer-teams-in-south/1100605
* 1983-4 Wings Yearbook, Steve Schaad, Editor
* Wichita Wings 1987-8 Media Guide
* www.fifa.com
* www.rsssf.com
* www.nasljerseys.com
* Canadasoccer.com
* www.11v11.com
* http://www.ussoccer.com/stories/2014/03/17/14/02/u-s-soccer-mourns-the-loss-of-glenn-mooch-myernick
* www.dbu.dk
* http://articles.philly.com/1992-05-20/sports/26012178_1_puerto-ricans-soccer-san-juan
* http://articles.baltimoresun.com/2007-08-29/news/0708280333_1_mcdonogh-blast-soccer
* www.ussoccer.com

Appendix B: Wings in English First Division (Premier League)

Sources for Appendix B include:

* www.footballdatabase.eu
* http://nifootball.blogspot.com/2007/09/vic-moreland.html
* http://www.sporting-heroes.net/football/queens-park-rangers-fc/barry-wallace-5152/league-appearances_a18823
* www.11v11.com
* http://www.sporting-heroes.net